D1072373

The
Clamorous
Malcontents

The
Clamorous
Malcontents

Criticisms & Defenses
of the Colony of Georgia
1741 – 1743

INTRODUCTION BY
TREVOR R. REESE

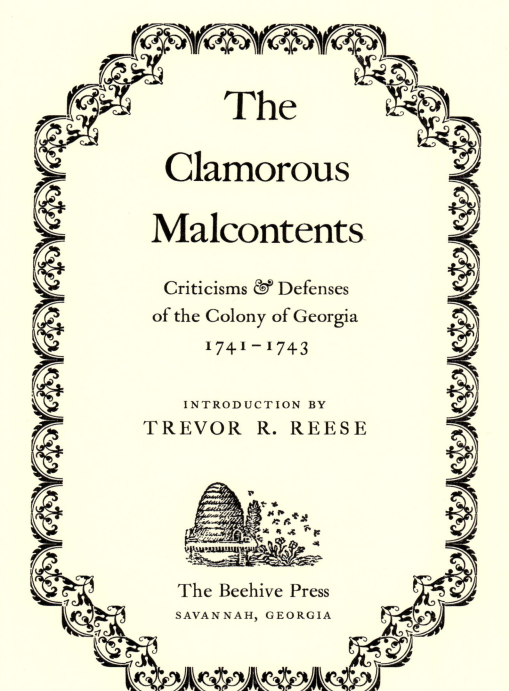

The Beehive Press
SAVANNAH, GEORGIA

Contents

Introduction

ITHIN a little more than two years of the first settlers arriving in Georgia in January 1733, the province's deficiencies in many of the ingredients of civil government were attracting the notice of inhabitants. By the spring of 1735 dissatisfaction was spreading, and there was common talk of returning to the mother country.[1] The main grievances related to Negroes, rum, and land. Many inhabitants believed slave labor to be essential if the province was to compete at all with South Carolina, which, in contrast to Georgia, possessed slave labor. The demand for the admission of Negroes arose very early in the history of Georgia and grew steadily in volume, and the refusal of the Trustees to permit it remained for many years a prominent cause of discontent. The demand emanated principally from settlers holding sufficient land to make Negro labor really useful, or from those possessing sufficient capital to make a slave trade profitable. Economic conditions and the proximity of South Carolina gave their arguments strength and conviction.

Another grievance was the prohibition of rum, a measure which

1. Dobree to Trustees, Feb. 6, 1734/5, C.O. 5/636 (Colonial Office Series 5, Vol. 636; Public Record Office, London), fol. 190. P. Gordon to Trustees, May 7, 1735, C.O. 5/637, fol. 9.

the Trustees were convinced was in the interests of the settlers themselves. It was impossible to enforce this law, and by 1738 rum shops were said to be as common in Georgia as gin shops used to be in London.[2] The land restrictions, too, were a source of unrest, and by 1738 several persons had declared their intention of leaving Georgia unless alterations were made to the system of land tenure.[3] In whichever direction the colonists turned there were restrictions, benevolently imposed by the Trustees but aggravating to the people who had to suffer them. The spring of 1737 seems to have been a particularly unfortunate period. There were no provisions in the public store at Savannah, purchasing power was practically nil, and some men were obliged to find employment in South Carolina to prevent their families' starving.[4] By 1739 the province was in such a poor condition that it became fashionable to ridicule it.[5] "It was a melancholy thing," wrote George Whitefield on his second voyage there, "to see the colony of Georgia reduced even to a much lower state than when I left it, and almost deserted by all except those who could not well go away."[6]

Discontent was organized and fostered by a group of disgruntled persons, mainly Scotsmen, in Savannah. The leader was Patrick Tailfer, a doctor from Edinburgh, who had moved to Georgia in 1734 with a group of settlers that paid its own costs in transportation and provisions. Tailfer had been granted land, but abandoned any idea of becoming a planter when he discovered it was a long way from Savannah. He rented a house in Savannah and conducted a successful practice as a physician and surgeon, gaining considerable prestige and social influence, especially after he married the

2. *Colonial Records of the State of Georgia*, ed. A. D. Candler (26 vols., Atlanta, 1904–16), iv, 122; hereafter cited as *Col. Rec. Ga.*

3. W. Stephens to Trustees, Dec. 20, 1737, C.O. 5/640, fols. 26–8. *Col. Rec. Ga.*, iv, ii, 29.

4. Brownfield to Trustees, May 2, 1737, C.O. 5/639, fols. 271–2.

5. Tracy to Verelst, Aug. 25, 1739, C.O. 5/640, fol. 360.

6. A. O. Aldridge, "George Whitefield's Georgia Controversies," *Journal Of Southern History*, ix (Aug. 1943), 360.

sister of a prominent and respected merchant, Robert Williams.[7] Tailfer appears to have been widely recognized as a leader, but he was ably assisted by a number of other highly intelligent settlers, notably David Douglas, a merchant who owned one of the largest houses in Savannah which for a time he rented to George White-field for use as an orphanage. Hugh Anderson, a cultivated man who arrived in Georgia in the summer of 1737 and became in-spector of the public garden, was another who was quickly disil-lusioned with his lot and his prospects and joined Tailfer in the campaign against the policies of the Trustees.

Tailfer formed his followers into a club which met regularly at Edward Jenkins's tavern, where, no doubt, indignation could be raised to fever heat under the stimulus of a tot of unlicensed rum. Their most bitter complaints were over land tenure, which they termed "a slavery under the Trustees," and the prohibition of Negro labor, and by various means they sought to persuade the other inhabitants into thinking with them.[8] They spread alarming rumors, or "bugbear tales" as the Trustees' representative acidly described them, about the Trustees' intentions and of imminent Indian attacks. They conducted an advertising campaign to at-tract supporters, and in June 1740 promoted horse racing with the idea of inducing the onlookers to adjourn after the race to the tavern, where Tailfer and his colleagues ranted about the colonists' alleged grievances to an audience naturally disposed to be recep-tive so long as their tankards were full.[9]

In December 1738 the club drew up a representation to the Trustees, setting forth the impossibility of the province's continu-ing with its present land system, its lack of slave labor, and its commercial disadvantages in comparison with other British col-onies. This quickly became the talk of the town and received 121

7. C. L. Ver Steeg, ed., *A True and Historical Narrative of the Colony of Georgia* (Wormsloe Foundation Publications No. 4, Athens, Ga., 1960), xii–xiii.

8. W. Stephens to Trustees, Dec. 20, 1737, C.O. 5/640, fols. 26–8 *Col. Rec. Ga.*, IV, 48–9.

9. *Col. Rec. Ga.*, IV, 48, 539, 542, 604–5.

signatures. The malcontents proposed to publish the representation in other parts of America and in England, and were encouraged by news of similar disaffection among the inhabitants of Darien, some sixty miles down the coast from Savannah, who had sent a deputation to James Oglethorpe to lay their grievances before him. The Highlanders of Darien, however, were not so refractory as Tailfer's supporters in Savannah, and the representation had a cool reception there.[10] Finding that their complaints made little impression on the Trustees either, some of the malcontents by the close of 1739 were preparing to cross over to the opposite banks of the Savannah into South Carolina, where they would be entitled to employ Negroes. Differences arose among them, Tailfer's authority was questioned by some, and he himself threatened to move to one of the West Indian islands. In July 1740 a few left for New York, among them the notorious Mrs. Townshend, who, with her husband Edward, had run a victualling house in Savannah without a license and had execrated the Trustees and been a nuisance in the town for several years. Finally, in September, the leaders carried out their long-proclaimed intent to leave the province.[11]

A caustic commentary on the activities of the malcontents was maintained throughout this period by William Stephens, who kept himself well informed by visits to Edward Jenkins's tavern. Stephens had been born in the Isle of Wight in 1671, and had represented one of the island's constituencies in Parliament for twenty years early in the eighteenth century.[12] In April 1737 he was appointed secretary in Georgia for the Trustees with the task of keeping them circumstantially and regularly informed of affairs there. In April 1741, when Georgia was divided into two counties, Savannah in the north and Frederica in the south, each under jurisdiction of a president and four assistants, Stephens became president

10. *Ibid.*, 239, 243, 264–5, 276.

11. *Ibid.*, 465, 624, 630–1, 655. Sarah B. Gober Temple and K. Coleman, *Georgia Journeys* (Athens, Ga., 1961), 188–92.

12. *Dictionary of National Biography*. E. Merton Coulter, ed., *The Journal of William Stephens 1741–1745* (Wormsloe Foundation Publications nos. 2–3; two vols., Athens, 1958–9), I, xiii–xv.

of the northern county.[13] Then, in June 1743, when he was over seventy, infirm and encumbered with domestic bereavements, Stephens was made president of the whole colony.[14]

Stephens loyally supported the Trustees in the controversy with the malcontents. His reports in this period were couched in terms designed to stiffen the Trustees' resolve to adhere to their original policies, and he consistently threw doubt on the motives and arguments of the critics. The day after he arrived in Savannah in November 1737 he wrote to the Trustees about Tailfer and his companions, who, he said, met in parties "and cabal how to rectify and reform matters according to their several caprices."[15] From the very beginning of his appointment in Savannah his detailed reporting of affairs in the colony contained a mordant commentary on the malcontents and their ways, and he rejoiced when the leaders left in September 1740.[16] Two months later he called a meeting in Savannah and asked the colonists to sign a memorial entitled *A State of the Province of Georgia, attested upon oath in the court of Savannah, November 10, 1740.* The memorial was a statement and vindication of the Trustees' policy and drew a roseate picture that the colonists evidently found unrecognizable, for only a small number of signatories was collected. It was significant, however, in that it stimulated the malcontents who had left the province to issue a reply, which they published in Charleston in 1741.[17]

A True and Historical Narrative of the Colony of Georgia is dedi-

13. The intention was that Oglethorpe should become president of the southern county, but no appointment was ever made. Martyn to Stephens, April 24, 1741, C.O. 5/668, pages 10–11 *Col. Rec. Ga.*, II, 367–8. See also *Manuscripts of the Earl of Egmont: Diary of the First Earl of Egmont (Viscount Percival), 1730–1747*, ed. R. A. Roberts (3 vols., Historical Manuscripts Commission, London, 1920–3) III, 171–2; hereafter cited as *Egmont Diary.*

14. *Col. Rec. Ga.*, I, 419. G. White, *Historical Collections of Georgia* (3rd. edn., New York, 1855), 180.

15. Stephens to Trustees, Nov. 2. 1737, C.O. 5/639, fol. 418.

16. See *Col. Rec. Ga.*, IV and Suppl., The Journal of William Stephens (1737–41).

17. Ver Steeg, *op.cit.*, xxiv–xxv, xxx.

cated with mock admiration and excessive deference to James Oglethorpe, whose vanities it ridicules, and the tone of the entire piece is sarcastic and bitter. As a satire and exposé of conditions in colonial Georgia it has won, somewhat surprisingly, and perhaps not wholly deservedly, a niche in the history of early American literature. One authority considers that "its authors display an urbane cultivation, a familiarity with contemporary culture, and a detachment unusual in eighteenth century controversial writings."[18] Another American authority in the nineteenth century describes it as "one of the most expert pieces of writing to be met with in our early literature. Its mastery of the situation is everywhere maintained, through the perfect mastery on the part of the authors, of their own temper. It never blusters or scolds. It is always cool, poised, polite, and merciless; and it passes back and forth, with fatal ease, between dreadful fact and equally dreadful invective and raillery."[19] This regard for the quality of the pamphlet has been echoed by an American historian, whose own conclusion, more modest than that of the literary critics, and historically undeniable, is that it holds "a distinctive place in the literature of early Georgia."[20]

In essence, *A True and Historical Narrative of the Colony of Georgia* is a partisan statement of grievances expressed with vigor and feeling. It sets out in detail all the encumbrances under which the province is alleged to be laboring. The reasons for Georgia's slow and disappointed progress are listed as the sanguine and misleading description of its soil and climate by the Trustees; limitation of land tenure to tail-male; restrictions on a proprietor selling or leasing property; the impossibility of supporting a family on the permitted maximum of fifty acres; the high rate of quit-rents; the prohibition on Negro labor; anomalies in the legal system, especially Oglethorpe's assumption of the power to nominate magis-

18. Robert E. Spiller, *et al.*, eds., *Literary History of the United States* (revised edition in one volume, New York, 1953), 48–9 (Louis B. Wright).

19. Moses Coit Tyler, *A History of American Literature 1607–1765*, (New York, 1878; revised edn., Ithaca, N. Y., 1949), 516.

20. Ver Steeg, *op. cit.*, xi.

trates; ill-judged methods of encouraging the production of silk and wine; and the assigning of definitive tracts of land without regard to its quality or to the settlers' capabilities. Although the pamphlet is abusive, especially against Oglethorpe and Thomas Causton, the keeper of the public stores, much of its criticism was well-founded. The early propaganda put out by the Trustees had, in truth, been sanguine, and the criticisms directed at the land and property regulations were demonstrably valid. The labor problem was real, although the need for slaves could be questioned. Oglethorpe's expanding authority had become a source of uneasiness to the Trustees themselves, who distrusted his independence and his tendency to put his own construction on their orders and enforce them at his own discretion.[21] The injustice involved in the assignment of land, regardless of its qualities or the capabilities of the tenant, was to recur as a cause of complaint under the royal government after 1754. The criticism of the high rate of quit-rents, however, does not ring true nor bear examination, for payment did not commence until ten years after the grant and none of the settlers in Georgia had yet paid one penny in quit-rent.

The Trustees answered the malcontents' attacks by issuing Stephens's memorial of November 1740 in pamphlet form and publishing two items prepared by their secretary in London, Benjamin Martyn. *An Impartial Enquiry into the State and Utility of the Province of Georgia* appeared early in 1741. It was designed both to counteract the derogatory reports being circulated by Tailfer and others about the province's condition and progress, and to serve as a piece of promotional literature in the now-vital campaign to secure financial assistance from Parliament. *An Account shewing the Progress of the Colony of Georgia in America from its first Establishment* is more clearly a direct reply to *A True and Historical Narrative*, and is as bitter and venomous in style and tone as its target. It answers the complaints of the malcontents by cataloging the various motives which lay behind the policy of the Trustees in

21. *Egmont Diary*, III, 169. 171.

the matters the critics had mentioned. The result is a logical, persuasive, and convincing pamphlet which considers each issue in turn and presents in forceful language the case for the Trustees. As a lucid factual statement and piece of logical reasoning it is of a high order, and the Trustees could not have wished for their case to be better argued. It answered their purpose admirably, and all historians of early Georgia have used it as the most reliable contemporary account available.

The very persistence of the malcontents was bound to attract the attention they desired. Through friends in Savannah they spread reports of inevitable ruin, "tickling each other at the hellish imagination of."[22] Their influence became still more dangerous when they managed to acquire supporters in the mother country, where criticism of the province was increasing, especially in Parliament. The critics began to find their ammunition in the allegations sedulously publicized by the malcontents of the colony itself, and their main source of information was Thomas Stephens, the wayward son of William Stephens. Thomas Stephens had followed his father to Georgia in 1737, but returned to England in October 1739 determined to bring the situation in Georgia to public notice. Except for a few months at the end of 1741, when he revisited the province, he disseminated for over three years accounts of deplorable conditions prevailing in the colony as a result of its government and laws.[23] William Stephens was so aggrieved by his son's activities that he persuaded the Trustees to regrant his land in order to deprive Thomas of his inheritance.[24]

Thomas Stephens answered Martyn's pamphlets with *The Hard Case of the Distressed People of Georgia* in 1742, and in the following year with *A Brief Account of the Causes that have retarded the Progress of the Colony of Georgia*, both hard-hitting attacks on the Trustees and their policies. In April 1742 a petition from Stephens came

22. *Col. Rec. Ga.*, XXIII, 4.
23. *Egmont Diary*, III, 82, 84, 105, 118, 139, 176, 200, 205, 264.
24. *Col. Rec. Ga.*, I, 431.

before the Privy Council in London.[25] It alleged that the failure and impracticability of the Trustees' schemes in Georgia had been "properly represented" to them from time to time and the necessary alterations recommended and requested of them for nearly seven years. It argued that the Trustees' refusal to redress the grievances of the inhabitants had reduced the colony to a condition in which it was incapable of fulfilling the purposes of its establishment. The petition was debated in the House of Commons, a committee of which resolved in June 1742 that it contained "false, scandalous and malicious charges tending to asperse the characters of the Trustees," and that the preservation and support of Georgia was necessary and advantageous to Great Britain. The culprit was brought to the bar of the House, where, on his knees, he was reprimanded by the Speaker and compelled to admit the errors of his ways.[26]

The resolutions of the House of Commons in 1742 condemning Thomas Stephens were, no doubt, gratifying to the Trustees, but the fact could not be disguised that the Georgia project was falling into disrepute. By the early 1740s the colony was a disappointment to many people, and its record provided no valid reason why its existence should be maintained, except in the capacity of a buffer between Florida and South Carolina. None of the original expectations had materialized and there was little indication that it would ever contribute much of value to the imperial system. Many of the grievances aired by Tailfer and his associates were not fabricated; they definitely existed. The complaints regarding the absence of Negro labor, the regulations for land tenure, and the prohibition on rum did not come only from the malcontents; responsible and industrious inhabitants voiced the same objections. Much of the disaffection was founded on genuine misery, discomfort, and want. However proper the Trustees' economic policies may have seemed

25. P.C. 2/97 (Privy Council Registers, Series 2, Vol. 97, Public Record Office, London), 119. *Col. Rec. Ga.*, I, 396.

26. *Journals of the House of Commons*, xxiv, 192, 268, 285, 288. *Egmont Diary*, iii, 265; v, 641. Ella Lonn, *The Colonial Agents of the Southern Colonies* (Chapel Hill, N.C., 1945), 46–9.

in theory, they were patently harmful in practice. Although the malcontents did not secure a great number of active supporters, many sympathized with their views, and it cannot be said that in the end they were altogether unsuccessful. Their constant pressure, reinforced by arguments from more responsible and respected quarters, gradually proved to the Trustees that a wrong start had been made and that modifications in their policy were essential.

A State of the
Province of *Georgia*.

A

STATE

OF THE

Province of *Georgia,*

Attested upon OATH

IN THE

COURT of SAVANNAH,

November 10, 1740.

L O N D O N:
Printed for W. MEADOWS, at the *Angel* in *Cornhill.*
MDCCXLII.

A State of the
Province of *Georgia*.

Attested upon Oath in the Court of *Savannah, Nov.* 10, 1740.

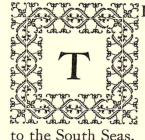T H E Province of *Georgia* lies from the most Northern Stream of the River *Savannah* (the Mouth of which is in the Latitude of 32 Deg.) along the Sea-Coast, to the most Southern Stream of the *Alatamaha* (the Mouth of which is 30½ Deg.) and Westward from the Heads of the said Rivers, respectively in direct Lines to the South Seas.

This Province was Part of *South-Carolina*; but the Eastern and Southern Parts of it, inhabited by the *Creek Indians*; the Northern by the *Cherokees* and *Chickesaws*; the Western by the *Chactaws*; the *Blew-mouths*, and other *Indian* Nations, to the *South-Sea*. The *Creek Indians*, who always acknowledged the King of *England* for their Sovereign, yet made War with the People of *Carolina*, to obtain Satisfaction for Injuries done by their pedling Traders: The War was concluded by a Peace, which obliged the People of *Carolina* not to settle beyond the River *Savannah*; and no *Englishman* was settled within this District, that we know of, when the first Colony of *Georgia* arrived. The Country was then all covered with Woods. Mr. *Oglethorpe* agreed with the *Indians*, and purchased of them the Limits mentioned in the Treaty.

The Town of *Savannah* was laid out, and began to be built, in which are now 142 Houses, and good habitable Huts. The Soil in general, when cleared, is productive of *Indian* Corn, Rice, Peas, Potatoes, Pumpions, Melons, and many other Kinds of Gourds, in great Quantities; Wheat, Oats, Barley, and other *European* Grains, 'tis found by divers Experiments, may be propagated in many Parts (more especially in the Uplands toward *Augusta*) with Success. Mulberry-Trees and Vines agree exceeding well with the Soil and Climate, and so does the Annual Cotton, whereof large Quantities have been raised; and it is much planted: But the Cotton, which in some Parts is perennial, dies here in the Winter; which nevertheless the Annual is not inferior to in Goodness, but requires more Trouble in cleansing from the Seed. Cattle, Hogs, Poultry, and Fruit-Trees of most Kinds, have increased even beyond Imagination.

Ships of about three hundred Tons can come up to the Town, where the Worm (which is the Plague of the *American* Seas) does not eat; and the River is navigable for large Boats, as far as the Town of *Augusta*, which lies in the Latitude of 33 D. 5 M. and is 250 Miles distant from *Savannah* by Water; small Boats can go 300 Miles further, to the *Cherokees*.

There is already a considerable Trade in the River; and there is in this Town a Court-House, a Goal, a Store-House, a large House for receiving the *Indians*, a Wharf or Bridge, a Guard-House, and some other publick Buildings; a publick Garden of ten Acres cleared, fenced, and planted with Orange-Trees, Mulberry-Trees, Vines, some Olives which thrive very well, Peaches, Apples, &c.

It must be confessed, that Oranges have not so universally thriven with us, as was expected, by Reason of some severe Blasts by Frosts in the Spring; yet divers with proper Care have preserved them; and as we see them grow and thrive well, with many of our Neighbours of *Carolina* to the Northward, we are convinced that they will with us also, as soon as we are become more perfect in the Knowledge of propagating them in a right Manner; in order to which frequent Experiments are making; and we have already discovered not only what Kind of Soil agrees best with them, but also that they flourish most when they grow under Forest Trees, whereby we imagine they are protected from Blasts; and 'tis observed, that they take no Harm from the Droppings of any, except the Pine, which suffers nothing to grow near it, unless of its own Kind.

Notwithstanding the Quantity of Silk, hitherto made, has not been great, yet it increases, and will more and more considerably, as the Mulberry-Trees grow, whereof there are great Numbers yearly planted.

Vines likewise of late are greatly increased, many People appearing to have an Emulation of outdoing their Neighbours; and this Year has produced a considerable Quantity of very fine Grapes, whereof one Planter in particular made a Trial, to see what Kind of Wine they would make, which he put into a large Stone-Bottle, and made a Present of it to the General; who upon tasting, said he found it to be something of the Nature of a small *French* White Wine, with an agreeable Flavour; and several Persons here, who have lived formerly in Countries where there are a Plenty of Vineyards, do affirm, that all young Vines produce small Wines at first, and the Strength and Goodness of it increases as the Vines grow older.

Three Miles up the River there is an *Indian* Town, and at six Miles Distance are several considerable Plantations: At ten Miles Distance are some more, and at fifteen Miles Distance is a little Village, called *Abercorn*.

Above that, on the *Carolina* Side, is the Town of *Purysburgh*, twenty-two Miles from *Savannah*; and on the *Georgia* Side, twelve Miles from *Purysburgh*, is the Town of *Ebenezer*, which thrives very much; there are very good Houses built for each of the Ministers, and an Orphan-House; and they have partly framed Houses, and partly Huts, neatly built, and formed into regular Streets; they have a great deal of Cattle and Corn-Ground, so that they sell Provisions at *Savannah*; for they raise much more then they can consume.

Thirty Miles above *Ebenezer*, on the *Carolina* Side, lies the *Palachocolas* Fort: Five Miles above the *Palachocolas*, on *Georgia* Side, lies the *Euchee* Town (or *Mount Pleasant*) to which about a hundred *Indians* belong; but few of them stay now in the Town, they chusing rather to live dispersed. All the Land from *Ebenezer* to the River *Briers* belongs to those *Indians*, who will not part with the same, therefore it cannot be planted.

One hundred and forty-four Miles above *Mount Pleasant*, on the *Carolina* Side, is *Silver Bluff*, where there is another Settlement of *Euchee Indians*: On both Sides of the River are Fields of Corn planted by them.

Thirty Miles above *Silver Bluff* is *New Windsor*, formerly known by the Name of *Savannah* Town, or *Moore's* Fort, where there are but two or three Families on the *Carolina* Side, and a small Fort.

Seven Miles above *New Windsor*, on the *Georgia* Side, lies the Town of *Augusta*, just below the Falls; this was laid out by the Trustees Orders in the Year 1735, which has thriven prodigiously; there are several Warehouses thoroughly well furnished with Goods for the *Indian* Trade, and five large Boats belonging to the different Inhabitants of the Town, which can carry about nine or ten thousand Weight of Deer-Skins each, making four or five Voyages at least in a Year to *Charles-Town*, for exporting to *England*; and the Value of each Cargo is computed to be from 12 to 1500 *l.* Sterling. Hither all the *English* Traders, with their Servants, resort in the Spring; and 'tis computed above two thousand Horses come thither at that Season; and the Traders, Packhorse-men, Servants, Townsmen, and others, depending upon that Business, are moderately computed to be six hundred white Men, who live by their Trade, carrying upon Packhorses all Kinds of proper *English* Goods; for which the *Indians* pay in Deer-Skins, Bever, and other Furs; each *Indian* Hunter is reckoned to get three hundred Weight of Deer-Skins in a Year. This is a very advantageous Trade to *England*, since it is mostly paid for in Woollen and Iron.

Above this Town to the North-West, and on the *Georgia* Side of the River, the *Cherokees* live, in the Valley of the *Appelachin* Mountains; they were about five thousand Warriors; but last Year it is computed they lost a thousand, partly by the Small-pox, and partly (as they themselves say) by too much Rum brought from *Carolina*. The *French* are striving to get this Nation from us, which if they do, *Carolina* must be supported by a vast Number of Troops, or lost: But as long as we keep the Town of *Augusta*, our

Party in the *Cherokees* can be so easily furnished with Arms, Ammunition and Necessaries, that the *French* will not be able to gain any Ground there.

The *Creek Indians* live to the Westward of this Town. Their chief Town is the *Cowetas*, two hundred Miles from *Augusta*, and one hundred and twenty Miles from the nearest *French* Fort. The *Lower Creeks* consist of about a thousand, and the *Upper Creeks* of about seven hundred Warriors, upon the Edge of whose Country, the *French* Fort of *Albamahs* lies: They are esteemed to be sincerely attached to his Majesty's Interest.

Beyond the *Creeks* lie the brave *Chickesaws*, who inhabit near the *Missisipi* River, and possess the Banks of it; these have resisted both the Bribes and Arms of the *French*, and Traders sent by us live amongst them.

At *Augusta* there is a handsome Fort, where there is a small Garrison of about twelve or fifteen Men, besides Officers; and one Reason that drew the Traders to settle the Town of *Augusta*, was the Safety they received from this Fort, which stands upon high Ground on the Side of the River *Savannah*, which is there one hundred and forty Yards wide, and very deep; another Reason was the Richness and Fertility of the Land. The great Value of this Town of *Augusta* occasioned the General to have a Path marked out, through the Woods, from thence to *Old Ebenezer*; and the *Cherokee Indians* have marked out one from thence to their Nation, so that Horsemen now can ride from the Town of *Savannah* to the Nation of *Cherokees*, and any other of the *Indian* Nations, all on the *Georgia* Side of the River; but there are some bad Places which ought to be causewayed and made good, and which the General says he has not yet Capacity to do. This Road begins to be frequented, and will every Day be more and more so, and by it the *Cherokee Indians* can at any Time come down to our Assistance.

At *Old Ebenezer* there is a Cow-Pen, where the Trustees have a great Number of Cattle, and 'tis hoped with Care they will amount to six or seven hundred Head in another Year: But they were much neglected, there not being Horses or Men sufficient to drive up the young and outlying Cattle.

This is the Situation of the Settlements upon the River, at the Mouth of which lies the Island of *Tybee*, with the Light-House, which has been of the greatest Use to all Ships falling in with this Part of *America*. But from *Savannah* Southward, there are several Plantations (besides the Villages of *Hampstead* and *Highgate*) several of which are settled by such of the Inhabitants of the Town, as being able to purchase Cattle, have petitioned for Leases of Lands, and are settled upon those Lands by the General's Permission, until the Trustees Pleasure be known concerning the Leases: The Terms they propose, is the Lease to be for twenty-one Years, renewable every seven Years, upon paying one Year's Purchase of the improved Value; the first seven Years to be free, and no Fine paid for the first Renewal. Besides these Settlements, there are some others of five hundred Acres *per* Grant from the Trust, which extend as far as the *Ogeechy* River; upon which River lies *Fort Argyll*, in such a Situation, as is intended thereby to command all the Passes in that Part of the Province.

The next is *Darien*, where the *Scots* Highlanders are settled; the Buildings are mostly Huts, but tight and warm; and they have a little Fort: They have been industrious in Planting, and have got into driving of Cattle, for the Supply of the Regiment, *&c.* but this last Year most of them going voluntarily into the War, little was done at home, where their Families remained.

Below the Town of *Darien*, is the Town of *Frederica*, where there is a strong Fort, and Store-Houses, many good Buildings in the Town, some of which are Brick; there is a Meadow near adjoining that is ditch'd in, of about three hundred and twenty Acres, of which there is good Hay made. The People have not planted much there this Year, occasioned by the War so near their Doors, and being chiefly Tradesmen, who make more by working, or selling to the Camp, than they can by Planting. There are some little Villages upon the Island of St. *Simon*'s, and some very handsome Houses built by the Officers of the Regiment; and there has been Pot-Herbs, Pulse, and Fruit, produced upon the Island, of great Use towards supplying the Town and Garrison: But Corn, Beer, and Meat, they have from elsewhere.

Between this Island and *Jekyll Island*, is an Inlet of the Sea, called *Jekyll Sound*, which is a very fine Harbour, and is one of the best Entries the *English* have to the Southward of *Virginia*. This is an excellent Station for Ships to cruize on the *Spaniards*, it commanding the homewardbound Trade, which must come through the Gulph of *Florida*, and near St. *Simon*'s; the Entry lies in 31 D. 10 M. The Place is barred, but upon the Bar there is Water sufficent every Tide to carry in Twenty-Gun Ships; and taking the best Opportunity, Forty-Gun Ships may be carried in to refit; — a great Conveniency to a Squadron in this Place. Upon *Jekyll Island* there is but very little good Land, not above three or four hundred Acres, the rest being sandy Sea-Beach. Mr. *Horton* has his Lot upon this Island, and has made great Improvements there. To the Southward of *Jekyll* lies the Island of *Cumberland*, and the Fort of St. *Andrew*'s, situated upon a fine commanding Ground; and on the S. E. of the same Island, is another strong Fort called *Fort William*, which commands *Amelia Sound*, and the inland Passage from *Augustine*. The next Island is *Amelia*; beyond that is St. *John*'s, one of the *Spanish* Outguards; and between forty and fifty Miles from that is *Augustine*.

We are now fully acquainted with the Colony, and what it will produce; the inland Part is hilly, till it rises into Mountains, where all Kinds of Timber grow. Near the Sea the Ground is more level and flat, where Laurels, Cedars, Cyprus, Bays, and Live Oak, are of the Size of Timber-Trees: Among the Shrubs, some of the principal are Pomegranates, which will grow well in Hedges, Myrtle, prickly Pears, Shumach, Sassafrass, China Root, several Sorts of Snake Root, &c. There is commonly black Mould in the low Lands; the rising Ground is frequently Clay, where Oak and Hickery mostly grow; as it also does in a great Part of the flat Land that is dry, where Walnut, Ash, Gum-Tree, Oak of several Kinds, Hickery, Beech, wild Cherries, &c. are in great Plenty to be found. The higher Lands are of a sandy Surface, where Pines usually grow, all Parts producing Trees of some Kind or other, except the Savannahs, and Marshes, which bear Grass; and many of the low Land Swamps covered with Canes, which are excellent Feed for

[9]

Cattle in the Winter. Where the Oak and Hickery grow, the Soil is in general of a strong Nature, and very well esteemed for Planting, being found by Experience to produce the best Crops of *Indian* Corn, and most Sorts of Grain, except Rice, which thrives best in swampy Ground: This is only spoken of the lower Parts of *Georgia*, which reaches from the Sea-Shore to the Foot of the Hills, being a flat Country of sixty or seventy Miles, or more, in Breadth. The Hill Country is very different, there being Marble, Chalk, Gravel, Rocks, and all the same Variety of Soil that is in Europe; with respect to the Proportion of the different Kinds of Soil, it cannot be given, unless the Whole were surveyed; but the *American* Dialect distinguishes Land into Pine, Oak and Hickery, Swamp, Savannah, and Marsh. Near the Town of *Savannah* we have found Stone, which is dug for Building; as there is also good Clay, whereof Bricks are made; and a Pottery Work is carried on with Success, where common Ware for most Uses is made in good Plenty, and exported to the neighbouring Provinces; and the Master, who is of an enterprizing Genius, has undertaken, as soon as he has made proper Furnaces, to make a superfine Sort, of such as shall not be inferior to *Porcelian* itself; but a little Time will discover his further Performances.

The Coast is low, with a hard, sandy Beach: When we approach it at twenty-five Leagues Distance, we find Ground in twenty-five Fathom Water, and it shoals gradually to the Shore; the Sounding being so regular, makes it a safe Coast to fall in with, having good Anchoring all along, and no Rocks. The Mouths of the Rivers *Savannah* and *Alatamaha* make a great Number of Islands, and the Entries between them form good Harbours. To the Southward of *Tybee* are the following Entries, *viz. Wassaw, Ossebah,* St. *Catharine*'s, *Sapello, Doboy,* St. *Simon*'s, which is the North-Entry to *Frederica; Jekyll Sound,* which is the South-Entry to *Frederica,* to which Place the Channel is navigable, from the ordinary Place of Anchoring in the Sound, for Ships of a good Burden up to the Town.

The Staple of the Country of *Georgia* being presumed, and intended to be, principally Silk and Wine, every Year confirms more our Hopes of succeeding in those two, from the great Increase (as has been before observed) of the Vines and Mulberry-Trees, wherein Perseverance only can bring it to Perfection. Several other Things might be produced, and perhaps more immediately profitable to the Planters; but it is apprehended, that it is not any Business of this Colony, nor any Benefit to the Trade of *England*, to interfere with what other *English* Plantations have produced, such as Rice, *&c*.

As the Boundaries of the Colony are now known, together with the Climate, and Manner of Agriculture, more might be done henceforward in one Year, than could in several Years before we attained to that Knowledge; but our People are weak, being decreased, by great Numbers having been decoyed away to other Colonies: Many having taken to Idleness, upon shutting up the Store went away; but those who stayed, and now remain, are still a Body of the most valuable People, that find Means to live comfortably, some by their Trades, some by Planting, and raising live Stock, and some by their Labour, either by Land or Water; and one of those remaining, are worth three that left us, for such Work: And if an Embarkation was to come in with the next Year, it would be of great Service to the Colony, the *Saltzburghers* wishing for more of their Countrymen, and having been very industrious.

The Persons sent from *England* on the Charity were of the Unfortunate, many of whom have by their Industry proved that they deserved better, and have thriven; many also shewed they were brought into those Misfortunes by their own Faults; and when those who quitted their own Country to avoid Labour, saw Labour stand before their Eyes in *Georgia*, they were easily persuaded to live in *Carolina* by Cunning, rather than work: This has been a great Misfortune also upon many Persons, who brought over Servants indented to serve them, for a certain Number of Years, who being picked up in the Streets of *London*, or some such Manner, their Masters found them unfit for Labour, and many of them took such Opportunities as they could get, to desert and fly into *Carolina*, where they could be protected. Indeed, good and bad which came from *England*, were mostly Inhabitants of Towns there; but such seldom turn out good Husbandmen with their own Hands; yet some of them proved very useful in a new Colony, since they most readily compose Towns, which is the first Thing necessary to be a Receptacle for new Comers: And from thence, when all Demands of Labour, for Building and Trade are supplied, the laborious People may enlarge into the Country, and raise Provisions for the Use of the Towns: Whereas, if the first were all labouring Countrymen, they would naturally disperse to the most fertile Land, and perhaps succeed for a While; but for Want of Neighbourhood and Markets, would force most of them to remove, and the Country remain little or nothing the better improved, as it happened in *Virginia*, till the Government, with great Difficulty at last, raised Towns in that Province.

It ought not here to be passed over, how ready the Country is to receive a Number of *German* Families, accustomed to Husbandry, such as usually come once a Year down the *Rhine* to *Holland*, and embark thence for *America*, or the *East-Indies;* some of these we have already had Experience of, insomuch that the People here would take off a good Number of them: And it would be of great Service (as we apprehend) to this Colony, at present, to send a Ship over, loaden with *Germans*, on the same Terms Mr. *Hope* does to *Philadelphia*, only taking Care that Provisions for them on their Passage be more plentiful, and that they are less crowded than on board his Ships: The Terms are, they pay Half their Passage themselves on embarking, and six Weeks after their Arrival, to pay the other Half, which they generally do, with private Contracts to People; but in case they do not, then they may be bound by the Ship's Master for four or five Years, if they are above twenty-one Years of Age; but if under, they may be bound until the Age of twenty-one if Men, and eighteen if Girls. It must be at the same Time confess'd, that divers of these Foreigners have, during the Time of their Servitude, shewn themselves of a dogged Disposition, surly and obstinate, discovering an Averseness to their Masters Orders, which proceeds (as we imagine) from a Dislike of their being subject to Strangers; whilst others again have behaved well; but it may be alledged with Truth, that when, or wheresoever among us, any of them have worked for their own Benefit, they are indefatigable, and out-done by none, which joined with great Parsimony, fits them for excellent Settlers when free.

To enable the industrious *English* Settlers to go on with Planting, who are truly desirous of cultivating Land; we humbly conceive nothing could be a greater Inducement to it, than that the honourable Trustees would please to import yearly, so long as they see good, a Number of *English* or *Welch* Servants, such as are used to hard Labour in the Country, and Strangers to London, to be contracted with in *England*, to serve the Trustees for five Years, from two to four Pounds yearly Wages, according to their Ability, for finding themselves in Apparel. Those Servants, on their Arrival, to be hired by the Inhabitants for one Year, the Person hiring to pay over and above the contracted Wages, one Pound yearly to the Trustees, so that in five Years the Passage-Money will be paid. And to enable the Planters to pay the said Wages, it is humbly proposed, that a Bounty be settled on every Product of the Land, *viz.* Corn, Pease, Potatoes, Wine, Silk, Cotton, Flax, *&c.* to what Value the honourable Trust shall judge meet to be limited in the following, or any other Manner, *viz.* For the first   Years the said Bounty to be payable for Corn, Pease, Potatoes, *&c.* only; and thenceforward to cease wholly, and the Residue of Years wherein any Bounty should be allowed, to be payable only for Silk, Wine, Oil, *&c.* by which Means the Planter so assisted might be able to live, whilst at the same Time he propagates Vines, Mulberry-Trees, *&c.* from which he can expect no immediate Benefit before they come to some Maturity. A Rule to be made, that they who hire the said Servants shall employ them only in Plantation-Work of their own, and not let them out at Hire to work at handicraft Trades, or any other Business, *&c.* That each Servant shall serve one whole Year; and if they part at the Year's End, he shall find himself another Master within   Days to serve for one Year also, and so on to the End of their respective Times to serve; by which Means good Masters will not want good Servants, and 'twill be a great Means to make other Masters become good, in order to get good Servants, or else be content with the bad, or none. If any Disputes arise between Masters and Servants, such to be determined by the Magistrates, according to the Laws of *England*, wherein the Magistrate concerned as a Party shall not appear as a Judge, or offer to interfere with the Opinion of the others, but acquiesce in their Determination, if it happens to be in Favour of the Servant, whom they ought to defend from cruel Usage, and where they find such evil Treatment either thro' too severe Correction, or want of sufficient wholsome Food, according to the Custom of the Colony, the Magistrates to have Power of vacating such Services, and obliging the Servants to find another Master.

The kind Intention of the honourable Trustees to extend the Tenure of Lands in the Manner proposed (as signify'd to their Secretary here) gave great Satisfaction to all reasonable Persons who seem'd to desire no more, and only wish to find that ratify'd, which they apprehend to be not yet done, and that occasions some Anxiety about it.

Whether these Helps, or whatever other, the honourable Trustees shall be pleas'd to afford us, the Ability of the Inhabitants to support themselves must still in a great Measure depend on the Industry and Frugality of each. Divers in the Province who understand Planting, and are already settled, provided they can attain to some live Stock, can and do support themselves. Men working for Hire, Boat-men, Packhorse-men, *&c.* support themselves very well, if they will work; and more such would, were they to be found. Shopkeepers, Tradesmen, and Artificers, such as Tallow-Chandlers, Soap-Boilers, Brasiers, Sadlers, Shoemakers, Tanners, *&c.* live very well on their Business here, and many more might, were there more Merchants to import Goods for supplying the *Indian* Traders, which would increase the Resort to *Savannah;* whereas those Traders are now obliged to get the greatest Part of what they want from *Charles-Town* in *Carolina.* New Planters, and such as go on upon particular Improvements, such as Wine, Silk, *&c.* will need some Assistance. Magistrates, Constables, and Tything-men, and others whose Time is taken up in the publick Service, require some Allowance for the same. It is also needful for the Well-being of the Colony, that Roads should be maintain'd: Posts for communicating of Letters, and Forts upon the Frontiers, as well towards the *Indians* as *Spaniards*, be supported: As likewise other publick Works, which the People here are in no Degree able to bear.

When the East Part of the Province of *Georgia* was taken Possession of under the Trustees Charter by Mr. *Oglethorpe*, according to the Limits of the *British* Dominions in *America*, Forts were erected upon the Extremities to keep up Marks of Possession: The Strength and Materials were of such a Nature, as the Men he had with him could make, and sufficient for Defence against any Strength that could be brought against them by the neighbouring *Indians*, or *Spaniards* in *Florida*.

The first Foundation of the Colony was upon Tenures, by which each Lot was to be occupied by a Freeholder, obliged to take Arms for the Defence of the Colony; and this Militia, with the Assistance of our friendly *Indians*, held the Colony against all Attempts of the *Spaniards* from *Augustine*, who alarmed them almost every Spring, pretending a Claim, and therefore a Right to invade, without being said to infringe the Peace; but did not take one Foot of Ground from us.

In the Beginning of the Year 1738, great Preparations were made at the *Havannah*, and Troops were sent from thence and *Old Spain* to *Augustine*, for the taking Possession (as they call'd it) of that Part of *Carolina* in which *Georgia* was comprehended, and which they gave out belong'd to them. Upon the Trustees having early Notice of these great Preparations, they applied to his Majesty to take upon him the Protection of the Colony, which in its Infancy was unable to repel so great a Force. His Majesty thereupon ordered a Regiment to be raised, and posted on the *Spanish* Frontiers, since which the War is broke out, and that Regiment, with the Assistance of Troops and *Indians* raised in *Georgia* and *Carolina*, in Conjunction with a Squadron of Men of War, attack'd *Augustine*, and after raising the Siege of that Place, remain'd in the Possession of the Frontiers, as before the War; but for the Defence of the Colony now, it is necessary to have Vessels that can act in shoal Water, on so large and extended a Frontier towards the Sea, and Rangers who can ride the Woods; as also Artillery, and all other Things necessarily appertaining thereto, and Means for augmenting our Fortifications equal to the increas'd Strength of the *Spaniards*.

Savannah, Nov. 10, 1740.

We whose Names are hereunto subscribed, being duly sworn in open Court, do declare, that the above State of the Province of *Georgia* is true, according to the best of our own Knowledge, and from the most certain Informations we could obtain from others; and do desire, that the Seal of this Court may be affixed thereto.

* Pat. Graham	George Johnson
* Jos. Fitzwalter	Samuel Parker
* James Carwells	Thomas Palmer
* Thomas Upton	William Stephens
* Giles Becu	Henry Parker
* Thomas Egerton	Thomas Jones
* Thomas Cundell	Samuel Mercer
Anthony Camuse	James Campbell
John Burton	John Rae
Jos. Pavey	Noble Jones
Robert Hainks	Thomas Young
John Mellidge	Thomas Ellis.
Tho. Bayley (Smith)	

N. B. Those seven mark'd with *, at their own voluntary Desire, were admitted to sign it, and were sworn before the Magistrates out of Court.

The Deposition of Lieutenant George Dunbar, *taken upon the Holy Evangelists, before the Recorder of the Town of* Frederica, Jan. 20, 1738-9.

This Deponent says, That he arrived in *Georgia* the Beginning of *June* last, with the first Detachment of General *Oglethorpe's* Regiment; and from that Time, to the Beginning of *August*, all the Carpenters of the said three Companies, and a certain Number of other Soldiers, were employ'd in building Clap-board Huts for the said Companies, and the other Soldiers were employ'd in unloading Vessels and Boats loaded with Clap-boards, and other Necessaries for Building, and Provisions of different

Kinds, often up to their Necks in Water: They were also employ'd in carrying Clap-boards, &c. upon their Backs to the Camp, in clearing Ground from Roots of Trees, &c. for a Parade, burning the Wood and Rubbish upon it, carrying of Bricks, and burning Lime: And the Artists who were excused from these Works, wrought at their own Trades, without standing still, by Reason of Heat. The Hours of Labour were from Day-Light, till between Eleven and Twelve; and from between One and Two, and sometimes between Two and Three, till Dark. All that Time the Men kept so healthy, that often no Man in the Camp ailed in the least, and none died except one Man, who came sick on board, and never worked at all; nor did I hear, that any of the Men ever made the Heat a Pretence for not Working.

And this Deponent further says, That he has been often in *America*, and frequently heard, that in the Negro Colonies, the Hire of White Men is more than that of Negroes. And this Deponent knows, that in *South-Carolina* White Ship-Carpenters and Caulkers have about one Third more Wages than a Negro of the same Trade or Profession, this Deponent having often paid Wages to both; and also knows there is the aforesaid Difference in many Handicrafts, and verily believes it is so in all; and affirms, that the same is owing to the White Men exceeding the Negroes in the same Professions, both in Quantity and Quality of their Work.

GEORGE DUNBAR.

Sworn before me the
Day and Year above
written,
FRANCIS MOORE.

Extract of a Letter from Mr. Thomas Jones *at* Savannah *in* Georgia, *to the* Trustees Accomptant, *dated* July 1, 1741.

The Trustees *German* Servants in general behave well, and are industrious: Of these, eight or ten Families are more remarkably so, and have this last Year purchas'd a good Stock of Cattle, some having six Cows, the least two; and each having a Garden, where they raise some Corn, Pease, Pompions, Potatoes, &c. which with the Milk of their Cows is the chief Part of their Food: They are at little Expence in Cloathing; but this exposes them to the Envy and Hatred of our Negro-Mongers, and such who seek the Extirpation of the Colony, as well as the of drunken, idle Sort amongst us.

I am informed by *Francis Harris* and *William Russell* (who are very conversant with them, and can talk the *German* Tongue) That they have lately joined, in a Letter writ and sent to their Friends and Acquaintance in *Germany*, persuading them to come to *Georgia*, where they may, by their Industry, live in greater Plenty, and more comfortably than they can elsewhere.

These Servants are very desirous, That (when the Time of their Service is expired) they have may Lands allotted them within twelve or fifteen Miles of *Savannah*, where they may bring Things by Land-Carriage in a Vicinage, and that they may make one common Fence (as the People of *Ebenezer* have done) and be assisting to one another.

The Copy of a Letter from the Reverend Mr. Frederick Michael Ziegenhagen, German *Chaplain to his Majesty, dated at* Kensington, January 11, 1741-2, *and sent to the Trustees for Establishing the Colony of* Georgia *in* America.

Gentlemen,

Having seen Paragraphs in Print representing the *Saltzburghers* as being uneasy with their Settlement at *Ebenezer* in *Georgia*, and desirous to remove therefrom; and fearing such Reports (if credited) might give just Offence to your Honours their Guardians, as well as to their Benefactors in *Germany*, and thereby deprive them from having yours, and their Favours continued.

I thought it my indispensible Duty to acquaint your Honours, That by all the Letters and Journals I have received since their Settlement at *New Ebenezer*, they have express'd quite different Sentiments; and not to trouble you with many Particulars, I beg Leave herewith to inclose you two Extracts of the latest Accounts I received from them in *November* last.

Extract of a Letter from the Reverend Mr. Boltzius *at* Ebenezer, *dated the* 23d *of* July, 1741, *to the Reverend Dr.* Francke, *Professor of Divinity at* Hall.

Together with these spiritual Blessings, and the salutary Effect of the Word of God to the Conversion of many Souls, we enjoy also this Year, by the Mercy of God, many temporal good Things.

The present War, and the Burden of it, hath not affected us yet, and we don't feel the least of it; and in the great Dearness the Colony suffered last Year, we have not been in Want of necessary Provisions. As to the present Year, we have a very hopeful Prospect of a good Harvest, every Thing in the Fields and Gardens growing so delightful, as our Eyes hardly have seen in this Country before. *If *Isaac*, by the Blessing of the Lord, received from what he had sowed, an hundred Fold, I believe, I dare say, to the Praise of the great Mercy of God over us, our *Saltzburghers* will get thousand Fold, notwithstanding that the Corn, when it came out of the Ground, was eaten quite up two or three Times by the Worms, of which nobody can hardly form a right Idea, except he sees it with his own Eyes. Wheat, Rice, and other Grain, must be sowed very thin, because each Grain brings forth fifty, an hundred, or more Stalks and Ears. The Land is really very fruitful, if the Sins of the Inhabitants, and the Curse of God for such Sins, doth not eat it up, which was formerly the unhappy Case of the blessed Land of *Canaan*.

And I am heartily sorry to acquaint you, that I don't find in some of the Inhabitants of the Colony, a due Thankfulness for, and Contentment with the many Benefits bestowed on them for several Years together; although those who are industrious, and will labour for their Maintenance, may, as we do, live contentedly, and subsist under the Blessing of God, promised by St. *Paul, Heb.* xiii. 5. *I will never leave thee, nor forsake thee.* Which Blessing the Idle and Unthankful are not intitled to.

Extract out of the Journal of Mr. Boltzius, *Minister of the Gospel at* Ebenezer *in* Georgia.

The 10th of *August*, 1741. We have this Year Plenty of Peaches, and as this Fruit doth not keep, some of our People try to make a certain Sort of Brandy of them, others give them to the Swine: This is more than any body could have promised to himself, or others, some Years ago. Even at this Time, when I am writing this, a Man brings a large Dish of blue Grapes to me, grown wild in the Woods; they are of a sweet Taste, and pretty like our *European* Grapes; that I am very apt to believe, the wild Vine-Trees, if properly managed, would give good Wine. Thanks be to our gracious God, who gives us here every good Thing for our Support.

The 9th of *September*, 1741. Some Time ago I wrote to an honoured

* Gen. 26:12.

Friend in *Europe*, That the Land in this Country, if well managed and laboured, brings forth, by the Blessings of God, not only hundred Fold, but thousand Fold; and I this Day was confirmed therein. A Woman having two Years ago picked out of *Indian* Corn, bought at *Purysburgh*, no more than three Grains of Rye (called here *German* Corn) and planting them here at *Ebenezer*, one of these Grains produced an hundred and seventy Stalks and Ears, and the three Grains yielded to her a Bag of Corn as large as a Coat-Pocket, the Grains whereof were good and full grown; and she desired me to send Part of them to a kind Benefactor in *Europe*. One of our *Saltzburghers* brought to me also a like Bag of Beans, all grown out of one Bean.

True it is, notwithstanding the Fertility of the Land, the first Tillagers of it must undergo and struggle with great Difficulties; but them that come after them will reap the Benefit thereof, if they go on to do their Labour in the Fear of God.

The Land is able to provide every good Thing, and more particularly is Pasturage very plenteous.

Finis.

A True and Historical Narrative
of the Colony of *Georgia* in *America*

A True and Historical

NARRATIVE

Of the COLONY of

GEORGIA

In *America,*

From the firſt Settlement thereof until
this preſent Period :

CONTAINING

The moſt authentick Facts, Matters and Tranſ-
actions therein;

TOGETHER WITH

His Majeſty's Charter, Repreſentations of the
People, Letters, &c.

AND

A Dedication to his Excellency General OGLETHORPE.

By { PAT. TAILFER, *M. D.*
HUGH ANDERSON, *M. A.*
DA. DOUGLAS, *and others,*

Land-holders in Georgia, *at preſent in* Charles-Town *in* South-
Carolina.

——Qui Deorum
Muneribus ſapienter uti,
Duramque callet pauperiem pati,
Pejuſque letho flagitium timet:
Non ille pro caris amicis,
Aut patria timidus perire.   HOR. lib. iv. Ode 9.

CHARLES-TOWN, SOUTH-CAROLINA:
Printed by P. TIMOTHY, for the Authois, M.DCC.XLI.

A True and Historical Narrative
of the Colony of *Georgia* in *America*

To his Excellency James Oglethorpe, *Esq*; *General and Command-*
er in chief of his Majesty's Forces in South-Carolina *and* Georgia;
and one of the honourable Trustees for establishing the Colony of
Georgia *in* America, *&c.*

May it please your Excellency,

A S the few surviving Remains of the Colony of *Georgia* find it necessary to present the World (and in particular *Great Britain*) with a true State of that Province from its first Rise to its present Period, your Excellency (of all Mankind) is best entitled to the Dedication, as the principal Author of its present Strength and Affluence, Freedom and Prosperity: And tho' incontestable Truths will recommend the following *Narrative* to the patient and attentive Reader; yet your Name, *Sir*, will be no little Ornament to the Frontispiece, and may possibly engage some courteous Perusers a little beyond it.

That Dedication and Flattery are synonimous, is the Complaint of every Dedicator who concludes himself ingenious and fortunate, if he can discover a less trite and direct Method of flattering than is usually practised; but we are happily prevented from the least Intention of this kind, by the repeated Offerings of the *Muses* and *News-Writers* to your Excellency in the publick Papers: 'Twere presumptuous even to dream of equalling or increasing them; we therefore flatter ourselves, that nothing we can advance will in the least shock your Excellency's Modesty; not doubting but your

[23]

Goodness will pardon any Deficiency of Elegance and Politeness on account of our Sincerity, and the serious Truths we have the Honour to approach you with.

We have seen the ancient Custom of sending forth Colonies for the Improvement of any distant Territory or new Acquisition, continued down to ourselves; but to your Excellency alone it is owing, that the World is made acquainted with a Plan, highly refined from those of all former Projectors. They fondly imagin'd it necessary to communicate to such young Settlements, the fullest Rights and Properties, all the Immunities of their Mother Countries, and Privileges rather more extensive: By such Means indeed these Colonies flourished with early Trade and Affluence; but your Excellency's Concern for our perpetual Welfare could never permit you to propose such transitory Advantages for us: You considered Riches like a Divine and Philosopher, as the *irritamenta malorum*, and knew that they were disposed to inflate weak Minds with Pride, to pamper the Body with Luxury, and introduce a long Variety of Evils. Thus have you *protected us from ourselves*, as Mr. *Waller* says, by keeping all earthly Comforts from us. You have afforded us the Opportunity of arriving at the Integrity of the *Primitive Times*, by entailing a more than *Primitive Poverty* on us: The Toil that is necessary to our bare Subsistence must effectually defend us from the Anxieties of any further Ambition: As we have no Properties to feed Vain-glory and beget Contention, so we are not puzzled with any System of Laws to ascertain and establish them: The valuable Vertue of Humility is secured to us by your Care, to prevent our procuring, or so much as seeing any *Negroes*, (the only human Creatures proper to improve our Soil) lest our Simplicity might mistake the poor *Africans* for greater Slaves than ourselves: And that we might fully receive the spiritual Benefit of those wholesome Austerities, you have wisely denied us the Use of such spiritous Liquors as might in the least divert our Minds from the Contemplation of our happy Circumstances.

Our Subject swells upon us; and did we allow ourselves to indulge our Inclination, without considering our weak Abilities, we should be tempted to launch out into many of your Excellency's extraordinary Endowments, which do not so much regard the Affair in Hand; but as this would lead us beyond the Bounds of a Dedication, so would it engross a Subject too extensive for us, to the Prejudice of other Authors and Panegyrists; we shall therefore confine ourselves to that remarkable Scene of your Conduct, whereby *Great Britain* in general, and the Settlers of *Georgia* in particular, are laid under such inexpressible Obligations.

Be pleased then, *Great Sir*, to accompany our heated Imaginations, in taking a View of this Colony of *Georgia*, this Child of your auspicious Politicks, arrived at the utmost Vigor of its Constitution, at a Term when most former States have been struggling through the Convulsions of their Infancy. This early Maturity, however, lessens our Admiration that your Excellency lives to see (what few Founders ever aspired after) the great Decline and almost final Termination of it. So many have finished their Course during the Progress of the Experiment, and such Numbers have retreated from the Phantoms of Poverty and Slavery, which their cowardly Imaginations pictur'd to them, that you may justly vaunt with the boldest Hero of them all,

> ————*Like Death you reign*
> *O'er silent Subjects and a desart Plain.* B U S I R I S.

Yet must your Enemies (if you have any) be reduced to confess, that no ordinary Statesman could have digested in the like Manner so capacious a Scheme, such a copious Jumble of Power and Politicks. We shall content ourselves with observing, that all those beauteous Models of Government which the little States of *Germany* exercise, and those extensive Liberties which the Boors of *Poland* enjoy, were designed to concenter in your System; and were we to regard the Modes of Government, we must have been strangely unlucky to have miss'd of the best, where there was the Appearance of so great a Variety; for under the Influence of our *Perpetual Dictator* we have seen something like *Aristocracy, Oligarchy*, as well as the *Triumvirate, Decemvirate*, and *Consular Authority* of famous Republicks, which have expired many Ages before us: What Wonder then we share the same Fate? Do their

Towns and Villages exist but in Story and Rubbish? We are all over Ruins; our Publick-works, Forts, Wells, Highways, Lighthouse, Store and Water-mills, &c. are dignified like theirs with the same venerable Desolation. The Log-house indeed is like to be the last forsaken Spot of your Empire; yet even this, thro' the Death or Desertion of those who should continue to inhabit it, must suddenly decay; the bankrupt Jailor himself shall be soon denied the Privilege of human Conversation; and when this last Moment of the Spell expires, the whole shall vanish like the Illusion of some *Eastern Magician*.

But let not this solitary Prospect impress your Excellency with any Fears of having your Services to Mankind, and to the Settlers of *Georgia* in particular, buried in Oblivion; for if we diminutive Authors are allowed to prophesy, (as you know Poets in those Cases formerly did) we may confidently presage, That while the Memoirs of *America* continue to be read in *English*, *Spanish*, or the Language of the *Scots Highlanders*, your Excellency's Exploits and Epocha will be transmitted to Posterity.

Should your Excellency apprehend the least Tincture of Flattery in any thing already hinted, we may sincerely assure you we intended nothing that our Sentiments did not very strictly attribute to your Merit; and in such Sentiments we have the Satisfaction of being fortified by all Persons of Impartiality and Discernment.

But to trespass no longer on those Minutes, which your Excellency may suppose more significantly employed on the Sequel, let it suffice at present to assure you, that we are deeply affected with your Favours; and tho' unable of ourselves properly to acknowledge them, we shall embrace every Opportunity of Recommending you to higher Powers, who (we are hopeful) will reward your Excellency according to your MERIT.

> *May it please your Excellency,*
> *Your Excellency's*
> *Most devoted Servants,*
> The Land-holders of GEORGIA,
> Authors of the following *Narrative*.

PREFACE.

THE *Colony of Georgia has afforded so much subject of Conversation to the World, that it is not to be question'd, but a true and impartial Account of it from its first Settlement to its present Period, will be generally agreeable; and the more so, that the Subject has hitherto been so much disguised and misrepresented in* Pamphlets, Poems, Gazettes *and* Journals.

If it is ask'd, Why this NARRATIVE *has not been publish'd to the World sooner? We assign two Reasons, which (we doubt not) will be satisfactory.*

First, *A Number of Honourable Gentlemen* accepted the Charge of Trustees *for executing the Purposes in his Majesty's most gracious* CHARTER; *Gentlemen, whose Honour and Integrity we never did, nor yet do call in Question: But, to our great Misfortune, none of that honourable Body (excepting Mr.* OGLETHORPE) *ever had Opportunity of viewing the Situation and Circumstances of the Colony, and judging for themselves as to the Necessities thereof. How far Mr.* Oglethorpe's *Schemes were consistent with the Welfare or Prosperity of it, will best appear from the following* Narrative.

When Experience gradually unfolded to us the Alterations we found absolutely requisite to our subsisting, we made all dutiful and submissive Applications to these our Patrons, in whom we placed so much Confidence: This Course we judged the most proper and direct, and therefore repeated these our dutiful Applications, both to the Body of the Trustees and to Mr. Oglethorpe; *but alas! our Miseries could not alter his Views of things, and therefore we could obtain no Redress from him; and the honourable Board we found were prejudiced against our Petitions (no doubt) thro' Misinformations and Misrepresentations; and this (we are confident) a further Enquiry and Time will convince them of.*

The inviolable Regard we paid to the honourable Board kept us from

[27]

applying to any other Power for Redress, whilst the least Hopes could be entertained of any from them: And we make no doubt, but that our Moderation in this respect will recommend us to all Persons of Humanity.

A second *Reason is, That as we had daily Occasion of seeing our supreme Magistrates, who ruled over us with unlimited Power, exercising illegal Acts of Authority, by Threatnings, Imprisonments, and other Oppressions; therefore we had just Reason to apprehend, that any further Steps to obtain Relief might subject us to the like Effects of arbitrary Power; so, until now, that a handful of us have made our Escape to a* Land of Liberty, *(after having made Shipwreck of our Time and Substance in that unhappy Colony) we had it not in our Power to represent the State of that Settlement to the World, or make our Application to higher Powers for Redress.*

We are hopeful that the Perusal of the following Sheets will rectify two sorts of Readers in their Surprize in relation to the Colony of GEORGIA, viz. *Those of* Great Britain, *who have never known this Part of the World but by Description; and those of* America: *The* First *are no doubt surprized to think it possible, that so* pleasant and temperate *a Clime, so* fruitful *a Soil, such* extensive *Privileges, all which were publickly given out, and such considerable Sums of publick and private Benefactions, have not satisfied and enriched us: Them we refer to the* following Narrative *for Satisfaction. The* American Reader, *on the other hand, must be equally surprized to find that such Numbers should have been so* fooled *and* blindfolded, *as to expect to live in this Part of* America *by Cultivation of Lands without* Negroes, *and much more without Titles to their Lands, and laid under a* Load *of Grievances and Restrictions: And tho' these were redress'd, how could Persons in their Senses ever imagine, that* Fifty Acres of Pine-Barren, *not value Fifty Sixpences in Property, (and whereof many Thousands may be purchased at half that rate in the neighbouring Province) could maintain a Family of White People, and pay such Duties and Quit-rents in a few Years, as the richest Grounds in* Carolina, *or other Provinces in* America, *will never bear? To these last we shall only beg Leave to observe, that such* fatal Artifice *was used, (we shall not say by whom) such* specious Pretences *were made use of, and such* real Falsities *advanced, and the* smallest Foundations *of Truth magnified to* Hyperbole; *that we, who had no Opportunity of knowing otherways, or means of learning the real Truth, and being void of all Suspicion of Artifice or Design, easily believed all these, and fell into the Decoy.*

The Mind of Man is naturally curious and enterprizing; we easily feed our Wishes into Realities, and affect and look upon every Novelty in the most favourable Light; how easy then is it for Cunning and Artifice to lay hold on the weak Sides of our Fellow Creatures, as we catch Fish with a Hook *baited to their particular* Goût?

To prove this Charge, we shall only *transcribe some Passages from a Piece of* Prose, *and some from a Piece of* Poesie; *by which Specimens the Reader may judge of some considerable Number which were dispers'd and vended of the same Stamp.*

The First *are from a Pamphlet printed at* London 1733, *entituled,* A new and accurate Account of the Provinces of SOUTH-CAROLINA and GEORGIA. *The Author has not thought fit to favour us with his Name; but it is easy to conceive that we, who suspected no Artifice or Design, must conclude that it came from the best* Authority, *from the Circumstances of its being dispersed publickly, and not being contradicted, and from the Author's intimate Acquaintance (at least so pretended) with all the Trustees Measures and Designs. After a high Encomium upon the Trustees,* Page 7, *he says,*

The Air of GEORGIA is healthy, being always serene and pleasant, never subject to excessive Heat or Cold, or sudden Changes of Weather; the Winter is regular and short, and the Summer cooled with refreshing Breezes; it neither feels the cutting North-west Wind that the *Virginians* complain of, nor the intense Heats of *Spain, Barbary, Italy,* and *Egypt.* The Soil will produce any thing with very little Culture.

Page 19,
All Sorts of Corn yield an amazing Increase; one Hundredfold is the common Estimate, tho' their Husbandry is so slight, that they can only be said to scratch the Earth, and meerly to cover the Seed: All the best Sort of Cattle and Fowls are multiplied without Number, and therefore without a Price: Vines are Natives here.

Page 21,

The Woods near *Savannah* are not hard to be cleared, many of them have no Under-Wood, and the Trees do not stand generally thick on the Ground, but at considerable Distances asunder: When you fell the Timber for Use, or to make Tar, the Root will rot in four or five Years; and in the mean time you may pasture the Ground; but if you would only destroy the Timber, 'tis done by half a Dozen Strokes of an Ax surrounding each Tree a little above the Root, in a Year or two the Water getting into the Wound rots the Timber, and a brisk Gust of Wind fells many Acres for you in an Hour, of which you may make one bright Bon-fire. Such will be frequently here the Fate of the *Pine*, the *Walnut*, the *Cypress*, the *Oak* and the *Cedar*. Such an Air and Soil can only be described by a Poetical Pen, because there is no Danger of exceeding the Truth; therefore take *WALLER*'s Description of an Island in the Neighbourhood of Carolina, to give you an Idea of this happy Climate:

> The Spring, which but salutes us here,
> Inhabits there, and courts them all the Year:
> Ripe Fruits and Blossoms on the same Tree live;
> At once they promise what at once they give.
> So sweet the Air, so moderate the Clime,
> None sickly lives, or dies before his Time.
> Heav'n sure has kept this Spot of Earth uncurst,
> To shew how all things were created first.

Page 27,

The *Indians* bring many a Mile the whole Deers Flesh, which they sell to the People who live in the Country for the Value of *Sixpence* Sterling; and a Wild Turkey of Forty Pound Weight for the Value of *Two Pence*.

In Page 32, *the Author when recommending the* Georgia *Adventure to Gentlemen of decayed Circumstances, who must labour at home or do worse, states the following Objection, viz.* "If such People can't get Bread here for their Labour, how will their Condition be mended in Georgia?" *Which he solves in the following Manner.*

The Answer is easy; Part of it is well attested, and Part Self-evident; they have Land there for nothing, and that Land so fertile, that, as is said before, they receive an Hundredfold Increase, for taking a very little Pains. Give here in *England* ten Acres of good Land to one of those helpless Persons, and I doubt not his Ability to make it sustain him, and by his own Culture, without letting it to another; but the Difference between no Rent and rack'd Rent, is the Difference between eating and starving.

Page 32,

These Trustees not only give Land to the Unhappy who go thither, but are also impowered to receive the voluntary Contributions of charitable Persons, to enable to furnish the poor Adventurers with all Necessaries for the Expence of their Voyage, occupying the Land, and supporting them till they find themselves comfortably settled; so that now the Unfortunate will not be obliged to bind themselves to a long Servitude to pay for their Passage, for they may be carried *gratis* into a Land of Liberty and Plenty, where they immediately find them selves in the Possession of a competent Estate, in an happier Climate than they knew before, and they are unfortunate indeed, if here they cannot forget their Sorrows.

Nay, as if such Assertions as these were not powerful enough to influence poor People, Calculations are subjoin'd, to demonstrate, that a Family consisting of one poor Man, his Wife, and Child of seven Years old, may in Georgia *earn sixty Pounds Sterling* per Annum, *and this abstracted from Silk, Wine, &c.*

Page 41,

Now this very Family in *Georgia*, by raising Rice and Corn sufficient for its Occasions, and by attending the Care of their Cattle and Land (which almost every one is able to do in some tolerable Degree for himself) will easily produce in gross Value the Sum of sixty Pounds Sterling *per Annum*; nor is this to be wondered at, because of the valuable Assistance it has from a fertile Soil and a Stock given *gratis*; which must always be remembered in this Calculation.

 The Calculation of one Hundred such Families when formally extended, stands thus,

Page 43,

	l. s. d.
In *London* one Hundred poor Men earn }	500 00 00
One Hundred Women and One Hundred Children, }	500 00 00
	1000 00 00

[31]

In *Georgia* an hundred Families earn,
 One Hundred Men for Labour,   1200 00 00
Ditto for Care of their Stock at ⎱
 Leisure Hours,   ⎰ 1200 00 00
One Hundred Women and One ⎱
 Hundred Children,   ⎰ 2400 00 00
Land and Stock in themselves,   1200 00 00
        Total, 6000 00 00
       2. E. D.

But we must conclude this Head, lest we tire the Reader. We shall now beg Leave to quote a few Poetical *Accounts of this* Paradise *of the World, and of the Fatherly Care and Protection we might depend on from Mr.* Oglethorpe. *An hundred Hackney Muses might be instanced; but we shall confine ourselves to the celebrated Performance of the Rev. Mr.* Samuel Wesley, *where we might well expect a sufficient Stock of Truth and Religion, to counter-ballance a Poetical Licence.* Vide *a Poem entituled,* GEORGIA, *and Verses upon Mr.* OGLE-THORPE's *second Voyage to* GEORGIA. *Printed* London, 1736.

 See where beyond the spacious Ocean lies
A wide waste Land beneath the Southern Skies;
Where kindly Suns for Ages roll'd in vain,
Nor e'er the Vintage saw, or ripening Grain;
Where all things into wild Luxuriance ran,
And burthen'd Nature ask'd the Aid of Man.
In this sweet Climate and prolifick Soil,
He bids the eager Swain indulge his Toil;
In free Possession to the Planter's Hand,
Consigns the rich uncultivated Land.
Go you, the Monarch cries, go settle there,
Whom *Britain* from her Plentitude can spare:
Go, your old wonted Industry pursue;
Nor envy *Spain* the Treasures of *Peru.*

 But not content in Council here to join,
A further Labour, OGLETHORPE, is thine:
In each great Deed thou claim'st the foremost Part,
And Toil and Danger charm thy gen'rous Heart:

But chief for this thy warm Affections rise,
For oh! thou view'st it with a Parent's Eyes:
For this thou tempt'st the vast tremenduous Main,
And Floods and Storms oppose their Threats in vain.

He comes, whose Life, while absent from your View,
Was one continued Ministry for you;
For you were laid out all his Pains and Art,
Won every Will, and soften'd every Heart.
With what paternal Joy shall he relate
How views its Mother Isle your little State:
Think while he strove your distant Coast to gain,
How oft he sigh'd and chid the tedious Main!
Impatient to survey, by Culture grac'd,
Your dreary Wood-land and your rugged Waste.
Fair were the Scenes he feign'd, the Prospects fair;
And sure, ye *Georgians*, all he feign'd was there.
A Thousand Pleasures crowd into his Breast,
But one, one mighty Thought, absorbs the rest,
And gives me Heav'n to see (the Patriot cries)
Another BRITAIN in the Desart rise.

Again,

With nobler Products see thy GEORGIA teems,
Chear'd with the genial Sun's directer Beams;
There the wild Vine to Culture learns to yield,
And purple Clusters ripen through the Field.
Now bid thy Merchants bring thy Wine no more,
Or from th' *Iberian* or the *Tuscan* Shore:
No more they need th' *Hungarian* Vineyards drain,
And *France* herself may drink her best *Champaign*.
Behold! at last, and in a subject Land,
Nectar sufficient for thy large Demand:
Delicious Nectar, powerful to improve
Our hospitable Mirth and social Love:
This for thy jovial Sons—Nor less the Care
Of thy young Province, to oblige the FAIR;
Here tend the Silk-Worm in the verdant Shade,
The frugal Matron and the blooming Maid.

[33]

From the Whole, we doubt not, the Reader will look upon us as sufficiently punished for our Credulity: And indeed, who would not have been catch'd with such Promises, such Prospects? What might not the Poor Man flatter himself with, from such an Alteration in his Situation? And how much more might a Gentleman expect from a plentiful Stock of his own, and Numbers of Servants to set up with? Could a Person with the least Faith, have question'd the Committing his Interests to such Guardians, and such a tender Father as Mr. Oglethorpe was believed to be? Whether he has acted that generous, that humane, that fatherly Part, the following NARRATIVE *must determine.*

As for these Poetical Licences touching the Wine and Silk, we do not transcribe them as a Reflection upon the Author, but as a Satyr upon the Mismanagement of those Manufactures; since no Measures were taken that seem'd really intended for their Advancement.

We no wise question the Possibility of advancing such Improvements in GEORGIA, *with far less Sums of Money, properly applied, than the Publick has bestow'd: But not even the Flourishing of Wine and Silk, can make a Colony of* British Subjects *happy, if they are deprived of the Liberties and Properties of their Birth-right.*

We have endeavour'd to the Utmost to be tender of Characters; but as we undertake to write an Account of Facts and Truths, there is no help for it, when those Facts and Truths press home.

It is a common Satisfaction to Sufferers, to expose to the Publick the Rocks upon which they split, and the Misfortunes by which they suffered; and it may well be allow'd us, to publish the Causes to which we attribute the Ruin of that Settlement and ourselves; and more especially as we are Prosecutors for Justice from higher Powers; which we doubt not receiving as the Case deserves.

We hope the Truth of the following Narrative *will recommend itself to the Perusal of the candid Reader. The fatal Truths of this Tragedy hath already been seal'd with the Death of Multitudes of our Fellow-Creatures; but still (Thanks to the Providence of the Almighty) some survive to attest and confirm the Truth of what is herein contain'd, against any Persons or Names, however great, however powerful. Our Circumstances and Sincerity will excuse our want of that Politeness and* Accuracy *of* Stile, *which might have represented our* Case *to greater* Advantage *to the* Courteous Reader, *whom we shall no longer detain from the* Subject *in hand.*

A true and historical
NARRATIVE, *&c.*

NOTHING is more difficult for Authors than to divest themselves of Byass and Partiality, especially when they themselves are Parties or Sufferers in the Affair treated of.

It is possible this may be supposed the Case with us the Publishers of this *Narrative;* it may be imagined, that the Hardships, Losses and Disappointments we have met with in the Colony of *Georgia,* will naturally sowr our Humours, and engage us to represent everything in the worst Light.

As the Probability of those Surmises is very obvious to us, we have, to the utmost of our Power, guarded against the weak Side of ourselves; and to convince the World of our Sincerity, shall no further descend into the Grievances of particular Persons, than is absolutely requisite for making our *General Narrative* intelligible; and to a faithful Detail of publick Vouchers, Records, Extracts, Missives, Memorials and Representations, shall only adjoin so much of History as may be necessary to recount the most material Events, and compleat the Connexion.

We are hopeful, that an Information founded upon the strictest Truth will effectually introduce any further Steps that Providence shall enable us to take towards procuring the Redress of our Grievances. While we had the least Hopes of Redress from our immediate Superiors and Patrons, we would not; and when we began to despair of Relief by that Channel, we durst not make Application to any other Tribunal, unless we would expose ourselves to the dreadful Effects of the Resentment of those who had before reduced us to Poverty by Oppression: And indeed, in all the Applications we made for Redress, we were brow-beat, obstructed, threatend, and branded with opprobrious Names, such as proud, idle, lazy, discontented and mutinous People, and several other Appellations of that kind, and were always afterwards harrassed by all Means whatsoever; several Instances of which will appear to the Reader in the Sequel.

Our late Retreat from that Confinement to a *Land of Liberty* puts it in our Power to speak the Truth; and tho' our Endeavours are too late to relieve the dead, the dying, and those many now dispersed in all the Corners of his Majesty's Dominions; yet they may be the Means of ushering in Sympathy and Assistance to the Survivors, and to Multitudes of Widows and Orphans of the deceased from the humane and generous.

As our sole Design is to give *A plain Narrative of the Establishment and Progress of the Colony of* GEORGIA, *from its Rise to its present Period*, we shall court no other Ornaments than those of Truth and Perspicuity, and shall endeavour to carry the Reader's Attention regularly from the first to the last Motions we make mention of.

In the Year 1732 his Majesty was pleased to erect, by his ROYAL CHARTER, into a separate Province, distinct from *South-Carolina*, that Space of Land lying between the Rivers *Savannah* and *Alatamaha*, under the Name of *GEORGIA*.

As this gracious Charter is the Basis and Foundation of all the Transactions relating to this Province, which have so much amused and perplexed the World, and which our Endeavour is to set in a true Light, we cannot dispense with inserting the Charter at large, which, we are confident, for many Reasons, will be acceptable to the Reader.

GEORGE *the Second, by the Grace of God, of* Great Britain, France *and* Ireland, King, *Defender of the Faith, &c*. To all to whom these Presents shall come, Greeting. *Whereas* We are credibly informed, That many of

Our poor Subjects are, through Misfortunes and Want of Employment, reduced to great Necessity, insomuch as by their Labour they are not able to provide a Maintenance for themselves and Families; and if they had Means to defray their Charges of Passage, and other Expences incident to new Settlements, they would be glad to settle in any of Our Provinces in *America*; where, by cultivating the Lands at present waste and desolate, they might not only gain a comfortable Subsistance for themselves and Families, but also strengthen Our Colonies, and increase the Trade, Navigation and Wealth of these Our Realms. *And whereas* Our Provinces in *North-America* have been frequently ravaged by *Indian* Enemies, more especially that of *South-Carolina*, which in the late War by the neighbouring Savages was laid waste by Fire and Sword, and great Numbers of the *English* Inhabitants miserably massacred; and Our loving Subjects who now inhabit there, by reason of the Smallness of their Numbers, will, in case of a new War, be exposed to the late Calamities, inasmuch as their whole southern Frontier continueth unsettled, and lieth open to the said Savages. *And whereas* we think it highly becoming our Crown and Royal Dignity to protect all Our loving Subjects, be they never so distant from Us, to extend Our fatherly Compassion even to the meanest and most infatuate of Our People, and to relieve the Wants of Our above mentioned poor Subjects; and that it will be highly conducive for accomplishing those Ends, that a regular Colony of the said poor People be settled and established in the southern Territories of *Carolina*: *And whereas* We have been well assured, That if We would be graciously pleased to erect and settle a Corporation for the receiving, managing and disposing of the Contributions of Our loving Subjects, divers Persons would be induced to contribute to the Purposes aforesaid, *Know Ye therefore*, That We have, for the Considerations aforesaid, and for the better and more orderly carrying on the said good Purposes, of Our special Grace, certain Knowledge, and mere Motion, Willed, Ordained, Constituted and Appointed, and by these Presents, for Us, Our Heirs and Successors, do Will, Ordain, Constitute, Declare and Grant, That Our Right trusty and Well-beloved *John* Lord Viscount *Purcival* of Our Kingdom of *Ireland*, Our Trusty and Well-beloved *Edward Digby, George Carpenter, James Oglethorpe, George Heathcote, Thomas Tower, Robert Moor, Robert Hucks, Roger Holland, William Sloper, Francis Eyles, John Laroche, James Vernon, William Beletha*, Esqrs. A.M. *John Burton*, B.D. *Richard Bundy*, A.M. *Arthur Bedford*, A.M. *Samuel Smith*, A.M. *Adam Anderson* and *Thomas Coram*, Gentlemen, and such other Persons as shall

[37]

be elected in the Manner herein after mentioned, and their Successors to be elected in the Manner herein after directed, be, and shall be one Body Politick and Corporate, in Deed and in Name, by the Name of *The Trustees for Establishing the Colony of* Georgia *in* America; and them and their Successors by the same Name, We do, by these Presents, for Us, Our Heirs and Successors, really and fully Make, Ordain, Constitute and Declare, to be one Body Politick in Deed and in Name for ever; and that by the same Name they and their Successors shall and may have perpetual Succession; and that they and their Successors, by that Name, shall and may for ever hereafter, be Persons able and capable in the Law, to purchase, have, take, receive and enjoy, to them and their Successors, any Manors, Messuages, Lands, Tenements, Rents, Advowsons, Liberties, Privileges, Jurisdictions, Franchises, and other Hereditaments whatsoever, lying and being in *Great Britain*, or any Part thereof, of whatsoever Nature, Kind or Quality, or Value they be, in Fie and in Perpetuity; not exceeding the yearly Value of *One thousand Pounds*, beyond Reprises; also Estates for Lives, and for Years; and all other manner of Goods, Chattels and Things whatsoever they be, for the better settling and supporting, and maintaining the said Colony, and other Uses aforesaid; and to give, grant, let and demise the said Manors, Messuages, Lands, Tenements, Hereditaments, Goods, Chattels and Things whatsoever aforesaid, by Lease or Leases, for Term of Years, in Possession at the time of granting thereof, and not in Reversion, not exceeding the Term of *Thirty one* Years, from the time of granting thereof; on which in case no Fine be taken, shall be reserved the Full; and in case a Fine be taken, shall be reserved at least a Moiety of the Value that the same shall reasonably and *bona fide* be worth at the time of such Demise; and that they and their Successors, by the Name aforesaid, shall and may for ever hereafter, be Persons able, capable in the Law, to purchase, have, take, receive and enjoy, to them and their Successors, any Lands, Territories, Possessions, Tenements, Jurisdictions, Franchises and Hereditaments whatsoever, lying and being in *America*, of what Quantity, Quality or Value whatsoever they be, for the better settling and supporting, and maintaining the said Colony; and that by the Name aforesaid they shall and may be able to sue and be sued, plead and be impleaded, answer and be answered unto, defend and be defended in all Courts and Places whatsoever, and before whatsoever Judges, Justices and other Officers, of Us, our Heirs and Successors, in all and singular Actions, Plaints, Pleas, Matters, Suits and Demands, of what Kind, Nature or Quality soever they be; and to act and do all other Matters and Things in as ample Manner and Form as any other Our Liege Subjects of this Realm of *Great Britain*, and that they and their Successors for ever hereafter, shall and may have a *Common Seal*, to serve for the Causes and Businesses of them and their Successors; and that it shall and may be lawful for them and their Successors, to change, break, alter and make new the said Seal, from time to time and at their Pleasure, as they shall think best. *And We do further grant*, for Us, Our Heirs and Successors, That the said Corporation, and the Common Council of the said Corporation herein after by Us appointed, may from time to time, and at all times, meet about their Affairs when and where they please, and transact and carry on the Business of the said Corporation. *And for the better Execution of the Purposes aforesaid, We do,* by these Presents, for Us, Our Heirs and Successors, *give and grant* to the said Corporation, and their Successors, That they and their Successors for ever, may, upon the *third Thursday* in the Month of *March* yearly, meet at some convenient Place to be appointed by the said Corporation, or major Part of them who shall be present at any Meeting of the said Corporation, to be had for the appointing of the said Place; and that they, or *two Thirds* of such of them that shall be present at such yearly Meeting, and at no other Meeting of the said Corporation, between the Hours of *Ten* in the Morning and *Four* in the Afternoon of the same Day, chuse and elect such Person or Persons to be Members of the said Corporation, as they shall think beneficial to the good Designs of the said Corporation. *And Our further Will and Pleasure is,* That if it shall happen that any Persons herein after by Us appointed as the Common Council of the said Corporation, or any other Persons to be elected or admitted Members of the said Common Council in the Manner hereafter directed, shall die, or shall by Writing under his or their Hands respectively resign his or their Office or Offices of Common Council Man or Common Council Men; the said Corporation, or the major Part of such of them as shall be present, shall and may at such Meeting, on the said *third Thursday* in *March* yearly, in manner as aforesaid, next after such Death or Resignation, and at no other Meeting of the said Corporation, into the room or place of such Person or Persons so dead or so resigning, elect and chuse one or more such Person or Persons, being Members of the said Corporation, as to them shall seem meet: *And Our Will is,* That all and every the Person or Persons which shall from time to time hereafter be elected Common Council Men of the said Corporation as aforesaid, do and shall, before he or they act as Common

Council Men of the said Corporation, take an Oath for the faithful and due Execution of their Office; which Oath the President of the said Corporation for the Time being, is hereby authorized and required to administer to such Person or Persons elected as aforesaid. *And Our Will and Pleasure is*, That the first President of the said Corporation is and shall be Our Trusty and Well-beloved the said *John* Lord Viscount *Purcival*; and that the said President shall, within *Thirty* Days after the passing this CHARTER, cause a Summons to be issued to the several Members of the said Corporation herein particularly named, to meet at such Time and Place as he shall appoint, to consult about and transact the Businesses of the said Corporation. *And Our Will and Pleasure is, and We,* by these Presents, for Us, Our Heirs and Successors, *grant, ordain, and direct,* That the Common Council of this Corporation shall consist of *Fifteen* in Number; *and* We do, by these Presents, nominate, constitute and appoint Our Right Trusty and Well-beloved *John* Lord Viscount *Purcival,* Our Trusty and Beloved *Edward Digby, George Carpenter, James Oglethorpe, George Heathcote, Thomas Laroche, James Vernon, William Beletha,* Esqrs. and *Stephen Hales,* Master of Arts, to be the Common Council of the said Corporation, to continue in the said Office during their good Behavior. *And whereas it is Our Royal Intention,* That the Members of the said Corporation should be encreased by Election, as soon as conveniently may be, to a greater Number than is hereby nominated; *Our further Will and Pleasure is, and We do hereby,* for Us, Our Heirs and Successors, *ordain and direct,* That from the Time of such Increase of the Members of the said Corporation, the Number of the Common Council shall be increased to *Twenty four;* and that at the same Assembly at which such additional Members of the said Corporation shall be chosen, there shall likewise be elected, in the Manner herein before directed for the Election of Common Council Men, *Nine* Persons to be the said Common Council Men, and to make up the Number *Twenty four. And Our further Will and Pleasure is,* That Our Trusty and Well-beloved *Edward Digby,* Esq; shall be the first Chairman of the Common Council of the said Corporation; and that the said Lord Viscount *Purcival* shall be and continue President of the said Corporation; and that the said *Edward Digby* shall be and continue Chairman of the Common Council of the said Corporation, respectively, until the Meeting which shall be had next and immediately after the first Meeting of the said Corporation, or of the Common Council of the said corporation respectively, and no longer: At which said second Meeting, and every other subsequent and future Meeting of the said Corporation, or of the Common Council of the said Corporation respectively, in order to preserve an indifferent Rotation of the several Offices of President of the Corporation, and of Chairman of the Common Council of the said Corporation; *We do direct and ordain*, That all and every the Person and Persons Members of the said Common Council for the time being, and no other, being present at such Meetings, shall severally and respectively in their Turns, preside at the Meetings which shall from time to time be held of the said Corporation, or of the Common Council of the said Corporation respectively: And in case any Doubt or Question shall at any time arise touching or concerning the Right of any Member of the said Common Council to preside at any Meeting of the said Corporation, or at the Common Council of the said Corporation, the same shall respectively be determined by the major Part of the said Corporation, or of the Common Council of the said Corporation respectively, who shall be present at such Meeting. *Provided always*, That no Member of the said Common Council having served in the Offices of *President of the said Corporation*, or of *Chairman of the Common Council of the said Corporation*, shall be capable of being or of serving as President or Chairman at any Meeting of the said Corporation or Common Council of the said Corporation, next and immediately ensuing that in which he so served as President of the said Corporation, or Chairman of the said Common Council of the said Corporation respectively; unless it shall so happen, that at any such Meeting of the said Corporation there shall not be any other Member of the said Common Council present. *And Our Will and Pleasure is*, That, at all and every of the Meetings of the said Corporation or of the Common Council of the said Corporation, the President or Chairman for the time being, shall have a Voice and shall vote and shall act as a Member of the said Corporation, or of the Common Council of the said Corporation, at such Meeting; and in case of any Equality of Votes, the said President or Chairman for the time being, shall have a lasting Vote. *And Our further Will and Pleasure is*, That no President of the said Corporation, or Chairman of the Common Council of the said Corporation, or Member of the said Common Council or Corporation, by Us by these Presents appointed, or hereafter from time to time to be elected and appointed in Manner aforesaid, shall have, take or receive, directly or indirectly, any Salary, Fee, Perquisite, Benefit or Profit whatsoever, for or by Reason of his or their serving the said Corporation, or Common Council of the said Corporation, or President, Chairman or Common Council Man, or as being a Member of the said

Corporation. *And Our Will and Pleasure is*, That the said herein before appointed President, Chairman or Common Council Men, before he and they act respectively as such, shall severally take an Oath for the faithful and due Execution of their Trust, to be administred to the President by the *Chief Baron of Our Court of Exchequer* for the Time being, and by the President of the said Corporation to the rest of the Common Council, who are hereby authorized severally and respectively to administer the same. *And Our Will and Pleasure is*, That all and every Person and Persons who shall have, in his or their own Name or Names, or in the Name or Names of any Person or Persons in Trust for him or them, or for his or their Benefit, any Office, Place or Employment of Profit, under the said Corporation, shall be incapable of being elected a Member of the said Corporation; and if any Member of the said Corporation, during such Time as he shall continue a Member thereof, shall in his own Name, or in the Name of any Person or Persons in Trust for him, or for his Benefit, have, hold, exercise, accept, possess or enjoy any Office, Place or Employment of Profit under the said Corporation, or under the Common Council of the said Corporation, such Member shall, from the Time of his having, holding, exercising, accepting, possessing and enjoying such Office, Place and Employment of Profit, cease to be a Member of the said Corporation. *And We do*, for Us, Our Heirs and Successors, *grant* unto the said Corporation and their Successors, That they and their Successors, or the major Part of such of them as shall be present at any Meeting of the said Corporation, conveen'd and assembled for that Purpose by a convenient Notice thereof, shall have Power from time to time, and at all times hereafter, to authorize and appoint such Persons as they shall think fit, to take Subscriptions, and to gather and collect such Monies as shall be by any Person or Persons contributed for the Purposes aforesaid, and shall and may revoke and make void such Authorities and Appointments as often as they shall see Cause so to do. *And We do hereby*, for Us, Our Heirs and Successors, *ordain and direct*, That the said Corporation every Year lay an Account in Writing before the *Chancellor*, or *Speaker*, or *Commissioners for the Custody of the Great Seal* of *Great Britain*, of Us, Our Heirs and Successors, the *Chief Justice of the Court of Kings-Bench*, the *Master of the Rolls*, the *Chief Justice of the Court of Common-Pleas*, and the *Chief Baron of the Exchequer*, of Us, Our Heirs and Successors, for the Time being, or any *Two* of them, of all Monies and Effects by them received or expended for the carrying on the good Purposes aforesaid. *And We do hereby*, for Us, Our Heirs and Successors, *give and grant* unto the said Corporation and their Successors, full Power and Authority to constitute, ordain, and make such and so many *By-Laws, Constitutions, Orders* and *Ordinances*, as to them, or the greater Part of them, at their General Meeting for that Purpose, shall seem necessary and convenient for the well ordering and governing of the said Corporation, and the said *By-Laws, Constitutions, Orders* and *Ordinances*, or any of them, to alter and annul as they, or the major Part of them then present, shall see requisite; and in and by such *By-Laws, Rules, Orders* and *Ordinances*, to set, impose and inflict reasonable Pains and Penalties upon any Offender or Offenders who shall transgress, break or violate the said *By-Laws, Constitutions, Orders* and *Ordinances*, so made as aforesaid, and to mitigate the same as they, or the major Part of them then present, shall think convenient; which said Pains and Penalties shall and may be levied, sued for, taken, retained and recovered by the said Corporation and their Successors, by their Officers and Servants from time to time to be appointed for that Purpose, by Action of Debt, or by any other lawful Ways or Means, to the Use and Behoof of the said Corporation and their Successors; all and singular which *By-Laws, Constitutions, Orders* and *Ordinances*, so as aforesaid to be made, WE WILL, shall be duly observed and kept, under the Pains and Penalties therein to be contained; so always as the said *By-Laws, Constitutions, Orders* and *Ordinances, Pains* and *Penalties*, from time to time to be made and imposed, be reasonable, and not contrary or repugnant to the *Laws* or *Statutes* of this Our Realm; and that such *By-Laws, Constitutions* and *Ordinances, Pains* and *Penalties*, from time to time to be made and imposed; and any *Repeal* or *Alteration* thereof, or any of them, be likewise agreed to, be established and confirmed by the said General Meeting of the said Corporation, to be held and kept next after the same shall be respectively made. *And whereas* the said Corporation intend to settle a Colony, and to make an Habitation and Plantation in that Part of Our Province of *South-Carolina* in *America*, herein after described; *Know Ye, That We*, greatly desiring the happy Success of the said Corporation, *for their further Encouragement* in accomplishing so excellent a Work, *Have*, of Our foresaid Grace, certain Knowledge, and mere Motion, *Given and Granted, and* by these Presents, for Us, Our Heirs and Successors, *Do Give and Grant* to the said Corporation and their Successors, the Reservation, Limitation and Declaration hereafter expressed, *Seven undivided Parts*, the Whole in *Eight equal Parts* to be divided, of all those Lands, Countries and Territories situate, lying, and being in that Part of *South-Carolina*, in *America*, which lies from the most northern Part of a Stream or River there, commonly called *The Savannah*, all along the Sea-coast to the Southward, unto the most southern Stream of a certain other great Water or River called *The Alatamaha*, and westerly from the Heads of the said Rivers respectively in direct Lines to the *South Seas*; and all that Share, Circuit and Precinct of Land within the said Boundaries, with the Islands on the Sea lying opposite to the eastern Coast of the said Lands, within *Twenty* Leagues of the same, which are not inhabited already, or settled by any Authority derived from the Crown of *Great Britain*, together with all the Soils, Grounds, Havens, Ports, Gulfs and Bays, Mines, as well Royal Mines of Gold and Silver as other Minerals, precious Stones, Quarries, Woods, Rivers, Waters, Fishings, as well Royal Fishings of Whale and Sturgeon, as other Fishings, Pearls, Commodities, Jurisdictions, Royalties, Franchises, Privileges and Pre-eminencies within the said Frontiers and Precincts thereof, and thereunto in any sort belonging or appertaining, and which We by Our *Letters Patent* may or can grant; and in as ample Manner and Sort as We may, or any Our Royal Progenitors have hitherto granted to any Company, Body Politick or Corporate, or to any Adventurer or Adventurers, Undertaker or Undertakers of any Discoveries, Plantations or Traffick of, in, or unto any Foreign Parts whatsoever, and in as legal and ample Manner as if the same were herein particularly mentioned and expressed: *To have, hold, possess* and *enjoy* the said *Seven undivided Parts*, the whole into *Eight equal Parts* to be divided as aforesaid, of all and singular the Lands, Countries and Territories, with all and singular other the Premisses herein before by these Presents granted, or mentioned or intended to be granted to them the said Corporation and their Successors *for ever*, for the better Support of the said Colony; to be holden of Us, Our Heirs and Successors, as of Our Honour of *Hampton-Court*, in Our County of *Middlesex*, in free and common Soccage, and not *in Capite*; *Yielding and Paying therefore* to Us, Our Heirs and Successors, yearly for ever, the Sum of *Four Shillings* for every *Hundred* Acres of the said Lands which the said Corporation shall grant, demise, plant or settle; the said Payment not to commence or to be made until *Ten* Years after such Grant, Demise, Planting or Settling, and to be answered and paid to Us, Our Heirs and Successors, in such Manner, and in such Species of Money or Notes as shall be current in Payment by *Proclamation* from time to time in Our said Province of *South-Carolina*; all which Lands, Countries, Territories and Premisses hereby granted, or mentioned and intended to be granted, *We do*, by these Presents, *make, erect and create,* One independent and separate Province by the Name of GEORGIA, by which Name WE WILL the same henceforth be called; and that all and every Person or Persons who shall at any time hereafter inhabit or reside within Our said Province, shall be and are hereby declared to be free, and shall not be subject to, or be bound to obey any Laws, Orders, Statutes or Constitutions which have been heretofore made, ordered and enacted, or which hereafter shall be made, ordered or enacted by, for, or as the Laws, Orders, Statutes or Constitutions of Our said Province of *South-Carolina,* (save and except only the Command in chief of the Militia of Our said Province of *Georgia,* to Our Governor for the Time being of *South-Carolina,* in Manner hereafter declared) but shall be subject to and bound to obey such Laws, Orders, Statutes and Constitutions as shall from time to time be made, ordered and enacted, for the better Government of the said Province of *Georgia,* in the manner herein after declared. *And We do hereby,* for Us, Our Heirs and Successors, *ordain, will and establish,* That for and during the Term of *Twenty one* Years, to commence from the Date of these Our *Letters Patent,* the said Corporation assembled for that Purpose, shall and may form and prepare *Laws, Statutes* and *Ordinances,* fit and necessary for and concerning the Government of the said Colony, and not repugnant to the *Laws* and *Statutes* of *England,* and the same shall and may present, under their *Common Seal,* to Us, Our Heirs and Successors, in Our or Their Privy Council, for Our or Their Approbation or Disallowance; and the said *Laws, Statutes* and *Ordinances* being approved of by Us, Our Heirs and Successors, in Our or Their Privy-Council, shall from thenceforth be in full Force and Virtue, within Our said Province of *Georgia. And Forasmuch* as the good and prosperous Success of the said Colony, cannot but chiefly depend, next under the Blessing of GOD and the Support of Our Royal Authority, upon the provident and good Direction of the whole Enterprize; *and* that it will be too great a Burthen upon all the Members of the said Corporation, to be convened so often as may be requisite to hold Meetings for the Settling, Supporting, Ordering and Maintaining the said Colony: *Therefore We do will, ordain and establish,* That the said Common Council for the time being, of the said Corporation, being assembled for that Purpose, or the major Part of them, shall from time to time, and at all times hereafter, have full Power and Authority to dispose of, extend and apply all the Monies and Effects belonging to the said Corporation, in such Manner and Ways, and by such Expences as they shall think best to conduce to the carrying on and effecting the good Purposes herein mentioned and intended: *And also*, shall have full Power, in the Name and on the Account of the said Corporation, and with and under their *Common Seal*, to enter under any Covenants or Contracts for carrying on and effecting the Purposes aforesaid. *And Our farther Will and Pleasure is*, That the said Common Council for the time being, or the major Part of such Common Council which shall be present and assembled for that Purpose from time to time, and at all times hereafter, shall and may nominate, constitute and appoint a Treasurer or Treasurers, Secretary or Secretaries, and such other Officers, Ministers and Servants of the said Corporation, as to them or the major Part of them as shall be present, shall seem proper or requisite for the good Management of their Affairs; *and* at their Will and Pleasure to displace, remove and put out such Treasurer or Treasurers, Secretary or Secretaries, and all such other Officers, Ministers and Servants, as often as they shall think fit so to do, and others in the Room, Office, Place or Station of him or them so displaced, removed or put out, to nominate, constitute and appoint; and shall and may determine and appoint such reasonable Salaries, Perquisites and other Rewards for their Labour, or Service of such Officers, Servants and Persons, as to the said Common Council shall seem meet; and all such Officers, Servants and Persons shall, before the acting their respective Offices, take an Oath, to be to them administered by the Chairman for the time being of the said Common Council of the said Corporation, who is hereby authorized to administer the same, for the faithful and due Execution of their respective Offices and Places. *And Our Will and Pleasure is*, That all such Person and Persons who shall from time to time be chosen or appointed Treasurer or Treasurers, Secretary or Secretaries of the said Corporation, in manner herein after directed, shall, during such times as they shall serve in the said Offices respectively, be incapable of being a Member of the said Corporation. *And We do further*, of Our special Grace, certain Knowledge and mere Motion, for Us, Our Heirs and Successors, *grant*, by these Presents, to the said Corporation and their Successors, That it shall be lawful for them and their Officers or Agents, at all times hereafter, to transport and convey out of Our Realm of *Great Britain*, or any other Our Dominions, into the said Province of *Georgia*, to be there settled, and so many of Our loving Subjects, or any Foreigners that are willing to become Our Subjects and live under our Allegiance in the said Colony, as shall be willing to go to inhabit or reside there, with sufficient Shipping, Armour, Weapons, Powder, Shot, Ordnance, Munition, Victuals, Merchandize and Wares, as are esteem'd by the *wild People*, Cloathing, Implements, Furniture, Cattle, Horses, Mares, and all other Things necessary for the said Colony, and for the Use and Defence, and Trade with the People there, and in passing and returning to and from the same. *Also We do*, for Our Selves and Successors, *declare*, by these Presents, That all and every the Persons which shall happen to be born within the said Province, and every of their Children and Posterity, shall have and enjoy all *Liberties, Franchises* and *Immunities* of *Free Denizons* and *Natural Born Subjects*, within any of Our Dominions, to all Intents and Purposes, as if abiding and born within this Our Kingdom of *Great-Britain*, or any other Dominion. *And* for the greater Ease and Encouragement of Our loving Subjects, and such others as shall come to inhabit in Our said Colony, *We do*, by these Presents, for Us, Our Heirs and Successors, *grant, establish and ordain*, That for ever hereafter there shall be a LIBERTY OF CONSCIENCE allowed in the *Worship of GOD*, to all Persons inhabiting, or which shall inhabit or be resident within Our said Province, and that all such Persons, except *Papists*, shall have a *free Exercise of Religion*; so they be contented with the quiet and peaceable Enjoyment of the same, not giving Offence or Scandal to the Government. *And Our further Will and Pleasure is, and We do hereby*, for Us, Our Heirs and Successors, *declare and grant*, That it shall and may be lawful for the said Common Council, or the major Part of them assembled for that Purpose, in the Name of the Corporation, and under the *Common Seal*, to distribute, convey, assign and set over such particular Portions of Lands, Tenements and Hereditaments by these Presents granted to the said Corporation, unto such of Our loving Subjects Naturally born or Denizons, or others, that shall be willing to become Our Subjects, and live under Our Allegiance in the said Colony, upon *such Terms*, and for *such Estates*, and upon *such Rents, Reservations* and *Conditions* as the same may be lawfully granted, and as to the said Common Council, or the major Part of them so present, shall seem fit and proper. *Provided always*, That no Grant shall be made of any Part of the said Lands unto any Person being *a Member of the said Corporation*, or to any other Person in Trust for the Benefit of *any Member of the said Corporation*; and that no Person having any Estate or Interest in Law or Equity in any Part of the said Lands, shall be capable of being *a Member of the said Corporation*, during the Continuance of such Estate or Interest. *Provided also*, That no greater Quantity of Lands be granted, either entirely or in Parcels, to or for the Use or in Trust for any one Person than *Five Hundred* Acres; and that all Grants made contrary to the true Intent and Meaning hereof, shall be absolutely null and void. *And We do hereby grant and ordain*, That such Person or Persons for the time being, as shall be thereunto appointed by the said Corporation, shall and may at all times, and from time to time hereafter, have full Power and Authority to administer and give *the Oaths* appointed by an *Act of Parliament* made in the First Year of the Reign of Our late Royal Father, to be taken instead of *the Oaths of Allegiance* and *Supremacy*; and also *the Oath of Abjuration*, to all and every Person and Persons which shall at any time be inhabiting or residing within Our said Colony; and in like Cases to administer *the solemn Affirmation* to any of the Persons commonly called *Quakers*, in such manner as by the Laws of Our Realm of *Great Britain* the same may be administered. *And We do*, of our further Grace, certain Knowledge and mere Motion, *grant, establish and ordain*, for Us, Our Heirs and Successors, That the said Corporation and their Successors shall have full Power and Authority for and during the Term of *Twenty one* Years, to commence from the Date of these Our *Letters Patent*, to erect and constitute *Judicatories* and *Courts of Record*, or other Courts, to be held in the Name of Us, Our Heirs and Successors, for the Hearing and Determining of all manner of Crimes, Offences, Pleas, Processes, Plaints, Actions, Matters, Causes and Things whatsoever, arising or happening within the said Province of *Georgia*, or between Persons of *Georgia*; whether the same be *criminal* or *civil*, and whether the said Crimes be *capital* or *not capital*, and whether the said Pleas be *real*, *personal* or *mixed*; and for Awarding and Making out Executions thereupon; To which Courts and Judicatories, *We do hereby*, for Us, Our Heirs and Successors, *give and grant* full Power and Authority, from time to time, to administer Oaths for the Discovery of Truth, in any Matter in controversy or depending before them, or the *solemn Affirmation* to any of the Persons commonly called *Quakers*, in such manner as by the Laws of Our Realm of *Great Britain* the same may be administered. *And Our further Will and Pleasure is*, That the said Corporation and their Successors do from time to time, and at all Times hereafter, register or cause to be registred all such Leases, Grants, Plantings, Conveyances, Settlements and Improvements whatsoever, as shall at any Time hereafter be made by or in the Name of the said Corporation, of any Lands, Tenements or Hereditaments within the said Province; and shall yearly send and transmit, or cause to be sent or transmitted, authentick Accounts of such Leases, Grants, Conveyances, Settlements and Improvements respectively, unto *the Auditor of the Plan-*

tations for the Time being, or *his Deputy*, and also to *Our Surveyor* for the Time being of Our said Province of *South-Carolina*, to whom *We do hereby grant* full Power and Authority from time to time, as often as Need shall require, to inspect and survey such of the said Lands and Premisses as shall be demised, granted and settled as aforesaid, which said Survey and Inspection, *We do hereby declare* to be intended to ascertain the *Quit-Rents* which shall from time to time become due to Us, Our Heirs and Successors, according to the Reservations herein before mentioned, and for no other Purposes whatsoever; *hereby*, for Us, Our Heirs and Successors, *strictly enjoining and commanding*, That neither Our or their Surveyor, or any Person whatsoever, under the Pretext and Colour of making the said Survey or Inspection, shall take, demand or receive any Gratuity, Fee or Reward of or from any Person or Persons inhabiting in the said Colony, or from the said Corporation or Common Council of the same, on the Pain of Forfeiture of the said Office or Offices, and incurring Our highest Displeasure. *Provided always, and Our further Will and Pleasure is*, That all Leases, Grants and Conveyances to be made by or in the Name of the said Corporation, of any Lands within the said Province, or a Memorial containing the Substance and Effect thereof, shall be registred with *the Auditor of the said Plantations*, of Us, Our Heirs and Successors, within the Space of *One* Year, to be computed from the Date thereof, otherwise the same shall be void. *And Our further Will and Pleasure is*, That the Rents, Issues and all other Profits which shall at any Time hereafter come to the said Corporation, or the major Part of them which shall be present at any Meeting for that Purpose assembled, shall think will most improve and enlarge the said Colony, and best answer the good Purposes herein before mentioned, and for defraying all other Charges about the same. *And Our Will and Pleasure is*, That the said Corporation and their Successors shall from time to time give in to one of *the principal Secretaries of State*, and to *the Commissioners of Trade and Plantations*, Accounts of the Progresses of the said Colony. *And Our Will and Pleasure is*, That no Act done at any Meeting of the said Common Council of the said Corporation shall be effectual and valid, unless *Eight* Members at least of the said Common Council, including the Member who shall serve as Chairman at the said Meeting, be present, and the major Part of them consenting thereunto. *And Our Will and Pleasure is*, That the Common Council of the said Corporation for the Time being, or the major Part of them who shall be present, being assembled for that Purpose, shall from time to time, for and during and unto the full End and Expiration of *Twenty one* Years, to commence from the Date of these Our *Letters Patent*, have full Power and Authority to nominate, make, constitute, commission, ordain and appoint, by such Name or Names, Stile or Stiles, as to them shall seem meet and fitting, all and singular such Governors, Judges, Magistrates, Ministers and Officers, Civil and Military, both by Sea and Land, within the said Districts, as shall by them be thought fit and needful to be made or used for the said Government of the said Colony; *save always* and except such Officers only as shall by Us, Our Heirs and Successors, be from time to time constituted and appointed for the managing and collecting and receiving such *Revenues* as shall from time to time arise within the said Province of *Georgia*, and become due to Us, our Heirs and Successors. *Provided always, and it is Our Will and Pleasure,* That every Governor of the said Province of *Georgia*, to be appointed by the Common Council of the said Corporation, before he shall enter upon or execute the said Office of Governor, shall be approved by Us, Our Heirs or Successors, and shall take such Oaths, and shall qualify himself in such Manner in all Respects, as any Governor or Commander in chief of any of Our Colonies or Plantations in *America* are by Law required to do; and shall give good and sufficient Security for observing the several Acts of Parliament relating to *Trade* and *Navigation*; and to observe and obey all Instructions that shall be sent to him by Us, Our Heirs and Successors, or any acting under Our or their Authority, pursuant to the said Acts, or any of them. *And We do* by these Presents, for Us, Our Heirs and Successors, *will, grant and ordain,* That the said Corporation and their Successors shall have full Power, for and during and until the full End and Term of *Twenty one* Years, to commence from the Date of these Our *Letters Patent*, by any Commander or other Officer or Officers by them for that Purpose from time to time appointed, to train, instruct, exercise and govern a Militia for the special Defence and Safety of Our said Colony, to assemble in Martial-array the Inhabitants of the said Colony, and to lead and conduct them, and with them to encounter, expulse, repel, resist and pursue, by Force of Arms, as well by Sea as by Land, within or without the Limits of Our said Colony; and also to kill, slay and destroy, and conquer, by all fighting Ways, Enterprizes and Means whatsoever, all and every such Person or Persons as shall at any Time hereafter in any hostile Manner attempt or enterprize the Destruction, Invasion, Detriment or Annoyance of Our said Colony; and to use and exercise the Martial-Law in Time of actual War and Invasion or Rebellion, in such Cases where by Law the same may be used or exercised; and also from time to time to erect Forts, and fortify any Place or Places within Our said Colony, and the same to furnish with all necessary Ammunition, Provisions and Stores of War for Offence and Defence, and so commit from time to time the Custody or Government of the same to such Person or Persons as to them shall seem meet; and the said Forts and Fortifications to demolish at their Pleasure; and to take and surprize, by all Ways and Means, all and every such Person or Persons, with their Ships, Arms, Ammunition and other Goods, as shall in an hostile Manner invade or attempt the invading, conquering or annoying of Our said Colony. *And Our Will and Pleasure is, and We do hereby,* for Us, Our Heirs and Successors, *declare and grant,* That the Governor and Commander in chief of the Province of *South-Carolina,* of Us, Our Heirs and Successors, for the Time being, shall at all Times hereafter have the chief Command of the Militia of Our said Province hereby erected and established; and that such Militia shall observe and obey all Orders and Directions that shall from time to time be given or sent to them by the said Governor or Commander in chief, any Thing in these Presents before contained to the contrary hereof in any wise notwithstanding. *And,* of Our more special Grace, certain Knowledge and mere Motion, *We have given and granted, and* by these Presents, for Us, Our Heirs and Successors, *do give and grant* unto the said Corporation and their Successors, full Power and Authority to import and export their Goods at and from any Port or Ports that shall be appointed by Us, Our Heirs and Successors, within the said Province of *Georgia* for that Purpose, without being obliged to touch at any other Port in *South-Carolina.* *And we do* by these Presents, for Us, Our Heirs and Successors, *will and declare,* That from and after the Determination of the said Term of *One and twenty* Years, such *Form of Government* and *Method of making Laws, Statutes and Ordinances,* for *the better governing and ordering the said Province of* Georgia, *and the Inhabitants thereof,* shall be established and observed within the same, as We, Our Heirs and Successors, shall hereafter ordain and appoint, and shall be agreeable to Law; and that from and after the Determination of the said Term of *One and twenty* Years, the *Governor* of Our said Province of *Georgia,* and all *Officers* Civil and Military within the same, shall from time to time be nominated and constituted and appointed by Us, Our Heirs and Successors. *And Lastly, We do hereby,* for Us, Our Heirs and Successors, *grant* unto the said Corporation and their Successors, That these Our *Letters Patent,* or the Enrolments or Exemplification thereof, shall be in and by all Things, good, firm, valid, sufficient and effectual in the Law, according to the true Intent and Meaning therof, and shall be taken, construed and adjudged in all Courts and elsewhere, in the most favourable and beneficial Sense, and for the best Advantage of the said Corporation and their Successors, any Omission, Imperfection, Defect, Matter or Cause or Thing whatsoever to the contrary in any wise notwithstanding. *In Witness We have caused these Our Letters to be made Patent.* Witness *Ourself at* Westminster, *the* Ninth *Day of* June, *in the* Fifth *Year of Our Reign.*

By Writ of Privy Seal.

COOKS.

The gracious Purposes and ample Privileges contained in the foregoing CHARTER, are so obvious to every Reader, that we need only say they were suitable to a most generous and humane *British Monarch;* and had the Settlement of the Colony of *Georgia* been carried on conformable thereto, and no other Restrictions or Reservations made than what are therein mentioned, then would the Colony at this Time have been in a flourishing Condition, answerable to all those glorious Ends that were proposed and expected from it: But on the contrary, Laws and Restrictions being made, such as were never heard of in any *British Settlement,* the Colony is brought to the present melancholy Situation. But we shall say no more at present on this Head than what Mr. *Oglethorpe* said in Parliament relating to the Charitable *Corporation, viz.* * *The better the Design was, the more those deserve to be punished who have disappointed the Publick of reaping the Benefits that might have accrued from it.*

Inhabitants of all sorts, *Roman Catholicks* only excepted, from all Parts of the World, were invited to possess this *promised Land,* and large Sums of Money from the Parliament, as well as Contributions from private and publick Charity, were collected; the Country was laid out as an *Earthly Paradise,* the Soil far surpassing that of *England,* the Air healthy, always serene, pleasant and temperate, never subject to excessive Heat or Cold, nor to sudden Changes.

* *Vide* Lond. Mag. *p.* 379.

It was particularly set forth, and with a Shew of Reason enough, that this proposed Settlement could not fail of succeeding when the Nation was so *bountiful*, the King so *gracious*, * the Trustees so *disinterested* and *honourable*, who had, for the Benefit of Mankind, given up that Ease and Indolence to which they were entitled by their Fortunes, and the too prevalent Custom of their Native Country; and withal being able, by seeing the Mistakes and Failures of other Colonies, both to avoid and rectify them; and lastly, the universal Report of Mr. *Oglethorpe*'s matchless *Humanity* and *Generosity*, who was to conduct the first Embarkation, and who was, in all Appearance, to undergo the greatest Hardships, without any other View than to succour the distressed; and, despising Interest or Riches, was to venture his Life, his All, in establishing the intended Settlement. *Glorious Presages* of the future Happiness of that Colony! *Irresistable Temptations* to those whose Genius or Circumstances led them to leave their native Country!

No wonder then that great Numbers of poor Subjects, who lay under a Cloud of Misfortunes, embraced the Opportunity of once more tasting Liberty and Happiness; that *Jews*, attracted by the Temptation of Inheritances, flock'd over; that *Germans*, oppressed and dissatisfied at home, willingly joined in the Adventure, some as Settlers, and others as Servants to the Trustees; and lastly, that great Numbers of Gentlemen of some Stock and Fortune, willingly expended Part of the same in purchasing Servants, Tools, Commodities and other Necessaries, to *entitle* them to such respective Proportions of Land as the Trustees had thought proper to determine, and such Liberties and Properties as they had Reason to expect from his Majesty's *most gracious Charter:* But how much they were all disappointed the Sequel will shew. The *first* Thing that was done was the circumscribing the Rights and Titles given by his Majesty, and making many other various Restrictions, Services and Conditions, impossible for any human Person to perform; a few of which we shall here enumerate: In the first Place, there was an excessive *Quit-Rent* laid upon the Land, being a great deal more

* *Vide* a Pamphlet, entituled, *A new and accurate Account of the Provinces of* South-Carolina *and* Georgia.

[53]

than his Majesty's Subjects in the other *British* Colonies pay, *viz.* *Twenty Shillings Sterling* for every *Hundred* Acres, to be paid yearly; and if it, or any Part thereof, should be behind and unpaid by the Space of Six Calendar Months next after any Day of Payment on which the same became due, then the Land was forfeited, and returned to the Trustees; as it likewise did upon Failure in any of the following Conditions, *viz. One thousand* Mulberry-Trees always to be growing on every *Hundred* Acres; no Partnership or Company to be entred into for making Pot-Ash; not to assign or transfer the Land, or any Part or Parcel thereof, or any Estate or Interest in the same, for any Term of Years; not to hire, keep, lodge, board or employ within the Limits of the Province, any Black or Negro; and if the Person holding Land should die without Issue Male, or his Heirs at any Time should die without Issue Male, in that Case likewise the whole Land was forfeited and reverted to the Trustees; and if any Part or Parcel of any of the *Five hundred* Acre-Tracts should remain not cultivated, cleared, planted and improved after the Space of *Eighteen* Years, such Part to return to the Trustees. These were the chief Restrictions in all the Grants of Lands, which appeared very hard even to Strangers, who had not yet felt them, and who were ignorant of the Climate and Nature of the Place; but when any one complained of the Hardships of them, to palliate the Matter, it was given out, that Negroes were entirely useless and unprofitable, Wine, Silk, Olives, Gardens, and Manufactures for Women and Children, were the intended Improvements of the Colony; that the Restriction of the Rights of Lands were only temporary, to prevent the bartering or selling them by the unthinking People at an Undervalue; and concerning the Want of Male Issue it was asserted, that the Trustees being duly petitioned, would grant Continuation of the Land to the eldest Daughter, if any, *&c.* upon their good * Behaviour: That the *Laws of England*, and the *Administration of Justice*, in the most impartial Manner, and most adapted to the Nature of *a free British Government*, should be ever secured to the Inhabitants.

* How precarious must this Security be to such unfortunate Persons, when their behaviour must be judged of by Information and Representation.

The first of *February* 1732-3, Mr. *Oglethorpe* arrived at *Georgia* with the first Embarkation, consisting of *Forty* Families, making upwards of *One hundred* Persons, all brought over and supported at the publick Charge. The FIRST Thing he did after he arrived in *Georgia* was to *make* a kind of *solemn Treaty* with a Parcel of *fugitive Indians*, who had been formerly banished their own Nation for some Crimes and Misdemeanors they had committed, and who had, some Months before this, got Liberty from the Governor of *South-Carolina* to settle there*. Some of these he afterwards carried home with him under *the Title* of *Kings, &c.* and all of them have been ever since maintained at the publick Charge, at vast Expence, when many poor *Christians* were starving in the Colony for Want of Bread; and we may safely affirm, (and appeal to the Store-books for the Truth of it) that a larger Sum of Money has been expended for the Support of those *useless Vagrants*, than ever was laid out for the Encouragement of Silk, Wine, or any other Manufacture in the Colony.

SECONDLY, He *prohibited* the *Importation* of *Rum*, under Pretence that it was destructive to the Constitution, and an Incentive to Debauchery and Idleness. However specious these Pretences might seem, a little Experience soon convinced us that this Restriction was directly opposite to the Well-being of the Colony: For in the *first* Place, we were cut off from the most immediate and probable Way of exporting our Timber (the only poor Prospect of Export that we could ever flatter ourselves with) to the *Sugar Islands*, Rum being the principal Return they make. In the *second* Place, the Experience of all the Inhabitants of *America* will prove the Necessity of qualifying *Water* with some *Spirit*, (and it is very certain, that no Province in *America* yields *Water* that such a Qualification is more necessary to than *Carolina* and *Georgia*) and the Usefulness of this Experiment has been sufficiently evident to all the Inhabitants of *Georgia* who could procure *it*, and use *it* with Moderation. A *third* Reason which made this Restriction very hurtful to the Colony was, That tho' the Laws were in force against

* They built a small Number of Huts on a Bluff called *Yamacraw. Savannah* now stands on the same Bluff.

it, (which put it in the Power of the Magistrates to lay Hardships upon every Person who might be *otherwise* under their *Resentment*) yet great Quantities were imported*, only with this Difference, that in place of Barter or Exchange, the ready Money was drained from *the Inhabitants:* And likewise, as it is *the Nature of Mankind* in general, and of *the common Sort* in particular, more *eagerly* to desire, and more *immoderately* to use those Things which are most restrained from them, such was the Case with Respect to Rum in *Georgia.*

The THIRD Thing he did was regularly to *set out* to each Freeholder in *Savannah* Lots of *Fifty* Acres, in *three* distinct Divisions, *viz.* The *Eighth Part* of *One* Acre for a House and Garden in the Town; *Four* Acres and 7 Eighths at a small Distance from the Town; and *Forty five* Acres at a considerable Remove from thence. No Regard was had to the *Quality* of the Ground in the Divisions, so that some were altogether Pine-Barren, and some swamp and Morass, far surpassing the Strength and Ability of the *Planter:* And indeed what could be done at any Rate with such small Parcels of Land separate from one another? These Lots were likewise shaped in long pointed Triangles, which considerably increased the Extent of Inclosure, and rendred great Part of each Lot entirely useless. But these and many other Hardships were scarcely felt by the few People that came there, so long as Mr. *Oglethorpe* staid, which was about *Fifteen* Months: They work'd hard indeed in building some Houses in Town; but then they labour'd in common, and were likewise assisted by Negroes from *Carolina*, who did the heaviest Work: But at † Mr. *Oglethorpe's* going to *England*, the growing Fame of the Colony was thereby greatly increased, so that, as it has been before observed, People in abundance from all Parts of the World flock'd to *Georgia*. Then they began to consider, and

---

* *Viz.* From *Carolina* and *New England*, who would take Money only.

† Before he departed, a Vessel with about *twenty* Families of *Jews* arrived, all of whom had Lots assigned them; and likewise a Vessel with *Forty* transported *Irish* Convicts, whom he purchased, although they had been before refused at *Jamaica*, and who afterwards occasioned continual Disturbances in the Colony.

endeavour, every one according to his Genius or Abilities, how they might best subsist themselves: Some, with great Labour and Expence, essayed the *making of * Tar:* This, as it is well known to the Trustees, never quitted Costs: Others tried to *make Plank* and *Saw-Boards;* which, by the great Price they were obliged to sell them at, by reason of the great Expence of white Servants, was the chief Means of ruining those who thought to procure a Living by their Buildings in Town; for Boards of all kinds could always be bought in *Carolina* for half the Price that they were able to sell them at; but few were capable to commission them from thence, and those who were so were prevented from doing it, upon Pretence of discouraging the Labour of white People in *Georgia.* Those who had Numbers of Servants and Tracts of Land in the Country, went upon the *Planting of Corn, Pease, Potatoes, &c.* and the Charge of these who succeeded the best, so far exceeded the Value of the Produce, that it would have saved *three Fourths* to have bought all from the *Carolina* Market. The *Felling of Timber* was a Task very unequal to the Strength and Constitution of White Servants, and the *Hoeing the Ground,* they being exposed to the sultry Heat of the Sun, insupportable; and it is well known, that this Labour is one of the hardest upon the Negroes, even though their Constitutions are much stronger than white People, and the Heat no way disagreeable nor hurtful to them; but in us it created *inflammatory Fevers* of various kinds both *continued* and *intermittent, wasting* and *tormenting Fluxes,* most *excruciating Cholicks,* and *Dry-Belly-Achs; Tremors, Vertigoes, Palsies,* and a long Train of *painful* and *lingring nervous Distempers;* which brought on to many a Cessation both from Work and Life; especially as *Water* without any Qualification was the chief Drink, and *Salt Meat* the only Provisions that could be had or afforded: And so general were these Disorders, that during the hot Season, which lasts from *March* to *October,* hardly one half of the Servants and working People were ever able to do their Masters or themselves the least Service; and the yearly Sickness of each Servant, generally speaking, cost his Mas-

* Mr.*Causton,* the Trustees Store-keeper, mostly at their Charge, made a Tar-Kiln, which turned out to no Advantage.

[57]

ter as much as would have maintained a Negroe for *four* Years. These Things were represented to the Trustees in Summer 1735, in a Petition for the Use of Negroes, signed by about *Seventeen* of the better sort of People in *Savannah:* In this Petition there was also set forth the great Disproportion betwixt the Maintenance and Cloathing of white Servants and Negroes. This Petition was carried to *England* and presented to the Trustees by Mr. *Hugh Stirling*, an experienced Planter in the Colony; but no Regard was had to it, or to what he could say, and great Resentment was even shewn to Mr. *Thompson*, the Master of the Vessel in which it went.

Whilst we laboured under those Difficulties in supporting ourselves, our *Civil Liberties* received a more *terrible* Shock: For, instead of such a free Government as we had Reason to expect, and of being judged by the Laws of our Mother Country, a * *Dictator*, (under the Title of *Bailiff* and *Store-keeper*) was appointed and left by Mr. *Oglethorpe* at his Departure, which was in *April* 1734 whose *Will and Pleasure* were the only Laws in *Georgia:* In regard to this Magistrate, the others were entirely nominal, and in a Manner but Cyphers: Sometimes he would ask in publick their Opinion, in order to have the Pleasure of showing his Power by contradicting them. He would often threaten Juries, and especially when their Verdicts did not agree with his Inclination or Humour. And in order the more fully to establish his *absolute* Authority, the Store and Disposal of the Provisions, Money and publick Places of Trust, were committed to him; by which Alteration in his State and Circumstances he became in a Manner *infatuated*, being before that a Person of no Substance or Character, having come over with Mr. *Oglethorpe* amongst the first *Forty*, and left *England* upon account of something committed by him concerning his Majesty's Duties: However, he was fit enough for a great many Purposes, being a Person naturally *proud, covetous, cunning* and *deceitful*, and would bring his Designs about by all possible Ways and Means.

As his *Power* increased so did his *Pride, Haughtiness* and *Cruelty*, insomuch that he caused *eight* Freeholders, with an Officer, to at-

* Mr. THOMAS CAUSTON.

tend at the Door of the Court every Day it sat, with their Guns and Bayonets, and they were commanded by his Orders to *rest their Firelocks* as soon as he appeared; which made People in some Manner afraid to speak their Minds, or Juries to act as their Consciences directed them. He was seldom or never uncovered on the Bench, not even when an Oath was administred; and being perfectly *intoxicated* with Power and Pride, he threatned every Person without Distinction, Rich and Poor, Strangers and Inhabitants, who in the least opposed his *arbitrary* Proceedings, or claimed their just Rights and Privileges, with the *Stocks*, *Whipping-Post* and *Log-House*, and many times put those Threatnings in Execution; so that the *Georgia Stocks*, *Whipping-Post* and *Log-House*, soon were famous in *Carolina*, and every where else in *America* where the Name of the Province was heard of, and the very Thoughts of coming to the Colony became a Terror to People's Minds. And now the Province of *Carolina*, who had, in private and publick Donations, given us upwards of 1300 *l. Sterling*, seeing these Things, and how the publick Money was thrown away, began to despise the Colony, and out of a Regard to the Welfare of their Fellow Creatures, disswaded every Body they could from settling in it. That this *absolute* Power might be exercised without the least Interruption, the other Magistrates were such, that they either were unable or incapable to oppose it: It is true, in *December* 1734, Mr. *Causton* met with a little Interruption; for the Trustees then sent over to *Savannah* one Mr. *Gordon*, as chief Magistrate, who being a Person of a very winning Behaviour, affable and fluent in Speech, soon got the Good-will of every Body, and a great many of the People laid their Grievances and Hardships open to him, which seem'd a little to eclipse Mr. *Causton*; but he soon found out an Expedient to remove this Adversary, *viz.* by refusing him Provisions from the Store, which in a little Time rendred him incapable to support himself and Family, whereby he was obliged, after about *six* Weeks Stay, to leave the Place, *in order*, as he said, *to represent our Grievances to the Trustees*, and soon after returned to *London;* but he did not perform his Promise, for what Reason we shall not pretend to determine; and some time thereafter he either resigned or was dismissed from his Office of First Bailiff, and Mr. *Causton* was appointed in his Stead. As to Mr. *Henry Parker*, who was appointed Third Bailiff when Mr. *Gordon* came over, he was, in the *first* Place, a Man who had nothing to support himself and large Family but his Day-Labour, which was Sawing, and consequently as soon as his Time was otherwise employed he must be entirely dependent on the Store for his Subsistance. In the *second* Place, he was a Man of no Education; so that Mr. *Causton* soon moulded him to his own liking, and infused into him what Notions he pleased. *Thirdly*, he was and is an *absolute* Slave to Liquor, and he who plies him most with it (which *Causton* always took care to do, and whose Example has been since followed by his Successor *Jones*) has him, right or wrong, on his Side. As to Mr. *Christie* the Recorder, he was easily over-ruled by the other two, and the same Practice was always continued; for he who was appointed Third Bailiff after *Gordon*'s Dismission or Resignation, was one *Darn*, nigh *Seventy* Years of Age, crazed both in Body and Mind, who died not long after his Appointment, and his Successor *R. Gilbert* could neither read nor write; so that *Causton* had never after *Gordon*'s Departure any Opposition made by the other Magistrates to his *arbitrary* Proceedings. If we should allow ourselves to enter into a Detail of the particular Instances of such Proceedings, we should exceed much our proposed Bounds; we shall therefore confine ourselves to *two* only, which may serve as a Specimen of the many others. *One* is that of Capt. *Joseph Watson:* This Person having incurred Mr. *Causton*'s Displeasure, was indicted for stirring up Animosities in the Minds of the *Indians*, *&c.* tending to the Ruin and Subversion of the Colony. Upon his Trial the Jury in their Verdict found him only guilty of *some unguarded Expressions*, (altho' twice returned and hectored by Mr. *Causton*, who acted both as Witness and Judge in the Matter) and verbally recommended him by their Foreman to the Mercy of the Court, imagining or supposing he might be lunatick; (however, as it afterwards appeared, it was represented to the Trustees that the Jury found him guilty of *Lunacy* in their Verdict) whereupon he was immediately confined by Mr. *Causton*, (altho' sufficient Bail was offered) and kept Prisoner near *three* Years, without any Sentence. But, as we are informed this Affair now lies before a proper Judicature, we shall say no more of it.

The *other* Instance is that of Mr. *Odingsell*, who was an Inhabitant of *Carolina*, and had been a great Benefactor to the infant Colony of *Georgia*, having given several Head of Cattle and other valuable Contributions towards the promoting it. This Person having come to *Savannah* to see how the Colony succeeded, after he had been there a few Days, being abroad some time after it was Night, as he was going to his Lodgings was taken up in the Street for a Stroller, carried to the Guard-house, and threatned with the Stocks and Whipping-Post; the Terror and Fright of which (he being a mild and peaceable Man) threw him into a *high Fever* with a *strong Delirium*, crying out to every Person who came near him, *that they were come to carry him to the Whipping-Post;* and after lying *two* or *three* Days in this distracted Condition, he was carried aboard his Boat in order to be sent home, and died in the Way somewhere about *Dawfuskee* Sound.

Thus, while the Nation at home was amused with the Fame of the Happiness and Flourishing of the Colony, and of its being free from *Lawyers* of any kind, the poor miserable Settlers and Inhabitants were exposed to as *arbitrary* a Government as *Turky* or *Muscovy* ever felt. Very Looks were criminal, and the grand Sin of *withstanding*, or any way *opposing* Authority, (as it was called, when any Person insisted upon his just Rights and Privileges) was punished without Mercy. Nevertheless, we bore all these Things patiently, in full Hopes that the Trustees Eyes would soon be opened, and then our Grievances be redressed, and still continued exhausting our Substance in pursuing an impracticable Scheme, namely, cultivating Land to Advantage in such a Climate with white Servants only, not doubting but that the Parliament, who yearly repeated their Bounty, would make up our Damages: But alas! their Bounty was applied in *Georgia* rather to the Hurt than Benefit of the Colony, as we shall here briefly relate. First, a *Light-House* was set about; but before the Frame was erected it was almost half rotten, and has not been carried on any further, nor never even covered, which has likewise greatly contributed to its Decay; and now that lofty Fabrick, so highly useful to Vessels which make that Coast, is either fallen or must fall very soon. *Log-Houses* and *Prisons* of various Sorts were built and erazed successively, and most Part of them were fitter for *Dungeons* in the *Spanish Inquisition* than *British Goals. Irons, Whipping-Posts, * Gibbets, &c.* were provided to keep the Inhabitants in perpetual Terror; for Innocence was no Protection; and for some time there were more Imprisonments, Whippings, &c. of white People in that *Colony of Liberty*, than in all *British America* besides. *Corn-Mills, Saw-Mills, Publick Roads, Trustees Plantations*, (as they were called) *Wells* and *Forts*, in different Places were all set about, but, as is evident from the Event, with no Design to serve the Publick, but only to amuse the World, and maintain some Creatures who assisted in keeping their Neighbours in Subjection; for few or none of these Things were ever brought to Perfection; some of them were left off half finished, and of those that were finished some were erazed, (being found of no Service) and others fell of themselves for Want of proper Care. To carry on the Manufactures of *Silk* and *Wine*, a Garden was planted with Mulberries and Vines, which was to be a Nursery to supply the rest of the Province: But this was as far from answering the proposed End as every Thing else was; for it is situated upon one of the most barren Spots of Land in the Colony, being only a large Hill of dry Sand: Great Sums of Money were thrown away upon it from Year to Year to no Purpose. This was remonstrated to the Trustees, and they seem'd to be sensible of the Error, and gave Orders to chuse another Spot of Ground; but the *ruling Powers* in *Georgia* took no Notice thereof. And now, after so great Time and Charge, there are not so many Mulberry-Trees in all the Province of *Georgia* as many one of the *Carolina* Planters have upon their Plantations, nor so much Silk made there in one Year as many of those Planters do make: Nor could they ever in that Garden raise one Vine to the Perfection of bearing Fruit. And here it may be observed, That the *Silk* Mr. *Oglethorpe*

* It was a very usual Thing with General OGLETHORPE, when any Person had incurred his Displeasure, to threaten to hang them.

carried over for a Present to Queen *CAROLINE*, was most of it, if not all, made in *Carolina*. Tho' no proper Measures were ever taken for advancing the *Silk* and *Wine Manufactures*, yet private Persons made several Essays towards the Culture of *European Grapes;* but even such Attempts met with no suitable Encouragement from Mr. *Oglethorpe*, as will appear from the following Fact. *Abraham De Leon*, a *Jew*, who had been many Years a Vineron in *Portugal*, and a Freeholder in *Savannah*, cultivated several kinds of Grapes in his Garden, and, amongst others, the *Porto* and *Malaga* to great Perfection; of this he sent home an attested Account to the Board of Trustees, proposing further, *That if they would lend him, upon such Security as he offered*, Two hundred Pounds Sterling, *for* three *Years without Interest, that he would employ the said Sum, with a further Stock of his own, in sending to* Portugal, *and bringing over Vines and Vinerons; and that he should be bound to repay the Money in* three *Years, and to have growing within the Colony* Forty thousand *such Vines, which he would furnish the Freeholders with at moderate Rates.*

The Trustees were satisfied with the Security, and accepted the Proposal, and wrote him, *That they had remitted the* Two hundred Pounds *by Mr.* Oglethorpe *for his Use;* which he did not deny when applied to by the said *Leon* for the same, but said, that he could not advance more than *Twenty* or *Thirty Pounds*, in regard he had other Uses for the Money; and so that Design dropt.

In *February* 1735–6 Mr. *Oglethorpe* arrived in *Georgia* for the *second* Time, with great Numbers of People, in order to settle to the southward, where he soon after carried them. Upon the Island of *St. Simons* he settled a Town, which he called *Frederica;* and about *five* Miles Distance from thence, towards the Sea, he placed the independent Company which he removed from *Port-Royal* in *Carolina*, their former Station. On one of the Branches of the *Alatamaha* he settled the *Highlanders*, in a Village which was called *Darien*. Then he settled a Fort on *Cumberland*, which he named *St. Andrews;* and some time after he caused a Garrison of about *Fifty* Men to be placed on a sandy Island (without fresh Water) in the Mouth of St. *John's* River, opposite to a *Spanish Look-out*,

[63]

where Possession was kept for about *six* Months, and several Fortifications built; but at last he was obliged to abandon it, after several People had lost their Lives by the Inconveniencies of the Place, besides great Sums of Money thrown away in vain.

Whilst Things thus passed in the southern Part of the Province, Mr. *Causton* was not idle at *Savannah;* and one would have thought, that he made it his particular Design further to exasperate the People of *Carolina:* He stopt their Boats who were going up to *New-Windsor;* and not content with that, he caused them to be searched, and whatever Rum was found therein was directly staved, in pursuance of an Act, as he alledged, entituled, *An Act against the Importation of Rum into the Colony of* Georgia. To complain of this, and to represent the bad State of the *Indian Trade*, a Committee from the Assembly of *South-Carolina* arrived at *Savannah* in *July* 1736, where Mr. *Oglethorpe* then was: But their coming was of little Consequence; for after this the Differences and Animosities betwixt the two Provinces rather encreased than diminished; and we shall only observe, that one Thing is certain, that ever since Mr. *Oglethorpe* intermeddled in the *Indian* Trade, it has decayed apace, and at this time is almost entirely *good-for-nothing* either to the one or the other Province.

Thus while the Province of *Carolina* resented the bad Treatment they had met with from the Leading Powers in *Georgia*, against the Colony in general; the poor inhabitants were doubly unfortunate, being ill look'd upon by their nearest Neighbours and Friends, for the Actings of their Governors, while they themselves were still the greatest Sufferers by those very Actings.

Whilst Mr. *Oglethorpe* staid in *Georgia*, great Complaints were made against the *arbitrary* Proceedings of Mr. *Causton;* but to no purpose: Likewise several Persons endeavoured to shew the Impossibility of the Colony's succeeding, according to its then present Constitution: But if this was done in his Hearing, he either always brow-beat the Person or evaded the Discourse; if by Letters, he never made any Answer to them; even altho' he had given publick Orders, that every Person should give in their Grievances and Complaints to him in Writing, and that he would consider and answer the same. But that we might not be entirely ignorant of his Thoughts, Mr. *Causton*, who always spoke his Sentiments, publickly declar'd, *That we had neither Lands, Rights or Possessions; that the Trustees gave, and that the Trustees could freely take away:* And again, when he was told, that the Light-house wanted a few Spike-nails to fasten some of its Braces which were loose, and which might occasion the Downfal of the whole Fabrick; he answer'd, *That he would say as Mr.* Oglethorpe *said, It might fall and be d - - - d.* Mr. *Oglethorpe* staid in *Georgia* until *November* 1736, most of which Time he spent to the Southward, and then embark'd for *England*, leaving Mr. *Causton* with the same Authority he had formerly invested him with, and in the same Power he then exercised, and the Colony under the same Difficulties and Hardships.

In *March* thereafter we had Advice of the *Spaniards* Intentions of attacking the Colony from the *Havannah*. This put the whole Province in great Consternation, especially the Town of *Savannah;* they having neither *Fort, Battery,* or any other Place to shelter themselves in, in case of any actual Attack: Therefore they immediately set about building a *Wooden Fort,* and all sorts of People labour'd continually until it was in some measure finish'd; only Mr. *Causton* never came to the Work, but did all he could to retard it, making light of the Information, altho' it was sent Express by Commodore *Dent,* with a Letter directed to the *Commander in Chief of Georgia;* and has since been put out of all manner of Doubt, the *Spaniards* having at that time *Four thousand* Men embarqued and ready to sail, if an extraordinary Accident had not prevented * them. People now seeing the *little* Care that was likely to be taken in case of a real Attack; and likewise finding, to their Cost, that the *Improvement of Land* was a vain and fruitless Labour with white Servants only, and with such Restrictions and

* They were detain'd *eight* Days at the *Havannah*, by contrary Winds; (the Land Forces being on board all that Time) at the End of which there came Orders from *Old Spain*, to forbear Hostilities, the Convention being then agreed upon.

precarious Titles, many began to withdraw and leave the Colony, and very little was planted this Season.

And *Now* to make our Subjection the more compleat, a new kind of Tyranny was this Summer begun to be imposed upon us; for Mr. *John Wesly* who had come over and was 1737. receiv'd by us as a Clergyman of the *Church of England*, soon discovered that his Aim was to enslave our *Minds*, as a necessary Preparative for enslaving our *Bodies*. The Attendances upon Prayers, Meetings and Sermons inculcated by him, so frequently, and at improper Hours, inconsistent with necessary Labour, especially in an infant Colony, tended to propagate a Spirit of Indolence, and of Hypocrisy amongst the most abandoned; it being much easier for such Persons, by an affected Shew of Religion, and Adherence to Mr. *Wesly*'s Novelties, to be provided by his Procurement from the publick Stores, than to use that Industry which *true* Religion recommends: Nor indeed could the Reverend Gentleman conceal the Designs he was so full of, having frequently declar'd, *That he never desir'd to see* Georgia *a Rich, but a* Religious Colony.

At last all Persons of any Consideration came to look upon him as a *Roman Catholick*, for which the following Reasons seem'd pretty convincing. 1*st*, Under an affected strict Adherence to the Church of *England*, he most unmercifully damned all *Dissenters* of whatever Denomination, who were never admitted to communicate with him until they first gave up their Faith and Principles entirely to his Moulding and Direction, and in Confirmation thereof declared their Belief of the invalidity of their former Baptism, and then to receive a new one from him: This was done publickly on the Persons of *Richard Turner*, Carpenter, and his Son. Another Instance was that of *William Gaff*, who had once communicated and always conformed to his Regulations, but was at last found out by Mr. *Wesly* to have been baptized by a *Presbyterian Dissenter*, the same thing was propos'd to him; but Mr. *Gaff* not inclinable to go that length; was ever thereafter excluded from the Communion.

* According to his System.

2dly, While all *Dissenters* (whereof a considerable Number was in the Colony) were thus unmercifully damned, and shut out from Religious Ordinances, contrary to that Spirit of Moderation and Tenderness which the *Church of England* shews towards them; Persons suspected to be *Roman Catholicks* were received and caressed by him as his First-rate Saints.

3dly, A third Confirmation of this Suspicion arose from his Endeavours to establish Confession, Penance, Mortifications, Mixing Wine with Water in the Sacrament, and Suppressing in the Administration of the Sacrament the Explanation adjoyned to the Words of communicating by the *Church of England*, to shew that they mean a Feeding on Christ by Faith, saying no more than "The Body of Christ; The Blood of Christ;" by appointing Deaconesses, with sundry other Innovations, which he called *Apostolick Constitutions*.

4thly, As there is always a strict Connexion betwixt *Popery* and *Slavery;* so the Design of all this fine Scheme seem'd to the most Judicious to be calculated to debase and depress the Minds of the People, to break any Spirit of Liberty, and humble them with Fastings, Penances, Drinking of Water, and thorough Subjection to the Spiritual Jurisdiction which he asserted was to be established in his Person; and when this should be accomplished, the Minds of People would be equally prepared for the receiving Civil or Ecclesiastical Tyranny.

All *Jesuitical* Arts were made use of to bring the well concerted Scheme to Perfection; Families were divided in Parties; Spies were engaged in many Houses, and the Servants of others brib'd and decoy'd to let him into all the Secrets of the Families they belonged to; nay, those who had given themselves up to his Spiritual Guidance (more especially Women) were obliged to discover to him their most secret Actions, nay even their Thoughts and the Subject of their Dreams: At the same time he gave Charge to Juries; gave his Opinion in all Civil Causes that came before the Court: Nor could we imagine what all this would end in: Complain we might; but to no purpose: And Mr. *Causton* and he went *hand-in-hand*.

But the merciful Providence of GOD disappoints frequently those Designs that are laid deepest in Human Prudence.

Mr. *Wesly* at this time repulsed Mrs. *Sophia Williamson*, Neice to Mr. *Causton*, from the Sacrament. This young Lady was by her Friends put under the Ghostly Care of Mr. *Wesly*, who was pleased to make Proposals of Marriage to her: These she always rejected; and in some little time married Mr. *William Williamson* of *Savannah*, much contrary to Mr. *Wesly*'s Inclinations: After the said Marriage Mr. *Wesly* used all Means to create a Misunderstanding betwixt Mrs. *Williamson* and her Husband, by persuading her, that Mr. *Williamson* had no Right to regulate her Behaviour as to conversing with him, or attending Meetings as formerly; but at last finding he could gain nothing upon her, and that Mr. *Williamson* had forbid him any Conversation with his Wife out of his Presence; he took the foresaid Means, by repelling her from the Holy Communion, of shewing his Resentment. Mr. *Williamson* thought himself well founded in an Action of Damages; and *Mr.* WESLY (being no longer supported by Mr. *Causton*, who was highly nettled at the Affront put upon his Neice, and could now declaim as fluently against Spiritual Tyranny as any Person) was indicted before a GRAND JURY of *Forty four* Freeholders, and *Thirteen* Indictments were found against him; *one* concerned *Mr. Williamson* and his Spouse; the others concerning the Grievances we felt by his Measures, and the Exercise of his Ecclesiastical Functions, as above related: These last were given in to the Magistrates, to be by them laid before the Trustees, that these our Grievances might in time coming be properly redressed, (we having no other Jurisdiction, either Civil or Ecclesiastical, that we could make Application to:) Then the Grand Jury began to consider and think, that as it was not probable a greater Number of the *better Sort* of People could ever be legally met together; so this was a fit Time to represent their Grievances and Hardships to the Trustees: Which they did in the following Manner.

An Abstract of the Representation of the Grand Jury of SAVANNAH to the Honourable the Trustees.

WE the Grand Jury duly sworn on the 22*d* of the last Month, and having divers Matters laid before us, which we humbly conceive cannot properly be presented to this Court, because several of the said Matters touch the Proceedings of the Magistrates of the said Court, and contain sundry Articles, setting forth many publick Necessities and Hardships, which can only be remedied by your Honours Authority: *THEREFORE,* We the said Grand Jury having examined several Witnesess, do, upon our Oaths, represent to your Honours the following *Grievances, Hardships* and *Necessities.*

That as the Inhabitants of this Town and County have been and are still subject to many Inconveniencies, for Want of a Body of the Laws and Constitutions of this Province; it being exceeding difficult in many Cases, both for Grand and Petit Juries, to discharge in a proper manner the great Duties that are incumbent on them by their Oaths; so we hope your Honours will assist us, that we may be enabled well and truly to execute our Duties as aforesaid.

That *Thomas Causton,* by his *arbitrary* Proceedings, hath endeavoured to render the Power and Proceedings of Grand Juries ineffectual, especially this Grand Jury, by intruding upon it when inclosed and about Business, and using the Members thereof with great Haughtiness and Ill-nature, and threatning to dissolve them.

That the said *Thomas Causton,* by his Office of Store-keeper, hath the dangerous Power in his Hands of alluring weak minded People to comply with unjust Measures; and also over-awing others from making just Complaints and Representations to your Honours; and the known *Implacability* of the said *Causton,* and his frequent *threatning* of such People, is to many weak-minded tho' well-disposed Persons, a strong Bulwark against their seeking Redress, by making proper Complaints and just Representations to You their *Benefactors, Patrons* and *Protectors.*

That the said *Causton* has made great Advancements on Provisions and Goods sold out of the Trustees Store to the Inhabitants, contrary to Mr. *Oglethorpe*'s Promise when he first settled this Colony, and contrary, as we apprehend, to your Honours good Intentions, and greatly detrimental to the Prosperity of the Colony; and that he hath refused to pay the Publick Debts otherwise than in Provisions at those dear Rates, and sometimes bad and unwholsome, out of the Publick Store, whereby the

Inhabitants were *greatly* distressed, and some have been obliged to leave the Province.

That whereas one *John White*, who had been committed for Felony, at the Suit of *William Aglionby*, and he the said *Aglionby* was bound to prosecute the same at next Court: Notwithstanding he the said *White* was removed before that time by a Warrant under the Hand and Seal of *Thomas Christie*, and as we think, by the Advice and Command of *Thomas Causton*; by which means we imagine the Criminal has escaped Justice, to the great Encouragement of enormous Offenders, contrary, as we conceive, to the Laws of our Country, the Peace of our Sovereign Lord the King, his Crown and Dignity, and particularly to the Welfare of this your Colony.

That the said *Causton* did greatly discourage the Inhabitants of this Town and County, in the Measures they had taken for the Defence and Safety of this Place in the late Alarm from the *Spaniards*; for altho' almost every Body, Masters and Servants, labour'd continually in making a Fort to defend themselves, in case of Necessity; yet he the said *Causton* never came nigh the Work, but by his Words and Behaviour did all he could to prevent *it*; until at last the People were obliged to leave off the Work unfinished, contrary to the Welfare and Safety of this Colony.

That the said *Causton* hath greatly prevented and discouraged the *Cultivation of Lands*, by his hindring People to settle on the Tracts that were allotted to them by the Trustees; whereby several People have been greatly distressed, and some almost ruin'd, contrary (as we humbly conceive) to your Honours good Intention, and the principal Part of your glorious Undertaking.

That the said *Thomas Causton*, in order to colour his illegal Proceedings, hath uttered Words to this or the like Purpose, *We do not stand upon our Feet; we do not know either our Laws or Liberties, nor what the Trustees intend; a Magistrate cannot act to strict Forms, but may dismiss Matters of Petty Felony in the easiest Manner;* thereby claiming to himself (as we humbly conceive) a dispensing Power, fatal to the Liberties of *British* Subjects, and contrary, *&c.*

The Want of *Publick Roads* hath been greatly detrimental to many who have Settlements at any Distance from this Place; and some have lost, and are still liable to lose a great part of their Crops, through the Difficulty of passing to and from their Plantations.

That the great Want of *Servants* in this Town and County, doth render the Freeholders thereof incapable of proceeding with proper Vigour in the

Cultivating their Lands; and as the Honourable *James Oglethorpe*, Esq; did generously promise, that your Honours would be pleas'd to give this Colony continual Assistance, by sending over Servants to the said Freeholders at reasonable Rates: *Therefore*, we do, with all Humility, lay before your Honours the great and general Want of Servants in this Town and County; not doubting your timely Assistance therein.

That the Town of *Savannah* stands in the utmost Need of having a good Wharff and Crane, for the Conveniency of both Strangers and Inhabitants, they being at *double* Pains and Costs in landing and getting their Goods up the Bluff.

That the Light-House of *Tybee*, which with great Labour and, as we humbly conceive, vast Expence to your Honours, remains unfinish'd and uncover'd; by reason of which, that most necessary and lofty Structure is subject to all the Injuries of Weather, and may totally decay if not in time prevented, which will be greatly detrimental to the Trade, Navigation and Welfare of this Colony.

That the Inhabitants of this Town and County are at vast Expence in time of Sickness, especially they who have most Servants; it being a general Misfortune, that during the *hot* Season of the Year, hardly one half of the Servants are able to do their Masters any Work, by reason of the *violent* Sicknesses; which hath very much prevented the Inhabitants from making Improvements.

It is without the least personal Resentment to Mr. *Causton*, or any other Person, that we do, with the most profound Respect and Duty, lay before your Honours the foregoing *Grievances*, *Hardships* and *Necessities*; and it is not the Persons or personal Infirmities of any of the Magistrates we blame; but such of their Actions and Words as, we humbly conceive, tend to the Subversion of our Laws and Liberties; and we are firmly persuaded, that Mr. *Causton* would not have impannelled *this* Grand Jury, on an Affair that so nearly concerned him as that of his Niece's did, if he had not believed the several Persons of this Grand Jury, to be Men of strict Integrity, and no way prejudiced against him; and as we the said Grand Jury are, for the time being, appointed for the solemn Representation of Truth, we humbly hope your Honours will consider *this* our *Representation*, as proceeding from a strict, impartial and sound Enquiry.

In Witness, &c. — *this first Day of* September, 1737.

The Original of this was signed by all the *Forty four*, and sent home; but was taken no notice of by the Trustees for any thing ever we heard; and we hope it will appear evident to every judicious Reader, that this Jury was neither *byassed* nor *intimidated* by *Causton*, to the Prejudice of any Person whatsoever, as Mr. *Wesly* asserts in his Journal printed at *Bristol*, 1739. He likewise says *there were a professed Athiest and Deist in the Number;* but for our Parts we know of neither: But a Man of Mr. *Wesly's* Principles, who makes no Scruple of writing wilful Falshoods (as may be seen by any Body that compares *this Narrative* with *his Journal*) and of damning every Person of a contrary Opinion with himself, may, *without* Hesitation, give People what Appellations come in his Head: However this put an End to any further Prosecution of Mr. *Wesly's* Schemes; for soon after this, he departed the Colony privately by Night, and went to *Charles-Town*, and from thence to *England*.

Mr. *Wesly* had Address enough (as he says in his forementioned Journal) to persuade several Persons who were Members of the Grand Jury, to retract (by some Paper which he drew up for them to sign) their former Sentiments; but this, if it was at all, proceeded entirely from the solemn Assurances which he gave them, *that his main Design home was to represent the Grievances and Oppressions which the poor Colony laboured under;* and upon this Account was charged with divers Letters and Papers from private Persons, relating to the Colony; which he undertook faithfully to deliver: But as we have since found, that all Mr. *Oglethorpe's* Interest was employed to protect Mr. *Wesly;* it is no Wonder those Promises were never fulfilled; nor indeed could it ever be ascertained that even the private Letters which he carried were so much as delivered.

On the other Hand Mr. *Causton* ever after bore a mortal Hatred to the Members of this Grand Jury, and took every Opportunity to shew his Resentment; and we doubt not but he prevailed upon *three* or *four* of them to make a Recantation, having either terrified or starv'd them into a Compliance: But we bore these Things the more patiently, as being satisfied the Trustees were Gentlemen who had our Interest at Heart, and who would hear and redress our Grievances in due Time, and that Mr. *Oglethorpe* might still be a Friend to the Colony; but at last we heard *He* had procured a

Regiment for its Defence, of which he was made Colonel, and that *He* was likewise made General and Commander in chief over all his Majesty's Forces in *South-Carolina* and *Georgia*. This News was confirmed by *William Stephens*, Esq; who was sent over as Trustees Secretary, to represent the State and Condition of the Colony as it really was, and to assist and consult with the Magistrates: But Mr. *Causton* soon found the Means to bring over the old Gentleman to his Interest, or at least to *acquiesce* in every Thing he said or did; for he had still the Command of the Cash and Stores, and Mr. *Stephens* had nothing to live upon but his Salary, which he could stop the Payment of at Pleasure; so our Secretary remained passive until *Causton*'s Government ended.

At last Mr. *Oglethorpe* comes over for the *third* time, in *September*, with the Remainder of his Regiment, the other Part having come with Colonel *Cochran* in *May*; but alas! this Regiment was of no Service, otherwise than to strengthen us in case of an Attack; for we could neither furnish them in Cloaths, Provisions, nor any one Thing they wanted: And to put us out of all Hopes of bettering our Condition, Mr. *Oglethorpe* was pleased to declare in the Courthouse of *Savannah*, *That as long as he had any thing to do with the Colony, there should neither be Allowance of Negroes, nor Alteration in the Titles of Land; and if any such thing should happen, he would have no farther Concern with it.* The People thus seeing there was no Hope of Redress, left the Colony daily; and the Trustees Credit receiving a great Shock by their refusing Mr. *Causton*'s certified Accounts, and an entire Stop being put to the publick Store, many poor Wretches died of Hunger; for at this Time Mr. *Causton* was turned out of all his Places, and the Store was ordered to be sold, in order, as was said, to pay off the Trustees Debts. One *Thomas Jones*, a Favourite of Mr. *Oglethorpe*, whose Character we shall have Occasion to give afterwards, was put in his Place as Cash and Store-keeper, only with a different Title, *viz.* that of *Magazine-keeper*; for none but the Trustees Servants were to be supplied from it: But the contrary soon appeared; for the *Sola Bills* that were sent over were ordered to be issued out in the Names of *William Stephens*, Esq; Mr. *Thomas Christie* and Mr. *Thomas Jones*, or any *two* of them; but the other *two* agreeing together entirely excluded *Christie*, and paid them to whom, and for what Purpose they thought convenient: They bought *New-York* Cargoes, and any other Commodities that could be got in Quantities, and put them into the Magazine, where they were sold out by *Jones* in Wholesale and Retail for ready Money, at *exorbitant* Rates. This Trade they have carried on ever since to their vast Advantage, but to the no small Distress of the poor People, who are obliged to give at the Rate almost of *cent. per cent.* for their Provisions. Thus, under the Colour of *no Store*, these *two* keep as open a one as ever *Causton* did; and by having the publick Money at their Disposal, the Payment of all Salaries and Pensions coming through their Hands, they are become as *absolute;* with this Difference, that Mr. *Causton*'s Power in every Respect extended over the whole Colony, when it was most populous and Money most plenty; but *theirs* seems only to affect the *wretched* Remains of *Savannah*.

We might have imagined that the Trustees were somewhat moved with our *repeated* Complaints, and that Mr. *Causton*'s Removal was owing thereto; but alas! in this we were mistaken; nothing (as ever we could understand) was laid to his Charge on our Account; and it was of small Benefit to us whether the Mismanagement of Money, which was the Reason of his Dismission, lies at his or Mr. *Oglethorpe*'s Door: And we *cannot but* here take notice, that Mr. *Causton*'s Case fortifies the common Observation, *That those who prostitute themselves to carry on illegal and oppressive Schemes, when they have once stuck in the Mire, they are forsaken by their Employers, and dispised by all the World besides.*

Mr. *Oglethorpe* staid not long at *Savannah*, his common Residence being at *Frederica*, where they had, in Imitation of us, built a few Houses, and cleared some Land; but finding Planting not answer, they left it off, and as soon as the Regiment came, almost every Body betook themselves to the keeping publick Houses; and in this Manner do the few that now remain live.

All the publick Work being put a Stop to, and clearing of Land, being found impracticable, by which most of us had ruined ourselves, we were in a miserable Condition; and all Hope from Mr.

Oglethorpe being at an End, we could hardly tell *what to do:* But still thinking that the Trustees might be ignorant or misinformed of the present Condition of the Colony, we at last resolved to set forth our Grievances in a short and general *Representation*, to be signed by all the Freeholders in the Colony, of which the following is an exact Copy.

To the honourable the Trustees for establishing the Colony of Georgia *in* America

   May it please your Honours,
WE whose Names are underwritten, being all *Settlers, Freeholders* and *Inhabitants* in the Province of *Georgia*, and being sensible of the great Pains and Care exerted by you in endeavouring to settle this Colony, since it has been under your Protection and Management, do unanimously join to lay before you, with the utmost Regret, the following Particulars: But in the *first* Place, we must beg leave to observe, *that* it has afforded us a great deal of Concern and Uneasiness, that *former Representations* made to you of the same Nature have not been *thought* worthy of due Consideration, nor even of an Answer. We have most of us settled in *this* Colony in pursuance of the Description and Recommendation given of it by you in *Britain*; and from the Experience of residing here several Years, do find that it is impossible that the Measures hitherto laid down and pursued for making it a Colony can succeed. None of all those who have planted their Land have been able to raise sufficient Produce to maintain their Families in Bread-kind only, even tho' as much Application and Industry have been exerted to bring it about, as could be done by Men engaged in an Affair on which they believed the Welfare of themselves and Posterity so much depended, and which they imagined required more than ordinary Pains to make succeed; so that by the accumulated Expences every Year of Provisions, Cloathing and Medicines, for themselves, Families and Servants, several have expended all their Money, nay even run considerably in Debt, and so been obliged to leave off Planting and making further Improvements; and those who continue are daily exhausting more and more of their Money, and some daily increasing their Debt, without a *Possibility* of being reimbursed, according to the *present* Constitution. This being now the general *State of the Colony*, it must be obvious that People cannot subsist by their Land

according to the present Establishment; and this being a Truth resulting from Trial, Practice and Experience, cannot be contradicted by any *theorical* Scheme or Reasoning. The Land then, according to the present Constitution, not being capable to maintain the Settlers here, they must unavoidably have Recourse to, and depend upon Trade; but to our *woful* Experience likewise, the same Causes that prevented the *first* obstruct the *latter*; for tho' the Situation of this Place is exceeding well adapted for Trade, and, if it was encouraged, might be much more improved by the Inhabitants, yet the Difficulties and Restrictions which we *hitherto have*, and *at present do* labour under, debar us of that Advantage. Timber is the only Thing we have here which we might export, and notwithstanding we are obliged to fell it in planting our Land, yet we cannot manufacture it for a foreign Market but at double the Expence of other Colonies: As for Instance, the *River of May*, which is but *twenty* Miles from us, with the Allowance of Negroes, load Vessels with that Commodity at one half of the Price that we can do; and what should induce Persons to bring Ships here, when they can be loaded with one Half of the Expence so near us? Therefore the Timber on the Land is only a continual Charge to the Possessors of it, tho' of very great Advantage in all the Northern Colonies where Negroes are allowed, and consequently Labour cheap. We do not in the least doubt but that in time *Silk* and *Wine* may be produced here, especially the former; but since the Cultivation of Land with white Servants only cannot raise Provisions for our Families, as before mentioned, *therefore* it is likewise impossible to carry on these Manufactures according to the *present* Constitution. It is very well known that *Carolina* can raise every thing that this Colony can, and they having their Labour so much cheaper, will always ruin our Market, unless we were in some Measure on a Footing with them; and as in *both* the Land is worn out in *four* or *five* Years, and then fit for nothing but Pasture, we must be always at a great deal more Expence than they in clearing new Land for planting. The *Importation* of the Necessaries of Life come to us at the most *extravagant* Rate, Merchants in general, especially of *England*, not being willing to supply the Settlers here with Goods upon Commission, because no Person here can make them any Security of their Lands or Improvements, as is very often practised in other Places to promote Trade, when some of the Employers Money is laid out in necessary Buildings and Improvements fitting for the Trade intended, without which it cannot be carried on: The Benefit of Importation *therefore* is all to *transient* Persons, who do not lay out any Money amongst us, but on the contrary carry every Penny out of the Place; and their chief Reason for enhancing the Price is because they cannot get any Goods here either on Freight or Purchase for another Market: If the Advantage accruing from Importation centred in the Inhabitants, the Profit thereof would naturally circulate amongst us, and be laid out in Improvements in the Colony. Your Honours, we imagine, are not insensible of the Numbers that have left this Province, not being able to support themselves and Families any longer; and those still remaining, who had Money of their own and Credit with their Friends, have laid out most of the *former* in Improvements, and lost the *latter* for doing it on such precarious Titles. And upon account of the present Establishment, not above *two* or *three* Persons, except those brought on Charity and Servants sent by you, have come here for the Space of *two* Years past, either to *settle* Land or *encourage* Trade, neither do we hear of any such likely to come until we are on *better* Terms. It is true his Majesty has been graciously pleased to grant a Regiment for the Defence of this Province and our neighbouring Colony, which indeed will very much assist us in defending ourselves against all Enemies, but otherwise does not in the least contribute to our Support; for all that Part of their Pay which is expended here is laid out with transient People, and our Neighbours in *Carolina*, who are capable to supply them with Provisions and other Necessaries at a moderate Price, which we, as before observed, are not at all capable to do upon the present Establishment. This then being our present Condition, it is obvious what the Consequences must be.

But we for our Parts have entirely relied on, and confided in your good Intentions, believing you would redress any Grievances that should appear; and now by our long Experience, from Industry and continual Application to Improvement of Land here, do find it impossible to pursue it, or even to subsist ourselves any longer, according to the *present* Nature of the Constitution; and likewise believing you will agree to those Measures that are found from Experience capable to make this Colony succeed, and to promote which we have consumed our Money, Time and Labour; we do, from a sincere Regard to its Welfare, and in Duty both to you and ourselves, beg leave to lay before your immediate Consideration the *Two* following chief Causes of these our *present* Misfortunes, and this *deplorable* State of the Colony, and which, we are certain, if granted, would be an infallible Remedy for *both*.

1*st*, The Want of a free Title or Fie-simple to our Lands, which, if granted, would both induce great Numbers of new Settlers to come amongst us, and likewise encourage those who remain here chearfully to proceed in making further Improvements, as well to retrieve their sunk Fortune as to make Provisions for their Posterity.

2d, The Want of the Use of Negroes, with proper Limitations; which, if granted, would both occasion great Numbers of white People to come here, and also render us capable to subsist ourselves, by raising Provisions upon our Lands, until we could make some Produce fit for Export, and in some Measure to balance our Importation. We are very sensible of the Inconveniencies and Mischiefs that have already, and do daily arise from an unlimited Use of Negroes, but we are as sensible that these may be prevented by a due Limitation, such as so many to each white Man, or so many to such a Quantity of Land, or in any other Manner which your Honours shall think most proper.

By granting us, *Gentlemen*, these *Two* Particulars and such other Privileges as his Majesty's most dutiful Subjects in *America* enjoy, you will not only prevent our impending Ruin, but, we are fully satisfied, also will soon make this the most flourishing Colony possessed by his Majesty in *America*, and your Memories will be *perpetuated* to all future Ages, our latest Posterity *sounding* your Praises, as their *first* Founders, Patrons and Guardians; but if, by denying us these Privileges, we ourselves and Families are not only ruined, but even our Posterity likewise, you will always be mentioned as the *Cause* and *Authors* of all their Misfortunes and Calamities; which we hope will never happen.

Savannah, *9th* Dec. 1738.	*We are, with all due Respect, your Honours most dutiful, and obedient Servants,*

Henry Parker,
His
Robert R G *Gilbert,* } Magistrates.
Mark.
Thomas Christie,

John Fallowfield,
John Brownfield,
William Woodroofe,
Patrick Tailfer,

Andrew Grant,
Robert Williams,
Samuel Mercer,
Patrick Grhame,
David Douglass,

Thomas Bailie,
Hugh Anderson,
James Williams,
Edward Jenkins,
Thomas Ormston,

Joseph Wardrope,
George Bunckle,
Adam Loyer,
Peter Joubart,
John Burton,
Robert Hows,
William Meers,
Thomas Salter,
James Bailow,
James Anderson,
Thomas Trip,
Samuel Holms,
James Muer,
William Parker,
John Grhame,
James Papot,
John Smith,
William Calvert,
Stephen Marrauld,
Richard Mellechamp,
Isaac Young, sen.
James Dormer,
William Carter,
Henry Moulton,
Jacob Watts,
Henry Manley,
Samuel Parker,
Stephen Mounfoord,
David Gender,
James Chainsae,
James Landry,
Lewis Stamon,
William Starflichet,
Simon Rieuwere,
John Young,
Samuel Lacy,
Peter Bailow,
Peter Emry,
William Elbert,

William Greenfield,
Christopher Greenfield,
Thomas Young, sen.
Henry Green,
Peter Tector,
Hugh Frazer,
John Sallie,
James Carwells,
John Lyndall,
Joseph Fitzwater,
Elisha Foster,
Walter Fox,
John Penrose,
David Snook,
Edward Townsend,
John Desborough,
—— Gorsand,
Andrew Duchee,
James Gallway,
John Kelly,
Joseph Stanley,
Thomas Young,
Thomas Cross,
Richard Davis,
Thomas Tibbet,
James Dean,
Donald Stewart,
John Dudding,
William Ewen,
Henry Loyd,
John Amory,
James Houston,
Isaac Young,
Robert Hanks,
Archibald Glen,
Thomas Neal,
Stephen Tarrien,
James Smith,
Samuel Ward,

Pierre Morelle,	*Giles Becou,*
John Desborough, jun.	*Francis Brooks,*
Edward Bush,	*John Clark,*
Benjamin Adams,	*George Rush,*
Charles Britain,	*Andrew Walker,*
John Rae,	*John Miller,*
William Colthred,	*Thomas Andrews,*
Thomas Wattle,	*William Sterling,*
Thomas Bailie,	*Thomas Gantlet,*
James Corneck,	*Richard Rogers.*
James Burnside,	
John Teasdale,	In all 117.

This *Representation* was signed with the greatest Willingness by the above *One hundred and seventeen* Freeholders in the County of *Savannah*, and only a very few of the General's Favourites declined to subscribe the same, so strong appeared to all of them the Truths therein contained, and the *absolute* Necessity of such an Application. The *Jews* applied for Liberty to sign with us, but we did not think it proper to join them in any of our Measures: We likewise did not allow Widows and Orphans to subscribe, because, as the Representation contained the absolute Necessities of the Colony, it might be objected to us, that they were no proper Judges. As for the People of *Ebenezer*, the Subscribers did particularly appoint some of their Number to wait upon Mr. *Boltzius* their Pastor, and to shew him the Representation, which was done; and Mr. *Boltzius* declared, That the *Saltzburghers* were equally dissatisfied with their Rights and Restrictions as the other Freeholders, and he doubted not their Willingness to join in petitioning for Redress, engaging to consult them, and to bring their Answer, which he never did; and being thereafter questioned thereupon by Mr. *Anderson* (one of the Persons commissioned to commune with him as is above related) in the Presence of several Gentlemen, he the said *Boltzius*, after some frivolous Excuses, confessed that the honourable Mr. *Oglethorpe* had both given them Satisfaction, and engaged him to write home to *Germany* for a further Supply of his Countrymen.

This Gentleman (we observe it with Regret) has been made the Instrument of imposing upon many *British* Subjects, by publishing Journals and Letters (to which we refer) most inconsistent with Truth.

Neither did we admit of Servants to sign the same, lest it should be objected, that they were under the Influence of their Masters. By this our Conduct it will appear to every Person of Impartiality how far we were from using Arts * to extort by Clamour a Redress of our Grievances.

A Copy of the Representation was immediately sent to *Frederica,* and another to *Darien;* the *last* was sent to Mr. *John More M'Intosh,* and under the same Cover a Letter to Mr. *Benjamin M'Intosh;* but the *first* kept up the other's Letter, and sent his own with the Representation to the General, who immediately dispatched Lt. *George Dunbar,* (who speaks the *Highland* Language, and has a very fluent and artful Way of talking) who, with the Assistance of *More M'Intosh,* and Promises to the poor People of Cattle, (which they afterwards got) with several other Considerations, soon perswaded them to sign a Paper, the Design of which, they were told, was to oppose the People of *Savannah,* who being Enemies to the General, were petitioning against him. As for their Leader *M'- Intosh,* he was immediately set up in a Store, and plentifully supplied with all Kinds of Goods, and had often declared, *That if, by acting as he did, he could live well himself, he did not care what became of the rest of the Colony; and as for his Children, they might go wander in the woods with the Indians.* As soon as it was heard that the Representation was come to *Frederica,* the Inhabitants were called together, and told, *That the People of* Savannah *were going to throw off the Government of the Trustees, and had associated together for that Purpose; and therefore advis'd them to beware of any Snare that might be laid by these People, which if they were caught in would ruin them.* And thus was the Design of the Representation quash'd both in *Darien* and *Frederica.* Some time after this a Copy of the Representation was sent to Mr. *Oglethorpe,* together with

* *Vide* Trustees Answer.

the following Letter, which was wrote by an anonymous Author; which we think is partly an Explanation of the Representation, and likewise a *true* View of the Situation of the Colony at that time, with the Character Mr. *Oglethorpe* then bore in it; and for these Reasons we here insert it: It was directed,

To the Honourable James Oglethorpe, *Esq; General and Commander in Chief over all his Majesty's Forces in* South-Carolina *and* Georgia, *&c.* — *at* Frederica.

SIR,

IT is the common Misfortune of all who act in the higher Stations of Life to be surrounded with Flatterers, who consult rather the Humours, Passions and Prejudices of their Patrons, than their Honour and Interest: This should induce every Person in such Station, who regards his own Honour, Interest or Fame, to lend an open and attentive Ear to Truth, in whatever Shape or from whatever Hand delivered. I who use this Freedom with your Excellency, being an anonymous Author, have no other Byass, Motive or Interest in view, further than as I am a Member of the Colony, and a Well-wisher to the Happiness of Society, unless a real and sincere Regard to your Honour and Welfare, and an earnest Desire to restore you to that Quiet of Mind and the now suspended Affections of the People, which the present State of Affairs must necessarily deprive you of; it is not therefore of Consequence to enquire *who* writes, but *what* is wrote: I am, *Sir*, a Plain-Dealer, and shall, with the greatest Respect, use you with more *Sincerity* than *Ceremony*; and if my Arguments can attain the desired Effect, you will, I doubt not, think me your and the Colony's real Friend. When a skilful Physician would relieve his Patient of a Disease, he traces it from the Beginning, and examines the Sources and Progress of it, in order that by finding out the Cause, he may the more certainly apply a Remedy: In the Body Politick the same Process is necessary to effect a Cure. The present languishing and almost desperate Condition of the Affairs of this Province, is too obvious to your Excellency to need a Description: Be pleased then, laying aside Prepossession and Prejudice, to retire unto your self, and examine impartially whence the present Misfortunes take Rise; in order to which, let me present your Excellency with a View of the Nation's Designs in establishing this Colony; and indeed they were and are nothing unsuitable to a *British* or *Roman* Spirit; to wit, *The establishing a strong and numerous Settlement as a Barrier and Safeguard of* British America: *To employ those Persons in effecting this End who were least useful at home, and others who from the Reasonableness of the Proposals, should voluntarily profer their Service: To restore Liberty and Happiness to those who, oppressed by the common Misfortunes of Mankind, were groaning under the Consequences of those Misfortunes, and incapable to serve themselves or Country at home: And* lastly, *to set a-foot such new Manufactures as might be most useful to support the Colony, or tend to rectify the Balance of Trade of* Great Britain *with neighbouring Nations.* A Design truly great, founded on the justest Policy, and practicable: To suggest that any low private Design was ever laid down, that might tend to make the Adventurers Slaves, or, at best, Tenants at Will; or that it was a Concert to leave the Industry and Substance of the Settlers exposed to satisfy the Ambition or Covetousness of an After-Governor, or any particular Courtier or Party; or to imagine that the Honourable Board of Trustees, or any of them, could be capable of such a Concert, I say, *Sir,* that such a Thought were impious. What Wonder then, if Numbers of Persons, encouraged by his Majesty's most ample Rights and Privileges granted in his *Royal Charter* to the Honourable Trustees, for the Behalf of the Inhabitants; from the beautiful Description of the *Fertility* of the Soil and *Happiness* of the Climate; and *lastly,* from a View that Mr. *Oglethorpe,* a Gentleman of the *greatest* Humanity and Generosity, was willing to sacrifice his Ease, and all those Pleasures and Enjoyments which his easy Circumstances of Life *entitled* him to, in order to be the *Patron* and *Father* of the Distress'd, and the *distinguish'd Friend* of his Country, Society and human Nature; I say, *Sir,* no Wonder, if Numbers, upon those Views, embark'd their Persons, Families and Fates in such an Adventure. Shall any thing then intervene to render such a noble Design abortive, and frustrate those of their expected Happiness, or your Excellency of your deserved Honour? GOD FORBID!

This Colony consists of *two* Sorts of People; either *those* whom the Publick sent over and supported, or * *Volunteers,* who were not burdensome to the Publick; *both* now I look upon in the same Light; as either Party have exhausted their Support or private Stocks in endeavouring to prosecute the intended Plan; but it shall suffice for my Argument, that so many of each Kind have applied themselves to this Purpose, as are sufficient to confirm the Experiment, *that* it is impossible for us with

* By this Word was meant those Persons who settled in *Georgia* upon their own Expence.

British or *Foreign* Servants to afford the lowest Necessaries of Life, much less to increase our Stocks, or defray the many Exigencies and Disappointments that this Soil and Climate are *inevitably* exposed to: This I take to be granted; and would to God the Success of the Colony depended on the laying the most *satisfying* Proof of it! And as for Persons who, from selfish Views, have imposed upon the Credulity of the Honourable Trustees, by representing Things in Colours distant from Truth, it were superfluous to curse them. I do not say, but in time Manufactures may be founded more suitable to the *Strength* and *Constitution* of *British* Servants, that might support and enrich the Colony; I heartily pray for *that* happy Period; and should then condemn and dissent from any who would *not* be content with the *present* Regulation; but as in the *interim* Production of Necessaries is *absolutely* requisite, and under the *present* Establishment impracticable, it follows of course, *that* either the Scheme must be *altered*, or the Design *abandoned:* At the first *it* was a Trial, now *it* is an Experiment; and certainly no Man or Society need be asham'd to own, *that* from *unforeseen* Emergencies their *Hypothesis* did misgive; and no Person of Judgment would censure for want of Success where the Proposal was probable; but all the World would exclaim against that Person or Society who, through mistaken Notions of Honour or Positiveness of Temper, would persist in pushing an Experiment *contrary to all Probability*, to the Ruin of the Adventurers. How many *Methods* may be found out by the Wisdom of the Trustees, for remedying *this* Inconvenience, I know not; *One* only occurs to me, which is, the *Admitting* a certain Number of Negroes, sufficient to ease the white Servants from *those* Labours that are most fatal to a *British Constitution:* I am very sensible of the Inconveniencies of an *unlimited* Use of them in a Frontier Colony; but am as sensible, that *those* Inconveniencies may be prevented by prudent *Regulations*; and their Admission for executing the more laborious Parts of Culture made the Means to *attract* Numbers of white Servants, who would otherwise fly the Place as a *Purgatory* or *Charnel-House.* If our Labour and Toil is not capable of producing mere Necessaries by *Cultivation of Land*, much less by *Trade:* For as all the neighbouring Colonies, by reason of their Negroes, prosecute all Branches of it at a *sixth* Part of the Expence we can, they would for ever preclude us of any Benefit therefrom. And supposing what cannot be admitted, that the Nation would consent to give a *perpetual* Fund for making up *all those* Deficiencies, What Benefit could ever accrue to the Nation? or What to the Settlers but a present bare Sustenance? and What the certain Consequence but the bequeathing a numerous Legacy of Orphans to the Care of Providence, since no Period of Time can be affixed when such a Support would enable us to provide for ourselves? A *second* Reason which disables us to improve either by Land or Trade, is our *Want of Credit:* You know very well, that both the mercantile and mechanick Part of Mankind live more by *Credit* than *Stock*; and the Man who has a probable Scheme of improving Credit, is naturally entitled to it: As we have no Stock further to dispense, either in Cultivation or Trade, we are reduced to need the Support of Credit, which the present Restrictions of our legal Rights and Titles to our Land deprive us of: It is true indeed the Trustees have assured us, *That those and other Restrictions are only temporary, and for the Welfare of the first Settlement, until a proper Body of Laws, which was upon the Carpet, should be perfected*; and I am far from disputing the Reasonableness of that Resolution, while either the *publick* Support or *private* Stocks kept us from needing Credit; but that now the Case is alter'd, the Necessity of removing those Restrictions is arrived, to preserve the Remains of the Colony not *yet* dissolved, and far too late for Hundreds whom *Necessity* has dispersed in *other* Corners of the world: This is a Truth, *Sir*, too obvious to need *further* Enlargement.

Hence it is clear, we can insist on demanding our Privileges as *British Subjects* from the Trustees Promises; but we likewise claim them as *Law*, *Justice* and *Property*. Your Excellency was pleased, in the Court-House of *Savannah*, to use a Comparison to satisfy the Minds of the People, of *a Man who would lend his Horse but not his Saddle, which one refusing, another accepted of:* This, I humbly take it, no ways meets the Case; the King's Majesty was Owner both of *Horse* and *Saddle*, of *Lands* and *Rights*, and gave us both in his *Charter*; we ask but what is *there* given us. The Reliance on the Publick Faith brought us to *this* Colony; and to endeavour to obviate or disappoint the Effects of *those* Promises which tempted us here, were to justify the decoying us to Misery, under the Sanction of the *Royal Authority*, than which nothing could be more injurious to the *Fountain of Honour*. I shall suppose, that were full and ample Rights given, that *some* idle Persons, who had no *Judgment* to value or *Inclination* to improve their Properties, no *Affections* for their Families or Relations, might dispose of *their* Rights for a *Glass of Rum*; but I absolutely deny, *that* the Colony could lose by such an Exchange: I own such Persons were much safer *if bound* than *at Liberty*; but where the *Affection of the Parent* and the *Reason of the Man* die, the Person is a fitter Inhabitant for *Moorfields* than *Georgia*. I must notice further, That not only are Parents incapable, for *Want of Credit*, to provide for themselves, being necessitated to dispose of their Servants for want of Provisions; but if they could, only their eldest Son could reap the Benefit, their younger Children, however numerous, are left to be fed by Him who *feeds the Ravens*; and if they have no Children, their Labour and Substance descends to Strangers: How, *Sir*, could you, or indeed any *free-born* Spirit, brook such a Tenor? Are not our younger Children and Daughters equally *entitled* to our Bowels and Affections? And does human Nature end with our First-born, and not extend itself to the rest of our Progeny and more distant Relations? And is it not inverting the Order of Nature, *that* the eldest Son should not only enjoy a double Portion, but exclude all the younger Children? and having an Interest *independant* of the Parents, how natural is it he should withdraw that Obedience and Subjection which proceeds from *paternal* Authority and *filial* Dependance! The Trustees are but a Channel to convey to us the King's Rights, and *cannot* in Law or Equity, and, I dare say, *will not* abridge those Rights. Can we suppose *that* we are singled out for a *State of Misery* and *Servitude*, and *that* so many Honourable Personages are Instruments of it? Far be the Thoughts from us! The Genius of the *British Nation*, so remarkably zealous for *Liberty* and the *Rights of Mankind*, will never suffer *British Subjects*, who have not fled their Country for Crimes, but voluntarily proffered their Service, and risked their ALL, upon the Confidence of the *Publick Faith* and the *Trustees Honour*, to accomplish a Settlement upon the *most dangerous* Point of his Majesty's Dominions; I say, it will never allow such to be depriv'd of *publick* Promises, or the *natural* Liberties of *British* Subjects. As we are on a *Frontier*, where our Lives and Fortunes may more frequently come into dispute than other People's, our Privileges and Supports should be proportionably greater; for who would venture his Life to secure *no Property*, or fight to secure to himself *Poverty* and *Misery*? And no doubt our cunning and vigilant Adversaries, the *French* and *Spaniards*, would know how to make their own Advantage. The King has been very gracious, and your Endeavours generous and useful, in procuring a *Regiment* for our Protection; but let me add a Truth equally certain, that only the Flourishing of the Colony can support *that Regiment*; and not only the *Support* of the Soldiers, but your own *Honour*, *Glory* and *Reputation* are *intermixed* with the *Fate of the Colony*, and must *stand* or *fall* with *it*.

To come closer to the Point, please to consider the *Consequences* of refusing the *Representation* of the Colony, whereof your Excellency, as one of the honourable Board, will be furnished with a Copy, and how *these Consequences* may affect *the* COLONY, *the* NATION, *the* TRUSTEES, *the* MILITARY ESTABLISHMENT in this Province, *the* INDIANS, *and* YOUR EXCELLENCY.

As to the COLONY, the deferring *hitherto* the necessary Relief has already *too tragically* affected it, by dispersing a great Part of the Inhabitants, the Remainder, in a languishing Condition, supported more with *faint Hopes*, and a *continued Reliance* on the Honour of the Nation and Trustees, than *Victuals*, while *Want* and *meagre Famine* guard the Door of many, and render them equally incapable to stay or go: The Town, so beautifully situated to the Honour of the Contriver, bearing the most visible Signs of *Decay* and *Mortality* before it is *fully born*; and the once cultivated Plantations now overgrown with Weeds and Brush, are so many *Hic-jacets* of such and such Persons and Families! I with it were possible to draw a Veil over this *tragick* Scene! But, *Sir*, our *Case* is more *clamant* than a *thousand Tongues*, and will reach the *Ears* and pierce the *Hearts* of every *True Briton*. If such are the Effects of *Delay*, what will the *total Dissolution* of the Colony produce? Such a Body of miserable People, Orphans and Suppliants, will be heard by the *Justice of the Nation*; and if it shall appear, that the *too* positively adhering to an impracticable Scheme, and the refusing those obvious Means that would answer the proposed End, or withholding those just Rights which we are *entitled* to, have been the Cause, we should have Right to recover Damages from the Authors of our Miseries. In all Places where Settlements were attempted by the *English*, and found untenable, the Settlers were taken home upon publick Charge, their Losses recompensed, and they made otherwise useful to the Community; while we are neither allowed to do for ourselves here or elsewhere. As to the *second* Point, how the NATION would be affected by *it*, it is first obvious, that all the noble *Ends* and *Advantages* they proposed are lost, and Sums of Money expended to no Purpose but to inform the *French* and *Spaniards* of the Importance of a Pass which they would not fail to Possess. It were impossible to make a *second Settlement* upon the *present Plan*, and if it is to be *altered* in the Favours of others, why not of us who have risqued and spent our *All* in the *Adventure*? How the TRUSTEES may be affected by it in all Respects I shall not say; a *Parliamentary* Enquiry into their Management I no ways question but they could *entirely* satisfy; but all good Men will regret that so honourable a Body should lose *that* Glory and Fame which the prosperous Success of the Colony would have crowned them with. I have formerly asserted, that only the flourishing

State of the Colony can support the MILITARY; and indeed without a Colony it were easier to maintain a Garrison in *Tangier* on the Coast of *Africa* than in the South of *Georgia*. One Regiment would *little* suffice to withstand the Enemy; and yet so small an Handful may be reduced to *Discontent*, *Straits* and *Wants* notwithstanding all the Bounty of a King, or *Prudence* of a General. As to the INDIANS, what could we expect less than being scorned and despised? That *they* should immediately fall in with the tempting Proffers of the *French* and *Spaniards*, and so *Great Britain* cut off from that valuable Branch of the *Indian Trade*; for how indeed could they expect *Execution of Treaties* or *Protection* from People who, *without* the Force of any Enemy, could *not* preserve their *own* Schemes of Government from falling to Pieces? How the Tragedy must affect YOUR EXCELLENCY would be *Presumption* in me to determine, I only know, that to see *Those* you honour with the Name of *Children* in *Want* and *Misery*, *that Settlement* which should have *perpetuated* your Name to Posterity with the *greatest* Honour, become the *Foil* of all your great Undertakings; and the *Expectations* of all the World, from your promising Endeavours, *setting* in a *Cloud* and *Obscurity*, must affect your Excellency in a Way suitable to your humane and generous Disposition.

Sir, we still *love*, *honour* and *respect* you, (whatever low selfish-minded Persons, the Bane of Society, may surmise to the contrary) and will continue to do so while we can have any *Hopes* of your pursuing Measures consistent with *our Prosperity:* But, *Sir*, *Smiles* cannot be expected amidst *Disappointments* and *Wants*, and there is no altering the Course of Nature: *Love* and *Gratitude* are the Tribute of *Favours* and *Protection*, and *Resentment* the Consequence of *Injuries* received; and in *Disappointments* of this Nature much more reasonably than in those of *Love*, do the contrary Passions take place in the same Degree. What then remains, but that you embrace *those* obvious Measures that will *retrieve* our desperate Affairs; *restore* to us, in Mr. *Oglethorpe*, our Father and Protector, whose Honour and Affection was depended upon; *secure* to your self a Society that loves and honours you, and who will always be ready to sacrifice both Life and Fortune to your Honour and Protection, and your Name with Blessings will be *perpetuated*. If in this I have, by a *sincere* and *well-meant* Freedom, given Offence, I heartily ask Pardon, none was intended; and I only request, that, while *Truth* keeps the Stage, the *Author* may be allowed to remain *incog.* behind the Scenes.

I am, Sir, your, &c.

The PLAIN-DEALER.

This Year there was promised a *Bounty* of *Two Shillings Sterling* on every Bushel of Corn, and *One Shilling* on every Bushel of pease and Potatoes, raised in the County of *Savannah*: This induced some few to plant, but they were miserably deceived, for few or none of them ever received their *full Bounty*, and not many *any Part thereof*, (altho' if they had received it twice over it could not have answered the End.) People being thus, by a *Chain of Disappointments* and *Miseries*, most of them rendred incapable to subsist, and, toward the End of this Summer, beginning to despair of having any favourable *Answer* to their *Representation*, or Hopes of Redress, left the Colony faster than ever; and when the *Answer* (or rather Denial) came over, they went in such Numbers, that the whole Province of *South-Carolina* was overspread with them, and in and about the Town of *Charlestown* alone, this Autumn above *Fifty Georgians* died in Misery and Want, most of whom were buried at the publick Charge.

In *September* a printed Paper, entitled, *An Answer to the Representation*, &c. was sent over, and arrived at *Savannah*, and of which this is an exact Copy.

The Answer of the Trustees for establishing the Colony of Georgia *in* America, *to the Representation from the Inhabitants of* Savannah, *the 9th of* December 1738, *for altering the Tenure of the Lands, and introducing Negroes into* Georgia.

To the Magistrates of the Town of Savannah *in the Province of* Georgia.

THE Trustees for establishing the Colony of *Georgia* in *America*, have received by the Hands of Mr. *Benjamin Ball* of *London*, Merchant, an attested Copy of a Representation, signed by you the Magistrates and many of the Inhabitants of *Savannah*, on the 9th of *December* last, for altering the Tenure of the Lands, and introducing Negroes into the Province, transmitted from thence by Mr. *Robert Williams*.

The Trustees are not surprized to find unwary People drawn in by crafty Men, to join in a Design of *extorting by Clamour* from the Trustees an Alteration in the fundamental Laws, framed for the Preservation of the People, from those very Designs.

But the Trustees cannot but express their Astonishment, that You the Magistrates, appointed by them to be Guardians of the People by putting those Laws in Execution, should so far forget your Duty, as to put yourselves at the Head of this Attempt.

However they direct you to give the Complainants this Answer from the Trustees, That they should deem themselves very unfit for the Trust reposed in them by his Majesty on their Behalf, if they could be prevailed upon, by such an irrational Attempt, to give up a Constitution, framed with the greatest Caution for the Preservation of Liberty and Property, and of which the Laws against the Use of Slaves, and for the Entail of Lands, are the surest Foundations.

And the Trustees are the more confirmed in their Opinion of the Unreasonableness of this Demand, that they have received Petitions from the *Darien*, and other Parts of the Province, representing the Inconvenience and Danger which must arise to the good People of the Province from the Introduction of Negroes. And as the Trustees themselves are fully convinced, that, besides the Hazard attending that *Introduction*, it would destroy all Industry among the white Inhabitants; and that by giving them a Power to alien their Lands, the Colony would soon be too like its Neighbours, void of white Inhabitants, filled with Blacks, and reduced to be the precarious Property of a few, equally exposed to domestick Treachery and foreign Invasion; and therefore the Trustees cannot be supposed to be in any Disposition of granting this Request; and if they have not before this signified their Dislike of it, this Delay is to be imputed to no other Motives but the Hopes they had conceived, that Time and Experience would bring the Complainants to a better Mind: And the Trustees readily join Issue with them in their Appeal to Posterity, who shall judge between them who were their best Friends, *Those* who endeavoured to preserve for them a Property in their Lands, by tying up the Hands of their unthrifty Progenitors, or *They* who wanted a Power to mortgage or alien them: Who were the best Friends to the Colony, *Those* who with great Labour and Cost had endeavoured to form a Colony of his Majesty's Subjects, and persecuted *Protestants* from other Parts of *Europe*; had placed them on a fruitful Soil, and strove to secure them in their Possessions by those Arts which naturally tend to keep the Colony full of useful and industrious People, capable both to cultivate and defend it; or *Those* who, to gratify the greedy and ambitious Views of a few Negroe Merchants, would put it into their Power to become sole owners of the Province, by introducing their baneful Commodity, which, it is well known by sad Experience, has brought our Neighbour Colonies to the Brink of Ruin, by driving out their white Inhabitants, who were their Glory and Strength, to make room for Black, who are now become the Terror of their unadvised Masters.

Signed by Order of the Trustees, this
20th Day of June, 1739.

BENJ. MARTYN *Secretary.*

We shall not in this Place detain the Reader, to shew the Absurdity and Insufficiency of the Reasons made use of in the above Paper, or how improperly it is called *An Answer to the Representation*, but refer them to the whole Tenor of *this Narrative.* With this Paper came over new Commissions for Magistrates, *viz.* Messrs. *Thomas Christie*, First, *John Fallowfield*, Second, and *Thomas Jones*, Third Bailiffs, and Mr. *William Williamson*, Recorder: And, as if the Inhabitants had not been sufficiently punished before by the *arbitrary* Government of *Causton*, the *Two* Offices of Storekeeper and Magistrate were again joined in *One* Person, which infallibly renders him, whoever he is, *absolute* in *Savannah.* And indeed if the Miseries and Hardships of the People could have received any Addition, they must have done so from the Person appointed to execute those Offices, namely, Mr. *Thomas Jones* Third Bailiff, as before mentioned, who surpassed Mr. *Causton* in every Thing that was *bad*, without having any one of his *good* Qualifications: And that he might the more easily govern at Pleasure, Mr. *Oglethorpe* thought proper to supersede the Commissions of Messrs. *Thomas Christie* and *William Williamson*, and continued Mr. *Henry Parker* as First Magistrate, being sure he was a Person that would always be in the Interest of whoever was Store-keeper; and having no other Magistrate to cope with but Mr. *Fallowfield*, they were certain of over-ruling him, tho' his Sentiments were never so just. And when the General heard that some People justly complained *that the Trustees Commissions were of none effect*, he threatned an armed Force if they refused to comply.

William Stephens, Esq; Messrs. *Thomas Christie* and *Thomas Jones*, were likewise appointed to inspect into *Causton*'s Accounts; but *Christie* was altogether rejected by the other *two*; nor did they ever do any thing to the Purpose: Indeed *Jones* would sometimes hector and domineer over *Causton*, in as haughty a Manner as ever he had formerly done over the meanest Person in *Savannah*.

Although the Trustees say in their *Answer* to the Representation, *That they should think themselves very unfit for the Trust reposed in them, should they, by an irrational Attempt, alter the Entail of Lands;* yet not one Month after we had received the aforesaid Answer, over comes the following Paper, *viz.*

The Resolutions of the Trustees for establishing the Colony of Georgia *in* America, *in Common Council assembled this* 28th *Day of* August, *in the Year of our Lord* 1739, *relating to the Grants and Tenure of Lands within the said Colony.*

WHEREAS the Common Council of the said Trustees, assembled for that Purpose, in the Name of the Corporation of the said Trustees, and under their common Seal, *have*, in pursuance of his Majesty's most gracious *Letters Patent*, and in Execution of the Trusts thereby reposed in them, *granted and conveyed* divers Portions of the Lands, Tenements and Hereditaments in the said *Letters Patent* mentioned, to many of his Majesty's loving Subjects, natural born, and Denizens, and others willing to become his Subjects, and to live under Allegiance to his Majesty in the said Colony, *to hold* to them respectively, and to the Heirs Male of their respective Bodies, lawfully begotten or to be begotten, under the several Rents, Reservations, Conditions and Provisoes therein contained: *And whereas* it hath been represented to the said Trustees, that many of the Persons to whom such Grants have been made have no Issue Male of their respective Bodies, and that an *Alteration* in the Grants and Tenure of the said Lands, upon Failure of such Issue, and likewise a known certain Provision for the Widows of Tenants in Tail Male, would not only encourage all such Persons chearfully to go on with their several Improvements, but also be an *Inducement* and *Means* of inviting divers other Persons to resort to and settle in the said Colony, and greatly tend to the Cultivation of the Lands, the Increase of the People, and the Defence, Strength and Security of the said Colony, which the said Trustees most earnestly desire to promote as far as in them lies: *It is therefore* this Day unanimously *resolved* by the Common Council of the said Corporation, assembled for that Purpose, *That* the Grants of Lands or Tenements within the said Colony, heretofore made and hereafter to be made by the said Trustees to any Person or Persons whatsoever, shall be altered, made and established in Manner and Form following; *that is to say*, That,

If Tenant in Tail Male of Lands or Tenements in the said Colony, not having done or suffered any Act, Matter or Thing, whereby his Estate therein may be forfeited or determined, shall happen to die, leaving a Widow and one or more Child or Children, that then and in such Case the Widow of such Tenant shall hold and enjoy the Dwelling-house and Garden, (if any such there be) and one Moiety of such Lands and tenements for and during the Term of her Life; the said Moiety to be set out and divided, in case the Parties interested therein do not agree within the Space of *three Months*, by the Magistrates of the Town-court in *Georgia* nearest thereunto, or any *one* of them. And in case such Division be made by *one* of such Magistrates only, then any Person or Persons finding him, her or themselves aggrieved thereby, may within the Space of *three Months* appeal to the other *three* Magistrates of the said Town-court, whose Determination thereof shall be final. *And* if such Tenant shall happen to die, leaving only a Widow, and no Child or Children, then that such Widow shall hold and enjoy the said Dwelling-house, Garden, and all such Lands and Tenements, for and during the Term of her Life. *And* in case the Widow of any such Tenant, whether he die without Issue by her or not, shall marry again after his Decease, then such Person to whom she shall be so married, shall, within the Space of *Twelve Months* after such Marriage, give Security to the said Trustees, and their Successors, whether personal or otherwise, agreeable to such Instructions as shall be given by the Common Council of the said Trustees, for maintaining and keeping in repair, during such Marriage, the said Dwelling-house, Garden, and other the Premises, to which she shall be so entitled in right of her former Husband: And if such Security shall not be given in manner aforesaid, within the Space of *Twelve Months* after such Marriage, that then, and in such Case, the Provision hereby made or intended to be made for the Benefit of such Widow, shall cease, determine and be absolutely void, to all Intents and Purposes; and the said Dwelling-house and Garden, and all and singular the Premisses, shall be, and endure to such Child or Children, or to such other Person or Persons, who would be *entitled* to the same, in case the said Widow was naturally dead.

And if Tenant in Tail Male of Lands or Tenements in the said Colony, not having done or suffered any Act, Matter or Thing, whereby his or her Estate therein may be forfeited or determined, shall happen to die, leaving *one* or *more* Daughter or Daughters, and no Issue Male; then that such Lands and Tenements, if not exceeding *eighty* Acres, shall be holden in Tail Male by any *one* of the Daughters of such Tenant; and if exceeding *eighty* Acres, by any *one* or *more* of the Daughters of such Tenant in Tail Male, as such Tenant shall by his or her last Will and Testament in Writing, duly executed in the Presence of *three* or *more* credible Witnesses direct and appoint; and in Default of such Direction or Appointment, then that such Lands and Tenements shall be holden in Tail Male by the eldest of such Daughters; and in Default of Issue Male and Female, either born in the Lifetime of such Tenant in Tail Male, or within *nine Months* after his Decease, then that such Lands and Tenements, if not exceeding *eighty* Acres, shall be holden in Tail Male by any *one* such Person; and if exceeding *eighty* Acres, by any *one* or *more* such Person or Persons, as such Tenant in Tail Male by his other last Will and Testament in Writing, executed as aforesaid, shall direct and appoint; and in Default of such Direction or Appointment, then that such Lands and Tenements shall be holden in Tail Male by the Heir at Law of such Tenant; *subject nevertheless*, in all and every the said Cases, to such Right of the Widow (if any) as aforesaid, *Provided* that such Daughter or Daughters, and all and every such Person or Persons so entitled to hold and enjoy any such Lands and Tenements, do within the Space of *twelve Months* after the Death of such Tenant, personally appear, if residing in *America*, and claim the same in any of the Town-courts in *Georgia*; and if residing out of *America*, then within the Space of *eighteen Months* next after the Death of such Tenant. *And Provided also*, That no such Devise or Appointment shall be made by any such Tenant of Lands exceeding *eighty* Acres, in any lesser or smaller Portion or Parcel than *fifty* Acres to *any one* Daughter, or other Person. *And* that no Daughter, or other Person shall be capable of enjoying any Devise, which may thereby increase his or her former Possession of Lands within the said Colony to more than *Five hundred* Acres; but such Devise to be void, and the Lands thereby given to descend in such manner as if no such Devise had been made. *And* in Default of such Appearance and Claim as aforesaid, That all and singular the said Lands and Tenements shall be and remain to the said Trustees and their Successors for ever. *Provided also*, That all and every such Estates hereby created or intended to be created, shall be subject and liable to the several Rents, Reservations, Provisoes and Conditions, as in the original Grants thereof are particularly mentioned and contained; *save and except* so much thereof as is hereby altered, or intended to be altered, in case of Failure of Issue Male, and the Provision hereby made or intended to be made for Widows.

And that in every Grant hereafter to be made by the said Trustees or their Successors of any *Lands* or *Tenements* in the said Colony, all and every Grantee therein named, not doing or suffering any Act, Matter or Thing whereby his or her Estate therein may be forfeited or determined, shall have good Right, full Power, and lawful Authority to give and devise the same by his or her last Will and Testament in Writing, duly executed in the Presence of *three* or *more* credible Witnesses, in Manner and Form following; *that is to say*, Every Grantee of Lands not exceeding *eighty* Acres, to any *one* Son or any *one* Daughter in Tail Male; and every Grantee of Lands exceeding *eighty* Acres, the whole or any part thereof, but not in lesser Lots or Portions than *fifty* Acres to any *one* Devisee, to his or her *Son* or *Sons*, *Daughter* or *Daughters* in Tail Male; and in Default of such Devise as aforesaid, then that such *Lands and Tenements* shall descend to the eldest Son in Tail Male; and in Default of Issue Male, to the eldest Daughter in Tail Male; and in Default of Issue Male and Female, then that such *Lands and Tenements* shall be holden in Tail Male, if not exceeding *eighty* Acres, by any *one* such Person; and if exceeding *eighty* Acres, by any *one* or *more* such Person or Persons, but not in any smaller Lot or Portion than *fifty* Acres to any *one* Person, as such Grantee shall by his or her last Will and Testament in Writing, executed as aforesaid, direct and appoint; and in Default of such Direction or Appointment, then that such *Lands and Tenements* shall be holden in Tail Male by the Heir at Law of such Grantee; *subject nevertheless* to such Right of the Widow (if any) as aforesaid. *Provided always*, That no Son, Daughter, or other Person shall be capable of enjoying any Devise which may thereby increase his or her former Possession of Land within the said Colony, to more than *Five hundred* Acres; but such Devise to be void, and the Lands thereby given to descend in such manner as if no such Devise had been made. *Provided also*, That such Son or Sons, Daughter or Daughters, and all and every such Person or Persons entitled to hold and enjoy any such *Lands and Tenements*, do, within the Space of *twelve Months* after the Death of *such Grantee*, or of *those* under whom they claim, personally appear, if residing in *America*, and claim the same in any of the Town-courts in *Georgia*; and if residing out of *America*, then within the Space of *eighteen Months* next after such Death; and in Default of such Appearance and Claim as aforesaid, That all and singular the said *Lands and Tenements* shall be and remain to the said Trustees, and their Successors for ever. *And Provided also,* That all and every such Estates shall be subject and liable to the like Rents, Reservations, Provisoes and Conditions, as in the former Grants of Lands heretofore made, *save and except* so much thereof as is hereby altered, or intended to be altered, upon the Failure of Issue Male.

And it is hereby required, That publick Notice of these Resolutions be forthwith given by the Magistrates of the respective Town-courts in *Georgia*, and also by the Secretary of the said Trustees in *London*, that all and every the Grantees of Lands or Tenements within the said Colony may enter their respective Claims, either at the *Georgia-Office* near *Old Palace Yard* in *Westminster*, or in any of the Town-courts in *Georgia*, within the Space of *twelve Months* from the Date hereof, to the end that they may receive the Benefit hereby intended, and that proper Grants and Conveyances in the Law may be forthwith prepared and executed for that Purpose. And it is hereby expressly declared, That no Fee or Reward shall be taken for the Entering of any such Claim, directly or indirectly, by any Person or Persons whatsoever.

Signed by Order of the said Common Council,
BENJ. MARTYN. *Secretary.*

We believe this Paper will perplex most People, who have not thoroughly studied the Law, to make Sense of it; and as there were no Lawyers in *Georgia*, it would seem as if it had been sent over with no other End, than that it should not be understood; and indeed it rather tended to add to the Confusions in the Colony, than to promote the Benefit of it: We can only assure the *Reader*, that it had no good Effect in *Georgia*, and that it was kept up there as much as possible from the People, only a fictitious Abridgment thereof, with the same Title and the same Way signed, being publickly exhibited in Writing: But this was a needless Caution; for not *One* in *Twenty* of them would have understood any one Paragraph of it. In *October* 1739, the General issues out his Proclamation for granting *Letters of Marque and Reprisals;* and the Inhabitants being called together in the Court-house, he there makes them a very elaborate Speech, and, amongst other Things, tells them, *That he was design'd against* St. Augustine, *and if he did not take it, he would leave his Bones before the Walls thereof:* But he is now at *Frederica*, and, as we have too much Reason to believe, this Castle is still in the Hands of the *Spaniards*. A little after this we had another Instance how much our Benefactors had our Interest and Welfare at heart; for at this Time it was given out, *That all the Cattle that were unmark'd belong'd to the Trustees as Lords of the Mannor;* and Orders were given that they should be mark'd accordingly: But People strenuously insisting to the contrary, the Design was dropt for that Time. On the 4th of *November* Mr. *Oglethorpe* departed from *Savannah;* and he now seems to have entirely forgot it: And it is certain, that ever since the Affair of the Representation, according to his own Words, *the very Name of the Place is become hateful to him, as are all those who he thought were Ringleaders in that Affair;* some of whom he endeavour'd to threaten and bribe to a Recantation, but to little purpose; *two* or *three* being the most (to the best of our Knowledge) that he could gain, and even those, we believe, never gave anything under their Hands. One flagrant Instance of the indirect Practices he used to draw People into his Measures was as follows: * In Summer 1739, when it was thought the Representation would have succeeded, Messrs. *Grant, Douglass, Stirling* and *Baillie,* who had been old Settlers in the Colony, and who had in a manner ruin'd themselves, as others had done, either by Planting or Building, wrote to the Trustees for an Island, and at the same time applied to Mr. *Oglethorpe* for it; he appeared mighty glad at their Resolution, and told them, *That if they would agree to what he had to propose, the granting of an Island should be nothing in respect to what he would do for them:* They told him, *They would do any thing that was consistent with their Knowledge and Conscience:* Then they were dismissed, and the next Day they were to know his Mind; *that* being come, two of his Emissaries were sent separately with Proposals, which they afterwards wrote in order to be signed, but refused a Copy thereof: These Proposals

* There are particular Affidavits to prove this whole Affair.

were to the following Effect, *viz.* To acknowledge they were in the wrong for having any Hand in the making or signing the Representation; to ask the General's Pardon for so doing; and to assert that they believed the Colony might flourish according to the *then* present Constitution: These Things complied with, they should have what Money they were pleased to ask for, with Horses, cattle and every Thing else they wanted, together with the General's perpetual Friendship and Assistance; if not complied with, they might expect nothing but his highest Resentment. They answered, *That they never expected, nor did they think they ever asked for any Favours from the General; and as for his Resentment, they believed they had already felt the utmost of it.* In whatever Shape the General wrote home of this Affair is not known, but however, from what he wrote, the Trustees thought fit at first positively to deny their Request, in a Letter which came to their Hands in *July* 1740, of which this is an exact Copy.

To Messrs. Grant, Douglass *and* Baillie, *at* Savannah *in* Georgia.

Gentlemen, *Georgia-Office, March* 25, 1740.

THE Trustees for establishing the Colony of Georgia *have received and read your Letter of* May 26, 1739, *by which they find you have abandoned your Settlements upon the* Ogeeche *River, for the following Reasons,* Because you are not allowed to have black Servants to cultivate your Lands; *and* because you disliked the Tenure of your Grants.

As to the First, *You must have seen by the Trustees Answer to the Representation of some of the People, that they cannot, and will not break into the Constitution of the Province, by such an Introduction of Slavery in Blacks, and that upon the most mature Deliberation, and for the strongest Reasons, which indeed are obvious to every considering Man, and which they are confirmed in by the Danger which has lately threatned* South-Carolina *by the Insurrection of the* Negroes, *and would be more imminent in* Georgia, *it being a Frontier.*

As to the Last, *relating to the Tenure of Lands, the Trustees suppose you may have seen the Alteration which they have made since the writing of your Letter, and they have no doubt but you are satisfied therewith, as the rest of the Colony are.*

The Trustees have likewise received and considered your Petition to General Oglethorpe *for a Settlement on* Wilmington-Island, *and his Answers thereto, which they think are of great Force, and therefore they cannot make you a Grant there, but hope you will go on improving your Settlements on the* Ogeeche *River, which they perceive by your Letter* May 26, *that you had made a great Progress in.*

I am, Gentlemen,

Your very humble Servant,

BENJ. MARTYN *Secretary.*

To this they returned the following *Answer.*

To the honourable the Trustees for establishing the Colony of Georgia *in* America, *at their Office near* Old-Palace-Yard, Westminster.

Honourable Gentlemen,

WE have received a Letter signed by your Secretary, of the 25th *March* last, owning the Receipt of ours to the Trustees for establishing the Colony of *Georgia,* dated the 26th *May* 1739, in which we set forth the Expence we had been at in prosecuting our Settlement on the *Ogeeche* River, together with the Impossibility of carrying on any Settlement with Success in this Colony according to the present Constitution; as an additional Confirmation of which we then presented your Honours with an Account current, carried on from the Commencement of our Settlement on the *Ogeeche,* and continued till we were drove thence by the strongest Appearances of Destruction, arising from the having expended our *All* in the strenuous Prosecution of an impracticable Scheme: And here we must beg leave to observe, That it appears to us you have neither considered our Letter or Account, otherwise you never would have advised us to return to a Place on which we have already in vain consumed so much Time and Money.

We have seen and seriously considered every Paragraph of a printed Paper, entitled, *The Answer of the Trustees for establishing the Colony of* Georgia *in* America, *to the Representation from the Inhabitants of* Savannah; which, in our humble Opinion, is *no Answer at all,* but rather an *absolute* Refusal of Demands to which we are legally entitled, under the specious Pretences of Guardianship and fatherly Care, without having answered *one* Sentence, or confuted by Strength of Argument *any* Part of our Assertions.

[99]

Because our neighbouring Province (of which you are pleased to take notice) has by an Introduction of *too* great Numbers abused the Use of Negroes; or because an undoubted Property in our Land-Possessions might prove detrimental or hurtful to idle, profligate or abandon'd People; it does not at all follow that we should be debarred the Use of Negroes for the Field, or the more laborious Parts of Culture, under prudent Limitations; or that sober and virtuous Men should be deprived of just Titles to their Properties.

We are surprized that your Honours mention the Representations of the People of the *Darien*, as a Confirmation of the Unreasonableness of our Demands: For did your Honours know the Motives by which these People were induced to present you with one or more Petitions contradictory to our Representation, the Welfare of the Colony and their own Consciences, we are perswaded you never would have offered them as Reasons for rejecting the Representation from *Savannah*. They were bought with a Number of Cattle, and extensive Promises of future Rewards; a little *present* Interest made them forget or neglect their *Posterity*; whereas the People of this Place, duly sensible of the Miseries and Calamities they have suffered, and do still labour under, *freely* and *voluntarily* put their Hands to the Representation of this Part of the Province: No *artful* Means were used to induce them to it; no *artful* Man or Men, Negro-Merchants or others, perswaded them to it: *Dismal* Poverty and the most *absolute* Oppression were the *true* Fountains from whence our Complaints proceeded. But how miserably were these *inconsiderate* deluded Wretches rewarded? They were soon after carried against *St. Augustine*, placed on a dangerous Post, where they were all or most of them cut off or taken Prisoners by the Enemy, which has put a Period to the Settlement of *Darien*, of which so many great Things have been falsly reported.

With regard to our *Representation*, we shall only beg leave to make one Supposition, which it is almost impossible can have happened, *viz.* That this and all the other *Representations*, *Letters*, *Suits* or *Petitions*, made to the Trustees by private or a joint Number of Persons, have been entirely false and groundless: What can have reduced the Colony to the *Situation* in which it now is? What can have reduced its Inhabitants to *one sixth Part* of the Number which we have known to reside here? Or, *lastly*, to what is the starving and despicable *Condition* of the few that are now left owing? Is it not, as well as every other Matter which we have before urged, owing to, and occasioned by the unanswerable Reasons at different Times given and laid before your Honours, by honest Men (independent of you) who were and are the chief Sufferers in this Colony, and who could not be *bribed* to conceal, or *terrified* from declaring their Sentiments?

Your Honours may readily and safely join Issue with us in our Appeal to Posterity, *who were their best * Friends, &c.* for it is certain and obvious, that if the Trustees are resolved to adhere to their *present Constitution*, they or their Successors are in no great Danger of being called to any Account by our Posterity in *Georgia*.

We have likewise seen and read the Alterations Mr. *Martyn* mentions to have been made by your Honours with regard to the *Tenure of Lands*, together with a fictitious Abridgment of the same affixed to the most publick Places at *Savannah*.

Mr. *Martyn* in his Letter is pleased to tell us, *That your Honours imagine we are satisfied therewith, as the rest of the Colony are.* Some few perhaps may have expressed themselves satisfied; but we will say no worse of such few, than that your Honours will soon be sensible that even *they* are Deceivers. It is true such *Alterations*, and the Paper entituled, *An Answer to* our *Representation* above mentioned, are artfully penn'd, and will doubtless for a Time amuse even Men of the best Sense in *Europe*, or elsewhere, who are Strangers to the Colony of *Georgia*; but any Man of common Understanding, or the least Penetration, who by an *unfortunate* Experience has been well acquainted with *that* Colony, can easily demonstrate that those very Papers are further Snares to increase our Miseries, as it is impossible we can be enabled by these *Alterations* to subsist ourselves and Families any more than before, far less to put us in a Capacity of recovering our already sunk Fortunes and Lots of Time. Some time in the Summer 1739, (whilst we still expected agreeable Alterations to have succeeded our *Representation*) we applied more than once to General *Oglethorpe*, as one of the Trustees, for the same Tract of Land which we have since been refused by your Honours; but our Petitions and Applications were rejected; and for what Reason? because indeed we refused to *contradict* what we had before set forth in our *Representation*, and so become Villains, as, we have too much Reason to believe, some others on the same Occasion were: We would not accept of *Settlements, Sums of Money, Horses, Cattle* and *other valuable Considerations*, at the Expence of *betraying our Country* and *contradicting our Consciences*, by signing a

* *Vide* Answer to the Representation.

Paper, which was prepared and offered to us, purporting a *Repentance of the Measures* we had taken for our own and the Relief of other distressed *British* Subjects; and consequently an *Approbation* of a Scheme, which, by all Appearance, seems to have been calculated and prepared to form a Colony of Vassals, whose *Properties* and *Liberties* were *at all times* to have been disposed of at the Discretion or Option of their Superiors.

Such and many other *Methods of Corruption* have been *too often* practised in this Colony; but we refused and scorned such Actions, from Principles of which every honest Man ought to be possessed.

We are not surprized to find, that we have in vain applied to your Honours in several Affairs, when we see you have been hitherto prepossessed by a Gentleman of superior Interest, with Informations and Assertions full of *Resentment*, and which we well know cannot stand the Test of an *impartial Examination*; but we are amazed and sorry to find, that he has had for so many Years together the Interest of nominating *Those* who have been appointed from time to time for the *Administration of Justice*, and making an *impartial* Enquiry into, and informing your Honours of the *real* Situation of the Colony of *Georgia*; we say, such who have been *implicitely* obedient in carrying on his *arbitrary* Schemes of Government, and *oppressing* the Inhabitants, as well as *conniving* at the deceiving your Honours and the Nation.

Gentlemen, as we have no Favours to ask, or Resentments to fear, we may with the greater Freedom observe, that we are in full Hopes, *that all* we can *justly* ask will be granted us by a *British Parliament*, who, we doubt not, will soon make an Enquiry into the Grievances of *oppressed Subjects*, which have formerly inhabited, or do now inhabit the Colony of *Georgia*, that Colony which has cost so great an Expence to the Nation, and from which so great Benefits were promised and expected.

We are sensible of the Freedoms which have been used with our respective Characters in the *Misrepresentations* sent your Honours by *partial* Men; nor are we less sensible that the Majority of the Trustees have been kept in the dark with regard to our *just Complaints* and *Representations*, or that such *Complaints* have been communicated to them in Lights *distant from Truth*, insomuch that we have Reason to believe *two Thirds* of the honourable Board are either misinformed of, or are entire Strangers to the barbarous and destructive Schemes carried on in this miserable Colony.

We hope it will ere long appear to your Honours and the World, (whatever has been advanced to the contrary) that we are *honest* Men, free from any *base* Design, free from any *mutinous* Spirit, who have only *stood firm* for the Recovery of our *lost Privileges*, which have been secretly and under the most specious Pretences withdrawn from us by some *designing* and *self-interested* Men.

We should be sorry to write disrespectfully of any *one* of the Trustees; but when *distressed* and *oppressed* People arrive at the last Extremities, it must be supposed they will neither be *ashamed* to publish their Misfortunes, or *afraid* of imputing their Calamities to the Fountain from whence they spring.

Far be it from us in any Shape to reflect in general on the honourable Board, who we still believe are Gentlemen of *Honour* and *Reputation*, who would not be accessory to any *sinister* or *base* Designs; but we cannot help thinking that they are deluded, and brought to pursue Measures inconsistent with the Welfare and Prosperity of the Colony, by *some* who of the *whole* Corporation are only acquainted with the particular Situation of it, and who must therefore wilfully, and from Design, form and prepare destructive Schemes for the perishing Inhabitants of *Georgia*, and, by *unfair* Representations of Persons and Things, draw the *Approbation* of the greater Part of the honourable Board to such Measures for the *Oppression* of his Majesty's Subjects, which they would, if they were impartially informed, scorn to think of, far less agree to.

General *Oglethorpe* with all his Forces has been obliged to raise the Siege of *St. Augustine*, and we have Reason to believe the impending Ruin of this Colony will be thereby determined; for the *Spaniards* are reinforced, the General's Army harrassed and weakned, and the *Indians* provoked and discontented; so that every Thing *looks* with the *most dismal* Aspect. But as his *Conduct in*, and the *Consequences of* these Affairs, will be soon published to the World, and as we doubt not we have already incurred your Honours Displeasure, by reciting thus freely the many *Hardships* which we have here and formerly asserted to have been the Causes of our Ruin, we shall now forbear, and conclude by adding, That the *Extremity* of our Misfortunes has at last rendred us utterly incapable of staying here any longer; and tho' all the Money we have expended on Improvements in the Colony is now of no *Advantage* to us here, nor can be elsewhere, yet, poor as we are, we shall think ourselves happy when we are gone from a Place, where nothing but *Poverty* and *Oppression* subsists: Therefore we hope, if ever *this* or any *other* Paper or Letter of ours shall appear in Publick, your Honours will impute such Publication to have proceeded from no other Motives besides a thorough Knowledge of our Duty to ourselves, our Fellow-Subjects and Sufferers, and to prevent others for the future from being deluded in the same Manner as we have been, who are, with the greatest Respect,

Honourable Gentlemen,
Your most humble Servants,

<table>
<tr><td>Georgia, Savannah,
10 August 1740.</td><td>Signed, Da. Douglas,
Wm. Sterling, Tho. Baillie.</td></tr>
</table>

About the latter End of *May* 1740, Mr. *Oglethorpe* set out with his Regiment for *Florida*, and soon after the *Carolina* Forces, consisting of about *Six hundred* Men, joined him, with about *Three hundred Indians*, and *Sixty Highlanders* Volunteers from *Darien*, who were buoyed up by the General with the mighty Hopes of Reward, besides several Stragglers and Boatmen from other Parts of the Province and elsewhere; so that, exclusive of *Seven Men of War*, there might be about *Fifteen hundred* effective Men assisting at the Siege, as it was called, of the Castle of *St. Augustine*. But we shall take no further Notice of this Affair, than as it has affected or may still affect the Colony of *Georgia:* The Place being alarmed, the *Highlanders*, with some others, making in all *One hundred and forty one* Men, were posted at *Musa*, (this was a small Fort about a Mile distant from the Castle which had been abandoned by the *Spaniards* at the General's first Approach) where they were soon after attacked by a Superior Force of the Enemy, and a miserable Slaughter ensued, scarcely *one Third* of the Number escaping, the others being either killed or taken Prisoners. Thus these poor People, who, at the Expence of their Consciences, signed a Representation contrary to their own Interest and Experience, and gave themselves entirely up to the General's Service, by their Deaths at once freed his Excellency from his Debts and Promises, and put an End to the Settlement of *Darien;* for there are now in that Place not *one Quarter* Part of the Number who settled there at first, and *that* is made up chiefly of Women and Children; and a Scout-Boat is stationed before the Town to prevent any of them from going off.

This Siege was raised about the Beginning of *July;* the General with the Remainder of his Regiment returned to *Frederica;* the *Carolina* Forces were shipped off for that Province; the few *Georgians* that were left repaired, as soon as they were allowed, to their several Homes in a miserable Condition; and the *Indians* marched towards their respective Countries, very much weakned and discontented; the *Cherokees* returned, as they came, by *Savannah,* and of *One hundred and ten* healthy Men only about *Twenty* got to their Nation, the rest either perished by Sickness or were slain: And thus ended the Campaign in *Florida.*

During these Transactions *Savannah* decayed apace; and in *August* and *September* the same Year People went away by *Twenties* in a Vessel, insomuch that one would have thought the Place must have been entirely forsaken; for in these *two* Months about *One hundred* Souls out of the County of *Savannah* left the Colony; many others have since left it, and, we believe, more will leave it very soon.

The Boats with their Hands which the General employed at that unfortunate Expedition he neither will pay, subsist, or let depart from that Place; however they are stealing away by Degrees *:

October 1740. And at this Time of about *Five thousand* Souls, that had at various Embarkations arrived in the Colony of *Georgia,* exclusive of the Regiment, scarce as *many Hundreds* remain, and these consist of the *Saltzburghers* at *Ebenezer,* who are yearly supported from *Germany* and *England;* the People of *Frederica,* who are supported by means of the Regiment; the poor Remainder of the *Darien;* a few Orphans, and others under that Denomination, supported by Mr. *Whitefield;* together with some *Dutch* Servants maintained for doing nothing by the Trustees, with *Thirty* or *Forty* necessary Tools to keep the others in Subjection: And *Those* make up the poor Remains of the miserable Colony of *Georgia* †.

---

* We are now informed they are all got away, some of them being paid and some not.

† It is here to be observed, that we have excluded the Settlement of *Augusta,* it being upon a quite different Footing.

Having now brought down this Work to the Month of *October* 1740, being about the Time most of the Authors of this *NARRATIVE* were obliged to leave that *fatal* Colony, we shall conclude the whole with a geographical and historical Account of its present State.

GEORGIA lies in the 30 and 31 Degrees of North Latitude: The *Air* generally clear, the *Rains* being much shorter as well as heavier than in *England;* the *Dews* are very great; *Thunder* and *Lightning* are expected almost every Day in *May, June, July* and *August;* they are very terrible, especially to a Stranger: During those Months, from *Ten* in the Morning to *Four* in the Afternoon, the *Sun* is extremely scorching; but the *Sea-breeze* sometimes blows from *Ten* till *Three* or *Four:* The *Winter* is nearly of the same Length as in *England;* but the *Mid-day Sun* is always warm, even when the *Mornings* and *Evenings* are very sharp, and the *Nights* piercing cold.

The *Land* is of *Four* Sorts, *Pine-Barren, Oak-Land, Swamp* and *Marsh.* The *Pine* Land is of far the greatest Extent, especially near the Sea-coasts: The *Soil* of this is a dry whitish Sand, producing Shrubs of several Sorts, and between them a harsh coarse kind of Grass, which Cattle do not love to feed upon; but here and there is a little of a better kind, especially in the *Savannas,* so they call the low watry Meadows which are usually intermixed with Pine Lands: It bears naturally *two* Sorts of Fruit, *Hurtle-Berries* much like those in *England,* and *Chinquopin-Nuts,* a dry Nut about the Size of a small Acorn: A laborious Man may in *one* Year clear and plant *four* or *five* Acres of this Land: It will produce the *first* Year from *two* to *four* Bushels of *Indian Corn,* and from *four* to *eight* of *Indian Pease per Acre;* the *second* Year it usually bears much about the same; the *third* less; the *fourth* little or nothing. *Peaches* it bears well; likewise the *White Mulberry,* which serves to feed the Silk-Worms; the *Black* is about the Size of a *Black Cherry,* and has much the same Flavour.

The *Oak-Land* commonly lies in narrow Streaks between *Pine-Land* and *Swamps, Creeks* or *Rivers:* The *Soil* is a blackish Sand, producing several Kinds of *Oak, Bay, Laurel, Ash, Walnut, Sumach* and *Gum* Trees, a sort of *Sycamore, Dog* Trees and *Hickory:* In the choicest Part of this Land grow *Parsimon* Trees, and a few *Black Mulberry* and *American Cherry* Trees: The common *wild Grapes* are of *two* Sorts, both red; the *Fox-Grape* grow two or three only on a Stalk, is thick-skin'd, large ston'd, of a harsh Taste, and of the Size of a small Cherry; the *Cluster-Grape* is of a harsh Taste too, and about the Size of a white Curran. This Land requires much Labour to clear; but when it is cleared, it will bear any Grain for *three, four* or *five* Years sometimes without laying any Manure upon it: An Acre of it generally produces *ten* Bushels of *Indian Corn*, besides *five* of *Pease*, in a Year; so that this is justly esteemed the most valuable Land in the Province, white People being incapable to clear and cultivate the Swamps.

A *Swamp* is any low watry Place, which is covered with Trees or Canes: They are here of *three* Sorts, *Cypress, River* and *Cane* Swamps: *Cypress Swamps* are mostly large Ponds, in and round which Cypresses grow. Most *River Swamps* are overflown on every Side by the River which runs through or near them; if they were drained they would produce good Rice; as would the *Cane Swamps* also, which in the mean time are the best Feeding for all Sorts of Cattle.

The *Marshes* are of *two* Sorts; *soft wet Marsh*, which is all a Quagmire, and absolutely good for nothing, and *hard Marsh*, which is a firm Sand, but however at some Seasons is good for feeding Cattle. Marshes of both Sorts abound on the Sea-Islands, which are very numerous, and contain all Sorts of Land, and upon these chiefly, near Creeks and Runs of Water, Cedar Trees grow.

We shall only add to the above, That considering no Land can be sowed (or at least what is sowed preserved) till the same is inclosed, that *five* Acres is the utmost a very able and laborious Man can propose to manage, this being the Quantity allotted for the Task of a Negro in the neighbouring Province, which Negro works *four* Hours each Day more than a white Man can do.

It must next be noticed, that with regard to the above Returns, (suppose a prosperous Season without Disappointments, which is not the Case in such small Improvements as can be expected in an infant Colony *one* Year in *five*) either Drought burns, or Rain drowns the Corn, and makes the Pease fall out of the Pod; Deer, which no Fences can exclude, devour those little Settlements in a Night; Rats and Squirrels do the same; Birds eat the Seed out of the Ground, and dig up the Blade after it is spired; and Variety of Worms and Insects devour the one half of it: But let us suppose none of those Evils happened, let us view the Amount of the Produce valued at the highest Rate.

The Produce of five *Acres of Pine-Land raised by one Hand the first Year.*

	L.	s.	d. Sterling.
Indian Corn, 20 Bushels, at 10 *s.* Currency *per* Bushel,	1	05	0
Indian Pease, 40 Bushels, at *ditto*,	2	10	0
Total of *first* Year's Produce,	3	15	0

The *second* Year the same; the *third* less; the *fourth* little or nothing.

Best *Oak-Land*, five *Acres*, at 15 Bushels of Corn and Pease *per* Acre, is 75 Bushels at *ditto* Price, is 4 *l.* 13 *s.* 9 *d.* Sterling.

Let us next consider the Maintenance of every single white Servant *per annum* at the lowest Rate, and then the Reader will be able to judge whether white People can get their Livelihood by planting Land in this Climate without Negroes; and the Allowance to the Trustees *Dutch* Servants being the least at which any white Servant could be maintained in *Georgia*, we shall therefore take our Estimation from it, which is *Eight Pence Sterling per Day,* or 12 *l.* 3 *s.* 4 *d. Sterl. per annum;* so that at a Medium the Expence is three Times greater than the Produce, besides Tools, Medicines and other Necessaries.

We must likewise observe, that the Proportion of *Pine-Barren* to either good *Swamp* or *Oak* and *Hickory Land*, is at least *six* to *one;* that the far greater Number of the small Lots have none, or very little *Oak* Land; and if they had *Swamp* that would bear Rice, white People are unable to clear them if they are covered with Trees, and tho' only with Canes, which is the easiest to cultivate, it were simply impossible to manufacture the Rice by white Men, the Exercise being so severe, that no Negro can be employed in any other Work or Labour comparable to it, and many *Hundreds* of them, notwithstanding all the Care of their Masters, yearly lose their Lives by that necessary Work.

Savannah stands on a flat Bluff, (so they term a high Land hanging over a Creek or River) which rises about *Forty* Feet perpendicular from the River, and commands it several Miles *both* upwards and downwards; and, if it was not for a Point of Woods which, about *four* Miles down the River, stretches itself out towards the South-east, one might have a View of the Sea and the Island of *Tybee:* The Soil is a white Sand for above a Mile in Breadth South-east and North-west; beyond this, eastward, is a River Swamp; westward a small Body of Wood-land, (in which was the old *Indian* Town) separated by a Creek from a large Tract of Land, which runs upwards along the Side of the River for the Space of about *five* Miles, and, being by far the best near the Town, is reserved for the *Indians*, as General *Oglethorpe* declares, as are also some of the Islands in the River *Savannah*, and the three most valuable Islands upon all the Coast of that Province, *viz. Ossiba*, *St. Katharine* and *Sapula*. South-west of the Town is a Pine-Barren that extends about *fourteen* Miles to *Vernon* River.

On the East-Side of the Town is situated the *Publick Garden*, being ten Acres inclosed, on a barren Piece of Land, where it is hardly possible for what is planted to live, but impossible to thrive; and from this Garden were all the Planters to have been furnished with *Mulberry-Trees, &c.*

The Plan of the Town was beautifully laid out in Wards, Tithings, and publick Squares left at proper Distances for Markets and publick Buildings, the whole making an agreeable Uniformity.

The publick Works in this Town are, *1st*, A *Court-house*, being one handsome Room with a Piache on three Sides: This likewise serves for a *Church* for divine Service, none having been ever built, notwithstanding the Trustees in their publick Acts acknowledge the Receipt of about *Seven hundred Pounds Sterling* from charitable Persons for that express Purpose.

2dly, Opposite to the Court-house stands the *Log-house* or *Prison*, (which is the only one remaining of *five* or *six* that have been successively built in *Savannah*) that Place of Terror and Support of *absolute* Power in *Georgia*.

3dly, Nigh thereto is a House built of *Logs*, at a very great Charge, as was said, for the Trustees Steward; the Foundation below Ground is already rotten *, as the whole Fabrick must be in a short Time; for the Roof being flat, the Rain comes in at all Parts of it.

4th, The *Store-house*, which has been many times altered and amended at a very great Charge; and it now serves as a Store for the private Benefit of one or two, as before mentioned.

5th, The *Guard-house*, which was first built on the Bluff, soon decayed, as did a second through improper Management, this now standing being the *third*. Several *Flag-staffs* were likewise erected, the last of which, according to common Report, cost 50 *l. Sterling*.

6th, A *Publick Mill* for grinding Corn was first erected at a considerable Expence in one Square of the Town; but in about *three* Years Time, without doing the least Service, it fell to the Ground. In another Square of the Town a *second* was set up, at a far greater Expence, but never finished, and is now erazed and converted into a House for entertaining the *Indians*, and other such like Uses.

7th, *Wells* and *Pumps* were made at a great Charge; but they were immediately choked up, and never rendred useful, tho' this Grievance was frequently represented both to the General and Magistrates, the want of Wells obliging the Inhabitants to use the *River Water*, which all the Summer over is polluted with putrid Marshes, and the numberless Insects that deposite their *Ova* there, together with putrified Carcases of Animals and corrupted Vegetables; and this no doubt occasioned much of the Sickness that swept off many.

* In *August* 1740 a new Foundation was begun.

Several of the Houses which were built by Freeholders, for want of Heirs-male, are fallen to the Trustees, even to the Prejudice of the lawful Creditors of the deceased, and are disposed of as the General thinks proper.

At least *Two hundred* Lots were taken up in *Savannah*, about *One hundred and seventy* of which were built * upon; a great many of these are now ruinous, and many more shut up and abandoned; so that the Town appears very desolate, scarce *one quarter* Part of its Inhabitants being left, and most of those in a miserable Condition for want of the proper Necessaries of Life.

St. Simon's Island having on the East the Gulf of *Florida*, on the other Sides Branches of the *Alatamaha*, is about *One hundred* Miles South of *Savannah*, and extends in Length about *Twenty*, in Breadth from *two* to *five* Miles; on the West-side of it, on a low Bluff, stands *Frederica*, having Woods to the North and South, to the East partly Woods, partly Savannas and partly Marsh.

The Soil is mostly blackish Sand; the Fortifications are augmented since the Retreat from *Augustine*, and here ly most of the Remains of General *Oglethorpe's* Regiment. *Frederica* was laid out in Form of a Crescent, divided into *One hundred and forty four* Lots, whereof about *Fifty* were built upon; the Number of the Inhabitants, notwithstanding of the Circulation of the Regiment's Money, are not above *One hundred and twenty*, Men, Women and Children, and these are daily stealing away by all possible Ways. On the Sea-Point, about *five* Miles South-east of the Town, were *three* Companies of the Soldiers stationed before the Attempt upon *St. Augustine*, several pretty Houses were built by the Officers, and many Lots set off to the Soldiers, and entred upon by them, most, if not all, now desolate. Several of the Officers of the Regiment brought over Servants to cultivate Land, Col. *Cochran* 20 Servants, Lt. *Horton* at *Jekyl* 16 Servants, Capt. *Gascoign* at least as many, all gone, and, according to the best of our Information, about *Two hundred* of the Regiment are diminished.

About *Twenty* Miles North-west from *St. Simon's* is DARIEN,

* Several of these had more than one House upon them.

the Settlement of the *Scots Highlanders;* the Town is situate on the Main-Land, close to a Branch of the *Alatamaha* River, on a Bluff *Twenty* Feet high; the Town is surrounded on all Sides with Woods, the Soil is a blackish Sand: Here were upwards of *Two hundred and fifty* Persons settled, who in *Spring* 1736 built a large Fort for their own Protection; and the poor Remains of these are now no more than *Fifty three,* (above *two Thirds* of which are Women and Children) besides *eleven* of the Trustees Servants inlisted as Soldiers, and stationed there under the Command of an Officer, in order to keep the others from going away, who are nevertheless making their Escape daily.

The southermost Settlement in *Georgia* is FORT ST. ANDREWS, *Fifty* Miles South from *Frederica,* on the South-west Side of *Cumberland Island,* upon a high Neck of Land which commands the River both Ways; the Walls are of Wood, filled up with Earth, round which are a Ditch and Pallisade; two Companies of General *Oglethorpe's* Regiment were formerly stationed there, but are now mostly drawn to *Frederica.*

Opposite to *Frederica,* on the Main, were settled Messieurs *Carr* and *Carteret,* with above *Twenty* Servants, where they cleared a considerable Tract of Land; but that Plantation is now quitted, and their Servants either dead or dispersed. We have lately heard from *Frederica,* that the General having station'd ten or twelve Men upon this Place, they were attacked by *Spaniards* or *Spanish Indians,* four were killed, four carried off, and two left wounded.

NEW EBENEZER, to which the *Saltzburghers* removed from their former Habitation at *Old Ebenezer,* consists of about *One hundred* Persons, under the Government of Mr. *Boltzius* their Pastor; they live and labour in a kind of Community, and never commix or associate with Strangers; they have been *hitherto* liberally supported both from *Germany* and *England,* and their Rights and Privileges have been much more extensive than any others in the Colony: This Town lies six Miles Eastward from the *Old,* on a high Bluff upon the Side of *Savannah* River, and forty Miles from *Savannah.* Near to this Place, on a Creek of the same River, was built a Saw-Mill, which cost of the Publick Money above *Fifteen hundred Pounds Sterling;* but, like most other publick Works, is now entirely ruinous.

About *ten* Miles East of *Ebenezer,* on a Creek *three* Miles from the River, was the Village of *ABERCORN;* in the Year 1733 there were *ten* Families settled there, and several afterwards: In the Year 1737, Mr. *John Brodie* with *twelve* Servants settled there: But all those are gone, and it is now a Heap of Ruins.

Four Miles below *Abercorn,* upon the River side is *Joseph's Town,* which was the Settlement of some *Scots* Gentlemen with *thirty* Servants; but they have now left it, most of their Servants having died there.

A Mile below, on the River side, is the Settlement where Sir *Francis Bathurst,* with *twelve* in Family and Servants, was placed, now in Ruins, without an Inhabitant.

A quarter of a Mile below was the Settlement of *Walter Augustine* with *six* in Family: Within this Settlement was another Mill erected, at the Charge of above 800 *l. Sterling,* all now in Ruins, without an Inhabitant.

A Mile below is *Landiloe,* the Settlement of Mr. *Robert Williams,* with *forty* Servants, who made large Improvements there, and continued for the space of *four* Years, planting each Season with great Industry in various Shapes, still expecting (with the other Settlers) an Alteration in the Constitution; but at last having sunk a great deal of Money, he was obliged to leave it, with the Loss of above *Two thousand Pounds Sterling;* and it is now uninhabited, and very much decayed. Next below that is the *Five hundred* Acre Tract belonging to Dr. *Patrick Tailfer;* which was settled, but found impracticable to proceed upon, by reason of the Hardships and Restrictions in the Colony. Next to that is Mr. *Jacob Matthew's* Plantation (formerly Mr. *Musgrove's*) called the Cow-pen, who lived there some time with *ten* Servants; but has now left it, and keeps only *two* or *three* to look after his *Cattle.* Adjoining to this was Mr. *Cooksey's* Settlement, with *five* in Family; now entirely abandoned. Next to this was Captain *Watson's* Plantation, with a good House, now in Ruins. All these lie upon the side of the River. And upon the East and Southward were the Settlements of *Young,*

Emery, *Polhil* and *Warwick*; all forsaken. Next upon the River side is the *Indian Land* before mentioned, separated from the foregoing Settlements by a Creek, and running all along to the Town. A little below this Creek is a Place called *Irene*, where Mr. *John Wesly* built a pretty good House for an *Indian School*; but he soon wearied of *that* Undertaking, and left *it*. A little below this is the *Indian Town* called *New-Yamacra*, where the Remainder of *Tomo Chachi's Indians* reside.

Five Miles South-west of *Savannah*, on a small Rise, stands the Village of *Highgate*: *Twelve* Families were settled here in 1733, mostly *French*, now reduced to *Two*. A Mile Eastward of this is *Hampstead*, where several *German* Families were settled in 1733, and some others since, now reduced to none.

Five Miles South-east of *Savannah* is *THUNDERBOLT*, where there was a good Timber Fort, and *three* Families with *twenty* Servants were settled; but it is now all in Ruins and abandoned.

Four Miles South of this is the Island of *Skiddoway*, on the North-east Point whereof *ten* Families were settled in 1733; now reduced to none.

A Creek divides *Skiddoway* from *TYBEE* Island, on the South-east Part of which, fronting the Inlet, the Light-House is built: *Twelve* Families were settled here in 1734, who have now forsaken it.

Twelve Miles Southward by Land from *Savannah* is Mr. *Houston's* Plantation, kept with *one Servant*. And,

About thirty Miles from that, up the River *Ogeeche*, was the Settlements of Messrs. *Stirlings*, *&c.* with *twenty five Servants:* This Place, when they went there, was the Southermost Settlement in the Colony, and very * remote; so that they were obliged to build at their own Expence and at a considerable Charge, a strong Wooden Fort for their Defence. And the said Messrs. *Stirlings* having resided there about *three* Years with the Servants, they were obliged to leave it, after having exhausted their Fortunes to no purpose in the Experiment.

Twenty Miles above this, on a high Bluff on the same River,

* This was the only Spot allow'd them to settle upon, any other Place being refused.

stands *Fort Argyle:* * 'Tis a small square Wooden Fort, Musket-proof: *Ten* Families were settled here and about it, now all gone; and the Fort itself garrison'd by *one* Officer, *one Dutch* Servant, and *one* Woman, who were lately surprized, in the Officer's Absence, by *two* Prisoners that broke out of the *Log-house* in *Savannah,* and both murdered.

Near the Mouth of *Vernon* River, upon a kind of an Island, which is called *Hope Isle,* are the Settlements of Messrs. *John Fallowfield, Henry Parker* and *Noble Jones:* They have made some Improvements there, but chiefly Mr. *Fallowfield,* who has a pretty little convenient House and Garden, with a considerable stock of Hogs, and some Cattle, *&c.* and where he generally resides with his Family. Near adjoining to this, upon a piece of Land which commands the † *Narrows,* is a Timber Building called *Jones's Fort;* which serves for *two* Uses, namely, to support Mr. *Noble Jones,* who is Commander of it, and to prevent the poor People of *Frederica* from getting to any other Place, where they might be able to support themselves.

About three Miles South-east of *Savannah,* upon *Augustine Creek,* lies *Oxstead,* the Settlement of Mr. *Thomas Causton,* improven by many Hands, and at a great Charge, where he now resides with a few Servants. Betwixt *Oxstead* and the Town of *Savannah* lie, 1*st, Hermitage,* the Settlement of Mr. *Hugh Anderson,* who had *seventeen* in Family and Servants; but he was obliged both to leave that and retire from the Colony about *two* Years ago, upon account of the general Hardships. 2*dly,* The Settlements of Mr. *Thomas Christie,* and *six* others belonging to the Township of *Savannah;* all now forsaken. 3*dly,* The Settlements of the *Germans* of Count *Zinzendorff,* who were *twenty* Families; which are likewise now entirely abandon'd, they having all gone to other Colonies.

* This is the Place where a Body of Horse called the *Southern Rangers,* under the Command of Capt. *James Macpherson,* were station'd for several Years. They were paid by the Government of *Carolina;* but have been discharged for some time bypast.

† This is a narrow Passage, through which Boats are obliged to pass and repass, in going to and from the Southward.

Upon the West-side of *Savannah* lie the Township Lots of the *Jews*, now deserted, they having all gone to other Colonies, except *three* or *four;* as are all others on that Quarter, excepting *one* or *two.*

About three Miles from *Savannah*, on the South, the Settlement of Mr. *William Williamson* is in the same Condition: And also,

The Settlement belonging to the Trustees adjoining to Mr. *Williamson's*; which was committed by them to the Care of Mr. *William Bradly* their Steward, to be cultivated and improved by him at their Charge, as an Example to others, and to satisfy themselves what Improvements in Land were practicable by *white Servants.* The Event might have open'd the Eyes of any that would see: Upwards of *twenty*, sometimes *thirty* Servants were employ'd; above *Two thousand Pounds Sterling* expended in the Experiment; and never so much of any kind of Grain raised from it, as would have maintain'd the Numbers employed about it *six* Months: It now lies on a par with the most ruinous Plantation in *Georgia.* Part of their *Dutch* Servants have been employed last Year by Mr. *Thomas Jones*, upon a new Plantation about a Mile to the Southward of *Savannah:* They were *twenty five* in Number, and maintain'd at the Expence of 8 *d. Sterl.* each *per diem;* and we have lately been credibly informed, the whole Produce did not exceed *One hundred* Bushels of Corn.

The *Orphan-House* is situated about fourteen Miles South-east of *Savannah:* This famous Work was begun in *March* 1740; and during the space of *six Months* there were about *One hundred* People, Men, Women and Children, maintain'd and employ'd about it; and, according to their own Calculation, they have expended near *Four thousand Pounds Sterling:* But ever since Mr. *Whitefield* left *Georgia* the latter End of *August*, in the same Year, it has decayed apace; for, besides those he then carried to the Northward with him, a great many have since left them; and their Money growing short, they were soon obliged to discharge most of the Workmen; besides, of late, many Divisions have arisen amongst them: In short, the Design seems to be drawing near a Period, altho' at this Time the House itself is scarcely half finished: It is built upon a low Pine Barren, surrounded on one Side with a large Tract of *Salt Marsh*, extending to *Vernon* River, to which they have a Passage by Water, when the Tides are up, for small Craft; on the other Side it is surrounded with Woods: They have cleared about *ten* Acres of Ground, and have built several Houses and Huts. The Frame of the Orphan-House is up, the Roof shingled *, and the Sides weather boarded: It is *sixty* Feet in length, *forty* Feet wide: It has two Stories besides Cellars and Garrets; the Cellars are built of Brick, which likewise serves for a Foundation to the whole Build-ing: It would certainly be a fine Piece of Work, if finished: but if it were finished, where is the Fund for its Support? and what Service can an Orphan-House be in a Desart and a forsaken Colony?

About three or four Miles from the Orphan-House, on the Side of *Vernon* River, *William Stephens*, Esq; formerly mentioned, has a Plantation with five or six Servants, who have cleared about seven or eight Acres: However, if he reaps no Benefit from them, he is at as little Charge to maintain them †.

As it would be too tedious to mention particularly the Township or *five* and *forty five* Acre Lots, being in all about *One hundred* that were settled, we need only therefore in general say, that there are few or none of them but what are in the same Condition with those before specified, *viz.* ruinous and desolate.

The last Place we shall mention is *AUGUSTA*, distant from *Savannah* two hundred Miles up the River, on the same Side: It was founded in 1737, at a considerable Charge, under the Direction of one Mr. *Roger Lacy*, being at that time Agent to the *Cherokee* Na-tion: It is principally, if not altogether, inhabited by *Indian* Trad-ers and Store-keepers, the Number of whom may now be about *thirty* or upwards; and a considerable Quantity of Corn has been raised there. To account for this singular Circumstance, we shall only assign *two* Reasons; the first is the Goodness of the Land, which at so great a Distance from the Sea is richer than in the

---

* *Shingles* are small Pieces of Wood sawed, or more usually cleft to about an Inch thick at one End, and made like Wedges four or five Inches broad, and eight or nine Inches long. This Covering is expensive, but if made of good Oak and cleft, not sawn, is preferable to Thatch.

† The Trustees allow him so many Servants, and their Maintenance.

maritime Parts; the second and chief one is, that the Settlers there are indulged and connived at in the Use of Negroes, by whom they execute all the laborious Parts of Culture; and the Fact is undoubted and certain, that upwards of *eighty* Negroes are now in the Settlements belonging to that Place: We do not observe this, as if it gives us any Uneasiness that our Fellow-Planters are indulged in what is so necessary for their Well-being; but we may be allowed to regret, that we and so many *British* Subjects, who stood much more in need of them, should have been ruined for want of such Assistances.

Having now taken a Survey of the Colony of *Georgia*, we shall conclude this Treatise, by taking Notice of *two* or *three* of the most remarkable Transactions in it since *October* last.

On the 10*th* Day of *November* a Court was called at *Savannah*, where Colonel *Stephens* read a Paragraph of a Letter, which he said was from the Trustees, desiring the Inhabitants to set forth their Miseries, Hardships and Difficulties in Writing, in order to have the Seal of the Colony annexed thereto, and so transmitted to the Trustees: Whereupon Mr. *Stephens* gave the Recorder a Paper to read, in which the Colony was represented in a most flourishing Condition, (in the Town of *Augusta* alone, there were represented to be 600 white People, and 3000 Pack-horses belonging thereto, who were employed in the *Indian* Trade) enumerating the many useful, fine and curious Productions of it, such as Hedges with Pomegranates growing upon them, Wine, Silk, Oil, Wheat, *&c.* with many other *Hyperboles*. This Paper Mr. *Stephens* said he had been at great Care and Pains about, and which he took to be a just Answer to the Trustees Letter, with the true State of the Colony: But the poor People seeing the Absurdity and Falseness of it, soon discovered their Dislike thereof by their leaving the Court-house, and only *eighteen* Persons signed the same, every one of whom were supported in one Shape or other by the Publick. Mr. *Fallowfield*, then on the Bench, used what Arguments he could to perswade him, that it was reasonable every Person should represent his own Case to the Trustees, and he apprehended the Design of the Trustees was such; but *Stephens* in a Passion said, *Except they would sign* *this, they should have the publick Seal to no other Paper;* so it was to no Purpose what either he or the Recorder Mr. *John Py* could urge, who very soon left the Court, declaring their Dislike and Abhorrence of such Proceedings; but immediately they, with the rest of the Inhabitants, to the Number of above *sixty,* drew up a Remonstrance to the Trustees, in which they fully set forth the *true* State of the Colony, with their own miserable Condition in it: This Paper, and soon after a Petition to the King and Council, *&c.* were lately transmitted to the Authors hereof, who immediately forwarded them for *London;* but as the Issue thereof is now depending, we do not think it proper to expose them to the Publick.

On the 2d of *April* last a Fire broke out by Accident in a Smith's Forge in *Savannah,* which consumed almost one whole Square; and in the highest Rage of the devouring Flames Mr. *Thomas Jones* stood an idle Spectator with his Hands in his Bosom, and with the utmost Unconcernedness; insomuch that when he was applied to by several of the miserable People for a small Quantity of Gunpowder to blow up an adjoining House, in order to prevent the Fire from spreading, his Answer was, *I can do nothing in it, I have no Orders concerning such Matters.*

We have lately been informed from *Frederica,* that the General having stationed *twelve* Men upon the Place which was the Settlement of Messrs. *Carr* and *Carteret* before mentioned, they were attacked by *Spaniards* or *Spanish Indians,* and *four* were killed, *four* carried off, and *two* wounded.

A good many of the People have come away from *Frederica* lately, and in order to get off were obliged to make use of Stratagems, such as going a hunting upon the Islands, *&c.* We are informed that some Differences have happened betwixt the General and some of the Magistrates there, and that in the Place of one of them he has appointed one of his Waiting-boys. Several of the poor Remainder of the *Darien* People have likewise escaped, notwithstanding the Body of Forces stationed there to prevent them.

Having thus brought this historical *NARRATIVE* within the Compass proposed, and endeavoured to dispose the Materials in as distinct a Method and Series as the necessary Conciseness would allow, we readily admit that the Design is far from being complete. To have acquainted the World with all the Hardships and Oppressions which have been exercised in the Colony of *Georgia*, must have required both a larger Volume than we are capable of publishing, and more Time than we could bestow: We therefore satisfy ourselves that we have with Care and Sincerity executed so much of the Design as may pave the Way to any others who can descend more minutely to Particulars; and those who are best acquainted with the Affairs of that Colony will be most capable of judging how tenderly we have touched both Persons and Things.

It only remains that we in a few Paragraphs endeavour to exhibit to the View of the Reader the REAL Causes of the Ruin and Desolation of the Colony, and these briefly are the following.

1. *The representing the Climate, Soil, &c. of* Georgia *in false and too flattering Colours: at least the not contradicting those Accounts when publickly printed and dispersed, and satisfying the World in a true and genuine Description thereof.*

2. *The restricting the Tenure of Lands from a Fie-simple to Tail Male, cutting off Daughters and all other Relations.*

3. *The restraining the Proprietor from selling, disposing of, or leasing any Possession.*

4. *The restricting too much the Extent of Possessions, it being impossible that* fifty *Acres of good Land, much less Pine-Barren, could maintain a white Family.*

5. *The laying the Planter under a Variety of Restraints in clearing, fencing, planting, &c. which was impossible to be complied with.*

6. *The exacting a much higher Quit-Rent than the richest Grounds in* North-America *can bear.*

7. *But chiefly the denying the Use of Negroes, and persisting in such Denial, after by repeated Applications we had humbly remonstrated the Impossibility of making Improvements to any Advantage with white Servants.*

8. *The denying us the Privilege of being judged by the Laws of our Mother-Country, and subjecting the Lives and Fortunes of all People in the Colony to one Person or Set of Men, who assumed the Privilege,*

under the Name of a Court of Chancery, *of acting according to their own Will and Fancy.*

9. *General* Oglethorpe's *taking upon him to nominate Magistrates, appoint Justices of the Peace, and to do many other such Things, without ever exhibiting to the People any legal Commission or Authority for so doing.*

10. *The neglecting the proper Means for encouraging the Silk and Wine Manufactures, and disposing of the liberal Sums contributed by the Publick, and by private Persons, in such Ways and Channels as have been of little or no Service to the Colony.*

11. *The misapplying or keeping up Sums of Money which have been appointed for particular Uses, such as building a Church, &c. several* Hundreds of Pounds Sterling, *as we are informed, having been lodged in Mr.* Oglethorpe's *Hands for some Years bypast for that Purpose, and not one Stone of it yet laid.*

12. *The assigning certain fixed Tracts of Land to those who came to settle in the Colony, without any Regard to the Quality of the Ground, Occupation, Judgment, Ability or Inclination of the Settler, &c. &c. &c.*

By these and many other such Hardships the poor Inhabitants of *Georgia* are scattered over the Face of the Earth; her Plantations a Wild, her Towns a Desart, her Villages in Rubbish, her Improvements a By-word, and her Liberties a Jest; an Object of Pity to Friends, and of Insult, Contempt and Ridicule to Enemies.

THE END.

An Impartial Enquiry, &c.

A N

Impartial Enquiry

INTO THE

STATE and UTILITY

OF THE

Province of *Georgia*.

L O N D O N:

Printed for W. MEADOWS, at the *Angel* in *Cornhill.*.
MDCCXLI:
[Price One Shilling and Six-Pence.]

An Impartial Enquiry, &c.

THE many Reports, which have been industriously propagated to the Disadvantage of the Colony of *Georgia*, call for an Enquiry into the Reasons and Validity of them; especially at this Time, when the Importance of the Province is so necessary to be known. And this Enquiry will be made in the plainest Manner, as there is no Intention to amuse or deceive the Publick, but only to lay the naked Truth before them; or to persuade them into an Opinion of the Colony, but with Regard to the general Interest of *Great Britain*. The principal Objections consist of the following Particulars, *viz.*

1. That the Climate is unhealthy.
2. That the Soil is barren.
3. That no Produces for Trade can be rais'd in it.
4. That the Lands were granted upon improper Tenures and Conditions.
5. That it will be impracticable to render the Colony of any Value, without the Use of Negroes.

These Objections will be consider'd in Order; and as the first three of them relate to Matters of Fact, about the Country, they will be truly stated, and the Answers to them will be chiefly collected from the Evidence of Persons who have been in the Province; and the Evidence itself will be annex'd in an Appendix, as it was delivered upon Oath before a Magistrate in *Georgia,* or before some of the Masters in Chancery here. The Affidavits, which were made before the Masters in Chancery, are none of them confin'd to any particular Points; they branch out into several, as the Business or Curiosity of the Deponents led them into an Observation of them; and where they speak of the same Things, they agree.

In answer to the last Objection, I shall shew from his Majesty's Royal Charter, the first Design of the Establishment, and how inconsistent Negroes are with it, as likewise with the Welfare of *Georgia;* and, if *Georgia* should receive them, how prejudicial they would be to *South-Carolina:* How needless also they are for the Products which are designed to be raised there; and in Support of the Arguments, a Petition will be added, of many of the Inhabitants against them, in the Appendix.

In the last Place, I shall endeavour to make appear, upon the Oaths of experienced Persons, the Goodness and great Importance of the Harbours; and then give some Account of the present State of the Colony.

But first, it may be requisite to take Notice, that the Objections have been raised by different Sorts of People, from their different Views; but none of these Views seem to have been directed towards the true Interest either of *Great Britain,* or the Province itself.

The Agents of the Court of *Spain* have from the Beginning been industrious to make it thought of no Importance to us, perhaps from a true and just Sense of how much Use it might be made to them. They seemed to think, that, by undervaluing, they should make *Great Britain* more negligent of it, and more ready to give it up on Demand. But by this Demand they have given a Proof of its Value, and a strong Argument for our preserving it. The late *Spanish* Minister *Geraldino* has often declared, that his Master would as soon part with *Madrid,* as with his Claim to *Georgia.* The King of *Spain* did claim it by a Memorial from Monsieur *Geraldino, September* 21, 1736, and an Armament was sent from *Cuba,* at a great Expence, in the Beginning of the Year 1737, to take by Force what they had represented as a barren, useless Spot.

Some of the Objections have taken their Birth from the Discontent of a few of the Persons who were sent thither, but principally from others of a superior Rank, who went at their own Expence. These, being too sanguine in their Hopes, or idle in their Dispositions, formed romantick Scenes of Happiness, and imagined they could find the Conveniences and Pleasures of Life without any Labour or Toil. They did not consider the Hardships inseparable from the first Settlement of a new Country, uncultivated, and consequently requiring Industry and Time, before it could afford them Necessaries: Therefore, finding themselves disappointed, they grew uneasy in their Situation, and for their Uneasiness would assign some plausible Excuse.

The Difficulties, which attend the Beginning of a Settlement, are very great, especially beginning it with low and necessitous People. It is hard to form these into Society, and reduce them to a proper Obedience to the Laws. They always repine at the Preferment of any of their own Body to be Magistrates over them, and they think every Regulation a Grievance, how mild soever it may be, or evidently for their Welfare.

As they have never been used to look forward, they live but to the present Day, and are unwilling to labour for any Thing but an immediate Subsistance; they start at any Difficulties near, and are disheartned from attempting at any Profits which may be distant. In short, as Lord *Bacon* says, * "They consume Provisions, grow weary of the Place, and then write over to the Prejudice and Discredit of the Plantation."

Nothing has been omitted for the Welfare of the People, and to give them a Spirit of Industry. They were sent over in convenient Transports, where such Regard was had to their Provisions and Accommodation, that out of upwards of fifteen hundred Natives and Foreigners, who have been sent at the publick Charge, above six have not died in the Passage. They were furnished with Cloathing and Provisions for some Years. They were likewise supplied with Arms for their Defence, Working-Tools for their Labour, a

* Lord *Bacon's* Essays, Vol. III. p. 349.

Stock of Cattle, and Seeds of all Kinds for their Lands, which were judged proper for the Country.

As the Reader may perhaps be early in starting the following Objection, Why was not more Care taken in the Choice of the Persons who were sent? It may be proper here to observe, that the Intention was to make the Settlement principally with those, who were a Burden on the Publick at home. And tho' it was apprehended, that many of them would still continue idle, yet it was not doubted, but some would, as they do, prove industrious, and lay a Foundation for foreign Protestants and others to join them; and the Charity was confined to those, who were most indigent in Town, it being thought not so proper to take People from the Plough, or the necessary Labours of the Country, tho' these would have been more useful to the Province.

As the Objectors before-mentioned have propagated the Reports to the Discredit of the Province; many have been too easy in their Belief of them, and perhaps from a sincere Regard to the Publick. They have seen no great Quantity of any Produce, and therefore have concluded, that none can be raised. But besides the particular Disadvantages, under which *Georgia* has laboured, by the continued Alarms of Danger from the *Spaniards;* and by the Necessity the People were under to fortify themselves, as well as clear their Lands, build their Houses, and raise a Subsistance; it ought to be considered, that none of our most beneficial Colonies have yielded any early Profit. This has depended on, and must be owing to an Increase of the People: Experience has always justified it, as the Reason of it is obvious. Lord *Bacon* makes the following wise Observation, * "Planting of Colonies is like planting of Woods, for you must make an Account to lose almost twenty Years Profit, and expect your Recompence in the End. The principal Thing that has been the Destruction of most Plantations, has been the sordid and hasty catching at Profit in the first Years. It is true, quick Returns are not to be neglected, so far as consists with the Good of the Plantation, but no farther." Lord *Bacon* formed this

* Lord *Bacon's* Essays, Vol. III. p. 349.

Judgment upon the most solid Reasons, and he wrote this, upon observing People too sanguine in their Expectations, and too ready to condemn upon the first Disappointment of them. *Virginia* struggled long in her Infancy, before she grew to any Strength; many more Years, than *Georgia* has been established, had past, before any Returns were made for the great Sums which had been expended. Those, who were impatient, not seeing them so soon as they expected, raised and fomented Clamours against its Establishment. They declaim'd upon the Improbability of its Success, and the ill Consequences of drawing People from *England* only to perish for Want. By Letters from * discontented Persons there, and by others who were too credulous here, it was represented as a barren and unprofitable Country. These Clamours spread, and prevail'd, as Time advanced unladen with any Profits. Three several Contributions (of large Sums too) were made by the first Undertakers. One of them amounted to near 40,000 *l.* a very considerable Sum in those Days. For above forty Years no great Improvements were made, and till † the Government undertook to carry it on, and promoted it with Vigour, it continued in the same languishing Condition. But, if they had been intimidated with the Clamours, and had despair'd at the little Prospect of Success in the Spring of their Undertaking, they had lost the Harvest of their Hopes, and Labour, and *England* had been deprived of what has proved one of her richest Mines.

But to proceed to the Objections; and,

1. That the Climate is unhealthy.

The Reverse of this has been found by the People even in their first Settling, in both Parts of the Province, and this was the Time of Trial. No general Illness has at any Time prevailed there (even when *South Carolina* has suffered by them) unless when Rum and other spirituous Liquors have stoln into the Province. By drink-

* Declaration of the State of the Colony and Affairs of *Virginia.* By his Majesty's Council for *Virginia. London.* 1630.

† *Keith's* History of *Virginia.*

ing of Rum to an Excess one Year, many of the People were thrown into burning Fevers, which carried off several, and that was the Cause, as they confess'd at their Deaths. The Flux is a Distemper to which new Comers in most Countries are liable, and some of the People in *Georgia* had it. But it was chiefly owing to the Want of Reflection, how requisite it is for Men to regulate their Diet and Manner of Living, in a different Way in the Latitude of 31, from that which they were accustom'd to in the Latitude of 51, in which they may safely eat and drink those Things, which, if indulged, in *Georgia*, would give them a Fever, and consequently a Flux. The * Heat in *Georgia* is not greater than in the Southern Parts of *Europe*, and there is almost constantly in Summer a refreshing Breeze from the Sea, from eight in the Morning till twelve, and from three or four till Sun-setting, and the Night afterwards is free from those faint and gloomy Heats which are so troublesome in some Places. What must contribute to the Healthiness of the Place, is the great Quantity of fine running Water; for besides the large Rivers there are many Rivulets, and numberless Springs of Water, which is sweet, clear and cool. As the *Swamps* come to be drain'd and cultivated, and the Woods to be thinn'd or cleared, the Country will consequently grow still more healthful. But to proceed to the second Objection, which has been more generally and industriously propagated.

2. That the Soil is barren.
The Land has been found barren only by those, who would not take any Pains or Labour to make it fruitful. The Soil is different, as the Land is divided into high and lower Grounds. It consists of four Sorts, generally speaking, which are distinguished and commonly known by the Names of
>*Pine-barren*,
>*Oak* and *Hickary*, or mixt Land,
>*Savannah*, and
>*Swamps*.

* Appendix, No. I.

Pine-Barren.—This is so called from the Pines growing on it, with scarce any other Sorts of Timber; and the Soil, being dry and sandy, will not produce Grain like the other Lands. However there is a Grass upon it, which feeds Abundance of Cattle. This being high Ground is found a healthy Situation, and the Houses are generally built upon it.

Oak and *Hickary*, or mixt Land. There is the usual Proportion of this Sort, as in the neighbouring Provinces. It is not so high as the *Pine-barren*, nor so low as the *Swamps*. It takes the Name of *Oak* and *Hickary* from the great Number of those Trees growing on it, not but there is a Variety of others among them. It has a Clay Bottom, which in hot Countries is esteemed the best, as it keeps the Roots of Trees, *&c.* cool. It is covered with a fine Mold, is light and works easy, and most Things, which are planted on it, answer very well even in the first Year. It * produces, when cultivated, *Indian* Corn, Potatoes, Pease, Wheat, Barley and Rye with great Increase, Asparagus, Colliflowers, Cabbage, Carrots, and all Sorts of Garden Stuff in Abundance: Likewise Vines, black and white Mulberries, Apples, Peaches, Figs, and most Kinds of Fruits that grow in *England;* besides many other very useful ones, as Oranges, Olives, Pomegranats, Water Melons, *&c.* which will not thrive in our colder Climate.

Savannah Land.—This is extremely proper for Husbandry, a strong Grass grows naturally upon it, and by frequent Burning, the Grass becomes finer, and makes very good Hay, for Foddering the Cattle in Winter. This runs generally upon a Level, and sometimes into large Parcels of 500 Acres, and upwards; is free from Wood, and is always well supplied with Springs of Water.

Swamps are of two Sorts.

The *Cypress.*—They are so called from that Sort of Tree growing in them, there, is excellent Land when cleared, but being the lowest is difficult to drain and cultivate, and must be a Work of Time and Labour. And,

The *Cane.* These when clear'd (which is done with Ease) and

* Appendix, No. II.

[131]

cultivated, have a Land which is extremely rich, being a black and greasy Mold; and many Things grow on it beyond Imagination. Rice particularly thrives the best in these *Swamps*.

The Land is so far from being barren or even bad, that the greatest Part of it is fruitful and productive of almost every Thing requisite for Subsistance. And the Experience already made by some in the Colony, is the best Proof how well People may subsist by their Labour.

Besides the Indigent from *England*, many foreign Protestants and *Highlanders* were sent to the Colony: These, being accustom'd to Hardship, and Labour, were not afraid of it in *Georgia*, and they live by it very comfortably. In the Town of *New Inverness* in *Darien*, in the Southern Part of the Province, the *Highlanders* are settled, they at first applied themselves, with Success, to the raising of Corn, and have since taken to feeding of Cattle, as yielding a more immediate Profit, on Account of supplying General *Oglethorpe*'s Regiment and the Shipping with fresh Beef. In the Town of *Ebenezer*, situated in the Northern Part of the Province, the *Saltzburghers* are planted: They are a sober and industrious People, and do at present reap the Fruits of their * Industry. They have great Herds of Cattle, which are increasing; their Land lies very neat, and is well cultivated. They raise large Quantities of Corn, Pease, Potatoes, Pomkins, Cabbages and other Garden Stuff. They not only raise sufficient for their own Consumption, but are enabled to sell at the Town of *Savannah*. They are so contented with their Settlement, and so sensible of their Happiness, that they are frequently sending to their own Country Invitations to their Friends to go over to them, and have applied to the Trustees to send more Transports of their Countrymen to be settled with them.

The next Objection is,

3. That no Produces for Trade can be raised in the Colony.

And this is believ'd because no great Entries have been seen of any yet in the *Custom-House*, though the Charter was granted but

* Appendix, No. III.

in *June* 1732, and the Colony has, from its first Establishment, laboured under many unforeseen Difficulties. Raw Silk is the chief Article which the Trustees had, and have still in view. This is bought by *Great Britain* at present with ready Money in *Italy*, at a vast Price; and which, notwithstanding that Price, our Merchants cannot get by any Degree so much as is wanted for the few Engines which we have for Throwing. Nay, they are obliged to take much the greatest Part as ready thrown, which carries still a higher Price, to pay for the Labour of Foreigners. Though Raw Silk requires very little Labour, it is obvious, that the raising any great Quantity of it must depend upon a Number of People, and of those chiefly who are of little Use in other Products, *viz.* Women and Children; and of whom the Trustees could not send many, Men being the most necessary in the first Establishment of a Colony, especially on a Frontier. In the raising of Silk, even the Aged and Impotent are of use. Lord *Bacon* has mentioned it as one of the most profitable Works a Plantation can go upon. Mr. *Joshua Gee*, in his excellent Treatise, called *The Trade and Navigation of* Great Britain *considered*, has expatiated upon the great Advantages and Probability of raising it in these Parts of the Continent. * Other Authors have long ago given the same Judgment. Sir *Thomas Lombe* delivered his Opinion, "That it would be attended with as little Hazard and Difficulty; that it was as much wanted, and might as soon be brought to Perfection, as any Undertaking so considerable in itself, that he ever heard of." † Besides these Authorities, Experience (the best Authority) has shewn the Probability of Success. Some Silk (though indeed by the Negligence of the People, and Want of proper Hands, but a little) has already been produced in *Georgia*. Enough, however, for a Conviction, that it may in Time be brought to such Perfection, as may make the Colony of the highest Advantage to *Great Britain*. For if twenty Pounds of it can be raised there, any greater Quantity may like-

---

* *Virginia*, more especially the South-Part thereof, rightly and truly stated, *viz. Carolina*, printed 1650. *Virginia's* Discovery of Silk Worms with their Benefit, 1650.

† Appendix, No. IV.

wise with a proper Number of People. Some was brought over this Year by one Mr. *Samuel Auspourguer*, who has made an *Affidavit, that he saw the *Italian* Family winding it off from the Balls. It was view'd by Mr. *Zachary*, an eminent Raw Silk Merchant, and Mr. *Booth*, one of our greatest Weavers, who affirmed it to be as fine as any *Italian* Silk, or any they would wish to use, and that it was worth at least twenty Shillings a Pound. The former Gentleman's † Opinion may be seen in the Appendix.

GEORGIA, being the most Southward Part of the *English* Possessions upon that Continent, is the most proper for this Production the warmer a Country is, (if the Heat is not too intense, and by bordering upon the Sea, it is refreshed with pleasant Gales of Wind) the stronger the Worms are, they yield a greater Increase, and the Silk has a better Texture. For this Reason *Italy* has the Advantage over *France*, as the same Quantity of Eggs will produce there a double Quantity of Silk more than the most Northern Parts of *France* in which it is raised, and a proportionable Difference is found between these and the most Southern Provinces.

The Planter in *Georgia* has no Obstacle in his Way of this Undertaking, but his Impatience and Diffidence. He has many Advantages which the Peasant in *France* and *Italy* wants. The Country affords him Timber for his Fabricks at no Expence, but of a little Labour. It is found by Experience, that the Mulberry-Trees thrive in an extraordinary Manner in *Georgia*, and these being his own, the Profits from the Worms are so too. He may build his House of what Dimensions he likes best, and may therefore have more Rooms, and may make these more spacious and convenient for the Nursery of his Worms: Whereas in *Languedoc*, *Provence*, and likewise in many Parts of *Italy*, the Peasant has perhaps only a low-roof'd Cottage, with one or two Rooms at the most for his Family to sleep, dress their Victuals, and keep their Worms in; and besides, he is obliged to purchase his Mulberry-Leaves of the Nobility and Gentry, who receive a considerable Part of their Revenue from the Sale of them. In many Parts of *Italy*, for Instance,

* Appendix, No. V.
† Appendix, No. V.

the poor Man gives a Moiety of his Profits to the Rich, only for the Leaves which he gathers on his Grounds, which must be a great Discouragement to him.

The Production of Silk will but little interfere with the other Labours of the Planter in *Georgia*. The whole Business of it is compleated within three Months. A Man with his Son, or a Servant, may, without much Trouble, gather Leaves sufficient for as many Worms as he can keep. His Wife and Daughter, or a Servant-Maid, may feed and attend the Worms, as they are within Doors. A *Piemontese* Family are settled in the Colony only to instruct the People, and their Children, in the Care of the Worms, and in the Art of winding off the Silk, which must be done early from the Balls, as these are apt to decrease in their Weight and Value by being neglected any Time. The Planter will be sure of a ready, stated, and great Price for this Commodity: It will be brought to *England* at a less Expence, and will have less to pay for Freight than almost any other, as the Bulk of it is so small in Proportion to the Value.

Mr. *Gee* supposes, that even the *Indians* may be useful to us in this Article of Trade; and, to shew this is not chimerical, he produces the Examples of them both with the *Spaniards* and the *French*. * "If (says he) great Numbers of Mulberry-Trees were planted among the *Indian* Nations bordering on our Settlements, and some skilful, good-tempered Persons were employed to instruct them in the proper Seasons for gathering Leaves, and feeding the Worms, and should reward them bountifully for their Pains, those People might be brought to be very profitable Subjects to this Nation. The *Spaniards*, notwithstanding their Pride, have found Condescension enough to instruct the *Indians* under their Jurisdiction, to make them very serviceable in carrying on, and improving the Manufactures of Indigo, Cochineal, and several others, to the great Advantage of *New Spain;* and the *French*, in their Settlements about the River St. *Lawrence*, the great Lakes, and even to the *Missisippi*, take a great deal of Pains to instruct

* The Trade and Navigation of *Great Britain* considered, *p.* 97.

them in every Thing which they think may contribute to their Mother Country. If the *Spaniards* and *French* can draw these People to be serviceable to them, I do not see it is impossible, if Kindness, Justice, and Good-Nature were shewed them, but they might be brought to be very serviceable to us also." Upon the first Establishing of *Georgia*, the Trustees, from the Dictates both of Humanity and Prudence, endeavoured to secure the Friendship of the *Indians*. They were treated with all the Candour and Gentleness imaginable. They were made sensible, that the *English* had no Intentions to distress, or disturb, but would be ready to assist, and protect them upon all Occasions. They were assured of Redress for any Injuries offered them, upon their making Complaints to the Magistrates; upon which in Return they engaged never to take any Revenge themselves, which might occasion Misunderstanding between the *English* and them. And, as they have since found that Justice has always been done them upon any Complaint, they have been punctual in their Engagements. They have shewn an Affection to the Colony, and upon the first breaking out of the War with *Spain*, and ever since, they have been ready, and earnest to defend it. They intermix with great Freedom with our People, and two Years ago, when a Body of the *Chickesaw Indians*, who live at a Distance from our Settlements, came down to *Savannah*, they saw in one of the Houses the Silk Worms feeding; they were so delighted, that they went twice a Day to observe them; and when they were told the Use of them, they * said, That if Worms should be given them, they would engage to return a great Quantity of Balls of Silk every Year, for they had many Mulberry-Trees in their Nations.

Another Article, which shews a great Probability of succeeding, is † Wine. The Vines grow wild in *Georgia*, and in great Abundance; they run up to the Tops of Oaks with Fruit upon them. As by the Luxuriancy of their Growth, the Grapes are but indifferent, these will be improved by Pruning, and a proper Care of the Vines; and it has been found, that the Grafting upon these Vines has been

* Appendix, No. VI.
† *Vide* Appendix, No. IV and VIII.

attended with Success. The *Portugal*, and other Vines also, which have been transplanted thither, thrive in a very extraordinary Manner. One *Abraham de Lyon*, a *Portuguese Jew*, in the Year 1736, by Encouragement from the Trustees, planted about a Score, which he had received from *Portugal*, where he had been bred among the Vineyards: In the next Year, by his Skill in pruning and dressing them, they bore plentifully a beautiful large Grape, as big as a Man's Thumb, almost transparent, and in great Bunches. A Shoot, in one Year, grew from the Root of a Bearing Vine as big as a Walking Cane, and ran over a few Poles placed to receive it, at least twelve or fourteen Feet; and he has now a very promising Vineyard. If Wine can be made in the Colony, the Advantages of it must be obvious to every one. This will not interfere with the Products of our other Plantations. Though therefore no more could be raised than to supply these, it would be a vast Profit to *Georgia*, as well as them. They might purchase it at a cheaper Rate than they do from *Spain* and the *Canaries*. They would not be liable to be interrupted in the Purchase of it in a Time of War between us and the Nations, which now supply them; and the Money, which they are to pay for it, will still remain among the Subjects of *Great Britain*. But this Product must be a Work of Time, and must depend upon an Increase of the People.

Other beneficial Articles for Trade, which (it is found) can be raised there, are,

Cochineal. The prickly Pear Shrubs, (upon which the Fly feeds, from which is taken the Cochineal,) are in Abundance upon the Islands in the Southern Part of the Province; and the Fly has been taken upon them, which, being squeezed by some Persons between their Fingers, has dyed them with the fine red Colour which the Cochineal gives.

Indigo,
Olives and *Oil*.
Cotton (of which some has been brought over as a Sample) and

* Appendix, No. IV and VIII.

many Drugs, *viz.* Aloes, Sassafras, Shumack, Snake-root, and several others, the Shrubs of which grow wild, and in great Numbers.

The Timber in the Province is very fine. In the Inland Part of the Country, some of the Trees grow so high, that they would furnish * Masts for Men of War; and near the Sea, where the Ground is more upon a Level, there is a great Quantity of excellent Knee Timber. The Laurel, Cedar, Cypress, and Bay-Trees, grow in this Part to the Height and Size of Timber-Trees.

The fourth Objection is,

4. That the Lands were granted upon improper Tenures and Conditions.

In the Infancy of the Settlement, many Regulations and Restrictions were thought necessary; but these have since, for the Ease of the People, been either relax'd, or remov'd. One Condition in particular was, That the Lands, which were granted, should in Failure of Issue Male revert to the Trust. The Females, however, were to have the Value of the Improvements, and in Case of Marriage, the Lot was intended to be given to the Husband of the eldest Daughter (which was always complied with upon Application) in Case he was not possess'd of any Lot before. The Design of this Restriction was to keep up a Number of Men equal to the Number of Lots, for the Defence and better Improvement of the Province, and to preserve a proper Equality among them. But this Condition has been since releas'd, and the Daughter of a Freeholder, or any other Person, is made capable of enjoying, by Inheritance, a Devise of Lands, provided that it does not increase her or his Possession, to more than two thousand Acres.

Another Proviso in the Grants was, That no Person should alien his Land, or any Part of it, or grant any Term, Estate, or Interest therein to any other Person, without a special Licence. This was to prevent the Effects of Usury, and People's running into Debt, which might incite them to Idleness; and to keep the Lots entire and undivided, and to prevent any Person's engrossing too great a

* *Vide* Appendix, No. II. and VIII.

Quantity of Land. This Proviso likewise has been releas'd, and a general Licence has been granted, for all Possessors of Land in *Georgia* to make Leases of any Part of their Lots, for any Term not exceeding five Years, to any Person residing in *Georgia*, and who shall continue resident there during the Term of such Lease.

A third Condition in the Grants was, That if any of the Lands should not be planted, cleared, or fenced, within the Space of ten Years from the Date of the Grant, every Part thereof, not planted, cleared, or fenced, should revert to the Trust. This was intended, only to put the People under a Necessity of being early, and industrious in their Improvements. But however, to remove any Apprehensions, which they might have of losing their Lots, a general Release has since been passed, by which no Advantage is to be taken against any Possessors of Land in *Georgia*, for any Forfeitures incurr'd at any Time before *Midsummer* 1740, in Relation either to the Tenure or Cultivation of Land; and a much longer Time for cultivating is allow'd on the easiest Conditions, and such as were propos'd by a Gentleman of the Province, on Behalf of the Freeholders.

The last and principal Objection is,

5. That it will be impracticable to render the Colony of any Value without the Use of Negroes.

This will require a more particular Examination, as it has obtained a Credit with many Persons of Understanding, who have an Affection for the Colony. The Reason, which has principally guided them in this Belief, is, That our other Colonies have not prohibited them, but find them necessary, and therefore they think there is no Occasion for this Singularity. It cannot, however, be doubted, but these Persons will consider with Attention the particular Circumstances of this Province, and the Arguments which will be offered to shew, that Negroes are inconsistent with the Constitution of it, needless for the Produces which are to be raised there, and absolutely dangerous to *Georgia* in its present Situation, as well as to the adjacent Provinces.

The Preamble to his Majesty's Charter runs as follows:

WHEREAS WE are credibly informed, that many of our poor Subjects are, through Misfortunes, and Want of Employment, reduced to great Necessities, insomuch as by their Labour they are not able to provide a Maintenance for themselves and Families; and if they had Means to defray the Charge of Passage, and other Expences incident to new Settlements, they would be glad to be settled in any of our Provinces in *America*, where by cultivating the Lands at present waste and desolate, they might not only gain a comfortable Subsistance for themselves, and Families, but also strengthen our Colonies, and increase the Trade, Navigation, and Wealth of these our Realms.

And WHEREAS OUR Provinces in *North-America* have been frequently ravaged by *Indian* Enemies, more especially that of *South-Carolina*, which in the late War was laid waste with Fire and Sword; and great Number of the *English* Inhabitants miserably massacred, and our loving Subjects, who how inhabit there, by reason of the Smallness of their Numbers, will, in Case of any new War, be exposed to the like Calamity, in as much as their whole Southern Frontier continueth unsettled, and lieth open to the said Savages.

And WHEREAS WE think it highly becoming our Crown and Royal Dignity to protect all our loving Subjects, be they never so distant from us: To extend our Fatherly Compassion even to the meanest and most unfortunate of our People, and to relieve the Wants of our abovementioned poor Subjects; and that it will be highly conducive for accomplishing these Ends, that a regular Colony of the said poor People be settled and established in the Southern Frontier of *Carolina*.

Know ye, *&c.*

By this Preamble it appears, that the chief Purposes, for which the Charter was granted, were a Subsistance for those, who were indigent at home, and consequently a Burden on the Publick; and making a Barrier for *South Carolina*, which had suffered, and lay still exposed to Danger by the Smallness of the Number of her *English* Inhabitants.

If a great Number of Negroes could have made *South Carolina* secure, she would not have wanted such a Barrier; for she is computed to have at least 40,000 Blacks, whilst the white People are not above 5000; and these (by the large Portions of Land being in the Possession of but few Persons) at too great a Distance from one another for the publick Safety.

The greater Number of Blacks, which a Frontier has, and the greater the Disproportion is between them and her white People, the more Danger she is liable to; for those are all secret Enemies, and ready to join with her open ones upon the first Occasion. So far from putting any Confidence in them, her first Step must be to secure herself against them.

GEORGIA therefore was designed to be a new Frontier, and that she might be well stocked with white Inhabitants, who by their Property could only add a Strength to it, his Majesty in the Charter restrained the Trustees from granting more than 500 Acres of Land either entirely, or in Parcels to, or for the Use of, or in Trust for any one Person.

To each of the Poor, who were sent from hence, and who were provided with every Thing at the Expence of the Trust, no more than 50 Acres have hitherto been granted. This Quantity, if well cultivated, would yield not only a comfortable, but handsome Subsistance, but would not enable him to maintain a Number of Negroes.

In other Colonies the Planter, being well stocked with them, can afford to purchase Wives for his Negroes, and their Increase adds to his Property. He can stay for the Growth of their Children before they are fit to labour; he can dispense with the Mother's neglecting to work, whilst she attends her Infants; but the white Man in *Georgia* cannot be able to feed the Negroe, his Wife, and the Child or Children, when perhaps the first is the only one from whom he receives any Profit.

If it is thought that one Male Negroe will be sufficient for each white Man, the Value of an unseasoned Negroe's Life cannot be computed at more than seven Years Purchase. The Price of a Negroe, when delivered in *America*, is from 25 *l.* to 30 *l.* Sterling; at whose Expence then must the first and continued Cost of them be? If at the Expence of the Trust, there would be no End of it; for the white Man would be more careless of his Negroe, and if he should want at any Time an immediate Supply for any Necessities, he would sell his Slave, at perhaps half the Value, to a Purchaser in *South-Carolina*, then pretend he had run away from him, and would demand a new one. This would require such a Supply from the Publick, as might justly occasion great Murmuring, even tho' the Parliament should condescend to grant it. If the Negroe is to be purchased at the Expence of the Planter, when and how will he be enabled to pay for him? He sets out poor, and unprovided of every Thing, but Land and Tools; with a Family which will require some Time to gain a Subsistance for; if then he cannot lay down the Purchase Money, he must take him upon Credit from the Negroe-Merchant, to satisfy whom, he must make over the Profits of his Labour, by which he will become dispirited; or he must mortgage his Land, by which the Country will soon lose many of her Inhabitants.

In our other Colonies the Plantations are made by Persons who set out with a sufficient Stock of Wealth to purchase a Number of Slaves, and who can afford to keep white Servants to inspect their Labour, and force them to it. But let it be supposed, that the poor Man in *Georgia* can be able, after some Time, to purchase two Negroes; he cannot maintain however a white Servant merely to inspect them; his whole Time therefore must be employed in watching them, in order to oblige them to work, to prevent their running away, or to secure himself and his Family from Danger against them; consequently the Province will reap no Benefit from his own Labour; and if he finds them idle, he will be afraid to correct them, when he knows how easily they may overpower him. If he has but one Negroe, he will have little Profit from his Service; for he must be under the same Obligation, and be always at Hand to watch him for his own Security, and force him to work. Perhaps it is imagined, that by gentle Usage the Negroe may be made a trusty Servant; this cannot be depended on. Every Man is naturally fond of Liberty, and he will struggle for it, when he knows his own Strength, when he sees this is equal, at least very little inferior to his Master's. But let it be granted, that the white Man is not under a Necessity of watching his Slaves; he will think it hard however to be obliged to work as much himself, and will contract an Unwillingness to do it; so that as he at most can maintain but one or two, the Labour of the Black may be gained, but that of the White will on the other hand be lost.

Nine Parts in ten of the Inhabitants of the Province are Freeholders of only 50 Acre Lots: As therefore, by the Inability of the Planter, and the Smallness of his Plantation, the Number of Negroes cannot be much greater than the Number of white Men; the Want of them is much better supplied by Servants from *Germany*, and other Places in *Europe*. These serve for a Term of Years, and then are intitled to Lots themselves, upon a Certificate from their Master of their good Behaviour. The Planter pays nothing when he first receives one of these Servants, but for the Passage of him. His whole Expence consists in his Food, (which likewise the Negroe must have) and in some few Cloaths, which need not be costly. The Master can have a greater Confidence in them, than he can possibly have in his Slaves. The Servants will have no Temptation to run away; from the Hopes of a Property they will be more industrious, and when they attain this, each Man of them adds a Strength to the Colony.

Besides, the Produces, which are to be raised in *Georgia*, do not require the Labour of Negroes. In other Plantations these are necessary. Sugar, Rice, and Tobacco are Works of Hardship and Fatigue; and perhaps it would be impossible to get white People from any Parts of *Europe*, who would sustain the Labour of them. But Silk, Cotton, Cochineal, and the other designed Produces of the Colony, stand only in Need of a careful and tender Management. They are Works rather of Nicety than Labour, especially where the Culture of the Land is so easy. The making of Wine will perhaps be the Work of the greatest Fatigue, and yet we see by *France*, *Portugal*, and other Parts of *Europe*, that it requires no Negroes to carry it on.

It may probably be said, As *Carolina* admits Negroes, if *Georgia* does not, the former, by having so much greater a Number of People, will soon be able to raise much more Silk than her younger Sister. To this it is answered, If she should undertake it upon the Prospect of its Success in *Georgia*, *Georgia* would lose nothing by it, and *Great Britain* would reap the Advantages of the Emulation, who could take off a greater Quantity of raw Silk than both those Colonies could produce, and without interfering with the Importation of it, either from *China*, or *Turkey*, this last especially being of a different Sort and for different Uses. Therefore, though *Carolina* might exceed *Georgia* in the Quantity raised, this last however would be sure of a Market for hers also; and although the Province might not in general be so rich, every private Man in it would reap a sufficient Profit.

It is lastly to be considered, how much Negroes would affect the Safety of the Province in general, and the individual Inhabitants of it, as being so much nearer to the *Spaniards*. *South-Carolina*, though at a greater Distance, has often and lately found by Experience, that the *Spaniards* at *Augustine* will, even in Time of Peace, invite her Negroes to them, with Promises of Liberty, and Encouragement by giving them Tracts of Land to cultivate for their own Use. The Introduction of Negroes into *Georgia* would therefore furnish a constant Subject of Contention, and would perpetually endanger the Peace (when subsisting) between the two Crowns of *Great Britain* and *Spain:* For our Court could not but resent their inticing away and protecting our Slaves; and the Court of *Spain* would pretend it to be extremely difficult, if not impossible, to prevent their People at *Augustine* doing it. Then in a Time of War, as at present, or upon the least Appearance of one, the *Spaniards* would, as they have lately done in *South-Carolina*, use all their Arts, and neglect no Promises to draw them off. And the Negroes would undoubtedly fly from a certain Slavery to Liberty and a better Treatment. What therefore does the Planter in *Georgia* do by purchasing a Negroe? He lays himself under Difficulties to raise the Means of doing it; and when he has got him, he cannot be sure of his Continuance with him for a Day, and at his own Expence he strengthens the Enemy.

If a wealthy Planter in other Colonies loses a Slave, he loses only the Cost of him, as he can easily purchase another; but the poor Man in *Georgia*, would lose, with his Slave, his whole Strength, and the Work of his Plantation would be at a Stand, as it likewise would upon the Death, or even Sickness of the Negroe; and when the Planter dies himself, if he leaves a Widow with perhaps two or three small Children, their Danger must be very great from the Negroe; they not only have no Power to prevent his flying away, but have no Security for their own Lives against him, being in a Manner absolutely at his Mercy.

It has been lately seen in *Jamaica*, and *Antigua*, how apt the Slaves are to rise against their Masters, upon every Opportunity; yet they had no foreign Power to receive and protect them. All they could have in View was, either to conquer or die, or betake themselves to the Woods, where they must live in continual Warfare with the white People. Before they could effect this, their Design must be general, and must be communicated to so many, as would make it improbable to be kept secret. But in *Georgia*, where there is only a River to pass, the Negroe may run away with Safety, without discovering his Mind to any others, if his Master leaves his Plantation but half a Day, nay if he does not watch or secure him even in the Night.

It may perhaps be said, that the Insurrections of Negroes in *Jamaica* and *Antigua* have been owing to the great Disproportion of their Numbers, which is more than will be necessary in *Georgia*: To which is replied, if there is not a much greater Number of Negroes than of white Men in *Georgia*, the End in having them will not be answered; and if there is, there can be no Safety for this Province, where even an Equality of them would make them dangerous.

It may likewise be said, if you do not permit the poor Men to have Negroes, since he has No-body else to look after them, for an Encouragement however of People, who have some Fortune, to go and settle there, allow them to the Gentlemen, who take up 200, 300, or 500 Acres, and who can afford white Servants to take Care of them. But this would soon destroy the Labour of the industrious white People, for whom the Colony was principally intended. For can it be supposed, that the poor Planter will be contented, even on his own Lot, to work in the same Manner, in which Slaves are employed on others? Won't he be importunate with the Trustees to provide Negroes likewise for him? And when they will not, (as they certainly cannot) won't he think himself hardly dealt with? repine and complain, that he leads the Life of a Negroe? then grow dispirited, and be more disposed to forsake the Province?

The most industrious People in the Colony, are so sensible of the Inconveniences, and Dangers, to which they should be exposed by the Introduction of Negroes, that they have petitioned against them, particularly the *Saltzburghers* at *Ebenezer*, and the * *Highlanders* at *New Inverness* in *Darien*.

The Inhabitants likewise of *Frederica* (the chief Town in the Southern Part of the Province) upon an Application for Negroes from some in the Northern Part, (who were less exposed to the *Spaniards*,) prepared a Petition against them, but desisted from sending it, upon an Assurance that their Apprehensions of the Introduction of Negroes were entirely needless.

South-Carolina has already experienced the Benefit of *Georgia*'s not admitting Slaves, and perhaps is indebted to this for her Preservation at present. If a Negroe is seen in *Georgia*, he is immediately known to be a Run-away; and by an Act, approved of by his Majesty in Council in *April, 1735, for rendring the Colony of* Georgia *more defensible by prohibiting the Importation and Use of Negroes*, every one, who is found in *Georgia*, is apprehended, and if the Owner in *South-Carolina* claims him within three Months, the Court of the Town of *Savannah* is ordered to restore him. This has probably prevented, at this critical Juncture, a Desertion of the greatest Part of the *South-Carolina* Negroes. The *Spanish* Emissaries have these three or four Years past been busy in this Province, inciting them to rise, and inticing them away. Several Insurrections followed thereupon; which, tho' suppress'd with the Death of many of the Inhabitants, as well as of the Blacks, hindered not the Escape of some of these; but they were few, they could only go off in Pettiauguas and other little Boats by Sea; the Way by Land was shut against them, as they knew they should be secured in *Georgia;* whereas if Negroes had been here also, it would not have

* Appendix, No. VII.

been easy to distinguish them, and the *Carolina* Slaves would have found a readier and safer Way to *Augustine*. With this Prospect they would have been more generally tempted to rise, from which the Difficulty of getting off undoubtedly deterr'd many of them. In *January*, 1738, the Council, and Assembly of *South-Carolina* sent a solemn Deputation to *Augustine* to demand those, who had escaped by Sea; but they returned without Success; the *Spanish* Governor peremptorily refused to deliver them, and declared he had Orders from the King of *Spain* to receive and protect them.

In the Beginning of last *June*, there was a Conspiracy and Insurrection of above two hundred Negroes, not far from *Charles-Town*. As they had no Prospect of escaping through the Province of *Georgia*, their Design was to break open a Store-House, and supply themselves, and those who would join them, with Arms. The Conspiracy was happily discovered the Night before it was to be put in Execution, and when they appeared the next Day, fifty of them were seized, and these were hanged, ten in a Day, to intimidate the other Negroes.

From these several Considerations, it is submitted to the Publick, whether *Georgia* does not stand in a different Point of Light from any of our other Colonies; and whether the Admission of Negroes is necessary, or expedient; or whether on the contrary, it would not be injurious to the greater Number of Inhabitants, and hazardous for them all.

It may be proper now to shew in one or two Instances, where the Colony has been, and will be of great Advantage to the Publick. If People are still credulous of every Clamour, and incredulous of, and unattentive to the Evidence, That Products for Trade can be raised in *Georgia;* or if they are too narrow-sighted to be pleased with the Distance of the Prospect; yet they must see, that the Inhabitants can subsist there. Consequently there is Room for increasing the Number of our People, by carrying over more *Saltz-burghers*, and other persecuted or distressed Foreign Protestants. These can be carried thither, and settled at a less Expence than the former, who have gone as Harbingers, and provided a Settlement, and easier Means of Subsistance for them. By these, and by the

Highlanders from *Scotland* (even if no more of our poor People from *England* should be sent) one great End of his Majesty's Charter is obtained. A Barrier is fixed, and will be strengthening, for the Southern Provinces on the Continent; and these may more securely proceed in their Cultivation. *South-Carolina* has in this Particular some Time since found the Advantages of this Barrier; for the most Southward Parts, before the Establishment of *Georgia*, were so unsafe, that People were afraid to make any Settlements on them; but soon after, many thousand Acres of rich Land near *Port-Royal* were run out, the Land was raised to four Times the former Value, and the Exportation of Rice from that Province was vastly increased. The Publick have seen, that *Carolina* has likewise been free from the Ravages or Attacks of the *Indians*, to which she was always liable before, and by which she so frequently suffered. In this View, therefore, of a Barrier, abstracting the Hopes of any Improvements in our Trade, *Georgia* has already been a national Benefit.

The last Point, in which *Georgia* is to be considered, is with Regard to the Goodness of her Harbours; and in this Light she will prove of the highest Importance to *Great Britain*. *Spain* has seen her in this Light, and has therefore been so restless to gain her. From the Badness of the Harbour at *Augustine*, which is in a Manner choaked up, and cannot receive any Ships of above a hundred Tons, she is more sensible of what Consequence it is to *Great Britain* to have good ones in *Georgia*. She knows, that if a *British* Fleet can ride there in Safety, in a wholsome Air, and daily supplied with fresh Provisions, they may be a constant Check on the Galleons, and her homeward-bound Trade, in their Course from the Gulph of *Florida*; and may amply retaliate all the Injuries which she does us on the other Side of the Gulph. For this Reason the *Spaniards* at *Augustine*, when they first complained of *Georgia*, called it a *Gibraltar* in *America*. There is a * Harbour in 31 Degrees in the Southward Part of the Province, between St. *Simon*'s *Island*, and *Jekyll*'s *Island*, which is capable of holding twelve Men of War

* Appendix, No. VIII.

in the greatest Security. The Harbour is Land-locked, and the Entrance into it is free from any Rocks or Shoals; and on the Bar there is a Depth of Water of twenty-two Feet, so that a forty Gun Ship may pass very well over it, and the Ships in the Harbour lie under the Cannon of St. *Simon*'s Fort. The River, which runs by the Harbour, is so large and deep, that it is capable of receiving any Number of Ships which *England* can send thither; and where, being Land-locked also, they may ride in great Safety. In *Cumberland Sound*, which is Southward of *Jekyll*, and lies between the Islands of *Cumberland* and *Amelia*, it is said, that there is still deeper Water than in *Jekyll Sound*; but as no Affidavits have been made in Relation to this, and as the Captains, who founded the Entrance into *Jekyll*, never went so far, I shall not dwell upon it, being unwilling to deliver any Thing upon Uncertainty. In the Northern Part of the Province, upon the Bar at *Tybee Sound*, at the Mouth of the River *Savannah*, there is a Depth of fifteen Feet at low Water, and twenty-two at high Water; and the River *Savannah* communicating with it, will contain, in Safety, four hundred Ships in smooth Water. The Entrance is so safe, that Ships of four hundred Tons, without altering their Course, may run directly from the Sea over the Bar.

The whole Coast of *Georgia* is secure for Navigation, there being seven or eight Fathom Water within three or four Leagues from the Land, where Ships, if Necessity requires, may anchor with the greatest Safety, the Ground being all clean Sand, from one End of the Coast to the other.

A Report has prevailed, that the Colony is abandoned; and this has been propagated chiefly by those who have quitted it. It is undoubtedly true, that some in the Northern Division of the Province have left it; but it is as true, that great Numbers are still remaining, and that few or none of those, who were settled in the Southern Part of the Province have left their Plantations. Among the Necessitous, who first applied to be sent over, there were some, who had been reduced merely by Misfortunes, but still unused to Labour; and many by Idleness, who were as little accustomed to it. It was almost impossible to distinguish between them. The Trustees could only proceed in their Choice, upon Recommendations of them, or their Appearance, as great Objects of Charity. But the Idle, who fled from Labour in *England*, would as certainly fly from it in *Georgia*. A Store was kept open for the Subsistance of the People, much longer than was either promis'd, or intended. This was done upon several Considerations, *viz.* a Dearth, which happen'd one Year through almost all the Continent of *America;* the Interruptions given to the Inhabitants by the Attempts of the *Spaniards;* Compassion in general to the Settlers, and for an Encouragement of them to be industrious for the future. But when it was found absolutely requisite to shut up the Store, of which the People had been long forewarn'd; those, who had fix'd their Thoughts and Means of Subsistance only there, and found themselves unprovided, immediately left the Province; a few also, upon an Appearance of a War with *Spain*, deserted their Settlements, in order to be more remote from Danger. There were some People likewise, in the first Settling of the Colony, who came from other *American* Provinces to seek for Work. These, finding but little Business, after the publick and most of the private Buildings were finish'd, return'd, as is suppos'd, to their own Homes.

By authentick Accounts transmitted from *William Stephens*, Esq; (who has resided in *Georgia* these three Years, as Secretary for the Affairs of the Trust within the Province) and received the 26th of last *November*; it appears, that the Strength of the Northern Division of the Province has not, for a Year past, been impaired by the going away of laborious Men, particularly of Freeholders; the Absence of some, whose Idleness or Fear of the *Spaniards* obliged them to withdraw, being supplied by others more industrious. And that of those, who had quitted it, with Expectation of a better Support in *South Carolina*, some have return'd again, and that two Families more intended the same. Nay, even so late as the 28th of *July* last, when the News of raising the Siege of *Augustine* had been a Fortnight in the Town of *Savannah*, notwithstanding Endeavours were used to work up a Pannick among the People, and though Permits to leave the Colony were given to any who should ask them, three Men only had quitted the Province; and of these, one was superannuated, and went to a Relation in *Charles-Town* to be supported. The other two were *Jews*, who had no visible Way of living. It was found likewise, that among the Freeholders in that Town, notwithstanding many had gone as Voluntiers to the Camp, there were about seventy, who were able and willing to act for Defence of the Colony, exclusive of Servants, Inmates, *&c.* who were above double that Number, and without taking Notice of the Plantations, and the adjacent Villages, and of the Town of *Ebenezer* in particular, which alone could furnish sixty able Men of the *Saltzburghers*.

Though beginning a Settlement with indigent People is commonly disadvantageous for Reasons before-mentioned; the sending over others of them in small Numbers after the Settlement is made, may not, and probably will not be attended with the same Inconveniences. When they see a Society formed, and a Government ready established, at which they cannot have a Shadow of Reason to repine: When they see others, who had been in the same Condition with themselves, living happily upon the Fruits of their Industry, and have evident and ocular Proofs, that they may soon arrive at the same; and when they will not have Numbers to countenance them in their Idleness, they will in all Likelihood be more incited to Labour.

The following short Account of the State of the Province, will (it is hoped) satisfy the Publick, that, though some have deserted it, it is not in that miserable Condition, which some have taken Pains to represent it.

About ten Miles up the River, the Town of *Savannah* is situated upon a Bluff of Land, about forty Feet perpendicular from the Water. The Land about it, and on which it stands, is sandy, and after the hardest Rains immediately dry, and therefore healthy, and fit for Habitations. The Water about the Town is excellent. The Town is regularly built, with a large Street through it from the Landing-Place. There are at least one hundred and thirty Houses in it, (besides Warehouses and Huts,) which are built at some Distance from each other, to prevent the Spreading of any Fire, and to keep them more airy. These form several wide Streets, and spacious Squares. The Town is divided into six Wards, and every Ward into three Tythings, with a Constable and three Tything-Men appointed for each Ward. It is governed by three Bailiffs, and a Recorder, who are the Magistrates, and have full Power to judge in all Matters of Civil Right, as well as capital Offences in the Northern Part of the Province. There are in the Town, a Court-House, a Goal, a Store-House, a House for the Trust Servants, a Wharf, a Guard-House, and some other publick Buildings. There is likewise a publick Garden, which was designed as a Nursery for raising Trees and Plants to be delivered out to the People for their Plantations, *viz.* Mulberry-Trees, Oranges, Olives, Vines, Peaches, Apples, Pears, Plumbs, *&c.* By the Negligence of former Gardeners, these had met with very ill Treatment; but by the Care of some *Italian* Gardeners last Year, they recovered from it, and the Garden is now in a thriving Condition. The Town of *Savannah* is conveniently situated for Trade, as the Navigation of the River is very good, and runs several hundred Miles up into the Country, and Ships of three hundred Tons may lie close to the Town, where the Worm does not eat into them.

About six Miles Distance from *Savannah* up the River are several considerable Plantations, and at fifteen Miles is a Village called *Abercorn.* Ten Miles above that, on the *Carolina* Side of the River, is the Town of *Purysburgh,* which is a Settlement of *Swiss,* formed in the same Year that *Georgia* was established. Fifteen Miles from *Purysburgh,* on the *Georgia* Side, is *Ebenezer,* where the *Saltzburghers* are situated; their Houses are neat, and regularly set out in Streets, and the whole Economy of their Town, under the Influence of their Ministers, Mess. *Bolzius* and *Gronau,* is very exemplary. For the Benefit of their Milch Cattle, a Herdsman is appointed to attend them in the Woods all the Day, and bring them Home in the Evening. Their Stock of out-lying Cattle is also under the Care of two other Herdsmen, who attend them in their Feeding in the Day, and drive them into Cow-Pens at Night. This secures the Owners from any Loss, and the Herdsmen are paid by a small Contribution among the People. These are very industrious, and subsist comfortably by their Labour. Though there is no regular Court of Justice, as they live in Sobriety, they maintain great Order and Decency. In Case of any Differences, the Minister calls three or four of the most prudent Elders together, who in a summary Way hear and determine as they think just, and the Parties always acquiesce with Content in their Judgment. They are very regular in their publick Worship, which is on Week-Days in the Evening after their Work; and in the Forenoon and Evening on *Sundays*. They have built a large and convenient House for the Reception of Orphans, and other poor Children, who are maintained by Benefactions among the People, are well taken Care of, and taught to work, according as their Age and Ability will permit. The Number computed by Mr. *Bolzius* in *June* 1738, whereof his Congregation consisted, was one hundred forty-six, and some more have since been settled among them. They are all in general so well pleased with their Condition, that not one of their People has abandoned the Settlement.

At some Distance from hence is a Place called *Old Ebenezer*, upon a River which runs into the *Savannah*. Here the *Saltzburghers* were at first settled, and there are now some Plantations of *German* Families, as also a Cow-Pen, in which the Trust have a great Number of Cattle for the Use of the Publick, and for Breeding.

Beyond *Ebenezer* are several Settlements of *Uchee Indians*, on both Sides of the River *Savannah*, who have raised a Quantity of Corn.

At a considerable Distance from hence is a Town called *Augusta;* it is two hundred thirty-six Miles by Water from the Mouth of *Savannah* River, and large Boats are navigated from hence to the Town of *Savannah*. It was laid out in the Beginning of the Year 1736, and thrives prodigiously. It is the chief Place of Trade with the *Indians*. There are several Warehouses in it well furnished with Goods for the *Indian* Trade; and the last Year the People raised there above six thousand Bushels of *Indian* Corn, besides some Wheat for their own Use, which was very good. There are five large Boats which belong to different Inhabitants of the Town, and carry about nine thousand Weight of Deer-Skins each; and last

Year about one hundred thousand Weight of Skins was brought from thence. All the *Indian* Traders from both Provinces of *South-Carolina* and *Georgia*, resort thither in the Spring. In *June*, 1739, the Traders, Packhorse-men, Servants, Townsmen, and others depending upon that Business, made about six hundred Whites, who live by the Trade in the *Indian* Nation. Each *Indian* Hunter is reckoned to get three hundred Weight of Deer-Skins in a Year, which is a very advantagious Trade to *England;* for the Deer-Skins, Beaver, and other Furs, are chiefly paid for in Woollen Goods and Iron.

At *Augusta* the Trustees have hitherto maintained a little Garrison, in a Fort which they built: And the Security which the Traders receive from this Fort is their Inducement to go there. The Town stands upon a high Ground, upon the Side of the River. A Road has been marked out from thence to *Old Ebenezer*, so that Horsemen can now ride from the Town of *Savannah* to *Augusta*, as likewise to the *Cherokee Indians*, who are situated above *Augusta* to the North West, and on the *Georgia* Side of the River, in the Valleys of the *Appelachian* Mountains. The *Cherokees* have now between four and five thousand Warriors. The *French* have been using their utmost Endeavours to gain or destroy them: But as the Town of *Augusta* so easily furnishes them with Arms, Ammunition, and Necessaries, the *French* have not been able to get any Ground among them. The *Creek Indians* live to the Westward of *Augusta*, their chief Town is the *Cowetas*, at two hundred Miles Distance. The lower *Creeks* consist of about a thousand, and the upper *Creeks* of about seven hundred fighting Men; upon the Edge of whose Country the *French* Fort of *Albamas* lies. They are all sincerely attached to the *English* Interest, and they express the greatest Gratitude upon all Occasions, for the kind Reception which their Chiefs met with in *England*, and for the Justice with which all the *Indians* are treated in *Georgia*. Beyond the *Creeks* lie the *Chickesaws*, who are a very brave People: They inhabit near the *Missisippi* River, and possess the Banks of it: They are likewise great Friends of the *English*, and have resisted both the Bribes and Arms of the *French*. Some *Georgia* Traders live among them. Ten

Towns also of the *Choctaws*, who were formerly in Alliance with the *French*, trade with the People of *Georgia*.

Besides the Settlements upon the River *Savannah*, there are several Plantations to the Southward of the Town, as well as the little Villages of *Highgate* and *Hampstead*, which lie about four Miles Distance from it. Some of these Settlements extend as far as the narrow Passages near *Ogeechee*, which is an Inland River. At the narrow Passages is *Fort Argyle*, in a Situation that commands all the Province. This was built in the Year 1733. It is a large, strong Palisade, eleven Feet high, with Flankers and Loop-Holes for small Cannon at the Angles. Beyond this, in the Southern Part of the Province, is the Town of *New Inverness*, in the District of *Darien*. Here the *Highlanders* are settled. They raised, at first, a considerable Quantity of Corn. They feed (as has been said before) great Numbers of Cattle, and have many good Sawyers, who make an advantageous Trade of Lumber. Their Buildings are chiefly Huts, but tight and warm. They have a Minister, who has an Allowance from the incorporated Society in *Scotland*, and are a sober and laborious People. They have also a Fort below the Town.

About twenty Miles from hence is *Frederica*, on the Island of St. *Simon*'s, which is near the Sea upon a Branch of the *Alatamaha* River. There are many good Buildings in the Town, several of which are Brick. There is likewise a Fort and Store-house belonging to the Trust. The People have a Minister, who has a Salary from the Society for propagating the Gospel. In the Neighbourhood of the Town, there is a fine Meadow of 320 Acres ditch'd in, on which a Number of Cattle are fed, and good Hay is likewise made from it. At some Distance from the Town is the Camp for General *Oglethorpe*'s Regiment: The Country about it is well cultivated, several Parcels of Land not far distant from the Camp having been granted in small Lots to the Soldiers, many of whom are married, and fifty five Children were born there in the last Year. These Soldiers are the most industrious, and willing to plant; the rest are generally desirous of Wives, but there are not Women enough in the Country to supply them. There are some handsome Houses built by the Officers of the Regiment, and besides the Town of

Frederica, there are other little Villages upon this Island. A sufficient Quantity of Pot-herbs, Pulse, and Fruit is produced there to supply both the Town and Garison; and the People of *Frederica* have begun to malt and to brew; and the Soldiers Wives spin Cotton of the Country, which they knit into Stockings. At the Town of *Frederica* is a Town-Court for administring Justice in the Southern Part of the Province, with the same Number of Magistrates as at *Savannah*.

Beyond St. *Simon*'s is *Jekyll* Island, where there is but little good Land. Captain *Horton*, an Officer of the Regiment, however, who has a Lot upon this Island, has made great Improvements on it.

Southward of *Jekyll* lies the Island of *Cumberland*, upon which is a strong Fort called St. *Andrew*'s, built in the Year 1736: It is situated upon a fine commanding Ground. Two Companies of the Regiment are stationed here, and the Soldiers, who have Wives, have had Lots granted them; which they have improved very much. They have made a little Village called *Barrimacké*, where are about 24 Families with good Huts.

Beyond St. *Andrew*'s to the South, is the Island of *Amelia*, where the Orange-Trees grow wild in the Woods. Upon this Island are stationed the Trust *Highland* Servants, with their Scout Boats. They have a very good Plantation, and rais'd Corn enough last Year for their own Consumption. A little Fort is built here, and has a Serjeant's Guard. Upon this Island, as well as *Cumberland*, there is a Stud of Horses and Mares, and the Colts out of them are very good ones, and are bred without any Expence.

Beyond *Amelia* is St. *George*'s, which was quitted in the Year 1736, by Agreement with the *Spaniards;* and at a little Distance from this is St. *Juan*'s, where the *Spaniards* had two Forts, which were taken last Year; and between 40 and 50 Miles Distance from St. *Juan*'s is *Augustine*.

To sum up in short the present Situation of the Colony. The Trust is in Possession, in Behalf of his Majesty, from the Garrison of the *Okfuskees* in the upper *Creek* Nation (which they settled six Years ago) down to the Gulph of *Mexico* by the *Appellachees*, and from thence to *Amelia*. The Garrison of the *Okfuskees* is near 400 Miles from the Sea, and a Mark of Possession within 40 Miles of the *French* Fort. The commanding Officer there keeps up the *English* Interest with the *Indians*, and the *French* cannot incroach further without Hostilities. The Sea-Coast lies from *Amelia*, which is in 30 Deg. 30 Min. to the Mouth of *Savannah*, which is in 32 Deg. and is a Degree and a half upon the Globe; but is computed by the Boatmen, who row it, to be near 200 Miles by Water.

The *Creek Indians*, though they acknowledged the King of *Great Britain* for their Sovereign, made War with the People of *South-Carolina*, to obtain Satisfaction for Injuries done them by their Traders. The War concluded by a Peace, which obliged the People of *Carolina* not to settle Southward of the River *Savannah*, and no *Englishman* was settled within this District, when the first Colony of *Georgia* arrived. But the *Creek Indians* have since, by Agreement, conceded the Limits mention'd above. In this Province, which eight Years ago was cover'd with Woods, there are four Towns and other Settlements. It is almost every Part of it fit for Pasture; there is a good Stock of Cattle, and it discovers a great deal of rich Land fit for Agriculture.

Besides what the Land yields for Subsistance, and the tame Cattle, which multiply very fast, there are in the Province Abundance of Deer and Buffaloes. There is a vast Plenty of almost all Kinds of wild Fowl. And the Rivers abound with a great Variety of fine Fish, and particularly Sturgeon, which may prove a beneficial Trade. And in the Coast upon the Sea are Oysters, and many other Sorts of Shell-Fish. There are found likewise in hollow Trees large Quantities of excellent Honey.

As the Government, in the Beginning of our present Disputes with the Court of *Spain*, asserted the Nation's Right to the Possession of this Province; it may be some Satisfaction to the Reader to see this stated, which I shall endeavour to do in a few Lines. Besides the Concession of it by the *Indians*, who are the native Proprietors of it, *Great Britain* has the Right by the first Discovery.

This was made by *Sebastian Cabot*, under the Authority of Letters Patent from *Henry* the VIIth, dated *March 5*, 1495. In the

Year 1496 he coasted by the Shore of the Continent so far, that he had the Island of *Cuba* on his left Hand, as is particularly described in the Decades of the Ocean, written by *Peter Martyr*, (a famous *Spanish* Historian) and dedicated to the King of *Spain*, in the Year 1516.

This Discovery is testified not only by our own Historians, but likewise by other *Spanish* Writers, as *Oviedo*, *Herrera*, and *Gomara*, and also by *Ramusius*, Secretary to the Republick of *Venice*.

In the Year 1516, *Henry* the VIIIth sent *Sebastian Cabot* a second Time with Sir *Thomas Port*, Vice-Admiral of *England*, to coast the Continent, and take Possession thereof: And by Virtue of this Discovery and Possession, the Kings of *England* have from Time to Time exercis'd their Right to the Lands, by granting particular Portions thereof by their Letters Patent; some of which are as follow, *viz.*

June 11, 1578, Queen *Elizabeth* to Sir *Humphry Gilbert*.

March 25, 1584, Queen *Elizabeth* to *Walter Raleigh*, Esq; who, with Sir *Francis Drake*, in the next Year, in Time of War with *Spain*, drove the *Spaniards* from Fort St. *John*, and the City of *Augustine*, (where they had lately settled) and thereby maintain'd the *English* Rights even to *Augustine* itself.

On the 30th of *October* 1629, King *Charles* the 1st, by his Letters Patent to Sir *Robert Heath*, (then Attorney General) and to his Heirs and Assigns for ever, granted the Rivers *Matheo* and *Passamagno*, and all the Lands between the said Rivers, (the first of which is in 30 Degrees, and the last in 36 Degrees of North Latitude) and erected the same into a Province, called *Carolana*.

On the 24th of *March* 1662, King *Charles* the IId, by his Letters Patent to *Edward* Earl of *Clarendon*, *George* Duke of *Albemarle*, *William* Lord *Craven*, *John* Lord *Berkeley*, *Anthony* Lord *Ashley*, Sir *George Carteret*, Baronet, Sir *William Berkeley*, and Sir *John Colleton*, their Heirs and Assigns for ever, granted all that Territory or Tract of Land within his Dominions in *America*, not then cultivated or planted, extending from the North End of that Island called *Lucke* Island, which lies in the Southern *Virginia* Seas, and within 36 Degrees of Northern Latitude; and to the West as far as the South Seas; and so Southerly, as far as the River St. *Mathias*, which borders upon the Coast of *Florida*, and within 31 Degrees of North Latitude; and so West in a direct Line, as far as the South Seas aforesaid; and made them the true and absolute Lords and Proprietors thereof. And by the said Letters Patent erected the same into a Province, and called it *Carolina*.

On the 30th of *June* 1665, King *Charles* the IId, at the Request of the Lords Proprietors, extended the said Province to the Degree of 29 inclusive North Latitude, from the Degree of 36 and 30 Minutes North Latitude, and annex'd and united the said enlarged Territory to the said Province.

The River *Matheo*, or St. *Mathias*, which is Part of the Grant of King *Charles* the Ist, and of the first Grant of King *Charles* the IId, is the * same that is now commonly called St. *Juan*'s, where the two *Spanish* Forts were built, which were taken last Year; consequently the *Spaniards*, so far from having a just Claim to any Part of *Georgia*, are to be look'd on as Incroachers upon the *English* Dominions; and the Spirit of *Great Britain* is properly exerted in maintaining her own Rights, and checking their Pretensions.

If there are any Persons of Opinion, that *Georgia* is not worth the further Care of *Great Britain*, and that no more Supports should be granted for it; the following short Considerations are recommended to them. It is notorious, that before the Commencement of the War, *Spain* did claim this Province, and that she had made Preparations to take it by Force; and for the effectually carrying on her Designs, she endeavour'd privately to stir up Insurrections among the Negroes in *South-Carolina*, and openly granted them Protection. It is likewise well known, that *France* has a longing Eye on some Place on this Side of the Continent; that she has, at different Times, used all her Arts to gain, and Power to destroy those *Indians* in Alliance with us, and who have been a Sort of Barrier against them. If therefore *Georgia* should be abandoned or neglected, and if either of those Nations should become possessed of it, how troublesome, how dangerous, nay how ruinous must

* Appendix, No. IX.

the Neighbourhood be to *Carolina*, and the adjacent Settlements? If likewise the *Indians* should think that *Great Britain* could not, or see that she would not, assert and support her own Possessions, how much more apt would they be to enter into Friendship with those, of whom they must have a better Opinion? And how much more dispos'd, on any Provocation, to disturb, insult, and even ravage our other Plantations?

N.B. Since the greatest Part of this *Enquiry* was printed, an Account was received from *Georgia* on the 13th of this Month of *December*, That some Persons, who have been the chief Instruments in working up among the People, a Contempt of the Magistracy, a Repugnance to any Improvements, Apprehensions of immediate Danger from the *Spaniards*, and a general Dislike to the Colony, have lately gone from thence; and that some, who had fled into other Provinces, are now complaining, that they find a greater Difficulty of subsisting, than in *Georgia*, and are repenting, that they had been seduc'd to leave it.

To shew still further, that the Province is in a better Condition, than has been represented; Extracts of a Letter, received by a private Person Mr. *John Lyde*, from Mr. *Thomas Jones*, a Friend of his in *Georgia*, dated so late as the 18th of last *September*, are added in the * *Appendix*.

* No. X.

APPENDIX

Number I.

The Deposition of Lieutenant *Raymond Demare* taken by *Francis Moore*, Recorder of *Frederica* in *Georgia*, the 19th Day of *January* 1738–9.

This Deponent says, That he arrived here on the first Day of June 1738, *with a Detachment of the Regiment, and continued with the same to the Arrival of the second Detachment in* September *last; and that all the Soldiers that came over with him, were in their Turns employed to work in the Sun and Air in building Huts, burning Lime, carrying Clap Boards, and going into the Water up to their Necks to unload Boats; and that they usually work'd from five in the Morning till between eleven and twelve; and began again about half an Hour after one, and work'd till Night. And some also work'd in clearing the Ground from Roots of Trees, &c. for a Parade; and during all the said Term, the Men continued very healthy, not one Man dying, except an old Man, who came sick on board at* Gibraltar, *and who never work'd. This Deponent says, that during the whole Time he never knew any Man desire to be excus'd from Labour on Account of the Heat; and that the Recruits, who came from* England, *were more employed than the old Men who came from* Gibraltar. *This Deponent further says, that he was ten Years with my Lord* Harrington *in* Spain, *and that he often felt the Weather hotter there than in* Georgia; *and that the Peasants in* Spain *perform all the Works of Husbandry without the Assistance of Negroes.*

RAYMOND DEMARE.

The Deposition of Mr. *Hugh Mackay*, taken by *Francis Moore*, Recorder of *Frederica* in *Georgia*, the 19th Day of *January* 1738–9.

This Deponent declares upon Oath, That he had the Charge of seventeen of the Trustees Servants for the Term of two Years: The said Servants work'd

[161]

very hard, and that they never lay by in Summer, by reason of the Heat of the Weather. That they the last Summer work'd in the open Air and Sun, in felling of Trees, cross cutting and splitting of Timber, and carrying it on their Shoulders, when split, from the Woods to the Camp, and in building Houses for the King's Troops. And this Deponent further says, that the said Servants work'd willingly and chearfully, and continued in good Health; and that the said Labour did not occasion any Illness amongst them: And that when he left them about eight Days ago, they were then all in good Health, except one who was drown'd by Accident.

HUGH MACKAY.

There are other Affidavits to the same Purpose.

NUMBER II.

Deposition of *John Cuthbert*, taken upon Oath before *Francis Moore*, Recorder of *Frederica* in Georgia.

This Deponent says, That he planted three Crops in Georgia, and verily believes, that a white Servant may in six Months of the Year, after the Land is cleared, raise as much Corn, Pease, Potatoes, Pompions, &c. as will be more than sufficient for his Provisions and Cloathing: And in the other six Months, may be employed on Lumber; at which, by this Deponent's Experience, a white Servant can at least earn two Shillings Sterling per Diem: Also that Hogs, Cattle and Poultry, if taken Care of, increase at a great Rate, and with little Expence.

JOHN CUTHBERT.

Philip Delegal *the Elder, of the Parish of St.* Margaret Westminster *in the County of* Middlesex, *Lieutenant in Captain* Hugh Mackay's *Company of the Regiment of Foot in* Georgia *in* America, *aged fifty-five Years and upwards, maketh Oath, and saith; That he hath been in* Carolina *and* Georgia *for about fourteen Years last past; and saith, That the Climate of* Georgia *is very healthy, by Reason of the great Number of Rivers and Streams of running Waters within that Province, and by Reason of the fresh Breezes from the Sea, which blow in the Middle of the hottest Days. And further saith,*

That the Soil of Georgia *consists of four different Sorts of Land, the one of which is called* Pine-Barren (*a sandy Earth, which bears Pine-Trees*) *another* Oak *and* Hickary, *or mixt Land* (*being of a strong Nature fit for Grain*) *the third* Swamps, *whereon grow very large and high Trees; and the fourth* Savannahs, *whereon grow Canes and Grass, where the Cattle feed: And that there is a good Proportion in the whole Province of the said different Sorts of Soil. And this Deponent saith, That both the Black and White Mulberry-Trees grow wild in* Georgia, *and are more or less in every Plantation. That Vines grow also wild there; and that about twenty Miles up the Country from St.* Simon's, *the Trees for Masts for Shipping grow very tall. And this Deponent saith, That the Islands in* Georgia *are full of the prickly Pear Shrubs, which feed Flies; and that taking the Flies off, tho' green upon the Shrub, and squeezing them, they dye the Fingers with a deep Red, which even with Soap cannot easily be washed off; which this Deponent verily believes to be the Cochineal Fly. And this Deponent saith, That in the Beginning of the Year one Thousand seven Hundred and thirty-seven, on the late Alarms of the* Spaniards, *and before the Independent Company was incorporated into the Regiment, he made an Intrenchment, and fortified towards the Sea the South-East Point of St.* Simon's *Island about ten Miles from* Frederica, *with Gabions filled with sandy Earth; between which thirteen Pieces of Ordinance were placed. And this Deponent saith, There is an House palisadoed with a Battery of Cannon at* Amelia, *by Way of Look-out, where a Scout-Boat is stationed. And further saith, That in the Year one Thousand seven Hundred and thirty-six, in the West Part of* Cumberland *Island St.* Andrew's *Fort was erected. And that in the same Year, another Fort was built at* Frederica, *consisting of a strong Mud Wall, with Frizes all round, a Square with four regular Bastions, and a Spur-Work towards the River, and a dry Fossé palisadoed on the Outside, and stockaded in the Inside, defended by Cannon, and other Ordinance. And that in the same Year another Fort was erected at* Darien, *consisting of two Bastions, and two half Bastions, which is so strong, that thirty or forty Men are sufficient to maintain it against three hundred; and that it is also defended by several Pieces of Ordinance. And when this Deponent left* Georgia *to look after further military Preferment, for his long and faithful Services, which was in* June *one thousand seven hundred and thirty-nine, the said Forts were all in a defensible Condition. And this Deponent saith, That three Companies of General* Oglethorpe's *Regiment are in Quarters in a Corner of St.* Simon's *Island, near which the Soldiers, by joint Labour* (*when not on military Duty*) *clear and plant the Lands set out for them. And this Deponent lastly saith,*

That the Province of Georgia *is the Barrier and greatest Security to* Carolina, *and the other Northern Provinces in* America, *and of the greatest Importance to the* British *Nation; and that the Produces, which may be expected therefrom, will in Time become very beneficial to its Mother Country.*

PHILIP DELEGAL, Senior.

Sworn at the publick Office,
March 11, 1739, before
FRAN. ELD.

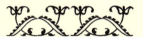

NUMBER III.

Extract of a Letter from the *Saltzburghers*, to his Excellency
General *Oglethorpe.*

Ebenezer, March 13, 1739.

WE Saltzburghers, *and Inhabitants at* Ebenezer, *that have signed this Letter, humbly intreat in our, and our Brethrens Name, your Excellency would
be pleased to shew us the Favour of desiring the Honourable Trustees for
sending to* Georgia *another Transport of* Saltzburghers *to be settled at* Ebenezer. *We have, with one Accord, wrote a Letter to our Father in God the
Rev. Mr.* Senior Urlsperger, *at* Augsburgh, *and in that Letter expressly
named those* Saltzburghers *and* Austrians, *whom, as our Friends, Relations,
and Countrymen, we wish to see settled here. We can indeed attest of them,
that they fear the Lord truly, love Working, and will conform themselves to
our Congregation. We have given them an Account of our being settled well,
and being mighty well pleased with the Climate and Condition of this Country, having here several Preferences in spiritual and temporal Circumstances
to other People in* Germany, *which your Honour will find in the inclosed
Copy of our Letter to Mr.* Senior Urlsperger. *If they fare as we do, having
been provided in the Beginning with Provisions, a little Stock for Bread, some
Tools, and good Land, by the Care of the Honourable Trustees; and if God
grant a Blessing to their Work, we doubt not but they will gain with us easily
their Bread and Subsistance, and lead a quiet and peaceable Life in all Godliness and Honesty. Tho' 'tis here a hotter Season than our native Country, yet
it is not so extreamly hot as we were told in the first Time of our Arrival. But
since we have been now used to the Country, we find it tolerable, and for work-*

[164]

ing People very convenient, setting themselves to work early in the Morning till Ten o'Clock, and in the Afternoon from Three to Sun-set. And having Business at Home, we do them in our Huts and Houses, in the Middle of the Day, till the greatest Heat is over. People in Germany *are hindered by Frost and Snow in the Winter from doing any Work in the Fields and Vineyards; but we have this Preference, to do the most and heaviest Work at such a Time, preparing the Ground sufficiently for planting in the Spring. We were told by several People after our Arrival, that it proves quite impossible and dangerous for white People to plant and manufacture any Rice, being a Work only for Negroes, not for* European *People; but having Experience of the contrary, we laugh at such a Talking, seeing that several People of us have had, in last Harvest, a greater Crop of Rice than they wanted for their own Consumption. Of Corn, Pease, Potatoes, Pumpkins, Cabbage, &c. we had such a good Quantity, that many Bushels are sold, and much was spent in feeding Cows, Calves and Hogs.*

We humbly beseech the Honourable Trustees, not to allow that any Negroes might be brought to our Place, or in our Neighbourhood; knowing by Experience, that Houses and Gardens will be robbed always by them; and white People are in Danger of Life from them, besides other great Inconveniencies.

Signed by forty-nine Men of the *Saltzburghers.* And lower,

> We Ministers of the *Saltzburghers at Ebenezer,* join with the *Saltzburghers* in this Petition, and verify, that every one of them has signed it with the greatest Readiness and Satisfaction.

> JOHN MARTIN BOLZIUS.
> ISRAEL CHRISTIAN GRONAU.

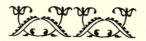

NUMBER IV.

To the Trustees for establishing the Colony of *Georgia.*

GENTLEMEN,

In writing this Answer to the Letter, which I had the Honour to receive from you, dated the 29th Instant, wherein you desire to know my Sentiments of an

Undertaking to raise Raw Silk in your new Settlement in Georgia: *Of the Probability of succeeding therein; the proper Steps to be taken to bring that Work to Perfection: And my Opinion of the Nature, Quality, and Use of the Raw Silk produced in* Carolina: *It is a great Pleasure to me, that from Experiments which I made some Years ago, I can now, besides my Opinion, give you some Information concerning that Silk, which may be depended on.*

The Value and Usefulness of the Undertaking will appear as soon as we consider, that all the Silk consumed in this Kingdom is now of foreign Growth, and Manufacture, which costs the Nation very great Sums of Money yearly to purchase, and that the raising our Supply thereof in his Majesty's Dominions in America, *would save us all that Money, afford Employment to many Thousands of his Majesty's Subjects, and greatly increase the Trade and Navigation of* Great Britain. *It appears to me as beneficial to this Kingdom, attended with as little Hazard or Difficulty, as much wanted, and which may as soon be brought to Perfection in a proper Climate, as any Undertaking so considerable in itself, that I ever heard of. I therefore think, there is a very great Probability of its succeeding, if such proper Measures are pursued, and such Assistance afforded to the poor People at their first Setting out, as are necessary to settle, instruct, and encourage them.*

The Silk produced in Carolina *has as much natural Strength and Beauty, as the Silk of* Italy, *(which is commonly called fine Silk,) and by the several Experiments I have tried with it, I am satisfied, it may be made to answer the same Purposes as* Italian *Silk now does, if it be reeled in short Skains, a fine, clean and even Thread; to effect which, if some experienced Persons are at first sent to teach the People, the Work will soon be made easy to the meanest Capacity, and the Value of the Silk will be thereby greatly increased.*

As for my own Part, if at any Time you should think I can be of Use to promote so good a Work, I shall be ready to execute your Commands, as far as I am able, and always remain,

OLD-JEWRY,
  Jan. 31, 1732.

GENTLEMEN,
Your most Obedient,
Humble Servant,
THO. LOMBE.

Number V.

Samuel Augspourguer, *of the Canton of* Berne *in* Switzerland, *Citizen, aged forty-two Years and upwards, maketh Oath, That in the Year of our Lord one thousand seven hundred and thirty-four, this Deponent went to* Purysburgh *in* South-Carolina; *and that in the Beginning of the Year one thousand seven hundred and thirty-six, this Deponent joined the Colony of* Georgia, *and with the Leave of the Honourable* James Oglethorpe, *Esq; laid out a Tract of Land in the Southern Part of the said Colony, which this Deponent has begun to improve for himself, and has two Men-Servants at Work thereon, with two Children belonging to one of them. That this Deponent left* Georgia *the eighteenth Day of* July *one thousand seven hundred and thirty-nine, on his Return to* Switzerland, *to settle his private Affairs, and to get some of his own Country Servants to return with him to* Georgia, *to go on with the Cultivation of his said Tract of Land, consisting of five hundred Acres. That the Climate of* Georgia *is very healthy, there being Quantities of running Water, and constantly fine Breezes from the Sea in the Middle of the hottest Days. That the Soil, which this Deponent knows the true Nature of, is* Pine-barren (*a sandy Earth which bears Pine-Trees*) *and also* Oak *and* Hickary, *or mixt Land, and* Swamps. *And that there is a good Proportion of the said different Sorts of Soil in* Georgia. *That the Climate and Soil is very fit for raising Silk, Wine and Cotton; for that the white Mulberry-Trees thrive exceeding well, as also the Vines, which have been cultivated there, bear exceeding good Grapes, which this Deponent tasted in* July *last in great Perfection; and being ripe so soon, can be gathered before the Rains fall, which generally happen in* September, *or* October. *And that the Cotton, by this Deponent's own Experience, who has planted the same there, grows very well in* Georgia, *a Specimen of which Cotton this Deponent brought over with him, and produced before the Trustees. All which Produces this Deponent saith can be raised by white Persons, without the Use of Negroes. And this Deponent saith, That the Day he left* Georgia *in* July *last, he received from the Hands of Mr.* Thomas Jones, *the Trustees Store-Keeper at* Savannah, *a Parcel of Raw Silk to be delivered to the Trustees in* England, *which the said Store-Keeper said was the Produce of* Georgia. *And this Deponent also saith, That he has seen the* Italian *Family at* Savannah *in* Georgia *winding off Silk from the Coquons, and that they have been there about four or five Years. And this Deponent further saith, That there are great Numbers of prickly Pear Shrubs in* Georgia, *and that he hath seen the Fly feeding on the Leaves, which this Deponent verily believes to be the Cochineal, he having squeezed*

[167]

the Flies, and tried them, and found the Juice of them a deep Red. And this Deponent saith, That by Industry People may raise a comfortable Subsistance; and by Encouragement to go on with these useful Produces, may obtain thereby the other Necessaries of Life, and benefit themselves, as well as Great Britain, *by producing in Time Quantities thereof for Export. And lastly, this Deponent saith, That in the Year one thousand seven hundred and thirty-six, he built the Fort at* Frederica, *to which there is four Bastions, a Ditch palisadoed, and a covered Way defended by fifteen Pieces of Cannon: And that he has also seen the Fort at St.* Andrew's, *built the same Year by Captain* Hugh Mackay, *which is a Star-Work, with a Ravelin at the Bottom, defended by nine Pieces of Ordinance. And that when this Deponent came from* Georgia, *he left them in a defensible Condition.*

SAMUEL AUGSPOURGUER.

Sworn at the publick Office,
   February 13, 1739, before
   W. SPICER.

   SIR,
The Silk you was so kind to send to have my Opinion of, is of as good a Quality, in all Appearance, as any we have from Italy: *It is already as well sorted as it can be; indeed the finer the more valuable, as it is so well cleaned. The Price of raw Silk is variable, but at present being dear, I think the greatest Part of it is worth* 20 s. per lb.

I am, SIR,

King-street, Cheap-
   side, January 16,
   1739–40.

To Mr. HARMAN VERELST.

Your most humble Servant,

JOHN ZACHARY.

Number VI.

Extract of a Letter from Mrs. *Martha Causton* to the Trustees.

Savannah, Jan. 16, 1737.

It is not without Fear of presuming too far, that I trouble you with this, in order to inform you of the State of the Silk Worms, and the Progress they made last Season in this Province.

They hatch'd in March, *when the Mulberry-Trees had been about three Weeks in Leaf. They were kept in a House* 24 *Feet long, wherein were five Tables of the full Length and Width of the House: These Tables were wholly covered with the Worms, as are likewise the upper Floor. Their Number, regular Disposition, and Manner of working, drew many to see them, who looked upon the Whole as Matter worthy Admiration. The* Chickesaw In-dians, *who were here at that Time, were in an exceeding Manner delighted with them, never failing their Attendance at the House twice a Day, during their Continuance at* Savannah. *I ordered an Interpreter to inform them that Silk was for Cloaths, and one of them said, they had not those Worms in their Nation, but if they had, and knew the Method of keeping them, they could return us yearly Canoes laden with Balls, having a great Abundance of Mul-berry-Trees up in the Country, to supply them with Food.*

Number VII.

To his Excellency General *Oglethorpe.*

The Petition of the Inhabitants of *New Inverness.*

We are informed, that our Neighbours of Savannah *have petitioned your Excellency for the Liberty of having Slaves: We hope, and earnestly intreat, that before such Proposals are hearkened unto, your Excellency will consider our Situation, and of what dangerous and bad Consequence such Liberty would be of to us, for many Reasons.*

1. *The Nearness of the* Spaniards, *who have proclaimed Freedom to all Slaves, who run away from their Masters, makes it impossible for us to keep them, without more Labour in guarding them, than what we would be at to do their Work.*

2. *We are laborious, and know a white Man may be, by the Year, more usefully employed than a Negroe.*

3. *We are not rich, and becoming Debtors for Slaves, in Case of their running away or dying, would inevitably ruin the poor Master, and he become a greater Slave to the Negroe-Merchant, than the Slave he bought could be to him.*

4. *It would oblige us to keep a Guard Duty at least as severe, as when we expected a daily Invasion: And if that was the Case, how miserable would it be to us, and our Wives and Families, to have one Enemy without, and a more dangerous one in our Bosoms!*

5. *It is shocking to human Nature, that any Race of Mankind and their Posterity should be sentenc'd to perpetual Slavery; nor in Justice can we think otherwise of it, than that they are thrown amongst us to be our Scourge one Day or other for our Sins: And as Freedom must be as dear to them as to us, what a Scene of Horror must it bring about! And the longer it is unexecuted, the bloody Scene must be the greater. We therefore for our own Sakes, our Wives and Children, and our Posterity, beg your Consideration, and intreat, that instead of introducing Slaves, you'll put us in the Way to get us some of our Countrymen, who, with their Labour in Time of Peace, and our Vigilance, if we are invaded, with the Help of those, will render it a difficult Thing to hurt us, or that Part of the Province we possess. We will for ever pray for your Excellency, and are with all Submission, &c.*

Signed by eighteen Freeholders of *New Inverness*, in the District of Darien.

New Inverness,
Jan. 3, 1738–9.

Vide Letter from the *Saltzburghers*, No. III.

Charles Dempsy, *of the Parish of St.* Paul, Covent-Garden, *in the County of* Middlesex, *Esq; aged fifty four Years and upwards, maketh Oath, That in the Year one Thousand seven Hundred and thirty five, this Deponent went with the honourable* James Oglethorpe, *Esq. to* Georgia *in* America, *and was sent from thence by the said Mr. Oglethorpe to St. Augustine, with Letters for the Governor there. That this Deponent continued going to and from thence until November one thousand seven Hundred and thirty six. And this Deponent saith, That the Mulberry-Trees and Vines grow wild in Georgia, That he has tasted the wild Grapes, which are sweet and have a hard Skin; and this Deponent verily believes, that by transplanting and cultivating those wild Vines, they will produce fine Grapes for Wine. And this Deponent saith, That on the West Part of Cumberland Island the Star-Work Fort of St. Andrew is built, and at Frederica there is another Fort built with four regular Bastions, and a dry Ditch palisadoed on the Out-side, and stockaded in the Inside, both which were erected and mounted with Ordinance, before this Deponent left Georgia, which is extended so much to the Southward, that it is thereby the only and greatest Security to Carolina, and the other Northern Provinces in America, by being a Barrier to them all, and is of the greatest Use to prevent the Desertion of Negroes or others. And this Deponent further saith, That he verily believes the having no Negroes in Georgia is the Security and Strength of that Colony, and that no Negroes can be expected to stay in Georgia, were they to be permitted there, while any Part of Florida remains in the Hands of the Spaniards.*

CHARLES DEMPSY.

Sworn at the publick Of-
    fice, *March* 11, 1739.
    before FRAN. ELD.

NUMBER VIII.

Thomas Shubrick, *of* Ratcliff-Cross, *in the County of* Middlesex, *Captain of the Ship* Mary Anne, *aged twenty nine Years and upwards, maketh Oath, That in* March *last he sailed with Provisions for General* Oglethorpe's *Regiment, to be delivered at* Frederica *in* Georgia, *and arrived there the second Day of* June *following. That this Deponent touched first at* Charles-Town, *and took in a Pilot for* Frederica. *That he found the Coast of* Georgia *as capable and secure for Navigation, as any Coast whatever. That at most*

Places there is seven or eight Fathom Water within three or four Leagues from the Land, where any Ship may stand into, and if Necessity should require, may anchor with the utmost Safety, the Ground being all clean Sand from one End of the Coast to the other. That the Entry at Jekyll *Sound is very safe, and that he found upon the Bar there, as he sounded when he went over at young Flood, seventeen Feet Water; so that upon that Bar this Deponent computes at low Water to be at least fifteen Feet Water, and at high Water full twenty two Feet Water, whereby* 40 *Gun Ships may safely go over it, and when in the Sound, which is large and well land-locked, twelve Men of War may ride in Safety. And this Deponent saith, That the River in* Georgia *flowing from that Sound will contain a great Number of Ships in smooth Water. And this Deponent further saith, That upon the Bar at* Charles-Town *in* South-Carolina, *there is only eleven Feet at low Water, and eighteen Feet at high Water. And this Deponent lastly saith, That he has seen very fine Knee Timber in* Georgia, *fit for Shipping, which grows near the Sea; and when on Shore, and viewing the Soil in those Parts, saw exceeding rich Land there, having fine Mold about two Feet deep.*

THOMAS SHUBRICK.

Sworn at the publick Office,
    Feb. 20, 1739, before
        THO. BENNETT.

George Dymond, *of* Golden-Lane, London, *late Mate of his Majesty's Ship the* Princess Caroline, *aged forty six Years and upwards, maketh Oath, and saith, That he, this Deponent, has been three Voyages from* Europe *to* Georgia *in* America, *and one Voyage from* Georgia *to* Pensilvania, *and back on board the Ship* Peter *and* James, *whereof he was Master. That the last Time this Deponent left* Georgia *was in the Month of* January, *one Thousand seven Hundred and thirty seven; that by reason of his said several Voyages there, and of his having been employed as a Store-ship and Guard-ship in the Southern Part of* Georgia, *he was well acquainted with the Coast and Harbours and the Climate, and the then State and Condition of the said Colony; and saith, That about four Year ago, the Trustees erected, at the Island of* Tybee, *a very high Beacon or Land Mark, visible four Leagues at Sea, which is of the utmost Use to all Ships sailing on that Coast, there being no other Land Mark on that, or on the Coast of* Carolina; *whereby Ships not only know the Bar of* Tybee, *but have also a Direction by that, to know the Coast they are on, which, before that Beacon was erected, they were at a very great Loss to know. That the Bar at* Tybee *is a very safe Entrance, where*

Ships of four hundred Tons, without altering their Course, may run directly from the Sea over the Bar, whereon there is fifteen Feet at low Water, and twenty two Feet at high Water, and that Creek and the River Savannah *communicating therewith, will contain in Safety four hundred or five hundred Sail of Ships in smooth Water. That about six Years ago the Town of* Savannah *was erected on a Bluff, about ten Miles from* Tybee *Creek, to which Town Ships of three hundred Tons may safely go up. That when this Deponent was last there, he verily believes there were upwards of two hundred Houses built in the said Town, most of which were then inhabited. And this Deponent saith, That the Coast of* Georgia *is as convenient and secure for Navigation, as any Coast in the World; for that at most Places there is seven or eight Fathom Water within three or four Leagues from the Land, where any Ship may stand into, and if Necessity should require, may anchor with the utmost Safety, the Ground being all clean Sand from one End of the Coast to the other; and this Deponent saith, He never heard of any Ship put on that Shore by Stress of Weather, for that the Wind seldom or never blows hard upon the Land; and if any Ships have ever run on Shore there, it must have been chiefly owing to Mistakes, which the Beacon erected at* Tybee *may for the future very likely prevent. And this Deponent saith, That there is the same Depth of Water upon the Bar at* Jekyll *Harbour, as there is upon the Bar at* Tybee, *whereby forty Gun Ships may safely go over either of those Bars. That* Jekyll *Harbour is so large and land-locked, that twelve Men of War may securely ride therein; and that the River belonging to that Harbour is so large, and hath such a Depth of Water, as to be able to contain above one thousand Sail of Ships in smooth Water. That about three Years ago the Town of* Frederica *was erected, about six Miles on a straight Line from* Jekyll *Harbour, where several Houses were built, as also a very strong, defensible Fort; and another Fort was begun at St.* Simon's. *And this Deponent saith, That the Climate of* Georgia *is very healthy, the Latitude of* Tybee *being in thirty two Degrees, and of* Jekyll *in thirty one Degrees Northern Latitude, which Climate is capable of producing Silk, Wine and Cotton, for no Vegetables thrive faster any where, than the Mulberry-Trees in* Georgia; *and this Deponent verily believes, that Wine may be brought to as great Perfection in* Georgia, *as in* Spain, *and be much the same Sort, the Vines growing wild, and the Grapes therefrom being well tasted, which by transplanting and Cultivation will improve: And this Deponent has no Doubt but they will thrive very well; and this Deponent saith, He is the more satisfied thereof, for that several* Spaniards *of St.* Augustine, *who came from* Andalusia *in* Old Spain, *with whom this Deponent frequently convers'd, told him, that* Georgia *would produce every Thing that* Old Spain *did; and this Deponent brought over with him several good Pods of Cotton, which grew in* Georgia; *and this Deponent saith, the prickly Pear Shrubs grow wild in* Georgia, *and that he hath seen several of the Flies, which feed thereon, and believes they are the Cochineal, for by squeezing the Insect, though green to Appearances, yet the Juice of it is a fine Scarlet. And this Deponent saith, That he has seen very good Timber for Masts in* Georgia, *which grow very high, and near navigable Rivers to be floated down: That there are also great Quantities of live Oak in* Georgia, *fit for building Ships; and that the Carpenter of the King's Sloop the* Hawk, *stationed in* Georgia, *told this Deponent, that the Timber for Masts in* Georgia *were fit for the largest Men of War. And this Deponent further saith, That the Province of* Georgia, *being settled and fortified, is the greatest Barrier and Security, not only to* Carolina, *but to all the Northern Provinces in* America; *and that Colony having no Negroes (which this Deponent believes are no Way necessary for the raising Silk, Wine, Cotton or Cochineal) is thereby of the greatest Use and Consequence to* Carolina, *to prevent the Running away of their Negroe Slaves. And this Deponent lastly saith, That in his Judgment and Opinion the said Colony of* Georgia *is of great Moment and Importance to the* British *Nation, and that the Produce thereof will, in Process of Time, become very profitable and beneficial to its Mother Country.*

Sworn at the publick Office,
  March 7, 1739, before
  W. SPICER.

William Thomson, *of* London, *Mariner, aged thirty Years and upwards, maketh Oath, and saith, That he, this Deponent, has been six Voyages from* Europe *to* Georgia *in* America; *that this Deponent left* Georgia *in the Month of* March *last; that he is well acquainted with the Coast, Harbours and Climate of* Georgia; *that the Beacon or Land Mark at the Island of* Tybee, *erected by the Trustees, is visible above four Leagues at Sea, and is of the greatest Consequence to all Ships coming upon that Coast; that the Bar at* Tybee *is a very safe Entrance, whereon there is at least fifteen Feet at low Water, and twenty two Feet at high Water, in common Tides; that the Town of* Savannah *is about ten Miles up the River from* Tybee, *to which Place Ships of three hundred Tons may go up with Safety; that the Sea Coast from* Tybee *to* Jekyll, *four Leagues from the Land, is all even Ground, not less than seven or eight Fathom Water, and any Ship keeping in such a Depth of*

Water, may steer along that Coast with the greatest Safety, and anchor, if they have Occasion; for no dangerous Banks reach so far from Land; that on the Bar at Jekyll *there is much the same Depth of Water, as at* Tybee, *and when over the Bar, there is a very convenient Harbour for almost any Number of Ships; that the Town of* Frederica *is about ten Miles up the River from* Jekyll, *upon the Island of St.* Simon's, *and when this Deponent last left* Georgia, *the said Town was begun to be fortified round, but a Fort was before erected in the Front of the said Town, commanding the River both Ways, where the Town Guard was kept, which was built large enough upon Occasion to contain the Inhabitants of the said Town; that three Companies of General* Oglethorpe's *Regiment were encamped on the South Point of the said Island, and most of the Soldiers had Lots of Land set out near the Camp, which they cultivated, when not on Duty; that on the West Part of* Cumberland *Island the Star-Work Fort of St.* Andrew *is built; that the Climate of* Georgia *is very healthy, and the Soil much the same as in* South-Carolina; *and that Vines and Mulberry-Trees grow wild thereon; that the possessing* Georgia *so far to the Southward, and settling the same with white Inhabitants, is a very great Security to all his Majesty's Northern Colonies in* America, *and particularly to that of* South-Carolina.

WILLIAM THOMSON.

Sworn at the publick Office
   this 26th Day of *August*
   1740, before me
     M. THURSTON.

NUMBER IX.

Frederica in
Georgia } that is to say,

The Deposition of *John Fred*, Pilot on board his Majesty's Ship
   the *Flamborough*, taken before *Francis Moore*, Recorder
     of the Town of *Frederica*.

This Deponent says, That in the Year 1729, *he was taken Prisoner by a* Spanish *Guarda Coast from the* Havannah, *in about the Latitude of* 24 : 40;

*that the Guarda Coast, who took this Deponent Prisoner, instead of falling in
with St. Augustine, as they intended, fell into the Northward of that Port
about 14 Leagues, at the Mouth of the River St. Matthaeo. This Deponent
says, that he knows the said River to be Saint Matthaeo, and that the* Spaniards *on board the Guarda Coast, and those at* Augustine, *called it by the
same Name. And this Deponent knows, that the River St. John's is within the
Bar of* Augustine, *and that the River which the* Spaniards *now call St.
John's, is what was called St. Matthaeo; but why they have chang'd that
Name, he does not know. And this Deponent farther says, that his Knowledge of the River St.* Matthaeo *arises from Draughts, and from the Declaration of the* Spaniards *themselves; that he has made the Entrance of the said
River several Times, and saw the Sand Hills and Entrance of the said River
this Voyage.*

J O H N F R E D.

Sworn to before me the
   25th Day of *January*
   1739–40.
     F R A. M O O R E.

N U M B E R X.

Extracts of a Letter from Mr. *Thomas Jones* to Mr. *John Lyde,*
dated at *Savannah, September* 18, 1740.

When I arrived at Savannah, *I took Lodgings, and boarded at a Gentle-
woman's House,* (Mrs. Vanderplank) *where I have continued hitherto, but
intend shortly to remove to my own House in Town, or to an House of the
Trustees, now vacant; having a small, but agreeable Family,* viz. *a Man and
Maid Servant, also one Mr.* Harris, *recommended to me by your Friend in*
Fosket; *he is a Person of great Integrity, has been very serviceable to me, and
in some Measure made up the Disappointment I met with in others; and one*
William Russel, *a sober Youth, whom I employ in Writing for me. My little
Family (may we be more thankful) have been very healthy; we abound in the
necessary Conveniencies of Life, are well supplied with fresh Provisions,* viz.
Beef from 1d.½ *to* 2d.½ *per* lb. *Pork from* 2d. *to* 2d.½ *per* lb. *Veal from*
2d½ *to* 3d. *per* lb. *Mutton (being yet very scarce) is from* 4d.½ *to* 5d. *per* lb.

Tame Fowl we have Plenty of, therefore seldom buy any, nor Wild Fowl, and Fish, which we abound with.—Mr. Harris, *who is an expert Fowler, sometimes goes out with his Gun, and seldom fails of bringing in either Wild Turkey, Curlews, Rabbit, Partridge, Squirrel, Ducks or Geese, (in their Season) sometimes Venison, but that, and Bear, &c. the* Indians *supply us with often. As to our Liquors, we have Wine; chiefly* Madeira *or* Vidonia, *which cost us from* 3s. *to* 3s. 6d. *a Gallon; Strong Beer* 20s. *per Barrel, of* 30 *Gallons; Cyder* 10s. *per Barrel. Our Small Beer we brew of Molassas, and is cheap. Coffee about* 18d. *per* lb. *Tea from* 5s. *to* 7s. *per* lb. *The finest Wheat Flour is at* 1d. *per* lb. *I bake my own Bread generally with half Wheat, and half* Indian *Wheat Flour; the* Indian *Wheat is sold from* 10d. *to* 18d. *per Bushel, is well tasted, and very nourishing Bread. The finest Rice is sold here from* 3s. 6d. *to* 5s. *per Hundred Weight. We have good Store of Pulse, Roots, and Potherbs, such as Pease, and Beans of divers Kinds, (many of them yet unknown in* England) *Pompions, Musk and Water Melons, Potatoes, and generally all the Roots and Herbs used in* England. *As to our Fruit, the most common are Peaches and Nectarines, (I believe that I had an hundred Bushels of the former this Year in my little Garden in the Town) we have also Apples of divers Kinds, Chincopin Nuts, Walnut, Chesnut, Hickary and Ground Nuts; several Sorts of Berries, besides those common with you; very good Grapes, but no Oranges grow nearer than* Amelia *to the Southward; We have exceeding fine Water at* Savannah, *Fire Wood very reasonable; such as have Houses of their own, have no other Burthen than performing or paying for their Guard Duty in their Turn. There are no Taxes; all publick Buildings, and other such Works, such as Bridges, Roads, &c. have been carried on at the Expence of the Trustees. I have not seen any Part of the World, where Persons, that would labour, and used any Industry, might live more comfortably.*

Having mentioned Darien, *which is a Town inhabited by the* Highland Scotch, *under the Care of Mr.* McCloud, *the People live very comfortably, with great Unanimity: I know of no other Settlement in this Colony more desirable, except* Ebenezer, *a Town on the River* Savannah, *at* 35 *Miles Distance from hence, inhabited by* Saltzburghers *and other* Germans, *under the pastoral Care of Mr.* Bolzius *and Mr.* Gronau, *who are discreet, worthy Men; they consist of* 60 *Families or upwards.*—*The Town is neatly built, the Situation exceeding pleasant, the People live in the greatest Harmony with their Ministers, and with one another, as one Family; they have no idle, drunken, or profligate People among them, but are industrious, many grown wealthy; and their Industry hath been blessed with remarkable and uncom-*

mon *Success, to the Envy of their Neighbours; having great Plenty of all the necessary Conveniencies for Life (except Cloathing) within themselves; and supply this Town and other neighbouring Places with Bread Kind, as also Beef, Veal, Pork, Poultry, &c.*

Many Artifices have been made use of to gain over these Germans *and the* Darien *People, to join with the discontented Party here, in petitioning for Negroe Slaves; and since they could not be prevailed on, Letters have been writ to them from* England, *endeavouring to intimidate them into a Compliance.*

I have already exceeded the Limits of a Letter, and perhaps trespassed on my Friend's Patience, by entring into a Detail of Matters not very entertaining; yet I thought it necessary, lest my Friends should conclude, that if living, I was wholly deprived of my Reason, by remaining in a Country (represented to be) wholly destitute of the common Necessaries of Life; or that Necessity obliged me to continue in it, or else that an eager Desire of Wealth might tempt me to run any Hazard; this last, I am well assured my Friends, who have known my Conversation and Manner of Life in England, *would hardly believe to be the Case with me, whatever Instances may be given of Persons, who have run great Risques in their Healths and Lives on that Account.*

I hinted to you in my last, that I enjoyed a better State of Health since I came into this Colony, than I had for some Years past; my Friends here have the same, though many of the Inhabitants have had Fluxes or intermitting Fevers frequently, (often occasioned by Intemperance) yet few die of those Distempers. I have carefully enquired into the Account of our Births and Burials at Savannah, *and its Districts, for one Year past, and find the former has exceeded the latter, at three to two. I have not known any Town, or Place in* England, *where fewer have died in that Space of Time, in Proportion to the Inhabitants. I have this Day (that I might be at a greater Certainty) enquired at Mr.* Whitefield's, *(who has by far the largest Family of any in this Colony, consisting of near one hundred and fifty Persons) and received the following Account from Mr.* Habersham, *(who has the Care and Direction of the Family in Mr.* Whitefield's *Absence) that their Family consists of sixty Persons, including hired Servants, sixty one Orphans, and other poor Children, twenty five working Tradesmen, and others, in all* 146, *exclusive of many others, who have remained at their House a Month, two or three Months at a Time, (and have been accounted to be of their Family) and that all the Family are in good Health.*

FINIS.

An Account Shewing the Progress
of the Colony of *Georgia*

AN
ACCOUNT

Shewing the PROGRESS of the

Colony of *GEORGIA*

IN

AMERICA

FROM ITS

First Eſtabliſhment.

LONDON:
Printed in the Year M. DCC. XLI.

An Account Shewing the Progress
of the Colony of *Georgia*

HIS Majesty King *George* the Second, by his Letters Patent, bearing Date the Ninth Day of *June* One thousand Seven hundred and Thirty-two, reciting amongst other things, That many of his poor Subjects were, through Misfortunes, and want of Employment, reduced to great Necessities, and would be glad to be settled in any of his Majesty's Provinces in *America*, where, by cultivating the Lands waste and desolate, they might not only gain a comfortable Subsistence, but also strengthen his Majesty's Colonies, and increase the Trade, Navigation and Wealth of his Majesty's Realms; and that the Provinces in *North America* had been frequently ravaged by *Indian* Enemies, more especially that of *South Carolina*, whose Southern Frontier continued unsettled, and lay open to the neighbouring Savages; and that to relieve the Wants of the said poor People, and to protect his Majesty's Subjects in *South Carolina*, a regular Colony of the said poor People should be settled and established in the Southern Frontiers of *Carolina*; did, for the Considerations aforesaid, constitute a Corporation by the Name of, The Trustees for establishing the Colony of *Georgia* in *America*, with Capacity to purchase and take Lands, to sue and to be sued, to have a common Seal, and to chuse Members of the said Corporation on the Third *Thursday* in *March* yearly, with restraining Clauses, that no Member of the said Corporation should have any Salary, Fee, Perquisite, Benefit, or Profit whatsoever, for acting therein, or have any Office, Place or Employment of Profit under the said Corporation, with a Direction for the said Corporation every Year to lay an Account in Writing before the Lord Chancellor, Chief Justice of the King's-Bench, Master of the Rolls, Chief Justice of the Common-Pleas, and Chief Baron of the Exchequer, or any Two of them, of all Moneys or Effects by them received or expended for carrying on the good Purposes aforesaid, with a Power to make Bye-Laws, Constitutions, Orders and Ordinances: And granted, amongst other Things, to the said Corporation, and their Successors, under the Reservations therein mentioned, Seven undivided Parts (the Whole into Eight equal Parts to be divided) of all those Lands, Countries and Territories, situate, lying and being in that Part of *South Carolina* in *America*, which lies from the most Northern Stream of a River there, commonly called the *Savannah*, all along the Sea-Coast to the Southward unto the most Southern Stream of a certain other great Water or River, called the *Alatamaha*, and Westward from the Heads of the said Rivers respectively, in direct Lines to the *South-Seas*, To have and to hold the same, to them the said Corporation, and their Successors for ever, for the better Support of the said Colony, under the yearly Rent of Four Shillings Proclamation Money of *South Carolina* for every Hundred Acres of the said Lands for ever, which the said Corporation should grant, demise, plant or settle, but not to commence until Ten Years after such Grant, Demise, Planting or Settling: And erected and created the said Lands, Countries and Territories into one independent and separate Province, by the Name of *GEORGIA;* and made the Inhabitants, who should reside therein, free, and not subject to any the Laws, Orders, Statutes or Constitutions of *South Carolina*, except the Commander in Chief of the Militia; and authorized the said Corporation for the Term of Twenty-one Years from the Date of the said Letters Patent, to form and prepare Laws, Statutes and Ordinances for the Government of the said Colony, not repugnant to the Laws and Statutes of *England*, to be presented under their common Seal to his Majesty in Council for his Approbation or Disallowance, and that the said Laws, so approved of, should be in full Force and Virtue within the said Province: And impowered the Common Council for the Time being of the said Corporation, or the major Part of them, to dispose of, expend and apply all the Moneys and Effects belonging to the said Corporation, and to make Contracts for carrying on and effecting the good Purposes therein intended; and that they should from time to time appoint a Treasurer, Secretary, and such other Officers, Ministers and Servants of the said Corporation, as they should see proper, for the good Management of their Affairs, and at their Pleasure to remove them, and appoint others in their stead; and that they should appoint reasonable Salaries, Perquisites, or other Rewards, for their Labour or Services; and that such Officers should be sworn, before they act, for the faithful and due Execution of their respective Offices and Places; and declared, that the Treasurer and Secretary for the Time being should be incapable of being Members of the said Corporation; and granted to the said Corporation, that it should be lawful for them, their Officers or Agents, to transport and convey into the said Province, such of his Majesty's Subjects and Foreigners, as were willing to go, and inhabit and reside there; and declared all Persons born within the said Province, and their Children and Posterity, to be free Denizens, as if they had been born within any of his Majesty's Dominions: And impowered the said Common Council, in the Name of the Corporation, and under their common Seal, to distribute, convey, assign and set over such particular Portions of the said Lands, Tenements, and Hereditaments, unto such of his Majesty's Subjects, and others willing to live in the said Colony, upon such Terms, and for such Estates, and upon such Rents, Reservations and Conditions, as the same might lawfully be granted, and as to the said Common Council, or the major Part of them, should seem fit and proper; provided that no Grant should be made of any Part of the said Lands unto, or in Trust for, or for the Benefit of any Member of the said Corporation, and that no greater Quantity of the said Land be granted either intirely, or in Parcels, to, or to the Use of, or in Trust for any one Person, than Five hundred Acres; and declared that all Grants made contrary to the true Intent and Meaning thereof, should be absolutely null and void: And granted that the said Corporation, for the Term of Twenty-one Years from the Date of the said Letters Patent, should have Power to erect and constitute Judicatures and Courts of Record, or other Courts to be held in his Majesty's Name, for the hearing and determining of all manner of Crimes, Offences, Pleas, Processes, Plaints, Actions, Matters, Causes, and Things whatsoever arising or happening within the said Province, or between Persons inhabiting or residing there, and for awarding and making out Executions thereupon; and directed the said Corporation to register, or cause to be registerd, all Leases, Grants, Plantings, Conveyances, Settlements and Improvements whatsoever, as should at any time be made of any Lands, Tenements or Hereditaments within the said Province, and yearly to transmit authentick Accounts thereof unto the Auditor of the Plantations, or his Deputy, and to the Surveyor of *South Carolina*, to inspect and survey the same, to ascertain the Quit-rents which should become due, according to the Reservation before-mentioned; but not to have or take any Gratuity, Fee or Reward, for such Survey or Inspection, on Forfeiture of their Office; with a Proviso, that all Leases, Grants and Conveyances to be made of any Lands within the said Province, or a Memorial containing the Substance or Effect thereof, should be registred with the Auditor of the Plantations within One Year from the Date thereof, otherwise that the same should be void: And directed, That all Rents, Issues or Profits, which should come to the said Corporation, issuing or arising out of or from the said Province, should be laid out and applied in such manner as would most improve and inlarge the said Colony, and best answer the good Purposes therein mentioned, and for defraying all other Charges about the same; and directed the said Corporation, from time to time, to give in to one of the Secretaries of State, and to the Commissioners of Trade and Plantations, Accounts of the Progress of the said Colony: And directed that the said Common Council should, from time to time, for the said Term of Twenty-one Years, from the Date of the said Letters Patent, have Power to appoint all such Governors, Judges, Magistrates, Ministers, and Officers Civil and Military, both by Sea and Land, within the said District, as they should think fit and needful for the Government of the said Colony, (except such Officers as should be appointed for managing, collecting and receiving, such of his Majesty's Revenues as should arise within the said Province) with a Proviso, that every Governor so appointed should be approved by his Majesty, and qualify himself as other Governors in *America* are by Law required to do, and give Security for observing the Acts of Parliament relating to Trade and Navigation, and obeying all Instructions from his Majesty, or any acting under his Authority, pursuant to the said Acts: And granted that the said Corporation, for the said Term of Twenty-one Years, from the Date of the said Letters Patent, should have Power, by any Commander, or other Officer for that purpose appointed, to train, instruct, exercise and govern, a Militia, for the special Defence and Safety of the said Colony, to assemble in martial Array, and put in warlike Posture the Inhabitants of the said Colony, and in Time of actual War, Invasion or Rebellion, to use and exercise the Law Martial; and also to erect Forts, and fortify any Place or Places within the said Colony, and the same to furnish with all necessary Ammunition, Provision, and Stores of War, for Offence and Defence; and, from time to time, to commit the Custody and Government of them to such Person or Persons as to them should seem meet; declaring that the Governor or Commander in chief of *South Carolina*, should have the chief Command of the Militia of *Georgia*, and that they should observe his Orders; and granted that the said Corporation should have Power to import and export their Goods, at and from any Port or Ports, that should be appointed by his Majesty within the said Province for that Purpose, without being obliged to touch at any other Port in *Carolina*; and declared, That after the End of the said Twenty-one Years, such Form of Government, and Method of making Laws, Statutes and Ordinances, for the Government of the said Province, and its Inhabitants, should be established and observed within the same, as his Majesty, his Heirs or Successors, should ordain and appoint, and should be agreeable to

Law; and that after the End of the said Twenty-one Years, the Governor, and all Officers Civil and Military, within the said Province, should be appointed by his Majesty, his Heirs and Successors.

In pursuance of his Majesty's Charter, and in order to fulfil the good Intents and Purposes therein expressed, it was thought necessary for the Trustees to send over such poor People, and foreign Protestants, as were willing to live in *Georgia*, not only to cultivate the Lands, but at the same time to strengthen his Majesty's Colonies. For which Purposes they consider'd each Inhabitant, both as a Planter and as a Soldier; and they were therefore to be provided with Arms for their Defence, as well as Tools for their Cultivation, and to be taught the Exericse of both; and Towns were to be laid out for their Settlements, and Lands allotted to each of them for their Maintainance, as near to those Towns as conveniently could be, that they might never have Occasion to be too far distant from their Towns, which were to be regarded as their Garisons.

And as the Military Strength of the Province was particularly to be taken care of; it seemed necessary to establish such Tenures of Lands, as might most effectually preserve the Number of Planters or Soldiers, equal to the Number of Lots of Land; and therefore each Lot of Land was to be considered as a military Fief, and to contain so much in Quantity as would support such Planter, and his Family; and Fifty Acres were judged sufficient, and not too much, for that Purpose: And Provision was made to prevent an Accumulation of several Lots into one Hand, lest the Garison should be lessened; and likewise to prevent a Division of those Lots into smaller Parcels, lest that, which was no more then sufficient for one Planter when intire, should, if divided among several, be too scanty for their Subsistence.

And in the Infancy of the Colony, the Lands were granted in Tail Male, preferable to any other Tenure, as the most likely to answer these Purposes; for if the Grants were to have been made in Tail General, it was thought, that the Strength of each Township would soon be diminished, inasmuch as every Female Heir in Tail, who was unmarried, would have been intitled to one Lot, and consequently have taken from the Garison the Portion of one Soldier; and by Intermarriages several Lots might be united into one; and if such Tenant in Tail General had had several Daughters, his Lot must have been divided equally amongst them all as Coparceners.

Nor were these the only Inconveniencies, which were thought likely to arise from Estates in Tail General; for Women being equally incapable to serve on Juries as to act as Soldiers, these Duties, and many others, such as Watching and Warding, &c. would return so much oftener to each Man in Proportion as the Number of the Men in the Township was lessened; and by that means would become very burthensome to the remaining Male Lot-holders; and in case of any Attack from the *Indians*, *French* or *Spaniards*, the Township would be less able to make a Defence.

And as it was not thought proper to grant Estates in Tail General, it appeared to be more inconvenient to grant them in Fee-simple; which Estate would have been attended with all the Objections before-mentioned incident to Estates in Tail General, and to several others besides; for the Right of Alienation being inseparable from an Estate in Fee, the Grantee might have sold, mortgaged or aliened his Lands, to whomever he thought fit; which was a Power not to be trusted with the People sent over, for the following Reasons:

I. From considering their Condition.

II. From considering the Purposes they were sent for.

III. From considering the Persons, to whom Lands might be alienated. And,

IV. From considering, that it might occasion a Monopoly of Land, contrary to the Intent of the Charter.

As to the First: The Persons sent over were poor indigent People, who had for the most part so indiscreetly managed what they had been Masters of here, that it did not seem safe to trust so absolute a Property in their Hands, at least in the Infancy of the Colony, and before they had, by a careful and industrious Behaviour, given some Reason to believe, they would prove better Managers for the future.

As to the Second: They were sent over to inhabit, cultivate and secure, by a personal Residence, the Lands granted to them within the Province; and they voluntarily engaged so to do; and in Expectation that they would perform those Engagements, they were maintained at the Expence of the Publick, during their Voyage, and their Passage was paid for them; and they were provided with Tools, Arms, Seeds, and other Necessaries, and supported from the publick Store, many of them at least, for Four Years together, from their first Landing; in which respect, the Publick may be said to have purchased of these People, for a valuable Consideration, their personal Residence, and all the Industry and Labour they could bestow in the Cultivation of this Province, and to have given them even Pay for the Hazard they might run in the Defence of it.

As to the Third: It was thought unsafe to grant them such an Estate, as might be the very Means of introducing such Sorts of People, as might defeat what the Trustees had always at Heart; *viz.* the Preservation of the Protestant Religion in that Province; which was necessary to be taken care of, both on a Political and Religious Account; the *French* lying to the West, and the *Spaniards* to the South of the Province of *Georgia*.

As to the Fourth: A Monopoly of many Lots into one Hand, would necessarily have been the Consequence of a free Liberty of buying and selling Lands within the Province; which would have been directly contrary to the Intent of the Charter, whereby the Grant of Lands to any one Person is limited not to exceed Five hundred Acres.

A further Inconvenience seemed likely to arise in every Case where the Tenant in Fee died without any Children, or without having disposed of his Lot by Will; for the Heir General, who might have the Right to it, might not happen to be found out for many Years after, especially if it was one of the Foreign Protestants; and all that Time the House would have run to Decay, and the Land remain uncultivated, and become a Harbour for Vermin, to the great Annoyance and Damage of the neighbouring Lots.

But tho' the before-mentioned Restraints were intended for the Good of the Whole, yet, whenever particular Cases required it, they were taken off, or dispensed with: And upon any Application for Leave to alienate Lands, Licences were always granted for that Purpose; and when the Succession of Females became less dangerous to the Province, by the growing Strength and Increase of the People, and by the Security provided for it by his Majesty's Forces there, the Trustees resolved to inlarge the Tenures of the Lands to Estates in Tail General.

The Tenures being thus settled, it was thought necessary to require the Inhabitants to cultivate their Lands within a limited Time; and in order to raise raw Silk, which was intended to be one of the Produces there, a certain Proportion of white Mulberry-trees were to be planted: And in their respective Grants Ten Years were allowed for the Cultivation, and One hundred white Mulberry-trees were to be planted on every Ten Acres of Land, when cleared; with a Power for the Trustees to re-enter on the Parts that should remain uncultivated.

But as the People were not able to cultivate their Lands within the Time required by their Grants, by reason of the Alarms from the *Spaniards*, the Droughts in that Part of *America*, and other unforeseen Accidents; the Trustees resolved to release all Forfeitures on that Account, and to require the Cultivation of no more than Five Acres of the said Fifty Acres, within the Remainder of the said Term of Ten Years.

And as other Persons applied to the Trustees for Grants of Land, in order to go over, and settle there at their own Expence; particular Grants were made under the same Tenure, and on the following Conditions: *Viz.* That they should within Twelve Months, from the Date of their Grants, go to and arrive in *Georgia*, with one Man-servant for every Fifty Acres granted them, and should with such Servants abide, settle, inhabit, and continue there for Three Years: That they should within Ten Years clear and cultivate one Fifth Part of the Lands granted them, and within the next Ten Years clear and cultivate Three Fifth Parts more of the said Lands, and plant One thousand white Mulberry-trees, upon every One hundred Acres thereof, when cleared; and that they should not at any time hire, keep, lodge, board or employ, any Negroes within *Georgia*, on any Account whatsoever, without special Leave. Which Conditions were readily approved of, and Counterparts executed by them all; and to those, who desired to name their Successor, on Failure of Issue Male, special Covenants were entered into by the Trustees for that Purpose, agreeable to their own Propositions. And for an Encouragement to their Men-servants to behave well, like Covenants were entered into, to grant to every such Man-servant, when requested thereunto, by any Writing, under the Hand and Seal of the Master, Twenty Acres of Land under the same Tenure.

The Trustees were induced to prohibit the Use of Negroes within *Georgia*; the Intention of his Majesty's Charter being to provide for poor People incapable of subsisting themselves at home, and to settle a Frontier for *South Carolina*, which was much exposed by the small Number of its white Inhabitants. It was impossible that the Poor, who should be sent from hence, and the Foreign persecuted Protestants, who must go in a manner naked into the Colony, could be able to purchase or subsist them, if they had them; and it would be a Charge too great for the Trustees to undertake; and they would be thereby disabled from sending white People. The first Cost of a Negro is about Thirty Pounds; and this Thirty Pounds would pay the Passage over, provide Tools and other Necessaries, and defray the Charge of Subsistence of a white Man for a Year; in which Time it might be hoped that the Planter's own Labour would gain him some Subsistence; consequently the Purchase-money of every Negro, (abstracting the Expence of subsisting him, as well as his Master) by being applied that way, would prevent the sending over a white Man, who would be of Security to the Province; whereas the Negro would render that Security precarious.

It was thought, that the white Man, by having a Negro Slave, would be less disposed to labour himself; and that his whole Time must be employed in keeping the Negro to Work, and in watching against any Danger he or his Family might apprehend from the

Slave; and that the Planter's Wife and Children would by the Death, or even the Absence of the Planter, be in a manner at the Mercy of the Negro.

It was also apprehended, that the *Spaniards* at *St. Augustine* would be continually inticing away the Negroes, or encouraging them to Insurrections; that the first might easily be accomplished, since a single Negro could run away thither without Companions, and would only have a River or two to swim over; and this Opinion has been confirmed and justified by the Practices of the *Spaniards*, even in Time of profound Peace, amongst the Negroes in *South Carolina;* where, tho' at a greater Distance from *Augustine*, some have fled in Perriaguas and little Boats to the *Spaniards*, and been protected, and others in large Bodies have been incited to Insurrections, to the great Terror, and even endangering the Loss of that Province; which, though it has been established above Seventy Years, has scarce white People enough to secure her against her own Slaves.

It was also considered, that the Produces designed to be raised in the Colony would not require such Labour as to make Negroes necessary for carrying them on; for the Province of *Carolina* produces chiefly Rice, which is a Work of Hardship proper for Negroes; whereas the Silk and other Produces which the Trustees proposed to have the People employed on in *Georgia*, were such as Women and Children might be of as much Use in as Negroes.

It was likewise apprehended, that if the Persons who should go over to *Georgia* at their own Expence, should be permitted the Use of Negroes, it would dispirit and ruin the poor Planters who could not get them, and who by their Numbers were designed to be the Strength of the Province; it would make them clamorous to have Negroes given them; and on the Refusal, would drive them from the Province, or at least make them negligent of their Plantations; where they would be unwilling, nay would certainly disdain to work like Negroes; and would rather let themselves out to the wealthy Planters as Overseers of their Negroes.

It was further thought, That upon the Admission of Negroes the wealthy Planters would, as in all other Colonies, be more induced to absent themselves, and live in other Places, leaving the Care of their Plantations and their Negroes to Overseers.

It was likewise thought, that the poor Planter sent on Charity from his Desire to have Negroes, as well as the Planter who should settle at his own Expence, would (if he had Leave to alienate) mortgage his Land to the Negro Merchant for them, or at least become a Debtor for the Purchase of such Negroes; and under these Weights and Discouragements would be induced to sell his Slaves again upon any Necessity, and would leave the Province and his Lot to the Negro Merchant; in Consequence of which, all the small Properties would be swallowed up, as they have been in other Places, by the more wealthy Planters.

It was likewise considered, that the admitting of Negroes in *Georgia* would naturally facilitate the Desertion of the *Carolina* Negroes, thro' the Province of *Georgia*; and consequently this Colony, instead of proving a Frontier, and adding a Strength to the Province of *South Carolina*, would be a Means of drawing off the Slaves of *Carolina*, and adding thereby a Strength to *Augustine*.

From these several Considerations, as the Produces to be raised in the Colony did not make Negro Slaves necessary, as the Introduction of them so near to a Garison of the *Spaniards* would weaken rather than strengthen the Barrier, and as they would introduce with them a greater Propensity to Idleness among the poor Planters, and too great an Inequality among the People, it was thought proper to make the Prohibition of them a Fundamental of the Constitution.

When the Trustees had made these Dispositions, and were enabled by Benefactions from several private Persons, on the 3d of *October* 1732. it was resolved to send over One hundred and Fourteen Persons, Men, Women and Children; being such as were in decayed Circumstances, and thereby disabled from following any Business in *England;* and who, if in Debt, had Leave from their Creditors to go, and such as were recommended by the Minister, Church-Wardens, and Overseers of their respective Parishes. And *James Oglethorpe*, Esq; one the Trustees, went with them at his own Expence to settle them.

On the 24th of the same Month the People were all examined, whether any of them had any Objections to the Terms and Conditions proposed to them; which they all declared they had not, but that they were fully satisfied with them; and executed Articles under their Hands and Seals, testifying their Consents thereto; which are now in the publick Office belonging to the Trustees.

But Four of them desiring, that their Daughters might inherit as well as Sons, and that the Widow's Dower might be considered; the Trustees immediately resolved, That every Person who should desire the same, should have the Privilege of naming a Successor to the Lands granted to them; who, in case the Possessors should die without Issue Male, should hold the same to them and their Heirs Male for ever; and that the Widows should have their Thirds as in *England:* With which Resolutions the People being all acquainted, were very well satisfied.

The Trustees prepared Forms of Government, agreeable to the Powers given them by the Charter; they established under their Seal a Court of Judicature for trying Causes, as well Criminal as Civil, in the Town of *Savannah*, (the Name which was given to the first Town to be raised) by the Name and Style of *The Town Court;* they also appointed Magistrates there, *viz.* three Bailiffs and a Recorder, and inferior Officers, *viz.* Two Constables, and Two Tything-men: They chose for Magistrates such as appeared to them the most prudent and discreet; but amongst a Number of People, who were all upon a Level at their first setting out, it was impossible to make any Choice or Distinction, which would not create some future Uneasiness among them.

On the 16th of *November* 1732. when the One hundred and Fourteen Persons, and with them the Reverend Mr. *Herbert*, a Clergyman of the Church of *England*, and a Man from *Piedmont*, (engaged by the Trustees to instruct the People in the Art of winding Silk) embarked on board the Ship *Ann*, Captain *Thomas*, several of the Trustees went to *Gravesend*, called over the People, and made a strict Inquiry into their Accommodations and Provisions, and left the People very well satisfied. Soon after Fifteen more

Persons were sent, Eleven of whom were Sawyers, in order to assist the People in building their Houses.

At the Time of the Embarkation Five thousand Acres of Land were granted to Three of the Colonists, in Trust for them, or the Survivors or Survivor of them, to make Grants, from time to time to every Man of Twenty-one Years of Age, or upwards, (who should arrive in *Georgia*, and desire the same) Fifty Acres of Land, to hold to him and his Heirs Male.

The Common Council of the Trustees (in whom by the Charter the Disposal of Money was lodged) did resolve at their first Meeting, that the Bank of *England* should be desired to keep all the Money belonging to the Trust; which the Bank accepted, and have continued so to do, paying no Sums but by Draughts signed by Five of the Common Council.

The Trustees desired, by a Letter, Sir *Thomas Lombe*'s Sentiments of the Goodness of the Raw Silk produced in *Carolina*, and the proper Methods of carrying on that Undertaking with Success; on which they received * from Sir *Thomas Lombe* great Encouragement to proceed in it, by his Approbation of the Silk produced in that Climate, of which he had made Experiments.

On the 28th of *February* 1732. the Trustees received a Letter from Mr. *Oglethorpe*, dated the 13th of *January* 1732. on board the Ship *Ann*, off *Charles-Town* in *South Carolina*, giving an Account of his safe Arrival there with the People, with the Loss only of Two Children.

On the 18th of *April* 1733. they received another Letter from him, which is here inserted at Length, as it gives an Account of the Situation where he planted the People.

* Appendix No. I.

From the Camp near Savannah, the 10th of February 173⅔.

GENTLEMEN,

I Gave you an Account, in my last, of our Arrival at *Charles-Town;* the Governor and Assembly have given us all possible Encouragement. Our People arrived at *Beaufort* on the 20th of *January*, where I lodged them in some new Barracks built for the Soldiers, whilst I went myself to view the *Savannah* River. I fixed upon a healthy Situation, about Ten Miles from the Sea. The River here forms an Half-moon, along the South-side of which the Banks are about Forty Feet high, and on the Top a Flat, which they call a Bluff. The plain High ground extends into the Country Five or Six Miles, and along the River-side about a Mile. Ships that draw Twelve Feet Water can ride within Ten Yards of the Bank. Upon the River-side, in the Centre of this Plain, I have laid out the Town, opposite to which is an Island of very rich Pasturage, which I think should be kept for the Trustees Cattle. The River is pretty wide, the Water fresh, and from the Key of the Town you see its whole Course to the Sea, with the Island of *Tybee*, which forms the Mouth of the River, for about Six Miles up into the Country. The Landskip is very agreeable, the Stream being wide, and bordered with high Woods on both Sides. The whole People arrived here on the First of *February*; at Night their Tents were got up. 'Till the 7th we were taken up in unloading and making a Crane, which I then could not get finished, so took off the Hands, and set some to the Fortification, and began to fell the Woods. I have marked out the Town and Common; half of the former is already cleared, and the first House was begun Yesterday in the Afternoon. A little *Indian* Nation, the only one within Fifty Miles, is not only at Amity, but desirous to be Subjects to his Majesty King *George*, to have Lands given them among us, and to breed their Children at our Schools. Their Chief and his beloved Man, who is the Second Man in the Nation, desire to be instructed in the Christian Religion. I am,

Gentlemen, &c.

In this Month of *April* the Trustees, in another Embarkation of Seventeen Persons, sent some *Italians*, whom they had procured from *Piedmont*, in order to promote the Silk Business.

They received another Letter from Mr. *Oglethorpe*, dated the

20th of *February* 1732. of which the following Extract gives a further Account of the People and their Situation:

Our People are all in perfect Health. I chose the Situation for the Town upon an high Ground, Forty Feet perpendicular above High-water Mark; the Soil dry and sandy, the Water of the River fresh, Springs coming out from the Sides of the Hills. I pitched upon this Place, not only for the Pleasantness of the Situation, but because from the above-mentioned and other Signs, I thought it healthy; for it is sheltered from the Western and Southern Winds (the worst in this Country) by vast Woods of Pine-trees, many of which are an Hundred, and few under Seventy Feet high. There is no Morse on the Trees, tho' in most Parts of *Carolina* they are covered with it, and it hangs down Two or Three Feet from them. The last and fullest Conviction of the Healthfulness of the Place was, that an *Indian* Nation, who knew the Nature of this Country, chose it for their Situation.

The Trustees endeavoured very early to secure the Friendship of the *Indians*, who, by ranging thro' the Woods, would be capable of giving constant Intelligence, to prevent any Surprize upon the People, and would be a good Out-guard for the Inland Parts of the Province. For this Purpose they were treated with all possible Candour and Gentleness: They were acquainted, that the *English* had no Intentions to hurt or distress them, but would be ready to assist and protect them on all Occasions. They received several Presents from the Trustees, and were promised, that if any of the People in *Georgia* injured them, they should, upon their Complaints, and Proofs of it, find a ready Redress; for which in Return the *Indians* engaged never to take any Revenge themselves, as it might breed Ill Blood between the *English* and them. And as they have since found, that Justice has always been done to them upon proper Complaints, they have been true to their Engagements.

The *Indians* made a formal and voluntary Cession of that Part of the Country to Mr. *Oglethorpe* for the King of *Great-Britain:* by which a further Right and Title to it was acquired, and added to that of the first Discovery and Cultivation; and a Treaty of Friendship and Commerce with them was settled, which was soon after sent over to the Trustees for their Ratification.

In the Month of *May* 1733. the Trustees sent over Six Persons more.

The Number of People sent on the Charity from the Beginning to the 9th of *June* 1733. (on which Day of the Month the Trustees Accompt is yearly made up, which is directed to be delivered to the Lord Chancellor, and the other Persons named in the Charter) amounted to One hundred and Fifty-two, of whom One hundred and Forty-one were *Britons*, and eleven were Foreign Protestants, and Sixty-one were Men.

The Lands granted in Trust this Year, in order to be granted out in smaller Portions in *Georgia*, were the aforesaid Five thousand Acres.

The Lands granted within this Year to Persons going at their own Expence, were Four thousand Four hundred and Sixty Acres.

The Money received from private Persons this Year amounted to 3,723 *l.* 13 *s.* 7 *d.* whereof the Trustees applied 2,254 *l.* 17 *s.* 9 *d.* of which they exhibited an Accompt to the Lord Chancellor, and the Lord Chief Justice of the Common-Pleas, pursuant to their Charter; and carried the Remainder into their succeeding Accompt.

From the 9th *of* June 1733. *to the* 9th *of* June 1734.

BESIDES the several Works on which the People were employed at *Savannah*, as palisading the Town, clearing the Place from Pine-trees, *&c.* and building of Houses, some other Works were carried on; *viz.* a publick Garden was laid out, which was designed as a Nursery, in order to supply the People for their several Plantations with White Mulberry-trees, Vines, Oranges, Olives, and other necessary Plants; a Gardener was appointed for the Care of it, and to be paid by the Trustees. A Crane was made for landing of Goods on the Bluff; a Battery raised, which commands the River, some Distance below the Town; and on the Island of *Tybee*, at the Entrance of the River, a Beacon was erected Ninety Feet high, which has been of great Service, not only to the

Ships entering the River *Savannah*, but to those likewise which sail by the Coast, there being none like it all along the Coast of *America*.

A Fort was likewise built at the narrow Passages of an inland River (called *Ogeechee*) in order to protect the Settlement from any inland Invasion from *Augustine*. Two little Villages were laid out and settled at about Four Miles distant from *Savannah*, inland from the River, and a Mile from each other, which were called *Hampstead* and *Highgate*.

In the *Carolina Gazette* *, dated the 22d of *March* 1732. a further Account was given of the Settlement at *Savannah*, which was written by a Gentleman of *Charles-Town*, who with some others went thither out of Curiosity.

The Parliament having granted out of the Money arisen from the Sale of the Lands at *St. Christopher*, Ten thousand Pounds for the further settling and securing the Colony; the Trustees resolved to lose no Time in strengthening it with People; and accordingly in the Months of *September* and *October* 1733. they sent over two Embarkations of Persons, whose Numbers are entered at the End of this Year's Proceedings, and of whom many were persecuted Protestants from *Saltzburgh*.

As very pleasing Accounts of the Country, and the Settlement, were sent from several of the People there to their Friends, the Trustees were informed, that some Persons had gone about in several Parts of *England*, offering Money and Land in their Names, (but without their Knowledge or Authority) to any who should be desirous of going to *Georgia:* Therefore they published an Advertisement in some of the News-papers, in order to prevent the ill Consequences of drawing laborious People out of the Country with such Expectations; and they declared, that they had never given such Power to any Persons whatsoever; and that they never used any Solicitations to induce People to go over.

* Appendix No. II.

	Number sent	British	Foreign Protestants	Men
The Persons sent on the Charity this Year were	341 whereof	237 and	104 and in	135.
Those in the former Year were	152 whereof	141 and	11 and in	61.
The Number of Persons sent in the Two Years to the 9th of *June* 1734. were	493 whereof	378 and	115 and in	196.

The Lands granted in Trust this Year, in order to be granted out in smaller Portions in *Georgia*, were Eight thousand and One hundred Acres.

The Lands granted this Year to Persons going at their own Expence, were Five thousand Seven hundred and Twenty-five Acres.

The Money received this Year, pursuant to Act of Parliament was 10,000 *l.* and from private Persons 1502 *l.* 19 *s.* 3 *d.* whereof the Trustees applied 6863 *l.* 0 *s.* 10 *d.* of which they exhibited an Accompt to the Lord Chancellor, and Master of the Rolls, pursuant to their Charter, and carried the Remainder into their succeeding Accompt.

From the 9th of June 1734. to the 9th of June 1735.

IN the Month of *June* 1734. Mr. *Oglethorpe* arrived from the Colony, and with him came some of the principal *Indians* of the *Lower Creek Nation*, who live nearest to *Savannah*.

When these *Indians* were in *England*, they desired of the Trustees, that the Measures, Prices and Qualities of all Goods to be purchased by them with their Deer-skins, might be settled; as likewise the Weights, that no body might be allowed to trade with the *Indians* in *Georgia* without a Licence from the Trustees; in order that if they were in any respect injured or defrauded by the Traders, they might know where to complain. And they further desired, that there might be but One Store-house in each *Indian* Town for supplying them with the Goods they might want to purchase, from whence the Trader should be obliged to supply them at the fixed Prices.

The Reason which the *Indians* gave for this Application was, because the Traders with them had often, in an arbitrary Manner, raised the Prices of Goods, and defrauded them in the Weights and Measures; and, by their Impositions, had often created Animosities between the *English* and *Indians*, which had frequently ended in Wars between them, prejudicial to both.

The Trustees, having considered of their Request, and being informed, that the Council and Assembly of *South Carolina* had passed an Act the 20th of *August* 1731. intituled, *An Act for the better Regulation of the* Indian *Trade, and for appointing a Commissioner for that Purpose with Regulations*, which the Trustees hoped might be effectual in *Georgia*, prepared an Act, intituled, *An Act for maintaining the Peace with the* Indians *in* the Province of Georgia, *with the same Regulations and Provisions as were in the* Carolina *Act*; which Act ceased to be of Force in *Georgia*, since it was erected into a distinct independent Province, not subject to the Laws of *Carolina*.

The Trustees, receiving frequent Informations from the Colony, of the pernicious Effects of drinking Rum, and other spirituous Liquors, by not only creating Disorders among the *Indians*, (who had been plentifully supplied with it by the Traders) but also destroying many of the *English*, and throwing the People into various Distempers, prepared an Act, intituled, *An Act to prevent the Importation and Use of Rum and Brandies in the Province of* Georgia, *or any kind of Spirits or Strong-waters whatsoever*. At the same time they endeavoured to supply the Stores with Strong-beer from *England*, Melasses for brewing Beer, and with *Madeira* Wines, which the People might purchase at reasonable Rates, and which would be more refreshing and wholesome for them. The Magistrates of the Town of *Savannah* were likewise impowered to grant Licences to private Persons for retailing Beer, Ale, *&c.* and the Trustees have great Reason to believe, that the remarkable Healthiness of *Ebenezer* in the Northern Part, and *Frederica* in the Southern Part of *Georgia*, is very much owing to the Prohibition of the Use of Rum; for in those Parts where Rum, in Defiance of the Act, has been introduced, the People have not in general been so healthy and vigorous.

At the same time the Trustees, taking into Consideration the many Inconveniencies which would attend the Introduction of Negroes in a Frontier, for the several Reasons before specified, prepared an Act for rendering the Colony of *Georgia* more defensible, by prohibiting the Importation and Use of Black Slaves or Negroes into the same.

These Three Acts were laid before the King in Council, in the Month of *January* 1734. and after a Report from the Lords Commissioners for Trade and Plantations to the Committee of Council, that they were proper to receive his Majesty's Royal Approbation, they were ratified by his Majesty in Council.

Tho' the Lands granted by the Trustees were to revert to them on the Failure of Issue Male, in order to be regranted for keeping up a Number of Men; yet the Trustees, as Guardians of the People, when any such Failure happened, resolved, that the Value of the Improvements upon the Lands of the late Occupiers, should be settled and paid to or for the Benefit of the Female Issue, or next Relation: And the First Instance of such a Failure being on the Death of one Mr. *De Ferron*, the Value of the Improvements he had made on his Estate, was, on the 5th of *February* 1734. ordered and paid for the Use of his Daughter in *England*, who, being destitute, would have been absolutely unable to proceed in the Cultivation of her Father's Lot.

Two Embarkations were made this Year, whose Numbers are hereafter-mentioned, which consisted chiefly of *Saltzburghers*, who, with the *Saltzburghers* that went before, were settled in a Town called by them *Ebenezer*, upon the River *Savannah*, at some Distance above the Town, and by the Sobriety and Industry of the People, they prove a very thriving Settlement.

	Number sent		British		Foreign Protestants		Men
The Persons sent on the Charity this Year were	81	whereof	23	and	58	and in	43
Those in the former Years were	493	whereof	378	and	115	and in	196
The Number of Persons sent in the Three Years to the 9th of *June* 1735. were	574	whereof	401	and	173	and in	239

The Lands granted in Trust this Year, in order to be granted out in smaller Portions in *Georgia*, were Two thousand Five hundred Acres.

The Lands granted this Year to Persons going at their own Expence were One thousand Nine hundred Acres.

The Money received this Year in Benefactions amounted to 5,416 *l*. 7 *s*. 7 *d*. whereof given in *South Carolina* 464 *l*. 18 *s*. 2 *d*. the Amount in Sterling Money, and in *England* 4,951 *l*. 9 *s*. 5 *d*. which the Trustees applied, as also Part of their former Balance, to the Amount of 11,194 *l*. 9 *s*. 2 *d*. of which they exhibited an Accompt to the Lord Chancellor, and the Master of the Rolls, pursuant to their Charter, and carried the then Remainder into their succeeding Accompt.

From the 9th of June 1735. to the 9th of June 1736.

THAT all Persons who should be desirous of going to *Georgia*, might be apprised in Time of the several Conditions they were to perform, * Rules were drawn up and printed for those who

* Appendix, No. III and IV.

should be sent on the Charity, as well as those who should go at their own Expence; in which the Conditions were specified, as well as the Necessaries for their Subsistence, and their Labour.

The Parliament having in the Year 1735. granted Twenty-six thousand Pounds for the further settling and securing the Colony of *Georgia*, the Trustees thought it prudent to strengthen the Southern Part of the Province, by making a Settlement on the *Alatamaha* River, to which they were strongly induced, by a * Memorial sent to his Majesty from the Governor and Assembly of *South Carolina*, dated the 9th of *April* 1734. wherein, after thanking his Majesty for his peculiar Favour and Protection, and especially for his most benign Care, so wisely calculated for the Preservation of *South Carolina*, by his Royal Charter to the Trustees for establishing the Colony of *Georgia*, and after representing the Practices of the *French* to seduce the *Indians* in Amity with *South Carolina*, the Attention of the *French* to the Improvement of their Settlements, and their late Inlargement of them nearer to *Carolina*; the defenceless Condition of their Province, and the Danger of the Inhabitants from their own Negroes, and the ruinous Situation of the *West-India* Trade in case the *French* should possess themselves of *Carolina*; they add, That the Harbours and Ports of *Carolina* and † *Georgia*, enable his Majesty to be absolute Master of the Passage through the Gulph of *Florida*, and to impede, at his Pleasure, the Transportation home of the *Spanish* Treasure, which, should his Majesty's Enemies possess, would then prove so many convenient Harbours for them to annoy a great Part of the *British*

* Appendix, No. V.

† The Harbour in the southern Part of *Georgia*, the nearest to the Gulph of *Florida*, which has yet been founded, has been proved by the Affidavits of Three Captains of Ships who have been there, *viz*. Captain *Thomas Shubrick*, Captain *George Dymond*, and Captain *William Thomson*, to be capable of receiving Ships of Forty Guns, and to be safely Landlocked: And by the Affidavit of *Thomas Pearce*, Mariner, who was on the Coast of *Georgia* near Four Years, it appears, That Ships in this Harbour, may, in Twenty-four Hours from the Bar, run out into the Gulph Stream of *Florida*, through which Stream the *Spanish* Galleons (when not passing the Windward-Passage) always come.

Trade to *America*, as well as that which is carried on through the Gulph from *Jamaica*.

Upon which Inducements the Trustees resolved to make Embarkations for strengthening the Southern Part of *Georgia;* and to obviate any Objections which might be made by sending over any of our useful Poor from *England;* and as the Trustees found, that many of the Poor who had been useless in *England*, were inclined to be useless likewise in *Georgia*, they determined that these Embarkations should consist chiefly of Persons from the Highlands of *Scotland*, and persecuted *German* Protestants.

Whilst these Embarkations were preparing, the Trustees made Preparations for the new Settlement: They established the civil Government for the new Town (which was called *Frederica*) in the same manner as they had before at *Savannah*.

In the Month of *January* 1735. the *Highlanders* arrived in *Georgia* (and with them several of the same Country, as Servants to private Grantees). They were settled on the *Alatamaha* River, about Sixteen Miles distant by Water from the Island *St. Simon*'s (which is at the Mouth of the River). They soon raised convenient Huts, till their Houses could be built; and the Town, at their own Desire, was called *Darien;* which Name still remains to that District, but the Town is since named by them *New Inverness*.

On the 6th of *February* 1735. the Embarkation, under the Conduct of Mr. *Oglethorpe*, arrived in *Georgia;* they were settled upon *St. Simon*'s Island; the Town called *Frederica* was soon laid out, and the People were set to work in building their Houses. The *Creek Indians*, who went thither upon occasion of this new Settlement, agreed, That the *English* should possess *St. Simon*'s Island, with the others contiguous to it. The Land of the Island is very fertile, chiefly Oak and Hickary, intermixed with Savannahs, and old *Indian* Fields; and according to a Survey made of it, it is about Forty-five Miles in Circumference.

For a Communication between the Settlements in the Northern and Southern Part of the Province by Land, a Road was soon afterwards opened.

	Number sent	British	Foreign Protestants	Men
The Persons sent on the Charity this Year were	470 whereof	341 and	129 and in	224.
Those in the former Years were	574 whereof	401 and	173 and in	239.
The Number of Persons sent in the Four Years to the 9th of *June* 1736. were	1044 whereof	742 and	302 and in	463.

The Lands granted in Trust this Year, in order to be granted out in smaller Portions, were Twenty thousand Acres; And in Trust for religious Uses, to be cultivated with the Money arising from private Benefactions, given for that Purpose, in order to settle a Provision upon a Clergyman at *Savannah*, a Catechist, and a School-master, Three hundred Acres.

The Lands granted this Year to Persons going at their own Expence, were Nine thousand Three hundred Acres.

The Money received this Year, pursuant to Act of Parliament, was 26,000 *l.* and in Benefactions 2,164 *l.* 19 *s.* 6¾ whereof in *South Carolina* 411 *l.* 1 *s.* 1¾ the Amount in Sterling Money, and in *England* 1,753 *l.* 18 *s.* 5 *d.* whereof the Trustees applied 22,697 *l.* 5 *s.* 5¾ of which they exhibited an Account to the Lord Chancellor and Master of the Rolls, pursuant to their Charter, and carried the Remainder into their succeeding Accompt.

FOR the Security of the People, (who were settled in the last Year on *St. Simon's Island*) and the Southern Part of the Province, several Forts were built this Year; *viz.*

One at *Frederica*, with Four regular Bastions, and a Spur-work towards the River, and several Pieces of Cannon were mounted on it.

About Ten Miles from *Frederica* a large Battery is built, commanding the Entrance into the Sound, where Ten or Twelve Forty-gun Ships may safely ride, there being sufficient Water on the Bar called *Jekyll* for such Ships to go over, which Bar lies in 30 d. 40 m. and behind *Jekyll* Island there is Water, and Room enough for Shipping for Ten Miles up. The Battery is inclosed within a strong Wall, and has a Guard-house within the Wall capable of holding Twenty-four Men.

Another Fort was built on the South-west Part of the *Island of St. Peter's*, (now called *Cumberland*) which lies in 30 d. 30 m. under which Fort, on which are mounted several Pieces of Ordnance, pointed towards the River, all Sloops and Boats in the Inland Passage to this Island must come. Within the Palisade round the Fort, there are fine Springs of Water; and there is a well-framed Timber Log-house, Thirty Feet by Eighteen, with a Magazine under it, both for Ammunition and Provisions. A Scout Boat is stationed at this Island.

As these Precautions were taken for the Southern Part of the Province, Directions were given for a Fort to be built for the Security of the Northern Part, by way of an Out-guard against any Invasion by Land. This was at a Place called *Augusta*, which has proved a very thriving Town, it being now the chief Place of Trade with the *Indians*, and where the Traders from both Provinces of *South Carolina* and *Georgia* resort, from the Security which they find there. *Augusta* is about Two hundred and Thirty Miles by Water from the Town of *Savannah*, and large Boats, which carry about Nine thousand Pounds Weight of Deer-skins, can navigate down the River *Savannah*. The Town which stands upon a high Ground, near the River, is well inhabited, and has several Warehouses in it, furnished with Goods for the *Indian* Trade. A Road has been likewise made, so that Horsemen can now ride from this Town to *Savannah*, as likewise to the *Cherokee Indians*, who are situated above the Town of *Augusta*, and trade with it. A Garison has been kept in this Fort, at the Trustees Expence, 'till the Arrival of the Regiment his Majesty since ordered for the Defence of the Colony.

Whilst these Dispositions were making for the Safety of the Province, the Parliament gave Ten thousand Pounds this Year for the further settling and securing the Colony; but as the Expences of the Forts, and the Supplies which were sent for the Support of the Colony, were very great; and as many of the People in the Northern Part of the Province were as yet unable to subsist themselves, and out of Compassion to them and their Families, a Store was still kept open for their Subsistence; the Trustees sent over but few Persons this Year.

In the Beginning of the Year 1737. the *Spaniards* at *Augustine* made Preparations for attacking the Colony of *Georgia*. They laid in Quantities of Corn and Provision, bought up a great Number of Fire-arms; and large Bodies of regular Troops were sent thither from the *Havannah*.

The Lieutenant Governor of *South Carolina* informed the Magistrates of *Savannah* of these Preparations. This Advice, and the frequent Alarms which were otherwise given, drew the People off from their Labour in the Sowing-season, and the Improvements in their Plantations were neglected, and they were obliged to make Preparations for their Defence.

At the same time the *Highlanders* at *New Inverness*, who were exposed to Danger, built a Fort there, and Twelve Pieces of Cannon were mounted on it.

Tho' the People at *Savannah* were not so immediately exposed to Danger, they began to build a large Fort at their Town, of a Palisade-work with Bastions: But as the Trustees perceived, that this took off the People from their Cultivation, that the Work would be very chargeable, and they had not Money to support the Expence; they found themselves under a Necessity to put a Stop thereto.

	Numbers sent	British	Foreign Protestants	Men
The Persons sent on the Charity this Year were	32 whereof	32 and	and in	19.
Those in the former Years were	1044 whereof	742 and	302 and in	463.
The Number of Persons sent in the Five Years to the 9th of *June* 1737. were	1076 whereof	774 and	302 and in	482.

The Lands granted in Trust this Year, in order to be granted out in smaller Portions in *Georgia*, were Three thousand Acres; and in Trust to be cultivated with the Money arising from private Benefactions given for that Purpose, in order to raise a Maintenance for a Minister and School-master at *Frederica*, and other religious Uses, Three hundred Acres.

The Lands granted this Year to Persons going at their own Expence, were Four thousand Three hundred Acres.

The Money received this Year pursuant to Act of Parliament, was 10,000 *l.* and in Benefactions 3,627 *l.* 18 *s.* 7 *d.* whereof in *South Carolina*, the Amount in Sterling Money 333 *l.* 19 *s.* 6 *d.* and in *England* 3,293 *l.* 19 *s.* 1 *d.* which the Trustees applied, as also Part of their former Balance, to the Sum of 17,239 *l.* 11 *s.* 5 *d.* of which they exhibited an Account to the Lord Chancellor, and the Master of the Rolls, pursuant to their Charter, and carried the then Remainder into their succeeding Account.

THE Lieutenant Governor of *South Carolina* having acquainted the Trustees, by a Letter dated from the Council-Chamber in *Charles-Town* the 7th of *February* 1736–7. that he had received Advice from Commodore *Dent*, of Preparations made by the *Spaniards* at *Augustine* and the *Havannah*, in order to make an Attack on the Colony of *Georgia*; and the Trustees having, in a * Memorial to his Majesty, set forth the Inability of the Colony to protect themselves against such a Force as was preparing at the *Havannah* and *Augustine*; his Majesty was graciously pleased to order a Regiment of Six hundred effective Men to be raised, and sent to *Georgia*, for the Defence and Protection of it.

And as an Encouragement for the Soldiers good Behaviour, the Trustees resolved to give each of them a Property in the Colony. They therefore made a Grant of Land in Trust for an Allotment of Five Acres of Land to each Soldier of the Regiment to cultivate for his own Use and Benefit, and to hold the same during his Continuance in his Majesty's Service; and, for a further Encouragement, they resolved, That each Soldier, who, at the End of Seven Years Service from the Time of his enlisting in the Regiment, should be desirous of quitting his Majesty's Service, and should have his regular Discharge, and would settle in the Colony, should, on his commanding Officer's Certificate of his good Behaviour, be intitled to a Grant of Twenty Acres of Land.

The Parliament having taken into Consideration the great Expences which the Trustees had been at in making Roads through the Province, and the several Fortifications in it, and the Presents made to the *Indians* to engage them firmer in the *British* Interest; and likewise the Preparations which were making by the *Spaniards* in order to take or destroy the Colony; and having granted for this Year a Sum of Twenty thousand Pounds for the further settling and securing the Colony; the Trustees made another Embarkation, which consisted chiefly of persecuted *German* Protestants.

* Appendix No. VII.

	Number sent	British	Foreign Protestants	Men
The Persons sent on the Charity this Year were	298 whereof	135 and	163 and in	152
Those in the former Years were	1076 whereof	774 and	302 and in	482
The Number of Persons sent in the Six Years to the 9th of *June* 1738. were	1374 whereof	909 and	465 and in	634

By Accounts received from the Colony before the End of this Year, there appear to have been One thousand One hundred and Ten Persons in *Georgia*, besides those at *Tybee, Skidoway, Fort Argyll, Thunderbolt*, and *Augusta*, in the Northern Part; and those at *St. Andrew*'s and *Amelia* in the Southern Part.

The Lands granted in Trust this Year, in order to be granted out in smaller Portions in *Georgia*, were Three thousand Acres.

The Lands granted this Year to Persons going at their own Expence, were One thousand Acres.

The Money received this Year pursuant to Act of Parliament was 20,000 *l.* and in Benefactions 909 *l.* 19 *s.* 10½ whereof the Trustees applied 18,870 *l.* 13 *s.* 3½. of which they exhibited an Accompt to the Lord Chancellor, and the Master of the Rolls, pursuant to their Charter, and carried the Remainder into their succeeding Accompt.

From the 9th of June 1738. to the 9th of June 1739.

AS several Merchants and Captains of Ships had, for their own Interest, carried into the Colony, from *New York*, and other Places, large Cargoes of Provisions, &c. great Part of which (to save the Merchants from Losses) was taken in at the Store without a proper Authority from the Trustees; and an Expence created thereby which the Trustees could not estimate, nor have Ability to discharge, and for which certified Accounts were returned to them; the Trustees published an Advertisement in the *London Gazette*, and ordered it to be published in the *South Carolina Gazette*, and to be affixed upon the Doors of the Store-houses at *Savannah* and *Frederica:* That out of a due Regard to publick Credit, they had resolved, That all Expences which they had ordered, or should order, to be made in *America*, for the Use of the Colony, should be defrayed and paid for in *Georgia*, in Sola Bills of Exchange only, under their Seal; and they gave Notice, That no Person whatsoever had any Authority from them, or in their Name, or on their Account, to purchase or receive any Cargoes of Provisions, Stores or Necessaries, without paying for them in the said Sola Bills.

Upon a Petition of one *Abraham De Lyon*, a Freeholder of *Savannah* in *Georgia*, that he had expended a great Sum in the Cultivation of Vines, which he had carried from *Portugal*, and had brought to great Perfection; and several Certificates being produced of his great Improvements in cultivating them, and of the Goodness of the Grapes, and their thriving in the most barren Lands of the Province; the Trustees assisted him to proceed in his Improvements.

The Security of the Colony being provided for by the Regiment sent over by his Majesty, the Parliament gave Eight thousand Pounds for the further settling the Colony: Therefore the Trustees sent over an Estimate of all the Expences which they allowed to be made in the Province; by which several military Expences, which they have been engaged in for the Defence of the Colony, and which were very great, were reduced.

The Trustees this Year sent over the Reverend Mr. *Norris* to reside at *Frederica*, with a Salary of Fifty Pounds a Year, ordered a House to be built for him, and another for the Inhabitants to perform divine Service in, till a Church could be built there.

The Assembly of *South Carolina* having in the last Year passed an Ordinance for raising a Sum to indemnify their Traders in Opposition to the Act which was approved of by his Majesty in Council, for maintaining the Peace with the *Indians* in the Province of *Georgia*, upon a Memorial from the Trustees, complaining of the said Ordinance, and upon the Petition of the Council and Assembly of *South Carolina* against the said Act, there was a solemn Hearing before the Lords Commissioners for Trade and Plantations; and afterwards before a Committee of the Lords of his Majesty's Privy Council: Whereupon his Majesty was pleased to order, That the said Ordinance of the Assembly of *South Carolina* should be repealed, and declared void; and was pleased to send an Instruction to the Trustees to prepare a proper Act or Ordinance for settling the Trade carried on by the Provinces of *South Carolina* and *Georgia*, with the *Indians*, on such a Footing as might be for the mutual Benefit and Satisfaction of both Provinces; and his Majesty at the same time was graciously pleased to give an Instruction to *Samuel Horsey*, Esq; Governor and Lieutenant General of *South Carolina*, to recommend to the Council and Assembly there, to pass a Law for the like Purpose in that Province: But *Samuel Horsey*, Esq; dying soon after, and no other Governor having since gone to *South Carolina*, that Affair remains unsettled.

The Trustees immediately sent to Colonel *Oglethorpe* a Copy of his Majesty's Instructions, and desired, that he would consult with Lieutenant Governor *Bull* in *South Carolina*, that Plans of proper Acts might be prepared and sent over to the Trustees for their Consideration, in order to answer the Purposes of his Majesty's Instructions; and that in the mean time the Commissioners of *South Carolina*, and the Commissioners of *Georgia*, might proceed in their respective Provinces, in Concert with each other, to carry on a mutual Trade to the *Indians* in both Provinces.

Mr. *Stephens*, Secretary in *Georgia*, having informed the Trustees, That the Grand Jury at *Savannah* claimed a Right of administering Oaths, and making Inquiry thereon, into all such Matters, as they should think fit, and the Trustees having perceived, that, in a Representation of the said Grand Jury, they had pretended to such Right, sent a Letter to Mr. *Stephens*, to acquaint him, That the Trustees were sensible great Mischief might be done by ill-designing Men, who might procure themselves to be put upon the Panel, if this Claim of the Grand Jury was allowed of; and therefore the Trustees ordered him to acquaint the People, That the Grand Juries had no such Right, and that their Claim was intirely illegal.

As the Trustees, both by their Letters and Instructions to the Magistrates, had constantly exhorted and encouraged the People to a Cultivation of their Lands, on which they were to depend for their Support; and as they found, that many (as well of those whom they had sent over as Objects of Charity, as of others, who, at different Times, had gone into the Colony from other Plantations for a temporary Maintenance) still continued in their Idleness, and were a Burden upon the Trust; they gave Orders for striking off the Store, all such as, having had Time to cultivate their Lands, had neglected it. This carried from the Colony many of those who had gone thither, or joined it from other Parts of *America*, to gain a Subsistence for a Year or two; and of others, who had not considered the Hardships attending the first Settlement of a Country, and were tired of their Labour.

The Trustees receiving an Account, dated the 12th of *February* 1738. from their Secretary in the Province, of an Uneasiness amongst several Persons, upon the Tenure of their Lots being confined to Heirs Male; and they considering, that the Colony had been some time established, the People grown more numerous; and a Regiment being stationed in it for its Defence; whereby the former Tenures became less necessary; did on the 15th of *March* following, at their anniversary Meeting, resolve, That in Default of Issue Male, any legal Possessor of Land might by a Deed in Writing, or by his last Will and Testament, appoint his Daughter as his Successor, or any other Male or Female Relation; with a Proviso, That the Successor should, in the proper Court in *Georgia*, personally claim the Lot granted or devised, within Eighteen Months after the Death of the Grantor or Devisor.

This was soon after extended to every legal Possessor's being impowered to appoint any other Person as his Successor.

But whilst the Trustees were taking these Steps for the Satisfaction of the People; and whilst those in the Southern Part of the

Province (tho' exposed to greater Danger) were industrious and easy in their Settlements, many of those in the Northern Part, who had neglected the Cultivation of their Lands, drew up a * Representation, dated the 9th of *December* 1738. setting forth the Want of a Fee-simple to their Lands, and Negroes to cultivate them; but they were far from being seconded or supported by the People in the Southern Part of the Province in this Representation, who not only refused to sign it, but † petitioned the Trustees against the Use of Negroes; setting forth the Danger they should be in from the *Spaniards*, who had proclaimed Freedom to all Slaves who would resort to them; and that by this means they should be exposed to an Enemy without, and a more dangerous one in their Bosoms.

The industrious *Saltzburghers* also at *Ebenezer* (who are in the Northern Part of the Province, not far from *Savannah*) ‡ petitioned against Negroes, and set forth their Satisfaction and Happiness in their Settlement; that they had raised in the last Season more Rice, Pease, Potatoes, Pomkins, Cabbage, Corn, *&c.* than was necessary for their Consumption, and that they did not find the Climate so warm but that it was very tolerable for working People.

	Number sent		British		Foreign Protestants		Men	
The Persons sent on the Charity this Year were	9	whereof	2	and	7	and in	4.	
Those in the former Years were	1374	whereof	909	and	465	and in	634.	
The Number of Persons sent in the Seven Years to the 9th of *June* 1739. were	1383	whereof	911	and	472	and in	638.	

The only Return from *Georgia* this Year was an Account of the People at *Savannah*, who were One hundred and Nine Freeholders,

* Appendix, No. VIII.
† Appendix, No. IX.
‡ Appendix, No. X.

besides their Wives and Children, and besides Inmates and Servants, of the latter of which were a great Number, part of whose Passages were paid for in the next Year, on Representations made to the Trustees for that Purpose.

The Lands granted in Trust this Year, to be cultivated for the Maintenance of an Orphan-house in *Georgia*, were Five hundred Acres.

The Money received this Year, pursuant to Act of Parliament, was 8,000 *l.* and in Benefactions 473 *l.* 9 *s.* 4 *d.* which the Trustees applied, as also Part of the former Balance, to the Amount of 10,347 *l.* 4 *s.* 1 *d.* of which they exhibited an Accompt to the Lord Chancellor, and the Master of the Rolls, pursuant to their Charter, and carried the then Remainder into their succeeding Accompt.

From the 9th of June 1739. to the 9th of June 1740.

AT the time that some of the People of *Savannah* were so clamorous for Negroes, (for Seventy-five Land and Freeholders, of whom Fifty-two were Freeholders, did not apply for them) the Province of *South Carolina* was under frequent Alarms upon account of the Negroes there. They had Intelligence, that a Conspiracy was formed by the Negroes in *Carolina* to rise, and forcibly make their Way out of the Province, to put themselves under the Protection of the *Spaniards;* who had proclaimed Freedom to all who should run to them from their Owners. That this Conspiracy was discovered at *Winyaw*, the most Northern Part of that Province, from whence, as the Negroes must bend their Course, it argued that the other Parts of the Province must be privy to it, and that the Rising was to be universal. Whereupon the whole Province was upon their Guard; the Number of Negroes in *South Carolina* being computed to be about Forty thousand, and the Number of White Men, at most, not above Five thousand. As several Negroes, who were employed in Pettiauguas, and other like Craft, (which they carried off with them) had taken the Benefit of the *Spaniards* Proclamation, and gone to *Augustine*, the Government of *South Carolina* sent a solemn Deputation to demand their Slaves. This Deputation consisted of Mr. *Braithwaite*, a Member of the Council, Mr. *Rutlidge*, one of the Assembly, and Mr. *Amian*, Clerk of the Assembly; but the Governor of *Augustine*, tho' in Time of profound Peace, peremptorily refused to deliver them up, and declared he had Orders to receive all such as should come thither, and protect them.

Upon this, and the Petitions which were sent from the *Highlanders* at *Darien*, and the *Saltzburghers* at *Ebenezer*, representing the Danger and Inconvenience of the Introduction of Negroes, the Trustees sent, under their Seal, an * Answer to the Representation from some of the Inhabitants of *Savannah*.

Among the Persons to whom Grants of Lands were made in order to their settling at their own Expence in the Colony, some never went over; others were Gentlemen of *Carolina*, who neglected to take up their Lands, or even desire to have them laid out; and others, who quitted their Plantations, and went to reside at *Savannah* as Shopkeepers: *One* Man in particular, an Apothecary Surgeon, from the Beginning, neglected his Grant, and followed his Practice in the Town; *another* quitted his Plantation, and betook himself to selling of Rum: To these Two, almost all the Town of *Savannah* were indebted for Physick or Rum; and they first raised the Clamour, that Lands might be alienable, and Negroes admitted, which would have made them Possessors of the chief Part of the Lots. To these some others, who had gone at their own Expence, and had employed their covenanted Servants on their Plantations, joined themselves, taking their Servants from their Labour, and letting them out to Hire in the Town, for the sake of an immediate Profit, on which they lived in an idle and riotous manner; and even at the Time when their Servants were taken off from their proper Labour in their Plantations, they fomented the Clam-

* Appendix, No. XI.

our for Negroes, in order to carry them on. The Spirit of Idleness, which was very early introduced in the Town, many of the People were too ready to follow. Constant Clubs have been held, and Horse-races kept up by them, to amuse and divert the People from their Labour; and Delinquents (who have insulted the Laws, even in the Courts of Justice, and declared they would do their utmost to destroy the Colony) have, when committed to Prison, been abetted and supported by them. By these the before-mentioned Representation was formed, and many of the People by their own Inclination to Idleness, by the Power which the others had over them as Creditors, and by Hopes being given them, that if they stuck together, the Trustees must grant them Negroes, or see the Colony abandoned, were thus drawn in to sign the same; in which they in a manner demanded the Permission of Negroes, and an Alteration of their Tenures.

The Trustees, to make all the People as easy and contented as they could, published an Advertisement in the *London Gazette*, the 8th of *September* 1739. and other Papers, which was continued for several Days; and ordered it to be published in the *South Carolina Gazette*, that they had resolved to inlarge their Grants on Failure of Issue Male, and to make a certain Provision for the Widows of the Grantees, in the following manner; *viz.* That the Lands already granted, and such as should hereafter be granted, should, on Failure of Issue Male, descend to the Daughters of such Grantees; and in case there should be no Issue, Male or Female, that the Grantees might devise such Lands; and for want of such Devise, that such Lands should descend to their Heirs at Law; with a Proviso, that the Possession of the Person who should enjoy such Devise, should not be increased to more than Five hundred Acres; and that the Widows of the Grantees should hold and enjoy the Dwelling-house, Garden, and One Moiety of the Lands their Husbands should die seized of, for and during the Term of their Lives.

The Trustees directed in the Advertisement, that those who intended to have the Benefit given them, should enter their respective Claims, in order that proper Grants and Conveyances in the Law might be forthwith prepared and executed for that Purpose; and that no Fee or Reward was to be taken for the entering of any such Claim, directly or indirectly, by any Person or Persons whatsoever.

In the Month of *August* 1739. the Trustees received Advice from General *Oglethorpe*, that he had frequent Intelligence of the *Spaniards* endeavouring to bribe the *Indians*, and particularly the *Creek Nation*, into a Rupture with the *English;* which made it necessary for him to go to the General Assembly of the *Indian* Nations at the *Coweta-town*, about Five hundred Miles distant from *Frederica*, in order to prevent such Designs and Seditions amongst them; and that he had been obliged to buy Horses, and Presents to carry up to this Meeting, where the *Choctaws* (who are upon the Frontiers between the *English* and *French* Settlements) and the *Chickesaws* were to send their Deputies.

This Journey of General *Oglethorpe*'s has since appeared to be of great Service to the Publick; for on the 26th of *August* 1739. Mr. *Stephens* received an Express from Colonel *Bull*, Lieutenant Governor of *South Carolina*, that he had Intelligence from Lieutenant Governor *Clarke* of *New York*, concerning the *French* marching from *Mont Reall*, near *Quebeck*, with a Body of about Two hundred regular Troops, and Five hundred *Indians*, who were to be reinforced by *French* and *Indians* in their Journey: That this Army was designed against the *Indians* in Friendship with his *Britannick* Majesty's Subjects of *Carolina* and *Georgia*, who are situated near some Branches of the *Mississippi River*. Colonel *Bull* added, that he should immediately dispatch an Express to the *Creek* Nations, with Advice to General *Oglethorpe* of the Contents of Lieutenant Governor *Clarke*'s Letter; and that it was necessary, that both the Provinces of *Carolina* and *Georgia* should be on their Guard; though if the *Creek Indians* should prove true, the Danger would not be great. General *Oglethorpe*, by his Treaties with the *Indians* in this Journey, has confirmed them in the *British* Interest, and made a new Treaty with them; whereby their former Concession of Lands to *Great Britain* was confirmed and extended.

A Parcel of Raw Silk was brought this Year from *Georgia* by one Mr. *Samuel Augspourguer*, who made an Affidavit before a Master in Chancery, that he received it from the Hands of Mr. *Thomas Jones*, the Trustees Store-keeper at *Savannah*, who told him it was the Produce of *Georgia;* and the said *Samuel Augspourguer*, who resided in the Southern Part of the Province, said, That, when at *Savannah*, he saw the *Italian* Family there winding off Silk from the Coquons.

The Silk was shewed at the Trustees Office to Mr. *John Zachary*, an eminent Raw Silk Merchant, and Mr. *Booth*, one of the greatest Silk Weavers in *England*, who declared it was as fine as any *Italian* Silk, and that it was worth, at least, Twenty Shillings a Pound.

This Mr. *Samuel Augspourguer*, who joined the Colony in the Beginning of the Year 1736. left it in *July* 1739. with Two Men Servants, and their Children, on his Plantation; and came over to obtain a Grant of Five hundred Acres of Land, and to get some of his own Countrymen from the Canton of *Bearn* in *Switzerland*, to go with him as Servants, on his Return to *Georgia*, in order to proceed more effectually in the Cultivation of his Lands.

	Numbers sent	British	Foreign Protestants	Men
The Persons whose Passage were paid for on the Charity, were	138 whereof	4 and	134 and in	49.
The Persons sent on the Charity in the former Years were	1383 whereof	911 and	472 and in	638.
The Number of Persons sent in the Eight Years, to the 9th of *June* 1740. were	1521 whereof	915 and	606 and in	687.

The Lands granted this Year to be cultivated at the Expence of the Incorporated Society in *Scotland* for promoting Christian Knowledge, in order to raise a Maintenance for the *Scots* Minister at *New Inverness* in *Georgia*, were Three hundred Acres.

The Lands granted this Year, to be cultivated by a Person at his own Expence, were Five hundred Acres.

The Lands granted in Trust in the said Eight Years, in order to be granted out in smaller Portions in *Georgia*, were Forty-one thousand Six hundred Acres; to be cultivated for religious Uses, were Nine hundred Acres; and to be cultivated for the Maintenance of an Orphan-house, were Five hundred Acres.

The Lands granted in the said Eight Years, to Persons who were to cultivate them at their own Expence, were Twenty-seven thousand One hundred and Eighty-five Acres.

The Money received this Year pursuant to Act of Parliament, was 20,000 *l.* and in Benefactions 181 *l.* 4 *s.* 3½ whereof in *South Carolina* the Amount in Sterling Money 86 *l.* 6 *s.* 11½ and in *England* 94 *l.* 17 *s.* 4 *d.* whereof the Trustees applied 16,614 *l.* 2 *s.* 5½ of which they exhibited an Accompt to the Lord Chancellor, and the Lord Chief Justice of the King's-Bench, pursuant to their Charter; and the Remainder of all the Money they ever received being 5919 *l.* 7 *s.* 7 *d.* will be carried into their succeeding Accompt.

From the 9th of June 1740. *to the present Time.*

THE Trustees this Year took further Methods for the Satisfaction of the People in the Province; they extended the Tenures, by which the Daughter of a Grantee, or any other Person, was made capable of enjoying, by Devise or Inheritance, any Quantity of Lands which did not increase her or his Possession, to more than Two thousand Acres.

A Licence was likewise granted for all the present Possessors of Land in *Georgia*, to make Leases of any Part of their Lots, for any Term not exceeding Three Years, to any Person residing in *Georgia*, and who should reside there during the Term of such Lease.

A general Release was likewise passed, by which no Advantage was to be taken against any of the present Possessors of Land in

Georgia, for any Forfeitures incurred at any time before *Christmas* 1740. in relation either to the Tenure or Cultivation of Land. And the Possessors of Fifty Acres of Land were not obliged to cultivate more than Five Acres thereof in Ten Years, from their Grants; and those of under Fifty Acres, in Proportion: And the Possessors of Five hundred Acres of Land, were not obliged to cultivate more than One hundred and Twenty Acres thereof in Twenty Years, from their Grants; and those of under Five hundred Acres, and above Fifty Acres, in Proportion, to prevent any Forfeitures for want of cultivating the Quantities required.

Under these Circumstances it is presumed, That no Complaint can now with Reason be made against the Tenure by which the Inhabitants at this Time hold their Lands; since they have more Power than is generally given by Marriage Settlements, in which the Grantees are only Tenants for Life, incapable of mortgaging, or aliening, or making any Disposition by their last Will; whereas the Freeholders in *Georgia* are now become Tenants in Tail General, and may, with the Licence of the Common-Council of the Trustees, upon Application made to them for that Purpose, mortgage or alien; and further, without Application, have it absolutely in their Power, on Failure of Issue in Tail, to dispose thereof by their last Will.

By an Account received from the Secretary in the Province, it appears, That on the First of *August* 1740. about Seventy Freeholders of the Northern Part of the Province, delivered in the Town-court of *Savannah*, their Claims of Lots, under the Tenures which were advertised the last Year in the *South Carolina* and *London Gazettes*.

That on the Fifteenth of the same Month, as many or more appeared in the said Town-court on the same Occasion; and that on the Twenty-seventh of the same Month, divers more delivered in their Claims likewise.

The Trustees are informed by their Secretary in the Province, That in pursuance of their Orders, he had just finished an authenticated Account of the State of the Colony, with respect to the Number of Inhabitants in the several Towns and Villages; the

Number of Houses, and the Settlements made; the Progress which the several People had made in the Cultivation of their Lands, and their Ability or Inability to support themselves; and in any Case where the last appeared, the Reasons of it; the Proportions of the different Sorts of Soil, as near as could be computed; and an Account of the several Produces, which, by Experience or Appearance, could or might be raised for Trade. And the Trustees are in daily Expectation of receiving from him the said Account. But by the several Accounts before received, they are enabled to give, though an imperfect one, the following State of the Settlements, *viz.*

The Town of *Savannah* is about Ten Miles up the River *Savannah*; there are (besides Warehouses and Huts) at least One hundred and Thirty Houses in the Town. As these, for the sake of Air, and to prevent the spreading of any Fire, are built at some Distance from each other, they make several spacious Squares and wide Streets. There is a regular Magistracy settled in the Town, which the Trustees are obliged to be at the Expence of supporting, till the Colony arrives at sufficient Strength to do it. There are in the Town a Court-house, a Store-house, a Gaol, a House for the Trust-Servants, a Wharf, a Guard-house, and some other publick Buildings; a Church is at present building, and a Clergyman is settled there. The Town is excellently situated for Trade, the Navigation of the River being very secure; and Ships of Three hundred Tons can lie within Six Yards of the Town, and the Worm does not eat into them.

About Four Miles from *Savannah*, inland from the River, are the Two Villages *Highgate* and *Hampstead*, which lie at about a Mile distant from each: The People settled there apply themselves chiefly to Gardening, and supply the Town of *Savannah* with Quantities of Greens and Garden-stuff.

By the Account of Mr. *Thomas Stephens*, who, at his Father's Request, was sent over to assist him in his Business of Secretary in the Province, and continued with him there some short time, he states, That there are Twenty Plantations, within Twenty Miles round *Savannah*, which have each of them from Five to Thirty Acres of Land cleared.

About Fifteen Miles from *Savannah*, is a Village called *Abercorn;* about Twenty Miles further up the River, is the Town of *Ebenezer*, where the *Saltzburghers* are settled, with Two Ministers; One of whom computed, That the Number of his Congregation, in *June* 1738. consisted of One hundred and Forty-six. Therefore as the Infants could not be reckoned in the Computation, and as Seven more have since been sent and settled with them, it is believed the Number has been increased; especially since the Town is so healthy, that by a Letter sent to the Society for promoting Christian Knowledge, by the Reverend Mr. *Bolzius*, one of the Ministers at *Ebenezer*, dated the 26th of *June* 1740. he declared, That in a Year's Time one Person only had died, which was a Child of Four Years old. The People are industrious and sober; they raise not only a sufficient Quantity of Corn, and other Produces, for their own Subsistence, but they sell great Quantities to those at *Savannah*, who have not been so careful of their Plantations; they have great Herds of Cattle, and are in so thriving a Condition, that not one Person has abandoned his Settlement, or sent over the least Complaint about the Tenures or the want of Negroes. On the contrary, they in a Body petitioned against the Use of Negroes; and their Ministers have declared, That their signing that Petition was a voluntary Act: And at their Desire, another Embarkation of their Countrymen, who are willing to go from *Germany* and join them, is designed to be sent with all convenient Speed.

About Ten Miles from hence, upon a River running into *Savannah*, is a Place called *Old Ebenezer*, where is a Cow-pen, and a great Number of Cattle, for the Use of the Publick, and for Breeding.

At a considerable Distance from hence is the Town of *Augusta*, before described, which, from the great Resort of Traders and *Indians*, is in a thriving Condition, and is and will be a great Protection to both the Provinces of *Carolina* and *Georgia*, against any Designs of the *French*.

In the Southern Part of the Province is the Town of *New Inverness*, upon the River *Alatamaha*, where the *Highlanders* are settled.

And about Twenty Miles from hence, on the Island of *St. Simon's*, near the Sea, is the Town of *Frederica*, with a regular Magistracy, as at *Savannah*, supported at the Expence of the Trust: Strong Fortifications round the Town are almost finished; and at the South-East Point of the Island are Barracks for Three hundred and Thirty Men.

There are Settlements on the Islands of *Jekyll* and *Cumberland*, which lie at a small Distance from each other to the Southward of *Frederica*; and on the last, Two Forts are built, one of which was described before, and the other was finished in *April* 1740. upon the South End of the Island. It commands the Inlet of *Amelia* Sound, is strongly palisaded with Flankers, and is defended by Eight Pieces of Cannon.

Barracks are built upon this Island for Two hundred and Twenty Men, with Store-houses, which were finished in *October* 1738.

There are Six Forts in the Province, and a Battery of Cannon erected to secure the Harbour at *St. Simon's*, under which Ships may safely lie.

The *Indians*, from the Presents which they have annually received from the Trustees, and from the Justice and Humanity with which they have been treated, are secured in the *British* Interest, notwithstanding the Arts both of the *French* and the *Spaniards* to seduce them: By this *South Carolina* has been free from those Wars, in which (as the Preamble to his Majesty's Charter sets forth) they had frequently suffered, and so late as in the Year 1715. had been laid almost waste with Fire and Sword; and by the Security which *South Carolina* received by such a Frontier as *Georgia* is to it, very large Tracts of Land have been cultivated in the Southern Part of that Province, which no Person would venture to settle on before, and a great Quantity of Rice raised thereon.

As the People in *Georgia*, sent on the Charity, were supported, to enable them to raise their own Provisions, in the first Place, on the Lands they should clear, and to convert the Timber they should cut down in clearing those Lands into Lumber, which they might, to their great Advantage, export to the Sugar Colonies; and further, to raise Silk, Wine and Oil, for which the Climate was very proper; it was hoped from thence they would gain a comfortable Subsistence, and be of Service to their Mother-Country in raising such Produces, which at present are purchased from Foreigners with ready Money.

Having thus stated the Plan laid down for the Trustees by his Majesty's Charter; the several Steps taken by them for the Execution of that Plan, with their yearly Progress therein; the several Obstructions from unforeseen Accidents, which have checked that Progress, with the present Condition of the Colony, according to the latest and most authentick Accounts from thence; they submit the Whole to the Wisdom of this Honourable House, being intirely disposed to follow any Directions that shall flow from thence: And as they have no other View but the Service of their Country, by making this Colony as useful to the Interest of *Great-Britain*, as by its Situation and Climate it is capable of being, they heartily with the Trust in abler Hands, that those important Services might not be defeated thro' their Inability.

By Order of the TRUSTEES,

BENJ. MARTYN, *Secretary*.

APPENDIX.

NUMBER I.

To the Trustees for establishing the Colony of Georgia.

GENTLEMEN,
In writing this Answer to the Letter, which I had the Honour to receive from you, dated the 29th Instant, wherein you desire to know my Sentiments of an Undertaking to raise Raw Silk in your new Settlement in *Georgia*; of the Probability of succeeding therein; the proper Steps to be

taken to bring that Work to Perfection; and my Opinion of the Nature, Quality and Use of the Raw Silk produced in *Carolina*: It is a great Pleasure to me, that, from Experiments which I made some Years ago, I can now, besides my Opinion, give you some Information concerning that silk, which may be depended on.

The Value and Usefulness of the Undertaking will appear, as soon as we consider, that all the Silk consumed in this Kingdom, is now of foreign Growth and Manufacture, which costs the Nation very great Sums of Money yearly to purchase; and that the raising our Supply thereof in his Majesty's Dominions in *America*, would save us all that Money, afford Employment to many Thousands of his Majesty's Subjects, and greatly increase the Trade and Navigation of *Great Britain*.

It appears to me as beneficial to this Kingdom, attended with as little Hazard or Difficulty, as much wanted, and which may as soon be brought to Perfection in a proper Climate, as any Undertaking so considerable in itself, that I ever heard of. I therefore think there is a very great Probability of its succeeding, if such proper Measures are pursued, and such Assistance afforded to the poor People at their first setting out, as are necessary to settle, instruct and encourage them.

The Silk produced in *Carolina* has as much natural Strength and Beauty, as the Silk of *Italy* (which is commonly called Fine Silk); and by the several Experiments I have tried with it, I am satisfied, it may be made to answer the same Purposes, as *Italian* Silk now does, if it be reeled in short Skains, a fine, clean and even Thread: To effect which, if some experienced Persons are at first sent to teach the People, the Work will soon be made easy to the meanest Capacity, and the Value of the Silk will be thereby greatly increased.

As for my own Part, if at any time you should think I can be of Use to promote so good a Work, I shall be ready to execute your Commands as far as I am able; and always remain,

GENTLEMEN,

Old Jewry, Jan. 31.   *Your most obedient,*
    1732.   *humble Servant,*
                                                THO. LOMBE.

NUMBER II.

Extract of a Letter from South Carolina Gazette, *dated at* Charles-Town *the* 22d March 1732.

On *Tuesday* the 13th Instant I went on board a Canoe, in Company with Mr. *George Ducat* and Mr. *John Ballantine*, with Four Negroes; and about 10 o'Clock we set off from Mr. *Lloyd's* Bridge for *Georgia*, and passing by *Port Royal* on *Wednesday* Night, we arrived, on *Friday* Morning, an Hour before Day, at *Yammacraw*, a Place so called by the *Indians*, but now *Savannah*, in the Colony of *Georgia*. Some time before we came to the Landing, the Centinel challenged us, and understanding who we were admitted us ashore. This is a very high Bluff, Forty Feet perpendicular from High-water Mark. It lies, according to Captain *Gascoigne's* Observations, in the Latitude 31 : 58, which he took off *Tybee*, an Island that lies at the Mouth of the *Savannah* River. It is distant from *Charles-Town* S. W. according to the Course and Windings of the Rivers and Creeks, about 140 Miles; but, by a direct Course, 77, allowing *Suillivant's* Island to be in the Latitude 32 : 47 from *Augustine* N. E. and by E. about 140 Miles, and by the Course of the Rivers is distant from Fort *Moore* 300 Miles; but, upon a direct Line, but 115 Miles N. W. and by W. This Bluff is distant 10 Miles from the Mouth of the Rivers on the South Side; and *Purrysburgh* is 24 Miles above it on the North, and is so situated, that you have a beautiful Prospect, both up and down the River. It is very sandy and barren, and consequently a wholsome Place for a Town or City, There are on it 130 odd Souls; and from the Time they embarqued at *London*, to the Time I left the Place, there died but Two sucking Children, and they at Sea. When they arrived, there was standing on it a great Quantity of the best Sorts of Pine, most of which is already cut down on the Spot where the Town is laid out to be built. The Land is barren about a Mile back, when you come into very rich Ground; and on both Sides, within a Quarter of a Mile of the Town, is choice good Planting-land. Colonel *Bull* told me, That he had been Seven Miles back, and found it extraordinary good.

Mr. *Oglethorpe* is indefatigable, takes a vast deal of Pains; his Fare is but indifferent, having little else at present but salt Provisions: He is extremely well beloved by all his People; the general Title they give him is *Father*. If any of them is sick, he immediately visits them, and takes a great deal of Care of them. If any Difference arises, he is the Person that decides it. Two happened while I was there, and in my Presence; and all the Parties went away, to outward Appearance, satisfied and contented with his Determination. He keeps a strict Discipline; I neither saw one of his People drunk, or heard one swear, all the Time I was there: He does not allow them Rum, but in lieu gives them *English* Beer. It is surprising to see how chearfully the Men go to work, considering they have not been bred to it: There are no Idlers there; even the Boys and Girls do their Parts. There are Four Houses already up, but none finished; and he hopes, when he has got more Sawyers, which I suppose he will have in a short time, to finish Two Houses a Week. He has ploughed up some Land, part of which he sowed with Wheat, which is come up, and looks promising. He has Two or Three Gardens, which he has sowed with divers Sorts of Seeds, and planted Thyme, with other Sorts of Pot-herbs, Sage, Leeks, Skellions, Celeri, Liquorice, &c. and several Sorts of Fruit-trees. He was palisading the Town round, including some Part of the Common, which I do suppose may be finished in a Fortnight's Time. In short, he has done a vast deal of Work for the Time, and I think his Name justly deserves to be immortalized.

Mr. *Oglethorpe* has with him Sir *Walter Raleigh*'s written Journal, and, by the Latitude of the Place, the Marks and Tradition of the *Indians*, it is the very first Place where he first went ashore, and talked with the *Indians*, and was the first *Englishman* that ever they saw: And about half a Mile from *Savannah* is a high Mount of Earth, under which lies their chief King; and the *Indians* informed Mr. *Oglethorpe*, That the King desired before he died, that he might be buried on the Spot where he talked with that great good Man.

The River Water is very good, and Mr. *Oglethorpe* has proved it several Ways, and thinks it as good as the River of *Thames*. On *Monday* the 19th, we took our Leave of Mr. *Oglethorpe* at Nine o'Clock in the Morning, and embarked for *Charles-Town*; and when we set off, he was pleased to honour us with a volley of small Arms, and the Discharge of Five Cannon: And coming down the Rivers, we found the Water perfectly fresh Six Miles below the Town, and saw Six or Seven large Sturgeon leap, with which Fish that River abounds, as also with Trout, Perch, Cat and Rock Fish, &c. and in the Winter Season there is Variety of Wild Fowl, especially Turkeys, some of them weighing Thirty Pounds, and abundance of Deer.

NUMBER III.

RULES for the Year 1735.

The Trustees intend this Year to lay out a County, and build a new Town in *Georgia*.

They will give to such Persons as they send upon the Charity; *viz.*

To every Man.   A Watch Coat.

A Musquet, and Bayonet, to those who have
    them not of their own.

An Hatchet.

An Hammer.

An Handsaw.

A shod Shovel, or Spade.

A broad Hoe.

A narrow Hoe.

A Gimlet.

A drawing Knife.

And there will be a publick Grindstone to each
    Ward or Village.

He will also have an Iron Pot, and a Pair of
    Pot-hooks.

And a Frying-pan.

And for his Maintenance in the Colony for One Year, he will have

To be delivered in such Proportions, and at such Times, as the Trust shall think proper.

> 300 Pounds of Beef, or Pork.
> 114 Pounds of Rice.
> 114 Pounds of Pease.
> 114 Pounds of Flour.
> 44 Gallons of Strong Beer.
> 64 Quarts of Melasses for brewing of Beer.
> 18 Pounds of Cheese.
> 9 Pounds of Butter.
> 9 Ounces of Spice.
> 9 Pounds of Sugar.
> 5 Gallons of Vinegar.
> 30 Pounds of Salt.
> 12 Quarts of Lamp-oil, and a Pound of
>   Spun Cotton.
> And 12 Pounds of Soap.

And to the Mothers, Wives, Sisters, or Children of such Men, Provision will be given in the Colony for One Year, in the following Manner; *viz.*

To each Head of them; that is to say, to every Person of the Age of Twelve Years, and upwards, *viz.*

To be delivered as above
{
300 Pounds of Beef, or Pork.
114 Pounds of Rice.
114 Pounds of Pease.
114 Pounds of Flour.
 64 Quarts of Melasses for Brewing of Beer.
 18 Pounds of Cheese.
  9 Pounds of Butter.
  9 Ounces of Spice.
  9 Pounds of Sugar.
  5 Gallons of Vinegar.
 30 Pounds of Salt.
  6 Quarts of Lamp-oil, and half a Pound of Spun Cotton.
}
And 12 Pounds of Soap.

And for every Person above the Age of Seven, and under the Age of Twelve, half the said Allowance, being esteemed half an Head.

And for every Person above the Age of Two, and under the Age of Seven, One-third of the said Allowance, being esteemed One-third of an Head.

The Trustees pay their Passage from *England* to *Georgia*; and in the Voyage they will have the following Provisions, *viz.* In every Week, Four *Beef* Days, Two *Pork* Days, and One *Fish* Day; and their Allowance served out daily as follows: That is to say,

On the Four Beef Days.

Four Pounds of Beef for every Mess of Five Heads.
And Two Pounds and a half of Flour.
And half a Pound of Suet, or Plums.

On the Two Pork Days.

Five Pounds of Pork,
And Two Pints and half of Pease, } for every Five Heads.

And on the Fish Day.

Two Pounds and half of Fish, ⎫
And half a Pound of Butter, ⎬ for every Five Heads.
The Whole at Sixteen Ounces to the Pound.

And allow each Head Seven Pounds of Bread, of Fourteen Ounces to the Pound, by the Week.

And Three Pints of Beer, and Two Quarts of Water, (whereof one of the Quarts for Drinking, and the other for boiling Victuals) each Head by the Day, for the Space of a Month; and a Gallon of Water (whereof Two Quarts for Drinking, and the other Two for boiling Victuals) each Head by the Day after, during their being on their Passage.

The Heads to be accounted in this Manner: Every Person above the Age of Twelve Years, to be accounted a whole Head; all Persons of the Age of Seven Years, and under the Age of Twelve Years, to be accounted Two for One; all Persons above the Age of Two Years, and under the Age of Seven Years, to be accounted Three for One; and any Person under the Age of Two Years, is not to be accounted.

And the said Persons are to enter into the following Covenants before their Embarkation; *viz.*

That they will repair on Board such Ship as shall be provided for carrying them to the Province of *Georgia*; and, during the Voyage, will quietly, soberly and obediently demean themselves; and go to such Place in the said Province of *Georgia*, and there obey all such Orders as shall be given, for the better settling, establishing and governing the said Colony.

And, That for the first Twelve Months from landing in the said Province of *Georgia*, they will work and labour in clearing their Lands, making Habitations, and necessary Defences, and in all other Works for the common Good and publick Weal of the said Colony, at such Times, in such Manner, and according to such Plan and Directions as shall be given.

And, That they, from and after the Expiration of the said last-mentioned Twelve Months, will, during the Two next succeeding Years, abide, settle and inhabit in the said Province of *Georgia*, and cultivate the Lands which shall be to them, and their Heirs Male, severally allotted and given, by all such Ways and Means as, according to their several Abilities and Skills, they shall be best able and capable.

And such Persons are to be settled in the said Colony, either in new Towns, or new Villages.

Those in the Towns will have each of them a Lot, Sixty Feet in Front, and Ninety Feet in Depth, whereon they are to build an House; and as much Land in the Country as in the whole shall make up Fifty Acres.

Those in the Villages will each of them have a Lot of Fifty Acres, which is to lie all together, and they are to build their House upon it.

All Lots are granted in Tail Male, and descend to the Heirs Male of their Bodies for ever; and in case of Failure of Heirs Male, revert to the Trust, to be granted again to such Persons as the Common Council of the Trustees shall think most for the Advantage of the Colony. And they will have a special Regard to the Daughters of Freeholders, who have made Improvements on their Lots, not already provided for, by having married, or marrying Persons in Possession, or intitled to Lands in the Province of *Georgia*, in Possession or Remainder.

All Lots are to be preserved separate and undivided, and cannot be united, in order to keep up a Number of Men equal to the Number of Lots, for the better Defence and Support of the Colony.

No Person can lease out his House or Lot to another, without Licence for that Purpose, that the Colony may not be ruined by Absentees receiving and spending their Rents elsewhere. Therefore each Man must cultivate the same by himself or Servants.

And no Person can alienate his Land, or any Part, or any Term, Estate, or Interest therein, to any other Person or Persons, without special Licence for that Purpose, to prevent the uniting or dividing the Lots.

If any of the Land so granted shall not be cultivated, planted, cleared, improved, or fenced with a Worm-fence, or Pales Six Feet high, during the Space of Ten Years from the Date of the Grant, then every Part thereof not cultivated, planted, cleared, improved, or fenced as aforesaid, shall belong to the Trust; and the Grant, as to such Parts, shall be void.

There is reserved, for the Support of the Colony, a Rent-charge for ever of Two Shillings Sterling Money for each Fifty Acres, the Payment of which is not to commence until Ten Years after the Grant.

And the Reversion, or Remainder expectant on the Demise of such Persons without Issue Male, shall remain to the Trust.

But the Wives of the Freeholders, in case they should survive their Husbands, are, during their Lives, intitled to the Mansion-house, and One-half of the Lands improved by their Husbands; that is to say, inclosed with a Fence of Six Feet high.

All Forfeitures for Non-residence, High Treason, Felonies, &c. are to the Trustees for the Use and Benefit of the Colony.

Negroes and Rum are prohibited to be used in the said Colony; and Trade with the *Indians*, unless licensed.

None are to have the Benefit of being sent upon the Charity in the manner above-mentioned; but,

1*st*, Such as are in decayed Circumstances, and thereby disabled from following any Business in *England*; and who, if in Debt, must have Leave from their Creditors to go.

2*d*, Such as have numerous Families of Children, if assisted by their respective Parishes, and recommended by the Minister, Church-wardens and Overseers thereof.

The Trustees do expect to have a good Character of the said Persons given, because no Drunkards, or other notoriously vicious Persons, will be taken.

And for the better to enable the said Persons to build the new Town, and clear their Lands, the Trustees will give Leave to every Freeholder to take over with him One Male Servant, or Apprentice, of the Age of Eighteen Years, and upwards, to be bound for not less than Four Years; and will, by way of Loan to such Freeholder, advance the Charges of Passage for such Servant or Apprentice, and of furnishing him with the Cloathing and Provision hereafter mentioned; to be delivered in such Proportions, and at such Times, as the Trust shall think proper:

Viz. With

A Pallias, and Bolster, and Blanket, for Bedding.

A Frock and Trowsers of Lintsey Wolsey,
A Shirt, and Frock, and Trowsers of Osnabrigs, ⎫
A Pair of Shoes from *England*,   ⎬ for Cloathing.
And Two Pair of Country Shoes,   ⎭

And 200 Pounds of Meat,   ⎫
And 342 Pounds of Rice, Pease, or *In-*   ⎬ for Food for a Year.
  dian Corn,   ⎭

The Expence of which Passage, Cloathing and Provision, is to be re-paid the Trustees by the Master, within the Third Year from their Embarkation from *England*.

And to each Man Servant, and the Heirs Male of his Body for ever, after the Expiration of his Service, upon a Certificate from his Master of his having served well, will be granted Twenty Acres of Land, under such

Rents and Agreements as shall have been then last granted to any others, Men Servants, in like Circumstances.

Sign'd by Order of the Common Council of the Trustees for Establishing the Colony of Georgia *in* America, *this Second Day of* July 1735.

BENJ. MARTYN, Secretary.

NUMBER IV.

To such Persons who can carry Ten Men Servants, and settle with them in Georgia *at their own Expence, and whose Characters the Trustees, upon Inquiry, shall approve of, will be granted Five hundred Acres of Land in Tail Male, and descend to the Heirs Male of their Bodies for ever, under the yearly Rent of Twenty Shillings Sterling Money for every Hundred Acres, for the Support of the Colony; the Payment of which is not to commence until Ten Years after the Grant.*

And the Land is so granted, upon the following Conditions and Covenants.

That such Persons do pay the Rent reserved, as the same shall become due; and no Part to be unpaid for Six Months after due.

That they, within a Month from the Grant, shall register the same, or a Memorial thereof, with the Auditor of the Plantations.

That they, within Twelve Months from the Grant, shall go to, and arrive in, *Georgia*, with Ten able-bodied Men Servants, being each of the Age of Twenty Years, and upwards.

That they shall abide in *Georgia* with such Men Servants Three Years from the Registering the Grant there, building their Houses, and cultivating their Lands.

That they shall clear and cultivate, within Ten Years from the Grant, Two hundred Acres of Land, Part of the said Five hundred Acres, and plant Two thousand White Mulberry-trees or Plants thereon; and on every Hundred of the other Three hundred Acres One thousand White Mulberry-trees or Plants, when cleared, and preserve the same Quantity from time to time thereupon, the Trustees obliging themselves to furnish the Plants.

That they do not alienate the said Five hundred Acres of Land, or any Part, for any Term of Years, or any Estate or Interest in the same to any Person or Persons, without special Leave.

That they do not make Pot-ash in Partnership without Leave; but may make it themselves not in Partnership.

On the Determination of the Estate in Tail Male, the Land to revert to the Trust.

That they shall not depart the said Province without License.

All Forfeitures for Non-residence, High Treason, Felonies, &c. are to the Trustees, for the Use and Benefit of the Colony.

If any Part of the said Five hundred Acres of Land shall not be cultivated, planted, cleared, and fenced round with a Worm Fence, or Pales Six Feet high, within Eighteen Years from the Grant, all and every such Part shall revert to the Trust; and the Grant, as to such Part, to be void.

And the Common Council of the Trust, at the Expirations of the Terms such Men Servants shall be severally bound for, (being none less than Four Years) when requested by the Grantee, will grant to each of such Men Servants Twenty Acres of Land in Tail Male, under such Rents, Conditions, Limitations and Agreements, as shall have been then last granted to any others, Men Servants, in like Circumstances.

When the Land reverts to the Trust on the Determination of the Estate in Tail Male, it is to be granted again to such Persons, as the Common Council of the Trust shall think most for the Advantage of the Colony. And the Trust will have a special Regard to the Daughters of those who have made Improvements on their Lots, not already provided for, by having married, or marrying, Persons in Possession, or intitled to Lands in the Province of *Georgia* in Possession or Remainder.

And the Wives of such Persons, in case they should survive their Husbands, are, during their Lives, intitled to the Mansion-house, and One half of the Lands improved by their Husbands; that is to say, inclosed with a Fence Six Feet high.

Negroes and Rum are prohibited to be used in the said Province, and Trade with the *Indians*, unless licensed.

NUMBER V.

To the KING's Most Excellent Majesty,

The humble Memorial and Representation of the State and Condition of Your Majesty's Province of South Carolina, *from the General Assembly of the said Province.*

Your Majesty's most dutiful Subjects of this Province having often felt, with Hearts full of Gratitude, the many signal Instances of your Most Sacred Majesty's peculiar Favour and Protection to these distant Parts of your Dominions, and especially those late Proofs of your Majesty's most gracious and benign Care, so wisely calculated for the Preservation of this your Majesty's Frontier Province on the Continent of *America*, by your Royal Charter to the Trustees for establishing the Colony of *Georgia*, and your great Goodness, so timely applied, in promoting the Settlement of the *Swiss* at *Purrysburgh*; encouraged by such Views of your Majesty's wise and paternal Care, extended to your remotest Subjects, and excited by the Duty which we owe to your Most Sacred Majesty, to be always watchful for the Support and Security of your Majesty's Interest, especially at this very critical Conjuncture, when the Flame of a War, breaking out in *Europe*, may very speedily be lighted here in this your Majesty's Frontier Province, which, in Situation, is known to be of the utmost Importance to the general Trade and Traffick of *America*: We therefore, your Majesty's most faithful Governor, Council and Commons, convened in your Majesty's Province of *South Carolina*, crave Leave, with great Humility, to represent to your Majesty the present State and Condition of this your Province, and how greatly it stands in Need of your Majesty's gracious and timely Succour, in case of a War, to assist our Defence against the *French* and *Spaniards*, or any other Enemies to your Majesty's Dominions, as well as against the many Nations of Savages, which so nearly threaten the Safety of your Majesty's Subjects.

The Province of *South Carolina*, and the new Colony of *Georgia*, are the Southern Frontiers of all your Majesty's Dominions on the Continent of *America*, to the South and South-West of which is situate the strong Castle of *St. Augustine*, garisoned by Four hundred *Spaniards*, who have several Nations of *Indians* living under their Subjection, besides several other small Settlements and Garisons near the *Appellaches*, some of which are not Eighty Miles distant from the Colony of *Georgia*. To the South-West and West of us the *French* have already erected a consider-able Town near Fort *Thoulouse*, on the *Moville* River, and several other Forts and Garisons, some not above Three hundred Miles distant from our Settlements; and at *New Orleans* on the *Mississippi* River, since her late Majesty Queen *Anne's* War, they have exceedingly increased their Strength and Traffick, and have now many Forts and Garisons on both Sides of that large River, for several Hundred Miles up the same; and since his Most Christian Majesty has taken out of the *Mississippi* Com-pany the Government of that Country into his own Hands, the *French* Natives of *Canada* come daily down in Shoals to settle all along that River, where many regular Forces have of late been sent over by the King, to strengthen the Garisons in those Places; and, according to our best and latest Advices, they have Five hundred Men in Pay, constantly employed as Wood-Rangers, to keep their neighbouring *Indians* in Sub-jection, and to prevent the distant ones from disturbing their Settle-ments; which Management of the *French* has so well succeeded, that, we are very well assured, they have wholly now in their Possession, and under their Influence, the several numerous Nations of *Indians* that are situate near the *Mississippi* River, One of which, called the *Choctaws*, by Estimation, consists of about Five thousand fighting Men, and who were always deemed a very warlike Nation, lies on this Side the River, not above Four hundred Miles distant from our Out settlements, among whom, as well as several other Nations of *Indians*, many *French Euro-peans* have been sent to settle, whom the Priests and Missionaries among them encourage to take *Indian* Wives, and use divers other alluring Methods to attach the *Indians* the better to the *French* Alliance; by which Means the *French* are become throughly acquainted with the *In-dian* Way, Warring, and Living in the Woods, and have now a great Number of White Men among them, able to perform a long March, with an Army of *Indians*, upon any Expedition.

We further beg Leave to inform your Majesty, That if the Measures of *France* should provoke your Majesty to a State of Hostility against it in *Europe*, we have great Reason to expect an Invasion will be here made upon your Majesty's Subjects by the *French* and the *Indians* from the *Mississippi* Settlements. They have already paved a Way for a Design of that Nature, by erecting a Fort, called the *Albama* Fort, alias Fort *Lewis*, in the Middle of the *Upper Creek Indians*, upon a navigable River leading to *Moville*, which they have kept well garisoned, and mounted with Fourteen Pieces of Cannon, and have lately been prevented from erecting a Second nearer to us in that Quarter. The *Creeks* are a Nation very bold, active and daring, consisting of about Thirteen hundred fighting Men, (and not above One hundred and Fifty Miles distant from the *Choctaws*) whom tho' we heretofore have traded with, claimed, and held in our Alliance, yet the *French*, on account of that Fort, and a superior Ability to make them liberal Presents, have been for some time striving to gain them over to their Interest, and have succeeded with some of the Towns of the *Creeks*; which, if they can be secured in your Majesty's Interest, are the only Nation which your Majesty's Subjects here can depend upon as their best Barrier against any Attempts, either of the *French*, or their confederate *Indians*.

We most humbly pray Leave further to inform your Majesty, That the *French* at *Moville* perceiving, that they could not gain the *Indians* to their Interest, without buying their Deer-skins, (which is the only Commodity the *Indians* have to purchase Necessaries with) and the *French* not being able to dispose of those Skins, by reason of their having no Vend for them in *Old France*, they have found Means to encourage Vessels from hence, *New York*, and other Places, (which are not prohibited by the Acts of Trade) to truck those Skins with them for *Indian* trading Goods, especially the *British* Woollen Manufactures, which the *French* dispose of to the *Creeks* and *Choctaws*, and other their *Indians*; by which means the *Indians* are much more alienated from our Interest, and on every Occasion object to us, that the *French* can supply them with Strouds and Blankets, as well as the *English*; which would have the contrary Effect, if they were wholly furnished with those Commodities by your Majesty's Subjects trading among them. If a Stop were therefore put to that pernicious Trade with the *French*, the *Creek Indians* chief Dependence would be on this Government, and that of *Georgia*, to supply them with those Goods; by which means great Part of the *Choctaws* living next the *Creeks*, would see the Advantage the *Creek Indians* enjoyed by having *British* Woollen Manufactures wholly from your Majesty's Subjects, and thereby be invited in a short time to enter into a Treaty of Commerce with us, which they have lately made some Offers for, and which, if effected, will soon lessen the Interest of the *French* with these *Indians*, and by Degrees attach them to that of your Majesty.

The only Expedient we can propose to recover and confirm that Nation to your Majesty's Interest, is by speedily making them Presents, to withdraw them from the *French* Alliance; and by building some Forts among them, your Majesty maybe put into such a Situation, that, on the first Notice of Hostilities with the *French*, your Majesty may be able to reduce at once the *Albama* Fort, and we may then stand against the *French* and their *Indians*, which if not timely prepared for, before a War breaks out, we have too much Reason to fear, we may be soon over-run by the united Strength of the *French*, the *Creeks*, and *Choctaws*, with many other Nations of their *Indian* Allies; for, should the *Creeks* become wholly Enemies, who are well acquainted with all our Settlements, we probably should also soon be deserted by the *Cherokees*, and a few other small Tribes of *Indians*, who, for the sake of our Booty, would readily join to make us a Prey to the *French* and Savages. Ever since the late *Indian* War, the Offences given us then by the *Creeks* have made that Nation very jealous of your Majesty's Subjects of this Province. We have therefore concerted Measures with the Honourable *James Oglethorpe*, Esq; who, being at the Head of a new Colony, will (we hope) be successful for your Majesty's Interest among that People. He has already, by Presents, attached the *Lower Creeks* to the Service of your Majesty, and has laudably undertaken to endeavour the fixing a Garison among the *Upper Creeks*, the Expence of which is already in Part provided for in this Session of the General Assembly of this Province: We hope therefore to prevent the *French* from encroaching farther on your Majesty's Territories, until your Majesty is graciously pleased further to strengthen and secure the same.

We find the *Cherokee* Nation has lately become very insolent to your Majesty's Subjects trading among them, notwithstanding the many Favours which the Chiefs of that Nation received from your Majesty in *Great Britain*, besides a considerable Expence which your Majesty's Subjects of this Province have been at in making them Presents; which inclines us to believe, that the *French*, by their *Indians*, have been tampering with them: We therefore beg Leave to inform your Majesty, that the building and mounting some Forts also among the *Cherokees*, and making them Presents, will be highly necessary to keep them steady in their Duty to your Majesty, lest the *French* may prevail in seducing that Nation, which they may the more readily be inclined to, from the Prospect of getting considerable Plunder in Slaves, Cattle and Commodities, which, they very well know, they have among us. Several other Forts will be indispensably necessary, to be a Cover to your Majesty's Subjects settled backwards in this Province, as also to those of the Colony of *Georgia*, both which in Length are very extensive; for tho' the Trustees for establishing the Colony of *Georgia*, by a particular Scheme of good Management, painfully conducted by the Gentleman engaged here in that charitable Enterprize, have put that small Part of the Colony, which he has not yet been able to establish, in a tenable Condition against the *Spaniards* of *Florida*, which lie to the Southward, yet the back Exposition of those Colonies to the vast Number of *French* and *Indians*, which border on the Westward, must, in case of a War, cry greatly aloud for your Majesty's gracious and timely Succour. The Expence of our Safety on such an Occasion, we must, in all Humility, acquaint your Majesty, either for Men or Money, can never be effected by your Majesty's Subjects of this Province, who, in Conjunction with *Georgia*, do not, in the Whole, amount to more than Three thousand Five hundred Men that compose the Militia, and wholly consist of Planters, Traders, and other Men in Business.

Besides the many Dangers, which, by Land, we are exposed to from so many Enemies that lie on the Back of us, we further beg Leave to represent to your Majesty the defenceless Condition of our Ports and Harbours, where any Enemies of your Majesty's Dominions may very easily by Sea invade us, there being no Fortifications capable of making much Resistance. Those in *Charles-Town* Harbour are now in a very ruinous Condition, occasioned by late violent Storms and Hurricanes, which already cost this Country a great deal of Money, and now require several Thousands of Pounds to repair the old, and build new ones; to mount the Ordnance which your Majesty was graciously pleased to send us, which, with great Concern, we must inform your Majesty, we have not yet been able to accomplish, being lately obliged, for the Defence and Support of this your Majesty's Province and Government, to raise, by a Tax on the Inhabitants, a Supply of above Forty thousand Pounds Paper Currency *per Annum*, which is a considerable deal more than a third Part of all the Currency among us; a Charge which your Majesty's Subjects of this Province are but barely able to sustain. Since your Majesty's Royal Instruction to your Majesty's Governor here, an intire Stop has been put to the Duties which before accrued from *European* Goods imported; and if a War should happen, or any thing extraordinary to be further expensive here, we should be under the utmost Difficulties to provide additionally for the same, lest an Increase of Taxes, with an Apprehension of Danger, should drive away many of our present Inhabitants, as well as discourage others from coming here to settle, for the Defence and Improvement of your Majesty's Province, there being several daily moving, with their Families and Effects, to *North Carolina*, where there are no such Fears and Burdens.

We must further beg Leave to inform your Majesty, That amidst our other perillous Circumstances, we are subject to many intestine Dangers from the great Number of Negroes that are now among us, who amount at least to Twenty-two thousand Persons, and are Three to One of all your Majesty's White Subjects in this Province. Insurrections against us have been often attempted, and would at any time prove very fatal, if the *French* should instigate them, by artfully giving them an Expectation of Freedom. In such a Situation, we most humbly crave leave to acquaint your Majesty, that even the present ordinary Expences necessary for the Care and Support of this your Majesty's Province and Government cannot be provided for by your Majesty's Subjects of this Province, without your Majesty's gracious Pleasure to continue those Laws for Establishing the Negroes, and other Duties, for Seven Years, and for appropriating the same, which now lie before your Majesty for your Royal Assent and Approbation; and the further Expences that will be requisite for the erecting some Forts, and establishing Garisons in the several necessary Places, so as to form a Barrier for the Security of this your Majesty's Province, we most humbly submit to your Majesty.

Your Majesty's Subjects of this Province, with Fulness of Zeal, Duty and Affection to your most Gracious and Sacred Majesty, are so highly sensible of the great Importance of this Province to the *French*, that we must conceive it more than probable, if a War should happen, they will use all Endeavours to bring this Country under their Subjection: They would thereby be able to supply their Sugar Islands with all Sorts of Provisions and Lumber by an easy Navigation, which, to our great Advantage, is now not so practicable from the present *French* Colonies; besides the Facility of gaining then to their Interest, most of the *Indian* Trade on the Northern Continent, they might then easily unite the *Canadees* and *Choctaws* with the many other Nations of *Indians*, which are now in their interest. And the several Ports and Harbours of *Carolina* and *Georgia*, which now enable your Majesty to be absolute Master of the Passage through the Gulph of *Florida*, and to impede at your Pleasure the Transportation home of the *Spanish* Treasure, would then prove so many convenient Harbours for your Majesty's Enemies, by their Privateers or Ships of War, to annoy a great Part of the *British* Trade to *America*, as well as that which is carried on through the Gulph from *Jamaica*, besides the Loss which *Great Britain* must feel in so considerable a

Part of its Navigation, as well as the Exports of Masts, Pitch, Tar and Turpentine, which, without any Dependence on the Northern Powers of *Europe*, are from hence plentifully supplied for the Use of the *British* Shipping.

This is the present State and Condition of your Majesty's Province of *South Carolina*, utterly incapable of finding Funds sufficient for the Defence of this wide Frontier, and so destitute of White Men, that even Money itself cannot here raise a sufficient Body of them.

With all Humility we therefore beg Leave to lay ourselves at the Feet of your Majesty, humbly imploring your Majesty's most Gracious Care in the Extremities we should be reduced to on the breaking out of a War; and that your Majesty will be graciously pleased to extend your Protection to us, as your Majesty, in your great Wisdom, shall think most proper.

In the Council Chamber, the 9th of April 1734.

South Carolina.

ROBERT JOHNSON.
THO. BROUGHTON, President.
PAUL JENYS, Speaker.

NUMBER VI.

Thomas Pearce, aged Forty Years and upwards, of the *Dover* Man of War, Mariner, having been at *Georgia* in *America*, on board the *Peter and James*, Capt. *George Dymond*, in the Year One thousand Seven hundred and Thirty-five, and from that Ship on board the *Hawk Sloop*, stationed at *Georgia*, until the Beginning of the Year One thousand Seven hundred and Thirty-nine; and having sounded every Inlet from the Sea all along the Coast of *Georgia*, from *Jekyll* Sound to *Tybee* Sound, maketh Oath and saith, That the said Coast, Four Leagues from the Land, is all even Ground, not less than Seven or Eight Fathom Water; and any Ship keeping in that Depth of Water, may steer along the same with the greatest Safety, and anchor, if they have Occasion. That on the Bar at *Jekyll*, there is at least Thirteen Feet and a half at Low-water, and at High-water Spring-tides Twenty-four Feet: And on the Bar at *Tybee*, there is at least Sixteen Feet and an half at Low-water, and at High-water Spring-tides Twenty-five Feet and an half; and the Difference between the Spring and Neap Tides is generally between Three or Four Feet. And this Deponent further saith, That he is well assured, and would undertake by Sounding with a Boat, even at Neap Tides, to carry in Forty-gun Ships over either of the said Bars; and saith, That he has seen in the Sound at *St. Simon's* from *Jekyll* Bar Ten Sail of Ships at One time; and that Ten or Twelve Forty-gun Ships may safely ride there: But behind *Jekyll* Island there is Water and Room enough for Shipping for Ten Miles up; and that the Sound at *Tybee* is large enough to hold with Safety Seven or Eight Forty-gun Ships. And this Deponent further saith, That Ships in *Jekyll* Sound may in Twenty-four Hours, from the Bar, run out into the Gulph-stream of *Florida*, through which Stream the *Spanish* Galleons (when not passing the Windward Passage) always come.

Tho. Pearce.

NUMBER VII.

To the King's Most Excellent Majesty,

The humble Memorial of the Trustees for Establishing the Colony of Georgia *in* America.

Humbly Sheweth,
That they being intrusted by your Majesty with the Care of the Colony of *Georgia*, which was formerly Part of your Majesty's Province of *Carolina*; and your Majesty's Colony of *Georgia* being very much exposed to the Power of the *Spaniards*, and become on Object of their Envy, by having valuable Ports upon the homeward Passage from the *Spanish West-Indies*; and the *Spaniards* having increased their Forces in the Neighbourhood thereof, the Trustees, in consequence of the great Trust reposed in them by your Majesty, find themselves obliged humbly to lay before your Majesty their Inability sufficiently to protect your Majesty's Subjects settled in *Georgia*, under the Encouragement of your Majesty's Charter, against this late Increase of Forces; and therefore become humble Suppliants to your Majesty, on the Behalf of your Subjects settled in the Province of *Georgia*, That your Majesty will be pleased to take their Preservation into your Royal Consideration, that, by a necessary Supply

of Forces, the Province may be protected against the great Dangers that seem immediately to threaten it.

All which is most humbly submitted to your Majesty's great Wisdom.

Signed by Order of the Trustees, this 10th *Day of* August 1737.

BENJ. MARTYN, Secretary.

NUMBER VIII.

To the Honourable the Trustees for Establishing the Colony of Georgia *in* America.

May it please your Honours,

We, whose Names are underwritten, being all Settlers, Freeholders and Inhabitants in the Province of *Georgia,* and being sensible of the great Pains and Care exerted by you in endeavouring to settle this Colony, since it has been under your Protection and Management, do unanimously join to lay before you, with the utmost Regret, the following Particulars.

But, in the first Place, we must beg Leave to observe, That it has afforded us a great deal of Concern and Uneasiness, that former Representations made to you of the same Nature, have not been thought worthy of due Consideration, nor even of an Answer. We have most of us settled in this Colony, in pursuance of the Description and Recommendation given of it by you in *Britain*; and from the Experience of residing here several Years, do find, That it is impossible the Measures hitherto laid down and pursued for making it a Colony, can succeed. None of all those who have planted their Lands, have been able to raise sufficient Produce to maintain their Families in Bread-kind only, even though as much Application and Industry have been exerted to bring it about, as could be done by Men engaged in an Affair, on which they believe the Welfare of themselves and Posterity so much depended, and which they imagine must require more than ordinary Pains to make succeed; so that by the accumulated Expences every Year of Provisions, Cloathing and Medicines, &c. for themselves, Families and Servants, several have expended all their Money, nay, even run considerably in Debt, and so been obliged to give off Planting, and making further Improvements; and those who continue, are daily exhausting more and more of their Money, and some daily increasing their Debts, without a Possibility of being reimbursed, according to the present Constitution. This being now the general State of the Colony, it must be obvious, that People cannot subsist by their Land according to the present Establishment; and this being a Truth resulting from Trial, Practice and Experience, cannot be contradicted by any theorical Scheme or Reasoning. The Land then, according to the present Constitution, not being capable to maintain the Settlers here, they must unavoidably have recourse to and depend upon Trade: But, to our woeful Experience, likewise, the same Causes that prevent the first, obstruct the latter; for though the Situation of this Place is exceeding well adapted for Trade, and, if it was encouraged, might be much more improved by the Inhabitants, yet the Difficulties and Restrictions which we hitherto have, and at present do labour under, debar us of that Advantage. Timber is the only thing we have here which we might export; and notwithstanding we are obliged to fall it in planting our Land, yet we cannot manufacture it fit for a foreign Market, but at double the Expence of other Colonies; as for Instance, The River of *May*, which is but Twenty Miles from us, with Allowance of Negroes, load Vessels with that Commodity, at One half of the Price that we can do; and what should induce Persons to bring Ships here, when they can be loaded with One half of the Expence so near us? Therefore the Timber on the Land is only a continual Charge to the Possessors of it, though of very great Service in all the Northern Colonies, where Negroes are allowed, and consequently Labour cheap. We do not in the least doubt, but that in time Silk and Wine may be produced here, especially the former; but since the Cultivation of Land with White Servants only, cannot raise Provisions for our Families, as before-mentioned, therefore it is likewise impossible to carry on these Manufactures according to the present Constitution. It is very well known, that *Carolina* can raise every thing that this Colony can; and they having their Labour so much cheaper, will always ruin our Market, unless we are in some measure on a Footing with them; and as, in both, the Land is worn out in Four or Five Years, and then fit for nothing but Pasture, we must be always at a great deal more Expence than they, in clearing new Land for Planting. The Importation of Necessaries of Life comes to us at the most extravagant Rate; Merchants in general, especially of *England*, not being willing to supply the Settlers with Goods upon Commission, because no Person here can make them any Security of their Lands or Improvements, as is very often practised in other Places to promote Trade, when some of the Employer's Money is laid out in necessary Buildings and Improvements, fitting for the Trade intended, without which it cannot be carried on. The Benefit of the Importation therefore is all to transient Persons, who do not lay out any Money amongst us, but, on the contrary, carry every Penny out of the Place; and the chief Reason for their enhancing the Price is, because they cannot get any Goods here, either on Freight or Purchase, for another Market. If the Advantages accruing from Importation centred in the Inhabitants, the Profit thereof would naturally circulate amongst us, and be laid out in Improvements in the Colony. Your Honours, we imagine, are not insensible of the Numbers that have left this Province, not being able to support themselves and Families any longer; and those still remaining, who had Money of their own, and Credit with their Friends, have laid out most of the former in Improvements, and lost the latter for doing it on such precarious Titles; and upon account of the present Establishment, not above Two or Three Persons, except those brought on Charity, and Servants sent by you, have come here, for the Space of Two Years past, either to settle Land, or encourage Trade; neither do we hear of any such likely to come, until we are on better Terms.

It is true, his Majesty has been graciously pleased to grant a Regiment for the Defence of this Province, and our neighbouring Colony, which indeed will very much assist us in defending ourselves against all Enemies; but, otherwise, does not in the least contribute to our Support; for all that Part of their Pay which is expended here, is laid out with transient People, and our Neighbours in *Carolina*, who are capable to supply them with Provisions, and other Necessaries, at a moderate Price, which we, as before observed, are not at all capable to do, upon the present Establishment. This then being our present Condition, it is obvious what the Consequences must be.

But we, for our Parts, have intirely relied on, and confided in, your good Intentions, believing you would redress any Grievances that should appear; and now, by our long Experience from Industry, and continual Application to Improvement of Land here, do find it impossible to pursue it, or even to subsist ourselves any longer, according to the present Nature of the Constitution: And likewise believing you will agree to those Measures that are found from Experience capable to make this

Colony succeed, and to promote which, we have consumed our Money, Time and Labour; we do, from a sincere and true Regard to its Welfare, and in Duty both to you and ourselves, beg Leave to lay before your immediate Consideration, the Two following chief Causes of these our present Misfortunes, and this deplorable State of the Colony, and which, we are certain, if granted, would be an infallible Remedy for both.

I. The Want of a free Title or Fee-simple to our Lands; which, if granted, would both occasion great Numbers of new Settlers to come amongst us, and likewise encourage those who remain here, chearfully to proceed in making further Improvements, as well to retrieve their sunk Fortunes, as to make Provision for their Posterity.

II. The Want of the Use of Negroes with proper Limitations; which if granted, would both induce great Numbers of White People to come here, and also render us capable to subsist ourselves by raising Provisions upon our Lands, until we could make some Produce fit for Export, and in some measure to balance our Importation. We are very sensible of the Inconveniencies and Mischiefs that have already, and do daily arise, from an unlimited Use of Negroes; but we are as sensible, that these may be prevented by a due Limitation, such as so many to each White Man, or so many to such a Quantity of Land; or in any other manner which your Honours shall think most proper. By granting us, Gentlemen, these two Particulars, and such other Privileges as his Majesty's most dutiful Subjects in *America* enjoy, you will not only prevent our impending Ruin, but, we are fully satisfied also, will soon make this the most flourishing Colony possessed by his Majesty in *America*, and your Memories will be perpetuated to all future Ages, our latest Posterity sounding your Praises, as their first Founders, Patrons and Guardians; but if by denying us those Privileges, we ourselves and Families are not only ruined, but even our Posterity likewise, you will always be mentioned as the Cause and Authors of all their Misfortunes and Calamities; which we hope will never happen.

We are, with all due Respect,

Savannah *in* Georgia, De-　　*Your Honours most dutiful,*
　cember *the 9th* 1738.　　　*and obedient Servants,*

Henry Parker　　　　　　*John Brownfield*
Robert † *Gilbert* his Mark　*William Woodroofe*
Thomas Christie　　　　　*Pat. Tailfer*
John Fallowfield　　　　　*And. Grant*

Sam. Mercer
Robert Williams
Patrick Graham
Da. Douglas
Tho. Baillie
Hugh Anderson
James Williams
Edward Jenkins
Thomas Omaston
Joseph Wardrop
George Buncle
Adrian Loyer
P. Joubert
John Burton
Robert Hows
Wm. † Maiers his Mark
Thomas Salter
James Baillow
James Anderson
John Seillie
James Carwells
John Lyndall
Jos. Fitzwalter
Elisha Forster
Walter Fox
William Ewen
J. Amory
Ja. Houston
Jacob Mathews
Isaac Young
Robert Hainks
Archibald Glen
Tho. Neale
Stephen † Terrien his Mark
Sam. Ward
James † Smith his Mark
Pierre Morel
Stephen de Monford
David Gainder

James † Chensac his Mark
James † Landry his Mark
Simson † Rouviere his Mark
Louis Stamen
Thomas Tripp
Sam. Holmes
James Mure
William Parker
John Graham
James Papot
John Penrose
David Snook
Edward Townsend
John Desborough
Andrew Duche
James Galloway
John Desborough, jun.
Edward Bush
Benj. Adams
Charles Britain
John Rae
William Colthred
John Young
Samuel Lacey
Andrew Walker
John Miller
Richard Rogers
Thomas Gantlet
William Starfichet
Petre Baillou
Peter Emory
Henry Lloyd
Wm. Elbert
John Smith
Wm. Calvert
Stephen Marrauld
Richard Millechamp
Isaac Young, sen.
John Kelly

Jos. Stanley
Tho. † Young his Mark
Thomas † Cross his Mark
Richard Davis
Thomas Wattel
Thomas † Baillie his Mark
James Corneck
James Burnsides
Hugh † Frazer his Mark
Samuel Parker
William Stirling
Tho. Andrews
George Gorsand
John Stonehewer
John Teasdeall
Wm. † Greenfield his Mark
Charles † Greenfield his Mark
Thomas † Young his Mark

James Dormer
William Carter
Henry † Moulton his Mark
Thomas Tibbett
James Dean
Don. Stewart
Gille Becu
Francis Brooks
John Clark
Henry Green
Jacob Watts
John Dudding
George † Bush his Mark
Peter † Deshter his Mark
Henry † Manley his Mark
Head Gardiner
Kenody O Brien.

NUMBER IX.

We are informed, that our Neighbours of *Savannah* have petitioned your Excellency for the Liberty of having Slaves. We hope, and earnestly intreat, that before such Proposals are hearkened unto, your Excellency will consider our Situation, and of what dangerous and bad Consequence such Liberty would be of to us, for many Reasons;

I. The Nearness of the *Spaniard*, who have proclaimed Freedom to all Slaves who run away from their Masters, makes it impossible for us to keep them without more Labour in guarding them, than what we would be at to do their Work.

II. We are laborious, and know a White Man may be by the Year more usefully employed than a Negro.

III. We are not rich, and becoming Debtors for Slaves, in case of their running away or dying, would inevitably ruin the poor Master, and he become a greater Slave to the Negro Merchant, than the Slave he bought could be to him.

IV. It would oblige us to keep a Guard-duty at least as severe as when we expected a daily Invasion; and if that was the Case, how miserable would it be to us, and our Wives and Families, to have an Enemy without, and more dangerous ones in our Bosom!

V. It's shocking to human Nature, that any Race of Mankind, and their Posterity, should be sentenced to perpetual Slavery; nor in Justice can we think otherwise of it, than that they are thrown amongst us to be our Scourge one Day or other for our Sins; and as Freedom to them must be as dear as to us, what a Scene of Horror must it bring about! And the longer it is unexecuted, the bloody Scene must be the greater. We therefore, for our own sakes, our Wives and Children, and our Posterity, beg your Consideration, and intreat, that instead of introducing Slaves, you'll put us in the way to get us some of our Countrymen, who with their Labour in time of Peace, and our Vigilance, if we are invaded, with the Help of those, will render it a difficult thing to hurt us, or that Part of the Province we possess. We will for ever pray for your Excellency, and are, with all Submission,

New Inverness, 3d
   January 1738–9.

              Your Excellency's most obliged
                      humble Servants,

          John Mackintosh Moore
          John Mackintosh Lynvilge
          Ranald M'Donald
          H M Hugh Morrison's Mark
          John M'Donald
          John Macklean
          John Mackintosh Son to *L.*
          John M'intosh Bain
          James M'Kay
          Daniel Clark, First
          Alexander Clarke, Son to the above
          Donald Clark, Third, his Mark †
          Jos. Ƀ I *Burges* his Mark
          Donald Clark, Second
          Archibald A M B *M'Bain* his Mark
          Alexander Munro
          William Munro
          John Cuthbert.

To his Excellency General *Oglethorpe.*

NUMBER X.

Ebenezer, 13th of *March* 1739.

We, *Saltzburghers* and Inhabitants of *Ebenezer*, that have signed this Letter, intreat humbly, in our and our Brethrens Names, your Excellency would be pleased to shew us the Favour of desiring the honourable Trustees for sending to *Georgia* another Transport of *Saltzburghers* to be settled at *Ebenezer*. We have, with one Accord, wrote a Letter to our Father in God, the Reverend Mr. *Senior Urlsperger*, at *Augspurg*, and in that Letter expressly named those *Saltzburghers* and *Austrians*, whom, as our Friends, Relations and Countrymen, we wish to see settled here. We can, indeed, attest of them, that they fear the Lord truly, love Working, and will conform themselves to our Congregation: We have given them an Account of our being settled well; and being mighty well pleased with the Climate and Condition of this Country, having here several Preferences in spiritual and temporal Circumstances, for other People in *Germany*, which your Honour will find in the here inclosed Copy of our Letter to Mr. *Senior Urlsperger*; if they fare as we do, having been provided in the Beginning with Provisions, a little Stock for Breed, some Tools, and good Land, by the Care of the honourable Trustees; and if God grants his Blessing to their Work, we doubt not, but they will gain with us easily their Bread and Subsistence, and lead a quiet and peaceable Life, in all Godliness and Honesty. Though it is here a hotter Season than our native Country is, yet not so extremely hot, as we were told on the first time of our Arrival; but since we have been now used to the Country, we find it tolerable, and, for working People, very convenient; setting themselves to work early in the Morning, till Ten o'Clock; and in the Afternoon, from Three to Sun-set; and having Business at Home, we do them in our Huts and Houses, in the Middle of the Day, till the greatest Heat is over. People in *Germany* are hindered by Frost and Snow in the Winter, from doing any Work in the Fields and Vineyards; but we have this Preference, to do the most and heaviest Work at such a time, preparing the Ground sufficiently for planting in the Spring: We were told by several People, after our Arrival, that it proves quite impossible and dangerous for White People to plant and manufacture any Rice, being a Work only for Negroes, not for *European* People; but having Experience of the contrary, we laugh at such a Talking, seeing that several People of us have had, in last Harvest, a greater Crop of Rice than they

[251]

wanted for their own Consumption. If God is pleased to enable us by some Money for building such Mills, convenient for cleaning the Rice, as we use in *Germany*, for making several Grains, fit for eating, then the Manufacture of Rice will be an easy and profitable thing. For the present, we crave your Excellency's Goodness to allow, for the Use of the whole Congregation, some Rice Sieves, of several Sorts, from *Charles-Town*, which cannot be had at *Savannah:* We will be accountable to the Store for them. Of Corn, Pease, Potatoes, Pomkins, Cabbage, *&c.* we had such a good Quantity, that many Bushels are sold, and much was spent in feeding Cows, Calves and Hogs. If the Surveyor, according to his Order and Duty, had used Dispatch in laying out our Farms, (which we have got not sooner than last Fall) *item*, if not, we all were disappointed by long Sickness, and planting the yellow *Pensilvania* Corn; we would have been able, by the Blessing of God, to spare a greater Quantity of Grain for getting Meat-kind and Cloaths, of which we are in Want. It is true, that Two Acres of Ground, for each Family's Garden, are set out some time ago; but being there very few Swamps fit for planting of Rice, and some Part of them wanting a good deal of Dung, we were not able, in the Beginning, to dung it well; therefore we could not make such a good Use of those Acres, as we now have Reason to hope, by the Assistance of God, after our Plantations are laid out: Hence it will be, that we plant the good Ground first, and improve the other Soil then, when Occasion will require it, in the best manner we can. In the first Time, when the Ground must be cleared from Trees, Bushes and Roots, and fenced in carefully, we are to undergo some hard Labour, which afterwards will be the easier and more pleasing, when the hardest Trial is over, and our Plantations are better regulated. A good deal of Time was spent in building Huts, Houses, and other necessary Buildings, in Town, and upon the Farms; and since, we wanted Money for several Expences; several Persons of us hired themselves out for some Weeks for building the Orphan-house, and its Appurtenances; *item*, The Reverend Mr. *Gronau*'s House, which happened to be built in the hottest Summer Season; and now some of us are employed to build the Reverend Mr. *Bolzius*'s House; which Buildings have taken away some time from our Work in the Ground; but the fair Opportunity of earning some Money at Home, was a great Benefit to us; this now being so, that neither the hot Summer Season, nor any thing else, hinders us from Work in the Ground, and we wish to lead a quiet and peaceable Life at our Place. We humbly beseech the honourable Trustees not to allow it, that any Negro might be brought to our

Place, or in our Neighbourhood, knowing by Experience, that Houses and Gardens will be robbed always by them, and White People are in Danger of Life because of them, besides other great Inconveniences. Likewise we humbly beseech you and the Trustees not to allow to any Person the Liberty of buying up Lands at our Place, by which, if granted, it would happen, that by bad and turbulent Neighbours our Congregation would be spoilt, and poor harmless People troubled and oppressed: But we wish and long for such Neighbours to be settled here, whose Good-name and honest Behaviour is known to us and our Favourers. The Honourable Trustees have been always Favourers and Protectors of poor and distressed People; wherefore we beseech you and them, they would be pleased to take us further under their fatherly Care, that the Remembrance of their Benevolence and Kindness to our Congregation might be conveyed to our late Posterity, and be highly praised. We put up our Prayers to God for rewarding your Excellency, and the Honourable Trustees, manifold for all their good Assistance and Benefits, which are bestowed upon us, and beg humbly the Continuance of your and their Favour and Protection, being, with the greatest Submission and Respect,

> *Your Honours*
> *Most Obedient Dutiful Servants,*
> Inhabitants at *Ebenezer.*

We Ministers of the Congregation at *Ebenezer* join with the *Saltzburgers* in this Petition, and verify that every one of them has signed it with the greatest Readiness and Satisfaction.

To His Excellency   JOHN MARTIN BOLZIUS.
   General Oglethorpe.   ISRAEL CHRISTIAN GRONAU.

NUMBER XI.

To the Magistrates of the Town of Savannah *in the Province of* Georgia.

The Trustees for establishing the Colony of *Georgia* in *America* have received by the Hands of Mr. *Benjamin Ball*, of *London*, Merchant, an attested Copy of a Representation, signed by you the Magistrates, and many of the Inhabitants of *Savannah*, on the 9th of *December* last, for altering the Tenure of the Lands, and introducing Negroes into the Province, transmitted from thence by Mr. *Robert Williams*.

The Trustees are not surprised to find unwary People drawn in by crafty Men to join in a Design of extorting by Clamour, from the Trustees, an Alteration in the fundamental Laws, framed for the Preservation of the People from those very Designs.

But the Trustees cannot but express their Astonishment, that you the Magistrates, appointed by them to be Guardians of the People, by putting those Laws in Execution, should so far forget your Duty, as to put yourselves at the Head of this Attempt.

However, they direct you to give the Complainants this Answer from the Trustees: That they should deem themselves very unfit for the Trust reposed in them by his Majesty on their Behalf, if they could be prevailed upon by such an irrational Attempt, to give up a Constitution, framed with the greatest Caution for the Preservation of Liberty and

Property, and of which the Laws against the Use of Slaves, and for the Entail of Lands, are the surest Foundations.

And the Trustees are the more confirmed in their Opinion of the Unreasonableness of this Demand, that they have received Petitions from the *Darien*, and other Parts of the Province, representing the Inconvenience and Danger, which must arise to the good People of the Province from the Introduction of Negroes; and as the Trustees themselves are fully convinced, that besides the Hazard attending of that Introduction, it would destroy all Industry among the White Inhabitants; and that, by giving them a Power to alien their Lands, the Colony would soon be too like its Neighbours, void of White Inhabitants, filled with Blacks, and reduced to be the precarious Property of a Few, equally exposed to domestick Treachery, and foreign Invasion: And therefore the Trustees cannot be supposed to be in any Disposition of granting this Request; and if they have not, before this, signified their Dislike of it, their Delay is to be imputed to no other Motives, but the Hopes they had conceived, that Time and Experience would bring the Complainants to a better Mind. And the Trustees readily join Issue with them in their Appeal to Posterity, who shall judge between them, who were their best Friends, those who endeavoured to preserve for them a Property in their Lands, by tying up the Hands of their unthrifty Progenitors; or they who wanted a Power to mortgage or alien them; who were the best Friends to the Colony, those who, with great Labour and Cost, had endeavoured to form a Colony of his Majesty's Subjects, and persecuted Protestants from other Parts of *Europe;* had placed them on a fruitful Soil, and strove to secure them in their Possessions, by those Arts which naturally tend to keep the Colony full of useful and industrious People, capable both to cultivate and defend it; or those who, to gratify the greedy and ambitious Views of a few Negro Merchants, would put it into their Power to become sole Owners of the Province, by introducing their baneful Commodity, which, it is well known, by sad Experience, has brought our neighbour Colonies to the Brink of Ruin, by driving out their White Inhabitants, who were their Glory and Strength, to make room for Black, who are now become the Terror of their unadvised Masters.

Signed, by Order of the Trustees, this Twentieth Day of June 1739.

BENJ. MARTYN, Secretary.   (L. S.)

FINIS.

[255]

The Hard Case of the
Distressed People of *Georgia*.

THE HARD

CASE

OF THE

DISTRESSED People of GEORGIA.

The Hard Case of the
Distressed People of *Georgia*.

I N the Year 1732, his Majesty being graciously pleased to grant a large Tract of Land, now called *Georgia*, lying between the Northern Stream of the River *Savannah* (bounding on *South-Carolina*, Northward, and the Southern Stream of the River *Alatamaha*, Southward) to several Noblemen and Gentlemen, incorporated by the Name of the Trustees for establishing the Colony of *Georgia* in *America*, with full Powers and Authorities for settling a regular Colony thereon, and governing the same. And this Colony being designed for a Barrier and Place of Strength for our Northern *British* Provinces of *America*, as well as a Provision for Numbers of the distress'd industrious Poor of *Great-Britain*, who by raising such Produces and Commodities used here, which were of foreign Growth, such as *Silk*, *Wine*, *Oil*, *&c.* great Sums might in time be saved to this Nation, and the *Trade*, *Navigation*, and *Wealth* of his Majesty's Realms be greatly increased; annual Supplies were granted to it by Parliament, together with great private Benefactions and Donations.

Upon this View, and at the Expence of *Part* of this Money, Numbers of Unfortunate People were sent over by the *Trustees* on the *Charity*, and Numbers of Gentlemen and others who became Adventurers on their own Private Stock and Fortunes, went over with Servants, to settle and improve this Colony upon the *Plan* laid down by the *Trustees;* so that neither Industry nor Money was wanting to pursue and perfect the Scheme.

And Attempts have been made accordingly; but after *Nine Years* Experiments, 'tis evident, that the most zealous industrious Planter is incapable of making out a Livelihood by the Return of his Labour and Expence, *this Scheme being utterly impracticable* upon the Footing it has been attempted, and the farther Persons have endeavoured to pursue it, the farther they have pursued the *very Miseries and Wants*, which they were here placed to extricate themselves out of.

And this Disappointment is owing to the particular Circumstances in the Constitution and Government of the Colony, which have defeated all the *Intents* and *Purposes* of it; and the great Discredit which is grown upon it, by the Restrictions and Oppositions that have infested it, has not only discouraged its Increase by preventing Numbers from transplanting themselves hither, but also obliged Numbers to look for that Security and Ease in other Colonies which has been deny'd them here.

The Discouragements first complained of, and which were so prejudicial to the Fortunes and Encrease of *People* and *Trade* here, were the Conditions of the Tenures, in which the Lands were granted in Tail-male only, and the Daughters and younger Sons, as tho' illegitimate, deprived of the Right of Succession and Inheritance. And these Grants, filled with so many Conditions impossible to be comply'd with, made them all liable to Forfeiture, and raised *very* just Fears and Opinions of Uncertainty in their Possessions, and consequently an Unsteadiness in the Improvement of them. And as in many Instances, Advantage had been taken of these Forfeitures; and every Possessor made to depend so much on the Courtesy of the Trust, for being restored to the *Freedom* of his Lands, *&c.* no Man, in common Prudence or Justice to his Family, could any longer think of going on and laying out their Fortune on such a fluctuating Bottom as the Humours and Integrity of frail Men, and of sending his Children to beg that Bread and Inheritance, (the Purchase of his own Industry, *&c.*) as a Mercy from the gracious Hands of the Trustees, which they ought naturally and legally to succeed to, as the Sons of *Britons*, and Heirs to the Properties and Liberties of their Fathers.

And the Trustees more effectually to *secure* to themselves the Reversion of the Lands and Houses built and improved there, deny'd the Possessor the Liberty of selling or letting his Improvements: So that, though he should find it necessary to turn to any other Way of Life, or remove to another Country, he must forfeit all, and lose the Benefit of so much Labour and Money expended on them, or be content at last, to sit down and return to the same hopeful Measures of Industry, which, with his last Penny, and his last Breath, he must resolve (since he has once began) to spend in the Service of these Gentlemen.

If it be said, that 'twas necessary to tie up the Hands of their unthrifty Progenitors for fear of their selling and disposing of their Lands from their Families; such a *moral* Pretence, and *conscientious* Regard, no doubt, is truly justifiable, and will abundantly apologize for any Evil arising from it. But have our Children any better Security than the same good Pleasure of the Trustees, on which they are made absolutely to depend for every Thing they shall inherit of their Fathers? Moreover, are there not many who have no Families at all, and should not they have Liberty to adopt Heirs to succeed them? Should this Law, upon any Pretence, have extended beyond those sent over on the *Charity*, for whose Security alone it could be thought necessary to be enacted? Do not these Gentlemen hereby also sap a main Foundation of Civil Government, when by losing thus the Tie of filial Dependance, they dissolve that of paternal Authority, a Duty which from its Tendency, is a Matter of as much real Moment to the well being of Society, as any other moral or civil Ordinance whatsoever?

Besides, is it natural to suppose, that these Gentlemen can have greater Tenderness and Anxiety for the future Happiness of the growing Generation, than their Fathers, who could resolve to quit their dear and native Country, Friends and Relations, tempt the Dangers of the Seas, unnatural Climates and uncultivated Wilds, without having any Regard or Attention to making that comfortable and secure Provision for their Families here, which their un-fortunate Stars, against all their Endeavours, had defeated them in at home?

But, as there has been many Instances of unthrifty, unnatural Parents, and not one of a *Breach of Trust* in a charitable incorpora-ted Body, 'tis but reasonable and fit, that Men, who were not to be trusted with their own *Laws*, *Liberties*, and *Families*, should have *Guardians* and *Fathers* assigned to their *Estates* also.

The Planter moreover has been indispensably confined to the Assignment and Culture of such Lands, as by a regular Plan were annexed to the several Lots and Divisions in the Townships, *indis-criminately*, without any Regard had to the *Nature* of the Soil or *Conveniency* of the Planter; so that often these Lots fell upon Grounds ever under Water, often upon an ungrateful Sand, and often upon such Places as neither suited the Humour or Design of the Planter. Should this be imposed barely for the Hazard of an Experiment? Is it reasonable, where so much good Land lies un-occupied? Are the Planters Ease and Advantage Circumstances that ought not to be considered? Why are they wantonly put under such *insuperable*, yet unnecessary Difficulties? For whom are the Reservations of the best and improveable Lands thus kept up? Or by what better Right and Service can any, besides the first Adven-turers, make Pretensions and Titles to them?

The Quit-Rent of 3 *s.* *per* 100 Acres reserved for the Crown in the Royal Charter, in the Grants issued by the Trustees, amounts in some to 10*s.* and in others 20*s.* *per* 100 Acres; a Sum much greater than any other Lands in *America* are charged with, or are capable of paying. This surely can be only designed as an Acknowl-edgment for the blessed Security the People enjoy here, from the Advantage of a Frontier Country, and the Favour of having their Lands, *&c.* restored, as often as the *Long-suffering* Trustees shall please not to be tired out with the repeated Remittances of their Forfeitures.

Besides these Discouragements in the Nature of the Tenures, and the Planter expending his Time, Money and Labour, on Lands, which, in a Course of Years, must revert to the Trust, he is even excluded from the necessary Means of raising a present Sufficiency of any kind of Produce for his Subsistence. The Use and Labour of Negroes has been found indispensably requisite for the Climate and Cultivation of Lands in *America;* and if in a Point of publick Utility so much contested, it may be allowed to produce in its Favour an Authority, which it is presumed none will object to, General *Oglethorpe*, a Gentleman of the Trust, (and one, who to all Appearances was as obstinately prejudiced against Negroes as any Man could be) is offer'd; who, 'tis plain, is now become reconciled to their Usefulness, as he keeps a Number of them on his Plantation, bordering on *Georgia.*

And indeed the extraordinary Heats here, the extraordinary Expences in maintaining, hiring and procuring White Servants, the extraordinary Difficulty and Danger there is in clearing the Lands, attending and Manufacturing the Crops, working in the Fields in Summer, and the *poor Returns* of *Indian* Corn, Pease and Potatoes, which are as yet the only chief Produces of the Land there, make it indisputably impossible for White Men alone to carry on Planting to any good Purpose. Besides, our Neighbours having such an Advantage, as the Privilege of Negroes, can always under-sell us in any Manufacture or Produce, which they are as well qualified for as we, should we be ever able to raise more than is necessary for home Consumption without them. The poor People of *Georgia,* may as well think of becoming Negroes themselves (from whose Condition at present they seem not to be far removed) as of hoping to be ever able to live without them; and they ought best to know, and most to be believed, who have made the Experiment.

'Tis objected, indeed, that the Introduction of Negroes might destroy the Colony; this, as it has never been tried, is but an idle Insinuation. That the Colony is already ruined is certain and evident; and it can't be said, that the Introduction of Negroes has brought this about. Besides, they were never intended to be admitted, but under such Limitations, as the *Safety*, as well as the *Improvement* of the Colony, would be equally consulted and provided for.

'Tis said also, that Negroes being so near St. *Augustin* would desert thither. If they are as well and better treated in *Georgia* than they can be there, where is the Temptation? besides, their Desertion can affect but a few Individuals out of the Whole, except we admit it to be total; and their Labour is of general Use. Moreover, have we not a Land Army, Forts and Marines, and may not they be as honestly and usefully employed hereafter in *hunting* and *running down* fugitive Negroes, as they are now the distress'd *Georgians*, flying for Bread and Liberty to other Countries? May not these Troops also be of as important Service hereafter, as they have hitherto been judg'd, in defending Towns, *&c.* without Inhabitants, and protecting a People who have no Properties? Besides, it can be proved, that for every Negroe that has run away from *Augusta* in *Georgia*, or the Parts of *Carolina* bordering thereon (which are one hundred Miles distant from any Settlement on the Coast) that five to one white Servants have deserted their Masters, and even fled to *Augustin*, from the *meagre Hunger* and *frightful Oppressions*, which stared them in the Face in *Georgia*.

It is also presumed, that the admitting and substituting Negroes to the laborious Parts of Culture, *&c.* would make the white Men grow idle and lazy. It has been already shewn, that white Men are unequal to the Task, and yet it must be done. If, therefore, others may be found much fitter and abler for this Work, and who besides doing it better, shall save a Man all the Trouble, and put Money into his Pocket, is this a criminal or unreasonable Piece of Luxury? And as the Labours of the Field here supply but a small Share of that Variety and Stock, which goes to answer the common necessary Demands, may not white Men be still industrious, and to better Purpose, each Man furnishing that Part for which he is best qualified? Moreover, as the principal Springs to that Industry (which the Trustees so much contend for) besides Necessity, seem to be the *Possibility* of raising those Commodities which are necessary for Life, much cheaper and better at home; the Labour and Money therein employed, being thus turned to better Account, and the Assurance of Men enjoying themselves what they get, or of leaving it to their Children; has not this Government, in the very Foundation of it, entirely relaxed or broke off those Springs in every Motion? The only Difference between an industrious Man in their Sense, and an idle Man hitherto, has been that the former has taken the shortest Way to be ruined, and the latter may possibly hold out till he is put in a better.

It is lastly said, That this Colony, by the Numbers of white Men alone who should inhabit it, was design'd to be the Barrier and Strength to the Northern Provinces in *America*, whose Safety was apprehended, from their Negroes. It were better, indeed, that it could be so established; but besides the Confirmations of an Experiment already made, it may be asserted, that there is no visible Way of doing it, but by making it a Garrison, and taking every Landholder, *&c.* into Pay; which could not be made effectual neither, for a much greater Sum every Year than has been given to the Trustees hitherto.

The Prohibition laid against the Importation of Rum, tho' from whatever moral Motive, is greatly prejudicial to Trade, and injurious to the particular Circumstances of the People: For Lumber being the only Export the Planter is capable of making, and which, by clearing of his Lands for Planting, he is consequently supplied with, he must lose the Benefit of it, by being thus prohibited to barter it for the Growth and Manufactures of the *West Indies*, the only Market for Timber, and whose Commodities, such as Rum, Sugar, Molasses, *&c.* make so great and necessary a Part of the Consumption of his Family; and a considerable Branch also of the *Indian* Trade. Besides, it is a wrong and unreasonable Prejudice, to object that this Liquor is hurtful to the Healths of the People, as it is well known, that the Waters of these Countries require to be corrected by some Spirit; and Experience has approved no Liquor so universally agreeable to *Americans* as small Punch, which both in Point of Health and Cost, is better, and near as cheap, as small Beer. And what farther proves a *Weakside* herein is, that we have, instead thereof, adopted Wines, which are of foreign Growth, which come excessively dear, and can be paid for but in ready Money only by us.

The People have often humbly represented the injurious Nature of these Tenures, which, tho' they have been often alter'd by the

Trust, remain yet so obscure and perplex'd, that no safe or free Title is conveyed in them; and the same *terrifying Forfeitures* are still annex'd; but for what honest Purpose, or good Meaning, is yet inexplicable. Nor can it be conscientiously answer'd, 'tis presumed, why the People have not been made easy in so reasonable, so just Demands; or, when Alterations were about being made, they were not early and effectually done, for establishing the Peace and Safety of the Province, and removing such ill-boding, such unavoidable Apprehensions. Can it be thought more proper to reserve and defer those Alterations, till there are few or no People left in the Colony, to take the Benefit of them? Will any, even among these Gentlemen say, he had honestly discharg'd his Duty to himself and Children, when, by his own Act, he suspended their Birthright, on the mere Favour of a Set of Men, whom no Law could oblige to be honest in such a Trust; and whom no overt Act of their own has shewn they were willing, or designed, to approve themselves such.

Should it be said, that *Englishmen*, whose free Spirit rises at the least obscure, oblique Attempt on their Liberties and Properties at home, shall impose such Yokes, the very Badges of Infamy and Slavery, on their own, tho' unfortunate, Countrymen abroad, who have common and unalienable Rights to the same Privileges with them? Should they be envied or denied the Benefit of their native Laws, while they are gratefully and honestly struggling in an in-hospitable Climate and Land, to *relieve* their Families, and be *useful* to their Mother Country? And this, perhaps, is the *only Blessing* she can impart to them, without imparing her own in some Measure; and the *only Security* which they can have, of their not being made Properties to the Avarice, as well as Slaves to the Ambition and Government of designing Men in a foreign Land.

It is now humbly submitted, whether such discouraging Cir-cumstances, and which are made to arise from the *Nature of the Constitution*, and have the Countenance of Laws, however equit-able or political, to support them, have not fundamentally de-stroyed, to all Intents and Purposes, his Majesty's gracious De-signs and Expectations in the settling of this Colony?

Whether these Gentlemen qualiter Trustees have Powers and

Authorities for making such Laws, and whether these Laws are not repugnant to the Laws of *England?*

Whether the Trustees are not inexcusably culpable in not making those necessary and just Alterations in their Laws and Tenures, which the Success and Safety of the Colony so much depended on, and which, by the repeated Address and Remonstrances of the People, were humbly set forth and petitioned for?

Whether the Trustees, by their inflexible Adherence to these pernicious and impracticable Schemes and Maxims of Government, should not compensate for the Fortunes of so many Thousands of unhappy Adventurers, and account for the publick Money and Donations consumed therein?

Whether this Colony, the better to answer the Design, and to enable it to arrive at sufficient Strength of becoming a Frontier, where the Lives and Fortunes of People are necessarily more exposed, should not have principally conferred equal at least, if not superior, Rights, Privileges and Immunities, than other Provinces in *America* enjoy?

Whether 'tis reasonable and just that People should be placed here for no other Consideration than the mere Danger of such a Situation, and to fight for the Liberties and Properties of other People, when they have none of their own to lose? and lastly,

Whether the distress'd People of *Georgia* have not a Right to complain and to be heard, and should be stiled mutinous and rebellious, for seeking for a Redress of those intolerable Grievances which have entirely ruined them, and which, for many Years past, have been as lightly regarded, as they were wantonly imposed, by the Trustees?

Hitherto indeed it may be said, that the People have been legally ruined: But 'tis humbly hoped no insinuating Expediency of Government can be pleaded in Favour of those Oppressions, Violences, Frauds, Impositions and wicked Exercises of Power, which have fatally also concurred to the Destruction and Desolation of this Colony; and which, 'tis presumed, no provisional Acts have yet been made for their Countenance and Support. Wrong Measures in Government, tho' they may be great Evils, when they proceed from real Errors in Judgment, have somewhat pardonable in them; but if they proceed from *Principle*, against Conviction, against Remonstrance, against known and established Laws, against publick Faith, and publick Declarations to the contrary, they have somewhat too flagrant and criminal in them to interest themselves in the favourable Opinion of Mankind.

And if it be consider'd what Numbers have been sacrificed to the Ambition, Avarice, Tyranny and Pleasure of Men in Power there, that the Trustees have obstinately supported them in their Measures against the Complaints of the People; that false Accounts, both of the State and Expences of the Colony have been published to impose upon the World, and this Nation and Parliament in particular; that honest Men's Characters have been wickedly impugned, *designedly* to weaken their Authority and Evidence in these Matters; that the Trustees have not wanted good Information and personal Testimony to set them right, but have haughtily and contemptuously rejected them; that many People, by indirect Influence and Compulsion, signed the Petitions against Negroes, &c. which the Trustees have printed in their own Favour, especially the People of *Ebenezer*, by the Means of their unworthy and base Minister, who has made them belie both themselves and him; and the People of *Darien* by Threats and Promises from General *Oglethorpe*'s Officers and others; that the Trustees themselves, 'tis said, have ordered their Servants in *Georgia* to send none but good Accounts of the Colony to *England*; that Magistrates have been intimidated in the Execution of their Office, &c. and Officers removed for daring to do their Duty: That the Magistracy has been filled with *mean, illiterate* and *dishonest Men*, whereby Justice has been partially administered, and many Cruelties exercised on the People; that in some Towns Magistrates or Courts of Justices could not be obtain'd, tho' Application has been made for them: That Imprisonments and corporal Punishments have been illegally and arbitrarily inflicted by Persons acting under the General without legal Process, any Commission, or legal Qualification; that the Laws of *England*, whether *Common* or *Statute* Laws, were declared upon the Bench to be no Laws in *Georgia*; that there are no

Body of Laws prepared by the Trust for the Government of the Colony, nor Records duly kept; that the Verdicts of the Juries have been falsified by the Magistrates; that no Appeal is allowed from *Georgia* to the Trustees; that the People's Lands and Houses have been taken from them arbitrarily, and disposed of by the General without Pretence of Forfeiture; that some Inhabitants could get no Lands at all; that People of Substance who might strengthen the Colony have been ever discountenanced; that Numbers could get no Instrument of Writing, whereby to shew they have any Titles at all to their Lands, *&c.* that the Magistrates have been made the Storekeepers and Cashiers, which has supported an arbitrary Power; that an injurious Trade has been carried on with the Money granted by Parliament, *&c.* that the Profits arising from such Trade do not appear to be accounted for to the Trustees; that the publick Account Books are blotted, erased, interlined and torn, and the Vouchers destroyed by Mr. *Thomas Jones*, the Trustee's Storekeeper, Magistrate and Accomptant; that the said *Jones* has been heard publickly and frequently to declare he would give the Trustees 1000 *l.* a Year for the Profits of their Stores; that the Labourers and Artificers, *&c.* in the Trustee's Employment have been obliged to take their Debts out in Goods from the Stores at an extravagant Price; that the publick Debts contracted by the Trustees or their Agents are not paid; that the Accomptants in *Georgia* refer the People to the Trustees for Payment of their Bills, *&c.* and the Trustees refer them back again to *Georgia;* that Bounties or Premiums promised on Produces rais'd are not paid; that the People have been charged, in their private Accounts, for the Cattle and Servants which were given to the Colony and People *gratis*, and likewise for the Supply of Provisions out of the Stores; that the People's Cattle are taken from them by the Trustees' Agents and killed, and the Flesh thereof carried into their Store and sold to the People; that not only the live Stock of the People is arbitrarily ordered to be killed by the General, under false Pretence of Damage done by them, but Money is also exacted from the Proprietors as a Reward to those who killed the same; that Grand Juries have been arbitrarily dissolved by the Magistrates while the Court continued to sit, and while Matters of Felony lay before them; that the General, in Capital Cases of Felony, has sat upon the Bench as a Judge, examined Witnesses, and solely summ'd up and given the Charge to the Jury; that Magistrates, after they have been dismissed by the Trustees, have sat as Magistrates on the Bench for a Year or more, without any other than a verbal Commission from the General, who removes and creates Magistrates at Pleasure; that there is no Church built, and seldom a Clergyman in *Georgia*, notwithstanding the Money given here for Support thereof, except the *Lutherans* at *Ebenezer*, whose Expences are born by their own Country and the Society here; that there are not those defensible Forts and Fortifications in *Georgia* as have been mentioned in the printed Accounts, most of them are become useless, and were never perfected; that no Roads have been compleated; that the Publick Buildings were suffered through wilful and apparent Neglect, to run to Decay, tho' erected at a great Expence; that a Guard of Soldiers and Marines is set on the People to keep them in the Colony against their Inclinations; that People who were taken in making their way out of the Colony, were obliged to enlist; that an *Indian* War is threatned, the *Indians* being disgusted, notwithstanding 'tis said that much more than 10000 *l.* has been expended on them, and great Embassies made amongst them; that if these Things *are so*, surely the People's Case of *Georgia* is very hard, and deserves as much as the Attention and Assistance of their Mother Country to rescue them from these Chains, as the miserable Captives in the Dungeons, of the *Spaniards*.

Notwithstanding it is not to be suspected that the Trustees are in a Confederacy to ruin so many People, and that *some* of them have *distinguished* themselves by openly shewing their Dislike to the *Proceedings in Georgia*, yet as the Grievances of the People have been often represented to the Trustees, it is humbly submitted, whether it be not reasonable for such as have more immediately taken upon them the Administration thereof, to give Reasons for suppressing the Representations of the People, and giving no Answer to them, and persevering in Measures so apparently destructive to the Colony, instead of applying proper Remedies whilst they had sufficient Power and Means in their Hands for effecting the same.

Of all these Things the People in *Georgia* (now equally reduced, as well those who went thither on their own Bottoms, as they who were sent on the Charity) are so sensible, that they make it their Prayer,

> That unless the Constitution be altered, the Money which may here-after be granted for the Use of the Colony, may be applied for re-moving them to some other Part of his Majesty's Dominions, where they may be able to support themselves and Families, and be of use to the Publick, instead of a Burthen to it as they are now.

THOMAS STEPHENS,

London, April 26th, 1742.

Agent for the People of Georgia.

A
Brief Account
of the
Causes
that have retarded the
Progress
of the
Colony of Georgia, *&c.*

A

BRIEF ACCOUNT

OF THE

CAUSES

That have retarded the

PROGRESS

OF THE

Colony of GEORGIA,

IN

AMERICA;

Attefted upon OATH.

BEING

A proper CONTRAST

TO

A State of the Province of

GEORGIA.

Attefted upon OATH;

And fome other Mifreprefentations on the
fame Subject.

LONDON:
Printed in the Year M.DCC.XLIII.

A Brief Account of the Causes
that have retarded the Progress
of the Colony of Georgia, &c.

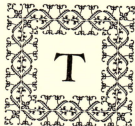

THE severe Grievances and Distresses of the Inhabitants of *Georgia*, had been so frequently and fruitlessly represented to the Honourable Body constituted, as they conceived, for the very purposes of preventing and redressing them, that their Application to a higher Power seemed the only * remaining Hope and Dependance of the unhappy People. After the Proofs produced at the Bar of the Honourable House of Commons, it can be thought no extravagant Assertion, that their Grievances and Oppressions were thought to be such, as were before unexampled under any *British* Government: And, if the Inexperience of their Agent in the Conduct of that Affair (where the Quality, Interest and Number of his Opponents might have discouraged a Person much better qualifyed) terminated, for that time, in some Censure upon himself, without the compleat Relief of his unfortunate Constituents; yet his Duty and their Distresses stimulate him sufficiently, to revive his Application in their Behalf, as he is satisfied, that the Justice and Compassion of a *British* Parliament will be extended to their present Grievances after further Information and

* Appendix, No. XXXIV.

Attention, and prevent, for the future, such Oppressions, as they have so long and unjustly languished under.

It may well be thought amazing, at the first View, that a Colony, which has been erected at such a considerable publick Expence to *Great Britain*, and further encouraged by such Numbers of private Donations, should be in a more indigent Condition, than any of those, which were settled at the Expence and Risque of private Adventurers, to the final Satisfaction and Happiness of Multitudes, and the reciprocal Benefit of their Mother Realms. And as it is impossible that any Settlement could ever be enterprized with greater Professions of Humanity, Compassion and Disinterestedness, than were the avow'd Views of sending a Colony to *Georgia*, it may seem as strange, that the Complaints they have proved were Oppressions of the *most essential* kind; and such as are really incompatible with the Nature, or *very Existence* of any *British* Government: But their Experience has discovered the Difference of Professions and Performances to be as wide, as that of Truth and Error; and indeed were it possible to *suppose* Affluence, where Property is unascertained and insecure, meer Abundance would never be deemed an Equivalent for the Want of those Rights and Liberties, which *British* Subjects consider as an unalienable Inheritance and Patrimony.

The Wisdom and Justice of the Regulations they have smarted under, are truly too profound for their Comprehension. If the Liberties of former Colonies had really prevented, or even retarded their own Increase and Prosperity, or their Benefit and Advantage to *Great-Britain*, some *political* Reasons, at least, might have been alledged for them; but when the *very contrary* is self-evident, whatever may have been the Designs of the many Discouragements they have felt, their ill Circumstances are too evidently owing, in a great Degree, to the Want of *that Liberty*, which has enriched and established the neighbouring Colonies, and extended the *British* Trade and Empire in Proportion.

To complain has been always deemed the wretched Privilege of the miserable; yet even this has been, as much as possible, obstructed; insomuch, that the *Georgians* are indebted to the Justice and Liberty of their neighbouring Province, for a Seal to many of the annexed Depositions, which they could never obtain in *Georgia*. And indeed any Magistrate, who has an Inclination to continue one, must be deaf to any Publick Complaint of the Discontented; which, it may be truly affirmed, all the Inhabitants, who are independent, and out of Office, with *great Reason* are, while they must be ever industrious to give a Sanction to all such Misrepresentations of the State of Things, as are contrary to Fact, and Insults on Reason itself. And under what Influence such Misrepresentations have been procured, will best be evinced from some of the following Depositions.

Bitterness is too naturally the Language of the Injur'd; But as their past Sufferings are irrevocable, they are more anxious to prevent their Continuance, than to perpetuate the disagreeable Remembrance of them by an unavailing Resentment; and it is with such a View the following Papers are tender'd to the worthy and unprejudiced. If a fair Account of their Hardships should inevitably infer any Thing disadvantageous to the Characters of any other, it has been their Misfortune, that it is in their Power to do it *with Justice*, and not in their Power to omit it without being unjust to themselves. They decline all Aggravation, both as difficult and unnecessary; they leave the Advantages of Art and Eloquence, to Persons and Things, which are better qualified to *divert*, than to *bear* Inspection; and rest the Validity of their Complaints upon the plain, but faithful Depositions of Men, who have been made to *feel* what they may be unable to express with the strictest Method and Propriety.

But before I proceed to these Proofs, I shall take the Liberty to make a brief and plain Enquiry into the principal Causes, that have either retarded, or totally prevented the Increase and Establishment of *Georgia*, which indeed amounts to a Consideration, how far his Majesty's most gracious Intentions, in the Settlement of *Georgia*, have been accomplished and fulfilled by those Persons appointed for that Purpose.

We find from the Preamble to his Majesty's Charter to the Trustees, that the professed Designs of establishing the Colony of

Georgia were for making Provision for the industrious Poor, for strengthening *South-Carolina*, and increasing Trade and Navigation.

To which end, his Majesty was pleased to grant in Trust (not as Proprietors) to several of the Nobility and Gentlemen, all the Soils, Grounds, *&c.* within the Limits of *Georgia*, together with all the Priviledges and Pre-eminences, which his Majesty by his Letters Patent might or could grant.

From which, it seems very natural to apprehend, that nothing *short* of the Rights and Liberties of other British Subjects or Colonies, were intended to be allowed such Settlers, who certainly took the same for granted, before their leaving *Great-Britain*, to go to *Georgia*. But in Consequence of such his Majesty's gracious Intentions, and from the Situation of that Frontier they were to defend, rather expected such further Immunities and Encouragements, as his Majesty, in his Royal Bounty and Goodness, could and might grant a Colony, honour'd with his Name, within the Limits of a British Constitution and Government, the *only one* they expected to be regulated by, and subject to. It seems to them, that the Trustees, thus empower'd and enjoyn'd to confer *all* the King's Rights, expressed in the Charter, could convey *no other* Rights, nor *no less;* and that every Grant or Tenure of theirs, short of such, was contrary to the Charter, and an illegal and unconstitutional Reserve. And that every other Act of theirs and their Magistrates there, contrary to the Laws and Usages of *Great-Britain*, and to the known Rights and Liberties of *English* Subjects, were oppressive and arbitrary, and directly destructive of the *express Intentions* of the Charter, and the *Settlement* of the Province, which has been but too evidently demonstrated by the present Condition of it.

The only Restraint the Charter expresses, is with Regard to the Quantity of Land to be granted to any Settler, which is limited to five hundred Acres. The Wisdom and Equity of this Limitation is undoubtedly very clear in the Main, as it is preventive of those unreasonable, and even impolitick Monopolies of Land, which have greatly retarded the Strength and Improvement of other

Places; and yet perhaps in some particular Cases, where a Settler might be both able and willing to cultivate and improve more, some further Allowance, in proportion to such Circumstances, might neither be unreasonable nor impolitick. But notwithstanding this Limitation of the *Quantity*, was the *only* Limitation warranted by the Charter; one of the first things done was, reserving the very best Lands, under a pretence that they were kept for the vagrant *Indians*, * who were brought over here, and imposed on the Publick for Kings; and so circumscribing and restraining the Rights and Titles of such others, as were not thought too good or valuable for the People, as to extinguish every Incitement to Industry and Improvement: By which means, almost all the best Lands continue unappropriated, to any Settler at least, and uncultivated to this Day. If this Method of establishing Colonies has nothing else to recommend it, we must allow it to be *new* at least, and acknowledge the Inhabitants would have been as unreasonable to expect any Advantages from it, as to hope for Miracles. But as if the Difficulties arising from indifferent Lands, and discouraging Tenures, were not sufficient to humble and prepare them, for the other Severities they have met with, they were totally prohibited the Importation, Use, or even Sight † of Negroes. In Spight of all Endeavours to disguise this Point, it is as clear as Light itself, that Negroes are as essentially necessary to the Cultivation of *Georgia*, as Axes, Hoes, or any other Utensil of Agriculture. So that if a Colony was designed able but to subsist itself, their Prohibition was inconsistent; if a Garrison only was intended, the very Inhabitants were needless: But all Circumstances considered, it look'd as if the Assistance of human Creatures, who have been called Slaves, as well as subject to the Treatment of such, were incongruous with a System, that proceeded to confer the Thing, but to spare the *Odium* of the Appellation. Experience would too soon have taught them the Parity of their Conditions, in Spight of a meer *nominal* Difference. The only *English* Clergy-

* See the Report of the Committee of *South Carolina*, appointed to examine into the Proceedings of *Georgia*.

† Appendix, No. XXIX.

men, who were ever countenanced there, declared they *never desired to see* Georgia *a rich, but a Godly Colony;* and the blind Subjection the poor *Saltzburghers* are under, to the Rev. Mr. *Boltzius*, who has furnished such extraordinary Extracts in some Accounts of *Georgia*, published here, will be too evident from some of the annexed Depositions to call for any Descant.

The pretended Content and Satisfaction of the People of *Ebenezer*, without Negroes, will plainly * appear to be the Dictates of spiritual Tyranny, and only the wretched Acquiescence of People, who were in Truth, unacquainted with the Priviledge of choosing for themselves.

It is acknowledged indeed that the present War, and late Invasion, may furnish the Enemies of the Colony, with the most plausible Objections that could occur, against the Allowance of *black* Slaves; but these Reasons have not always existed, nor have the Trustees ever declared any Resolution to admit them, at any other Juncture. But if it plainly appears that *Georgia*, as a Colony, cannot barely *exist* without them, surely an Admission of them under Limitations, suitable to the present Situation of Affairs, is absolutely necessary to its support; since Want and Famine must be more dreadful and insuperable Invaders, than any living Enemy: Besides, the Honourable Trustees were informed by a Letter from Mr. *Stirling* and others, of the Falshood, of the contented and comfortable Situation of the People of *Darien* were affirmed to be in; and that *they were* † *bought with a Number of Cattle, and extensive Promises of future Rewards*, when they signed their Petition against Negroes.

It is established also by their Charter, that the Trustees, *shall and may form and prepare Laws, Statutes and Ordinances, fit and necessary for and concerning the Government of the said Colony, and not repugnant to the Laws and Statutes of* England.

But notwithstanding this, and although the Trustees were apply'd to by the ‡ People, for a *Body of Laws for the Government of*

* Appendix, No. VIII. and IX.
† Appendix, No. V. VI. and VII.
‡ In a Representation from the Grand Jury.

the Colony; *as the want of them render'd it exceeding difficult, for either Grand or Petit Juries, to discharge in a proper Manner, the great Duties incumbent on them by their Oaths;* yet they never received, or heard of any other Laws except *the Salique Law, one for the Prohibition of Negroes,* and a third, *prohibiting the Use and Importation of spirituous Liquors;* any one of which was sufficient to prevent, or defeat the Settlement of a Colony in their Situation: Neither would the most judicious Application of the Money, advanced for its Establishment, have compensated for such fundamental Errors in the Constitution. It seems a little odd, that *three* Laws should be form'd, that had a visible Tendency to distress the Colony, and *not one* fairly calculated for its Increase and Encouragement; none that might make it seem *related* to a *British* Government. The Intention of this Omission, I shall not presume to explain, but 'tis certain that enacting and executing of Laws, *not* repugnant to the Laws of *England,* must have prevented a great deal of such Government, as the poor People have complained of; much indefinite and unwarrantable Imprisonment, Fining, Punishing and Forfeiting.

The Trustees are further impowered by their Charter, *to erect and constitute Judicatures and Courts of Record, or other Courts, for the hearing and determining of all manner of Crimes, Offences, Pleas, Processes, &c.* As well as to *appoint Governors, Judges, Magistrates, &c. for the Government of the Colony.*

We may very naturally infer, that this Power of constituting Courts of Justice, implys a due and regular Application of that Power, to be the Duty of the Trustees; and yet there is not so much as a Magistrate in two of the Towns (there being but five in the Province) *viz. Darien* and *Ebenezer,* * though one of them is thirty, and the other above 50 Miles off any Settlement, that has a Magistrate: The populous Town of *Augusta,* which is said to furnish out *two thousand Horses in the Spring,* and which, by the Trustees publish'd Account, was resorted to by *six hundred* white Men, †

---

* Appendix, No. VI and VIII.
† See a State of the Colony attested upon Oath.

employed on the *Indian* * Trade, had none, till lately one *Kent* was said to have a Commission given him by the Trustees, when 'twas expected they would have punished him, for having dared to act as a Justice of Peace, and imprison † and punish the People, without any but a verbal Commission from Mr. *Oglethorpe*, under whom he has a Military Command of Men: If they really believed this Town to be so populous, why was it without even one civil Magistrate? But for the real State and Poverty of this Place, we refer to the Affidavits of Mr. *O'Brien*, and *John Gardner*.

Savannah and *Frederica*, (the two principal Towns) must be allowed to have had extraordinary Magistrates indeed, some of whom may not have wilfully injured the People; tho' others have declared from the Bench, that *the Laws of* England *were no Laws in* Georgia;‡ made false Imprisonments, § discharged Grand Juries, whilst Matters of Felony lay || before them, ⚹ intimidated Petit-Juries; in short, stuck at nothing to oppress the People; neither has there been any Governor appointed, or any Records rightly kept for the People to appeal home from; which, whether it is so designed or not, prevents them from applying so regularly to his Majesty, for the Benefit and Redress of his distressed Subjects.

The Charter also enjoyns *the training, instructing and exercising the Militia for the Safety of the Colony, the Use of Martial Law in Time of actual War and Invasion, and the Erection of Forts for the Defence of the Colony;* notwithstanding which, it is said there has been no Muster there these four or five Years, and that there is not a defensible ** Fort in the Province. The Want of Martial Law they cannot indeed justly complain of, since they have had nothing else but that, or worse, in Time of Peace, which possibly may have

---

* Appendix, No. X and XI.
† See Petition of the Grand Jury, 1741.
‡ Appendix, No. XVIII.
§ Appendix, No. XXVI.
|| See Petition of the Grand Jury, 1741.
⚹ Appendix, No. XVIII.
** Appendix, No. II.

been one Reason for no Musters, * since it might be judged bad Politicks to train a People up to the Knowledge and Use of Arms, who were to be ruled by *nothing else*. Besides indeed frequent Musters would have exposed the real Scarcity of People in a Place, that has been so diligently misrepresented, as populous, and what not.

It is said, that the Trustees have altered the Tenures of the Lands; but are they yet so good as in any of the rest of his Majesty's Provinces, where Lands are granted in free and common Socage? Have any ill Effects attended such full Tenures? And have any good ones followed the Want of them? A sufficient Term has been allowed for the Experiment, and can the ill Success of it be an Argument for its Continuance in *any* Degree, or Shape, or upon any Pretence or Colour? And of the ill Tendency of this destructive Tenure, the Trustees had a very early Warning from a Gentleman of undoubted Integrity, and a Member of their own Body, which we shall take the Liberty to recite in his own Words.

Right Honourable the Lords and other Honourable Trustees for establishing the Colony of Georgia, *in* America.

I Conceive I am summoned hither at this Time, with the other *Trustees*, to hear and debate on *one* or *two dangerous Mistakes*, which have happened in the *Beginning* of Settling the Infant Colony of *Georgia*; the Good and Prosperity whereof no Man can have more at Heart than I have had: But, as I have often with Sorrow found at this Board, my Want of Eloquence hath caused the Motions of my sincere good Intentions for the Colony to pass *unregarded*, I hope you will therefore excuse the Liberty I now take, of delivering in writing, what I pray to say on those two *pernicious* Mistakes.

The *first* of those two Evils is, concerning the Portions of the Land granted, to each Man, Heads of the Families sent thither on the Charity or otherwise; which Land *is of no Value now, nor ever can be, until culti-*

* Appendix, No. XXXII.

vated and improved by their great Labour and Expence: Yet that Estate is limited to an *Intail Male,* whereby, upon any Failure of *Male* Issue, all the Females and their Posterity are entirely cut off from all Fruits and Advantages of their Parents Labour, and Industry, for one or more Ages; which is the Childrens *natural Right,* and ought in *Justice* to be secured to them. Moreover the subjecting the same Estate to so many *terrifying Forfeitures,* renders it the more precarious. There never was an Instance of any Lands ever granted in the *British* Plantations, under *such Limitations* and *Forfeitures,* before this, which will be attended with *many evil Consequences.*

It will not only *defeat* the charitable Intentions of those many good and generous Benefactors, who have contributed very liberally, and those who shall do so, for the comfortable Settlement, Provision and Support of many *poor distressed Families,* and their Children; but also *deprive* the Females of their *just* Right *given them by God and Nature:* This extraordinary Tenure will be a *great Means of de-peopling the Colony, as fast as you can people it;* for those poor People, who now gladly embrace *any* Terms or Conditions to be removed from their present Distresses *here,* will, as soon as the *Trustees* have done feeding them in *Georgia,* remove themselves into other Plantations, where they may have Lands *given them gratis,* under the *best Tenure the Crown could ever grant,* without paying *any Quit Rent,* or *other Consideration* for it.

Much more might be said to shew the *mischievous Effects,* which that *unreasonable Tenure,* by which the Lands are now granted to those, who are settled in *Georgia,* will *unavoidably have on that Colony.* But I beg Leave to say something of the *Jews,* who, to the Number of between Forty and Fifty, have procured themselves to be already settled there contrary to the Will, and without the Consent of the *Trustees,* and there are more of their Nation now going over to them.

I humbly conceive these shocking Matters require your most serious Attention; for unless you speedily take some vigorous Resolutions to suppress effectually the two great Evils aforesaid, *Georgia* will soon become a *Jewish* Colony, for that all the *Christians* there, will, for the Reasons aforesaid, fall off and desert it, as Leaves from a Tree in Autumn, until there will not be a valuable *Christian* remaining, except some few *Carpenters, Sawyers, Smiths, &c.* whom the *Jews* will find most necessary and useful, and encourage them to remain to be employed in their Buildings and otherwise, and that all *Christian* Benefactions for that *Colony* will soon cease. Therefore for these Considerations, I beg Leave to recommend the speedy entering into proper Measures for *preventing*, as well the *Ruin of the Colony of* Georgia, *as the Reproach and Scandal of the Trustees.*

> I am,
> with the greatest Respect,
> Right Honourable and Honourable,
> Your most obedient Servant,
> THOMAS CORAM.

Georgia Office, 27th
   March, 1734.

But it is farther to be observed, that many of the original Grants consist of one Contraction, a Figure, three Words, and the two initial Letters of the General's Name. And the Manner of declaring Lands forfeited, as well as taking from one, and giving to another, is really incredible. *

It was the Sense of the Commons of *Great-Britain*, that the *Georgians* ought to be allowed the Use and Importation of Rum, from which it seems a very natural Inference, that they meant the Importation of it on the *same* Terms, and with no other Restrictions, or Limitations, than it was imported into the other *British* Colonies. What Regard has been paid to this Opinion of that great Body, such true Friends to the Settlement, must best appear from the Act of the Trustees, in Conformity to that Report, which is said to be loaded with such Restraints, Difficulties, and Limitations, of which *their Magistrates* are to be Judges, as to be little better in Effect than a Prohibition, and has not been hitherto, as we are informed, approved of by the Right Honourable the Lords of Trade.

The Trustees alledge, in Extenuation of many past Abuses, that they have altered the Form of Government, having appointed a President and Assistants. Whereas the Charter requires the Appointment of a Governour to be *approved by his Majesty*, who is to give Security for a due Observation of the several Acts relating to Trade and Navigation, which has never been complied with in any

* Appendix, No. XIX. and II.

particular: And, as if this Evasion were not sufficiently inexcusable, to compleat the Farce, the Magistrates, so very liable to be justly *appealed from*, are the very Assistants, who must be *appealed to;* which, without the least Reflection, sufficiently explains this *notable* Amendment both of the Intention and Mode of Governing.

The Administrators of such a Polity should, in Propriety, be invested with some suitable Resemblance of Character and Equity: Mr. *Thomas Jones*,* who had not been a little active in procuring †️ several Informations against such Malecontents, as they were called (who must have been stupid to have been otherwise) was one of the venerable Bench; and Mr. *Henry Parker* another, who had signed a Complaint, was not restored, till he had contradicted the Truths he subscribed in it: Mr. *Fallowfield* was formerly a Magistrate, but for daring to *feel*, and to complain of it, and to allow others to do the same, he was immediately deemed unqualified for any Part of the Administration, and cast out as a Malecontent, as will appear from Mr. *Verelst*'s very solemn Notification of it to him in the Appendix. ‡️.

It is said the Trustees keep no Store now, but it is answered, that their Officers do in their Names, that only the Name of their *Store* is changed into their *Magazine*, by Virtue of the Key of which, *T. Causton* has formerly commanded §️ the whole Colony, as it is feared *Thomas Jones* does still, tho' it is reported the Trustees lately removed him from *some* of his Employments, to appease the People, with Regard to a Felony, which produced an Indictment against him; but from which his Brother Magistrates screen'd || him, till he went to *Frederica* (where the General is) for Protection.

As the Complainants of *Georgia* have been industriously represented, as a few clamorous, unreasonable People, spirited up by one Man, who stiles himself their Agent, their Number will best

---

* Late High Constable of, and well known in *Holbourn*.
†️ See the Secretary's Journals printed by the Trustees.
‡️ Appendix, No. XXXVI.
§️ Appendix, No. XXIII.
|| Appendix, No. XXIV. and XXV.

appear from the annexed List, which cannot be equall'd * by any Catalogue of Persons, the Trustees could reckon contented, tho' all their Magistrates and Dependants were to be included in it: As to his being able, or even desirous to foment a Clamour he has no particular Interest in, the Absurdity is Self-manifest, and sufficiently exposed, by former Complaints of the People,† when he was little known among them, and when he was in *England* before ‡. His joyning the People in Opposition to his Father's Conduct, has been thought a strong Objection to his own, with many: To this he takes Leave to say, that while he is conscious of all dutiful Affection and Regard for a Parent, he can see no Cause for his being insensible to the Suggestions of Truth and Reason, and of the Hardships of his Fellow Sufferers: If his Father's great Age, and several Misfortunes, dispose him to be contented with a poor Provision for *one*, his Son cannot discover, that filial Duty obliges him to think in the same manner; but were his Father's Concurrence necessary on such a Score, he might even appeal to his own Journals published by the Trustees, and to several Extracts of Letters to himself.

Much might be added very pertinently, to furnish a more strict and particular Account of the real Grievances of the People of *Georgia*, and the insuperable Impediments to its ever deserving the *Name* of a Colony on the present Foundation: In Truth it has the Force of a thousand Arguments to reflect, that for four Years past no Person has attempted to settle in *Georgia* at his own Expence, which never is the Case of any new Colony, where People are satisfied with the Plan and Scheme of the Conductors of it; and it is utterly opposite to common Sense, to conceive, that a People of depress'd Circumstances, with very few of Name or Interest, can find any Pleasure or *Account* in complaining, for the meer Sake

* Appendix, No. XXXV.

† A Letter in the Year 1735, signed by the principal Inhabitants of the Colony; a Representation 1737; another Representation 1738, signed by 117.

‡ A Petition, 1740, from the Servants out of their Time; a Remonstrance, 1740, from the People; a Petition to his Majesty, 1740; an Address to his Majesty, 1741.

of Complaint, in Opposition to Persons of Condition, Opulence and Reputation: If they really enjoyed the common Liberties of their Fellow Subjects, and murmured under those Circumstances of Government their Fellow Colonies are happy from, such an unreasonable Discontent might very justly be discountenanced. Let this *one fair* Experiment be made, and the People of *Georgia* little doubt, without being Burthensome to their Mother Country, to subsist themselves, and by Degrees to become useful Subjects to his Majesty: Whereas, far from being benefitted by any publick Contribution, on the *present Footing*, they can consider it as nothing, but strengthening a Sort of Government, that is an insupportable Plague * and Discouragement, instead of a Support and Protection. And, it is but too evident, that all Projects to devise a better Constitution of Government than the *British*, for *British* Subjects, has proved sad *Quack Politicks* in the Event, destroying or torturing the Patients, and disgracing the Prescriber: The People are convinced with Pleasure, that many Gentlemen of the Trust are far from intending the Oppression of their Fellow Creatures, or Fellow Subjects, and that some of them have publickly expressed their Aversion to all such Measures, as were injurious to the Colony, and *contrary* to the Charter: But Persons who have never been out of *England*, cannot be perfect Judges of the Encouragements necessary to the Establishment of a new Colony, in that Climate; nor easily discover the Truth, at so great a Distance; or they would no more continue in a known Error, than suffer such illegal Excesses of Power to be exercised over the People, to whom they are Guardians; nor ever permit so injurious a Trade to be carried on with the publick Money, without giving the Publick Credit in their Accounts, for what has been so extorted †, contrary to their Intention, from the poor People; for whose Benefit the Money so employed *was given:* But how can the Trustees account to the Publick, unless their Agents (whose Accounts were never made up) account to them? The only Trustee who is there, must be able indeed to form a pretty general Judgment of Affairs;

* Appendix, No. XV., XVI., XXVIII. and XXIX.
† Appendix, No. III., XVII., XX., XXI., XXII., XXIII.

but the People cannot forbear considering him, as the greatest Enemy to the Colony, who was called the Father of it, before the Regiment was obtain'd, which became necessary the sooner, from our Imprudence in provoking and alarming the *Spaniards* in Time of Peace, by erecting a Fort, garrisoned with upwards of 20 Men, directly opposite to, and in Sight of the *Spanish* Look-out on St. *Juans*, which is said to be without the Limits assigned by the Charter. And since which Appointment; there is scarcely any Species of Oppression, short of Life and Limb, which may not be unanswerably proved to have been arbitrarily exerted by this Gentleman, who has publickly appeared an Invader of the natural * Rights of Mankind, and the particular Priviledges of his Fellow Subjects; and if ever a Colony is to be effected under his Auspices, it must never consist of *Britons:* The Lands must be interdicted to his Majesty's Subjects, and instead of preventing the Importation of Slaves, they must import none but such: If these Affirmations be thought severe, let the actual and lawless Severities he has treated Multitudes with, be duly ponder'd, and the unavailing Privilege of complaining, must be thought a very poor Recompence. If it be said he is not present to defend himself, that is not the least Misfortune to the Colony of *Georgia, where he is;* they will never revoke any thing they have hitherto affirmed and approved against him, but have *much more* to add to it, whenever they shall be so happy as to be called on for that Purpose: Some light Specimens will appear in the following Affidavits voluntarily made, the Effect of no Art or Management; collected with no View to disguise or amuse, but to inform and convince, the natural and plain Language of oppressed Men, to which we refer the Reader.

* Appendix, No. I., II., IV., XXX., XXXI.

APPENDIX.

NUMBER I.

From FREDERICA.

SAMUEL PERKINS, late Inhabitant and second Bailiff of *Frederica*, in *Georgia*, aged thirty-nine Years and upwards, maketh Oath and saith, That he lived there five Years and upwards, and clear'd and fenced in five Acres of Land, whereof he planted one Acre and a half; built two good and habitable Houses in the Town of *Frederica*, and one good and habitable House on his five Acre Lot: That the Produce of the Land so clear'd, fenced in, and planted, was *never* sufficient to defray the Expence of maintaining his Servant who was employed thereon, and did well attend and keep clean the same, during the Season for Planting, for four Years together: That he kept a Store well furnish'd with Goods from his first Arrival, but that *James Oglethorpe*, Esq; who was either entrusted with, or took to himself, the *sole Command of All*, would not allow this Deponent, to sell Iron Goods, because Mr. *Lawley* sold such: That about two Years after his Arrival, he, this Deponent, sent *James Shepherd* to the Guard-House, for abusing this Deponent and Mr. *John Caldwell* third Bailiff, in the Execution of their Office, in order to be punished, unless he repented, and ask'd Pardon for his Fault: But that Mr. *Horton*, then Commander in Chief at *Frederica*, (Mr. *Oglethorpe* being absent) released the said *Shepherd*, and threatned this Deponent to *lock him to an Oar* in the Scout-Boat, and to *starve* the said *Caldwell*, for securing the Person of the said *Shepherd*. That finding he could not live by Cultivation, and being bred a Coach-maker, this Deponent would have wrought at his Trade, and had Chaises bespoke of him by Lieut. Colonel *Cockran*, and Captain *Gascoigne*, and in *Carolina*; but that the Honourable *James Oglethorpe*, Esq; Colonel of his Majesty's Regiment of Foot, continuing still the sole Commander of all Affairs in the Southern Division of *Georgia*, as well Civil as Military, *would not suffer him to work at his Trade*; and farther, That the said *Oglethorpe*, on or about *November*, 1738; did say to this Deponent, "*By G - - - I will burn the first Chaise you make;*" for which Reason this Deponent durst never make any during his stay in *Georgia*; nor so much as *Cart Harness* for his Neighbours, *that* being also forbid in the same manner; tho' a Sett was bespoke, Materials provided, and the Work begun.

[290]

That at a Court holden at *Frederica, February* 4, 1739–40, a Complaint was made by *William Allen*; That Mr. *Thomas Hawkins*, Chief Magistrate, owed him Eight Shillings and Six-pence; which the said *Hawkins* acknowledg'd in open Court to be due, and promised to pay the same; but the Plaintiff's suit being renew'd at sundry Courts, and the Money not being paid, this Deponent and Mr. *Francis Moore*, Recorder, on the 4th of *February* 1740, did, in Conjunction, write a handsome Letter to the said *Hawkins*, (who would not appear that Day either as Defendant or Magistrate) desiring him to shew Cause why his Goods should not be distrain'd; when he return'd for Answer, that his Health would not permit him to come to Court, and desired not to be condemn'd unheard: But this Deponent having seen him laughing and very merry, within an Hour before, as the Constable, by whom the Letter was sent did inform the Court, he was, when he deliver'd it; it was the Opinion of the Court and every one present, that a Distraint should be granted, for satisfying the said Complainant *William Allan*, which was done accordingly: But upon the Officer's putting the same into Execution, *the said* Oglethorpe, *sent for the said* Caldwall *Bailiff, when the Goods seiz'd were replevyed, and the said* Hawkins *did say he should appeal to the Trustees.*

That the said *Hawkins*, having, at times, done some very wrong things in Court, which had brought the Authority of it to a very low Ebb, insomuch *that the People were under no Government:* As for Instance, *James Bland* being taken into Custody, and kept a long while confin'd, for selling Rum to some Soldiers, who swam on board his Master, Mr. *Townsend*'s Vessel, and swearing they would have Rum, took it by force, drank thereof and returned ashore; but afterwards making a second Attempt, two of the said Soldiers were drown'd: After a long Confinement, the said *Bland*, at a Court held at *Frederica* aforesaid, did move for his Tryal; when the said *Hawkins* answer'd, *that he should not be tryed, for if the other Magistrates had no Bread to lose, yet he had; and that he would not disoblige the General for any Body:* wherefore, finding the said *Oglethorpe* did justify all such Proceedings of the said *Hawkins*, and condemn'd and villified whatever was done by this Deponent; he did in *August* 1740, lay down his Commission; as did Mr. *Francis Moore*, Recorder, at the same time, and *for the same Reasons*, as the said *Moore* did tell this Deponent and others.

That the said *Oglethorpe* did tell this Deponent, *That he would ruin him for distraining the said* Hawkins's *Goods, were he Lord Chief Justice.*

That *David Fellows*, Coxswain of the said *Oglethorpe*'s Boat, abused this Deponent in his own House; whereupon a Constable was sent for, and the said *Fellows* striking the said Constable, who got a Warrant for the said *Fellows*, and by Virtue of which did carry the said *Fellows* to the Guard-House; *for which the said* Oglethorpe *broke the said Constable.*

That at a Court held the 27th of *August*, 1740, *Thomas Herd*, and *Samuel Davidson*, returning *Samuel Lee*, *John Harding*, *Thomas Archer*, *John Shelleday*, *Richard Hart*, and *Samuel Gough*, who cohabited each with his respective Female unmarried, the Grand Jury found a Bill against them; and the said *Hawkins* did declare in open Court, *that the said* Oglethorpe *had got the Proceedings of the said Court, and did forbid the said* Hawkins *to proceed farther in that Affair*, adding, that the said General told him, *the Constables were indictable for returning, and the Grand Jury for finding a Bill against them, which violent Proceedings of the said* Oglethorpe *were blamed, even by the said* Hawkins.

That this Deponent having lived in good Repute among his Neighbours, and the Officers of the Regiment, was yet at last abandoned by them all, and *that by Order from the said* Oglethorpe, as Capt. *Desbrisay* and several others did confess to this Deponent and his Wife.

That in 1738, he received a *German* Family, consisting of a Man, his Wife, Son of nineteen, and Daughter seven Years of Age, *for which he gave Bond to the Trustees Store* for seventeen Pounds ten Shillings, Sterling, in Capt. *William Thomson*'s Name; *the same being to bear Interest at* 10 per Cent. after the Expiration of two Years, if unpaid. That the Trustees being indebted to this Deponent more than that Sum, he demanded the said Bond, before he left the Province, *but the said* Oglethorpe *refused to deliver him the same; tho' he the said* Oglethorpe *did, at the same time, acknowledge, that the Money for the said Family was paid.* That the said Bond is still out against this Deponent, *and* 10 per Cent. *for the same running on.* And moreover, the *said* Oglethorpe *having vow'd Revenge against this Deponent, for distraining the said* Hawkins's *Goods*, would not see him, nor *suffer his Account to be made up before he left the Colony of* Georgia, *tho' he did often apply to the said* Oglethorpe, in order thereto. And further Mr. *Thomas Jones* did inform this Deponent, *that the said* Oglethorpe *swore, he should never be paid one Farthing*, and that
　　is due from the Trustees; and for Boat-hire, and other Services done at the late Expedition against St. *Augustine.**

That having 18 tame Hogs, the said *Oglethorpe* issued an Order, after

* 90 *l.* the whole.

the Fortifications were begun, (and it was said were to be carried on round the Town) That no Hogs should be kept within it, when this Deponent sent his Hogs to his little Plantation, from whence they stray'd to Town in about six Months thereafter; where, without any Notice given, three Sows big with young, and three Barrows were shot by one *Pighly*, a Servant to the Trustees, (as this Deponent has been informed) the said *Pighly* being appointed for that Purpose.

That as this Deponent was getting the Remainder of the said Hogs into his Yard, *Thomas Hunt*, the *General*'s Servant Boy, did, at the same time, run with his Gun in Pursuit of them, and say *that he was ordered by the General to shoot them.*

That notwithstanding he was unable to live by cultivating Lands, on which he has built without a proper Title; that Promises made by the Trustees of supplying the People with Servants, of a Bounty on Produces raised, *&c.* were never fulfilled; and that the Complaints of these and many other Things were universal; yet, from his Hopes, that they might reach his Majesty's Ears, and the Colony be under his Royal Protection, he should not have forsaken his Improvements in *Georgia* so soon, *could he have borne the said* Oglethorpe's *Usage, who is become a Terror not to* Evil Doers, *but to* innocent Men.

SAMUEL PERKINS.

South-Carolina, ff.
    Sworn before me the
    28th of *Nov.* 1741,
OTHNIEL BEALE, J. P.

NUMBER II.

From FREDERICA.

JOHN ROBERSON, aged thirty-three Years and upwards, and *Joseph Cannon*, aged 20 Years and upwards, late of *Frederica* in *Georgia*, do make Oath and say, That in Company of 40 Families or more, commanded by *James Oglethorpe*, Esq; they did go to the said *Frederica*, at the first Settling thereof, which was in *March* 1735-6; when the said People did immediately build themselves *Palmetto Hutts*, by joint Labour, to shelter themselves from the Weather. That in *May* 1736, *by Command of the said* Oglethorpe, 22 of the said Inhabitants of *Frederica* went to making of

Bricks, sawing of Timber, and providing other Materials, in order to build 27 Brick-Houses, which Labour they continued till *December* following; when they had build only two Houses, which were left unfinished; and the poor People finding the Task too heavy for them were obliged to leave off, after having so lost thus much of their Labour, and having done nothing towards raising their own Provisions; tho' nine Months of their one Year's Provisions promised them by the Trustees were expended. That then 10 of the said Inhabitants of *Frederica* having petitioned the said *Oglethorpe* before he went for *England*, for one Tything of Land together, being a Mile Square, and obtaining the same in order to cultivate it; they made an Attempt to inclose the whole with a Worm Fence of six Foot high; and before it was finish'd, there being an Alarm that the *Spaniards* designed to invade them, Mr. *Horton*, Commander in Chief, in the said *Oglethorpe*'s Absence, ordered them not to go out of Sight of the Town, which happening in *February* 1736, hinder'd their Planting any thing considerable, or raising 20 Bushels of Corn, within that Tything that Year; *nor did* the Crop of all the other Inhabitants *far exceed* that Quantity.

That the said People did employ themselves in Cultivation and other Improvements the next Year, when their Corn was so destroy'd by the Drought, that it was the Opinion of every one, that the whole Settlement did not raise 100 Bushels.

That the said Inhabitants did *still* continue *to plant* with *great Pains* and *Industry* in the Year 1739, when the *best* Crop was raised of every Sort, that was seen at the said *Frederica* from the first Settling of it; and then Complaints were universal among the said Inhabitants, *that it did not answer the Expence of Planting, and attending it.*

That for the Encouragement of Planting this Year, Mr. *Thomas Hird* and *Samuel Davidson* went from House to House to acquaint the People, that General *Oglethorpe* said the Trustees had always allowed one Shilling *per* Bushel for any Sort of Grain *&c.* that was raised, and *that he would allow two that Year, but that these Deponents did never receive any such Bounty, nor hear of any that did.*

That in the Year 1740, being unable to support themselves by Cultivation, and complaining of the Restraints they were under, particularly the precarious Titles of their Lands, *the Publick Debts not being duly paid,* finding themselves dependant on the Trustees for a Support, *Falconer's* Lot being taken away, and a great, and the most valuable Part of the Common belonging to the Town; that many Things were promis'd by the

General and Trustees, whereof few were accomplished, *particularly Mulberry Trees; and the General interfering with the Magistrates, and obstructing the Course of their Proceedings*, with many Instances of Injustice and Oppression, to the great Injury of the Inhabitants, they began now to drop off, and many being engaged in the Expedition against St. *Augustine*, very little Planting was done this Year, and their Crop again complained of.

That in the Spring 1741, arbitrary Power having raged to a great Degree, and the Inhabitants in general having no Hopes of Redress, many of them left the Colony, as most of the others have done since, and are doing daily, *there being not above* 12 *of the first Settlers left, and none of them Planting*, but Mr. *Hawkins* and another or two at the most. *That some of the Lots of those gone off are filled with Officers of the Regiment, and the General's Servants.*

That on or about *August* 1740, Mr. *Hawkins*, first Magistrate, being adjudged by the Court to pay *William Allen 8s. 6d.* the said *Allen* went to him to demand the same; when the said *Hawkins* gave him abusive Language, which being returned by *Allen*, the said *Hawkins* ordered the Constable to carry him to Prison, for such his Behavior; but the Constable, as well as others, being wearied out with that trifling Debt, (which the said *Hawkins* would not pay, tho' he acknowledged it in several Courts to be due) loiter'd, and not punctually obeying the said *Hawkins* Command, where he was both Judge and Party; the said *Hawkins* then apply'd to Major *Cook* to send a Party of Soldiers, under Pretence that the People were rising in a Mob, and threaten'd to break open the Store; and accordingly a Party of Soldiers, consisting of 30 and upwards, were sent by the said *Cook*, and quarter'd 24 Hours at the Houses of *Samuel Davison* and Widow *Bennett*; for which the said *Cook* (finding that it was only a Dispute arising from the ill Conduct of the said *Hawkins*) was very angry, as was Ensign *Sutherland* the Officer sent with them. And further, *that the said Soldiers were posted Centinels, two at a Time, at the Door of the Court, which was then held by the Magistrates on Affairs of the Town.*

That *an Order was made by the said* Oglethorpe, *and publick Notice given, that no Hogs should come within the Town* after the First of *March*, 1739-40; and some Hogs belonging to the Inhabitants coming into the Town afterwards, *were shot by his own Servants, who did so by the said* Oglethorpe's *Order, notwithstanding they were a great Part of the People's Support*; and farther, that by the said *Oglethorpe's* Orders likewise, demanded of Mr. *Francis Moore* and others, who were Proprietors of the said Hogs, Four-pence a-piece for shooting them, and the Money was paid by the said Proprietors. That the only Pretence of some of them, for so destroying the Peoples Stocks, was, that they spoilt the Fortification, which *was only a Bank of sandy Earth with Puncheons and Fascines begun, but never finish'd, and great Part of it fallen down again.* That Major *Cook* the Engineer gave it as his Opinion, that the Hogs would do the Fortification no Damage, tho' it were compleated, *as once it was said to be intended.* That the Loss the People sustained hereby was considerable, tho' not to compare with that of the Soldiers killing such as were in the Woods: *Daniel Cannon,* who it is well known had a large Stock of them, having lost Fifty and upwards, as have others in Proportion, besides Black Cattle, *some of which being proved to be shot by the Soldiers,* there is great Reason to believe, that all that were lost were so destroyed by them, because they were out with their Guns; and *tho' Application has been made to the said* Oglethorpe, *even by Mr.* Hawkins *and others, he rather seem'd enclined to justify, than punish them, by saying poor Men! they must have the Liberty of going out with their Guns in this Country; and farther, that the said* Oglethorpe *did say they had a Title to come with their Guns on any Plantation fenced in.*

That Complaints of Grievances were universal and intolerable, or these Deponents would not have left their Improvements, which have never answer'd the Expence; nor, *if they are not seized by the General or Trustees,* they apprehend will never be of any Value to them now; unless his Majesty would be graciously pleased to save his Subjects from the Severities of the said *Oglethorpe,* and a Multitude of Evils arising from a Misconduct throughout the whole, by taking them under his Princely Care.

JOHN ROBERSON.
JOSEPH CANNON.

South-Carolina.
   Sworn before me this
   29th Day of *Nov.* 1741.
      OTHNIEL BEALE.

NUMBER III.

From FREDERICA.

SAMUEL DAVISON, late of *Frederica* in *Georgia*, aged forty Years and upwards, maketh Oath and saith, That whereas there was a Fort built on St. *George's* Island, about the time that *Frederica* was first settled, and (the said Fort being then garrison'd with 20 Men and upwards) that within ten Days after settling the said Fort, which was on or about *April* 1736, Captain *Ferguson*, Master of the Scout-Boat, employed by *James Oglethorpe*, Esq; being sent by the said *Oglethorpe*, to visit the said Garrison, did, conjunctly with Captain *Harmsdorff*, Commander of the said Garrison, withdraw the said Men therefrom, and bring them to the Island of *Amelia*; it being thought all the said Men were *in Danger of their Lives*, and *therefore it was their Request so to do*, as this Deponent was by some of them informed; as he was, that the said Fort was so near the *Spanish* Look-out, on St. *Juan's* River, where the *Spaniards were much more in Number than the said Garrison*, and that *the two Centinels could see each other from the said Fort, to the said Look-out.* That the said *Oglethorpe*, being angry with the said *Ferguson*, for having so done, he did send for this Deponent, then Constable, to warn the People at *Frederica*, and give them Notice of the Danger they were in; and did then say to this Deponent, that the said *Ferguson* was quite to blame; *"For what are a hundred Mens Lives to my Honour."*

That the said *Oglethorpe* did employ *Henry Manly* last Spring, as his Overseer, at *50 l. per Ann.* and fourteen Servants or more, besides him, to plough a Piece of the Common belonging to the Inhabitants of *Frederica*; and *which he the said* Oglethorpe *did take from them in the Year* 1739. And that the said Piece so plough'd, being planted with Corn, Pease and Potatoes, and attended by the said Men the whole Summer, *did not produce 20 Bushels of any Sort of Corn or Grain that was planted.*

That a small time before he left the said *Frederica*, which was in *October* last, the Inhabitants thereof, (*who never did raise their own Provisions*, and not being able to plant so much this Year, as the two or three preceeding Years for want of Servants, and through other Discouragements) *had nothing to feed on but Rice, brought from* Carolina; *which was sold dear*, till a Supply of eight Steers and eight or nine Barrels of Flower, (*which was sold at 26 s. Sterl. per hundred*) was brought thence, and sold to the Inhabitants.

MEMORANDUM, on the twenty-sixth Day of *November*, One thousand seven hundred and forty-one, before me *Abraham Croft*, Notary-Publick, in the Province of *South Carolina*, by lawful Authority, Admitted and Sworn, personally appeared Mr. *Samuel Davison*, and did on his Oath declare, that the foregoing Affidavit was just and true.

SAMUEL DAVISON.

Sworn before me the Day
  and Year aforesaid.   [L.S.]
ABRAHAM CROFT, N. P.

NUMBER IV.

From FREDERICA.

JOHN ROBERSON, late Bricklayer in *Frederica* in *Georgia*, maketh Oath and saith, That on or about the 9th of *August* last, being at Work on Mr. *Davison*'s House, adjoining to Mr. *Hawkins*'s, at the said *Frederica*; on which the said *Davison* was putting a new Roof, he did propose to the said *Hawkins*, to take up a few Shingles, and a Gutter belonging to the said *Hawkins*'s House, and put the said Gutter on the Party-Wall, to which the said *Hawkins* agreed; saying, that it would be a Benefit to him, because he must be obliged to alter the Roof of his own House soon; and the said *Davison* being to lay down a new Gutter at his own Expence, it would serve for both Houses, and which must save one half the Expence of the said Gutter to the said *Hawkins:* But the said *Hawkins* being out of Town, a Day or two after *General* Oglethorpe *sent to the said* Davison, *to forbid him to touch any thing belonging to the said* Hawkins*'s House*; tho' the said Gutter encroached 14 Inches on the said *Davison*'s Ground; and the said *Oglethorpe*'s own Carpenter said it might be done in a few Hours, and without harm to the * Doctor: That the said *Oglethorpe* did, soon after on the same Day, stand on the Sill of the said *Hawkins*'s Window, and put his Head up betwixt the Joice of the said *Davison*'s House, and *ordered Mr.* Cannon *to build the said Joice six Inches lower*; when the said *Cannon* told the said *Oglethorpe*, they were but six Inches deep; *when the said* Oglethorpe *replyed, he did not care, they might take it down, and build the House six Inches lower*; when the said *Cannon* said, that one Roof

* *Hawkins.*

would fall lower than the other, and that *therefore it would be impossible to make the said* Davison's *House tight, or keep it dry*; then the said *Oglethorpe* said, you might have thought of that before. And further, that the said *Oglethorpe* did then say to the said *Cannon*, if you touch a Shingle of what the Doctor (meaning *Hawkins*) has put down, I'LL SHOOT YOU, to which he added a great Oath, for you have done more than you can answer, in building so high, as to stop up the Doctor's Window. That the said *Davison*, being thus hinder'd from finishing his House, was forced to remove his Goods from the said House, (which was quite open) *and had only a Stable for his Family to be in, until this Deponent left the said* Frederica; which was on the 29th of *September*, 1741.

JOHN ROBERSON.

South-Carolina. ff.
   Sworn before me,
Nov. 28, 1741.
     OTHNIEL BEALE.

NUMBER V.

From DARIEN.

JOHN M'LEOD, late Minister of *Darien*, maketh Oath and saith, That the People settled in *Darien*, in the Province of *Georgia*, *January* 1735–6; expected something more than being able barely to support themselves and Families by clearing Land, and planting it, or feeding of Cattle: But in the Year *1738*, they found by Experience, *that the Produce of Land in* Georgia *did not answer the Expence of Time and Labour bestowed on it, either by themselves*, who had taken great Pains, *or indeed by any white Men at all*; even where neither Labour nor Money were wanting; tho' it has always proved ineffectual. *Therefore, it was then the Voice of the said People of* Darien, *to leave the Colony*, tho' the Improvements they had made were considerable; *and settle in some Province to the Northward, where they would be free from such Restraints, as rendered them incapable of subsisting themselves and Families.* That the Petition signed by some of them against Negroes, and in Opposition to the Representation from *Savannah*, dated the 9th of *December*, One thousand seven hundred and thirty-eight, (*which was afterwards signed by some of those who did sign the said Petition*) was wrote by a Person who had no Lott in *Darien, an Officer in General* Oglethorpe'*s Regiment, whom this Deponent has great Reason to believe, to have been sent by the said* General *to* Darien *on that purpose*; knowing that the said Person *had an Influence* on some of that People, he being their Countryman, and formerly Master of the Ship in which the said People came to *America.* That when this Deponent left the said *Darien*, in May last, the Widows and fatherless Children, then there, had a Promise of a *slender* Allowance of Provisions for some Months before; but *not being punctually given them, they were in a miserable Condition.* Nor where they suffered to go and get a livelyhood elsewhere, *which they were desirous of.* That the indented Servants, who survived the unhappy Action at *Musa,* when their time of Servitude was expired, *were under the Necessity of Listing in the Service of a bad Paymaster, or starving*; because *there was a Land-Scout and Water-Scout, to keep them from leaving the Place, by Land or Water*; and there were no others in the Place to give them Bread for their Labour, being then but four of the old Settlers there; and these being wearied of cultivating Ground for its Produce, *planted none last Season;* and the others (being about twenty in Number) were for the most part *Servants,* lately sent by the said *General* from another part of the Colony, *the rest being Servants* to the Trustees at *Darien.*

That all the People at the said *Darien are so strictly watched,* that this Deponent *could not get away* to *Frederica,* when he was coming off; nor from *Frederica* to *Savannah without a Permit:* And that the said *General refused* (as his then Secretary Mr. *Mariotte* told this Deponent) *to permit his indented Servant* to row his Boat from *Frederica* to *Savannah.* And farther this Deponent saith not.

JOHN M'LEOD.

South-Carolina. Personally appeared before me *Othniel Beale,* (one of his Majesty's Assistant Judges) the above-named *John M'Leod,* and made Oath, that the Contents above and foregoing, to which he subscribed his Name are true.

Sworn this 12th *Nov.* 1741.
   OTHNIEL BEALE.

Number VI.

From Darien.

Alexander Monroe, late of *Darien* in *Georgia*, aged thirty-five Years and upwards, maketh Oath and saith, That he arrived at the said *Darien*, together with his Wife, and one Child, in Company with near 40 Families more, in *February* 1735-6. That he cleared, fenced in, and planted five Acres of Land, built a good House in the Town, and made other Improvements, such as Gardening, *&c.* That he was never able to support his Family *by Cultivation*, tho' he planted the said five Acres three Years and had a good Crop. That he lived at *Darien* three Years, and might have continued there *longer*, tho' he never heard that any white Man was able to gain a *Livelihood by Planting*, had it not been for the Mismanagement of some People in Power, who exercised great Severity over the Inhabitants. That *John More M'Intosh*, who had the Care of the Trustees Stores kept at *Darien* for the Use of the People there, issued out the stipulated Allowance from the Trustees of Corn-kind, such as was *rotten*, tho', at the same time, there was good and wholesom Corn in the Stores, which the said *M'Intosh*, not only made Use of for himself and Family, but *fed his own Hogs* with the same, and this for two Months together. That their Allowance of Cheese was so bad, that the Inhabitants were obliged to throw it out to *Dogs*, tho' they *were starving* at the same time. That the said *M'Intosh* did employ this Deponent and others of the said Inhabitants in making a Fort, making a Landing-place, building a Store-house, Guard-house, and several other publick Works, promising in Behalf of the Trustees, that they should be paid for the same, but that this Deponent did never receive any *Money*, or other Consideration for such Service; tho' he, together with the others employed in the said Works, applied to Col. *Oglethorpe* in that Behalf.

That in the Year 1737, the Inhabitants of *Darien* were reduced to such *Distress* for Want of Provisions, having neither Corn, Pease, Rice, Potatoes, nor Bread-kind of any Sort, or Fish, nor Flesh of any kind in Store, after sending several Times to *Mr. Horton* at *Frederica* for a Supply, without being able to obtain it. That their *Necessity* pressed so much, that they were obliged, and did unanimously agree to go in a Body with the said *M'Intosh More* at the Head of them, and make a Demand of the said *Horton* to relieve their Wants; and, it being our *last Shift*, in Case we were not supplied there, to go from thence to *Savannah*, where we were informed was no Want in their Stores, and not to return *empty*, being one and all determined, that if we should meet with a Denial there, to break open the Stores in a publick Manner, *for Hunger will break thro' even Stone Walls*. But the said *Horton* not supplying us, sent us to Capt. *Gascoigne*, Commander of his *Majesty's Sloop* the *Hawk*, who spared us *two Barrels* of Flower, and *one Barrel* of Beef.

That Capt. *Hugh M'Kay* having exercised an *illegal* Power there, such as *judging* in all Causes, directing and ordering all Things according to *his* Will, as did the said *M'Intosh More*, by which *many unjust* and *illegal* Things were done. That not only the Servants of the said Freeholders of *Darien* were ordered to be *tyed up* and *whipt*; but also *this* Deponent, and *Donald Clark*, who themselves were *Freeholders*, were taken into Custody, and *bound* with Ropes, and threaten'd to be sent to *Frederica* to Mr. *Horton*, and there *punished by him*: This Deponent, *once* for refusing to cry *all is well*, when he was an Out-Centry, he having before advised them of the Danger of so doing, least the Voice should direct the *Indians* to *fire* upon the Centry, as they had done the Night before, and *again* for *drumming* with his Fingers on the Side of his House, it being pretended, that he had alarmed the Town. That upon Account of these, and many other *Oppressions*, the Freeholders applied to Mr. *Oglethorpe* for a *Court of Justice* to be erected, and proper *Magistrates* appointed in *Darien*, as in other Towns in *Georgia*, that they might have *Justice done* among themselves; when he gave them for Answer, *"that he would acquaint the Trustees with it;"* but that this Deponent heard no more of it. That in *December* 1738, the said Inhabitants of *Darien* finding, that from their first Settling in *Georgia* their Labours turn'd to no Account, that their *Wants* were daily growing on them, and being *weary* of *Oppression*, they came to a Resolution to depute two Men, chosen from amongst them, to go to *Charles-Town* in *South-Carolina*, and there to make Application to the Government, in order to obtain a Grant of Lands, to which the *whole Settlement* of *Darien* to a Man were to remove all together, the said *John M'Intosh More excepted*; but that it being agreed among them, first to acquaint the said *Colonel* with their Intentions, and their Reasons for such Resolutions, *John M'Intosh L.* was employed by the said Freeholders to lay the same before *him*, who returned them an Answer, *"That they should have Credit for Provisions, with two Cows and their Calves, and a breeding Mare, if they would continue on their Plantations."* That the People with the View of these Helps, and hoping for the further Favour and Countenance of the said *Colonel*, and being loath to leave their little All behind them, and begin the World in a strange Place, were willing to make another Tryal, if they could by any Means make out a Livelyhood in the Colony: But whilst they were in *Expectation* of these Things, this Deponent being at his Plantation two Miles from the Town in *December* 1738, he received a Letter from *Ronald M'Donald*, which was sent by Order of the said *M'Intosh More*, and brought to this Deponent by *William*, Son of the said *M'Intosh*, ordering him, the said Deponent, immediately to come himself, and bring *William Monro* along with him to Town, and advising him, that, "*if he did so, he would be made a Man of, but that if he did not, he would be ruined for ever.*" That this Deponent coming away without Loss of Time, he got to the said *M'Intosh More's* House about nine of the Clock that Night, where he found several of the Inhabitants together, and where the said *M'Intosh More* did tell this Deponent, "*that if he would sign a Paper, which he then offered him, that the said* Colonel *would give him Cattle* and *Servants from time to time, and that he would be a good Friend to as many as would sign the said Paper, but that they would see what would become of those that would not sign it, for that the People of* Savannah *would be all ruin'd, who opposed the said* Colonel *in it.*" That this Deponent did not know the *Contents* of the said Paper, but seeing, that some before him had signed it, his *Hopes on one Side, and Fears on the other, made him sign it also.* That upon his conversing with some of the People, after leaving the House, he was acquainted with the Contents and *Design* of the said Paper, which this Deponent believes to be the *Petition from the Eighteen*, which the Trustees have printed, and *that very Night* he became *sensible* of the *Wrong* he had done; and that his *Conscience did thereupon accuse him, and does yet,* for having so done. That upon a Promise from the said *Colonel*, that he would give this Deponent *12 l. Currency per* Month, he went to the *late Siege of St.* Augustine, as did *Sixty* other Inhabitants and Servants of *Darien*, of which *only thirty-two escaped the Massacre at* Moosa. That their Allowance of Provisions not being delivered as they ought, this Deponent, and the rest of their Company, were reduced to the *Necessity of feeding* on *Pallmetto Roots* to keep themselves from *starving.* That this Deponent was almost famished with Thirst on long Marches and Counter-Marches, and not allowed even to quench it with Water. That the said *Colonel* had this Deponent's *Boat* on that Service for *three Months*, promising him to purchase the same, but it was returned to him, and *no Pay at all* allowed for that, nor his *own Time*, except *one Month's Pay*, tho' he was out *three*, and had engaged, as others did, with the said *Colonel* for *four Months cer-*

tain; and was *all* he had to *support* his Family, his *Crop* being *lost* by his being absent. That in *November* 1740, this Deponent left the said *Darien*, and all his aforesaid Improvements, tho' not without Hopes, that a *Power superior to the Trustees* would take the *deplorable* Condition of these People into Consideration, and give Encouragement for him to return and reap the Benefit of his Labours.

That he left only *four* of the *Freeholders*, and about as many of their Servants there, besides a *few Servants* of the Trustees, and the Widows and Orphans of those *Slain* and taken *Prisoners* at *Moosa*, whom the said *Colonel* allowed *Two Pounds of Beef* and a *Peck of Indian Corn a Head per Week*, and who were desirous of coming away, but were *unable*; That this Deponent never heard of their petitioning the said *Colonel*, or any Body else, for a Supply of others of their Countrymen in the Room of those lost at *Moosa*, nor that they were desirous of it.

Alexander Monroe.

South Carolina. Sworn before me
  this 29th Day of *Nov. Anno*
  1741 ("the Words *and whole-*
  some in the first Page, and *Two*
  Pounds in the fifth Page being
  first interlined.")
  OTHNIEL BEALE.

NUMBER VII.

GEORGE PHILP, late of the Town of *Savannah* in *Georgia*, Merchant, aged twenty-three Years and upwards, maketh Oath and saith, That he this Deponent has been twice in *Georgia* in *America*: That the second Time he arrived there, which was in *September* 1738, *he found the Number of Inhabitants decreased*, and *the People in general uneasy*: That the Inhabitants of the South, both of *Frederica* and *Darien*, notwithstanding some of the latter did send a Petition to the Trustees, as some of the others are said to have signed one, which they did not send, yet *they are as uncapable of improving their Lands and raising Produces*, as the People in the Northern Division, as appears from the very small Quantity of *Indian* Corn which hitherto has been the chief and *almost only* Produce of the Province, some few Potatoes excepted; and as a Proof of which, this Deponent says, That he was in the South in *May* last, when the Season for planting was over, and *much less* was done at *Frederica* than in *former Years:* And that the People of *Darien* did inform him, that they *had not* of their own Produce to carry to Market, even in the Year 1739, which was the *most plentiful Year* they ever saw there, nor indeed any preceeding Year; nor *had they* (the People of *Darien*) *Bread-kind of their own raising*, sufficient for the Use of their Families from one Crop to another, as themselves, or some of them, did tell this Deponent: And farther, the said People of *Darien* were, in *May* last, repining at their Servants being near out of their Time, because the little Stock of Money they carried over with them was exhausted on Cultivation, which did *not* bring them a Return; and they were thereby rendered quite unable to plant their Lands, or *help themselves any way:* And further, that those of the Inhabitants in the South, who did sign the Petition, counter to the Representation of the 9th of *December* 1738, were some of them *ashamed* and *heartily sorry* for having so done, it being contrary to the *true* Interest of themselves and the whole Country, as *themselves did confess* to this Deponent; and, that the said Inhabitants in the South, or some of them, did confess and voluntarily say to him this Deponent, that they were *induced to sign the said Petition* by Promises of Credit being given them by the STORE, for Cattle, which they afterwards had, and *gave Bonds for their Value*; and that those that *refused* to sign the said Petition *praying against Negroes*, had *no* Cattle given them, *nor Credit for any*, as some of the said People who did sign the said Petition, counter to the said Representation, did tell this Deponent: And that in *September* last, Mr. *John M'Intosh*, Son of Mr. *Benjamin M'Intosh*, told him this Deponent, That his Father, at the Request of the *few People then remaining at* Darien, was to go soon into *South Carolina*, to look out for some new Settlement there for the said People of *Darien*, for that *they did intend to leave their Improvements in* Georgia, because they did not answer the Expence; nor were they able any *longer to subsist themselves in* Georgia: That he *never saw nor heard of* the *Saltzburghers* at *Ebenezer, their selling Provisions* in *Savannah*, nor *elsewhere*, except a few Calves; tho' he lived, and, for the most part, was in the most publick Part of the Town, and near the Place where the Provisions were commonly sold; but that he has often seen them fetch Provisions for their own Use, as supposed, from the *publick Stores* at *Savannah*, as also Bread and Flower from other private Stores in the Town; that he has *seen* and *known* a great many People in *Georgia*, and who were reputed to be the most industrious, to be *very laborious*, and to take Pains on their Lands, the Produce of which, does *not* answer the Expence of a *White-man's Labour*, as they themselves have told him; that this Deponent would not have left the Colony, had it not been so much upon the Decline, for that he liked the Place so well, that he would have taken up a Lot in the Town of *Savannah*, about the Month of *August* 1739, but General *Oglethorpe refused to grant him* one; because he said he would not have asked for one, had he not hoped that the Tenures would be altered.

George Philp.

Sworn at the Publick Office,
  16 Feb. 1740.
    W. SPICER.

NUMBER VIII.

From EBENEZER.

JOHN SPEILBEIGLER, late of *Ebenezer* in *Georgia*, aged 29 Years and upwards, maketh Oath and saith, That he arrived in *Georgia* on or about *March* 1735–6, and lived there till *March* 1740–1; that soon after his Arrival, his Countrymen, who were settled at *Old Ebenezer*, on their first coming to *Georgia*, (upon a Complaint, "*That the Land did not answer the Expence and Labour bestowed on it*") were removed several Miles farther up the River *Savannah*, to the Place now called *Ebenezer*, and where he left them, or the greatest Part of them when he came away; that he built a House, and fenced in his Lot, and made other Improvements in the Town, and clear'd and planted 4 Acres of Land, on which he never but once had so much as *Fifty* Bushels of Corn, and *Twenty* Bushels of Potatoes, which was *not Sufficient* to maintain himself and Mother in the common Necessaries of Life; (they having nothing to Drink but Water) nor did he buy any Cloaths, nor had he Money or any thing to give in Exchange for Drink or Cloaths, the whole five Years that he lived in *Georgia* except about thirty Yards of Oznabrigs that made him ten Shirts, and about ten Pair of Shoes, which cost Six Shillings a Pair; that he must have *gone naked*, had not he hired himself by the Month at *Savannah*, which enabled him to buy the said Shirts and Shoes; that the Inhabitants of the said *Ebenezer* in *general*, have often said to him, "That *they could not live were it not for the Assistance they received from their Friends in*

Europe *and the Trustees Store,*" which Mr. *Boltzius,* the Minister, distributed among them as *he* thought fit; That the said Inhabitants had *never* Corn, and Rice, or *any sort* of Bread-kind *sufficient* for the Use of their Families from Crop to Crop; tho' last Year some of them gave in *exchange* a small Quantity of *Indian* Corn for a little Flower, and some times, (perhaps) twice the last Year, three or four Fowls, a Calf, or small Pig among them: That he never had his Lands *conveyed* to him, nor a Grant or any sort of Writing to shew for the same; and that *all* the Inhabitants of the said *Ebenezer* in general, were frequently complaining that they had no sort of Writing to shew that they had Titles to their Lands; That the Inhabitants in general of the said *Ebenezer,* have often said to him, that they *wanted* and would be glad of *Negroes,* because they found that they were *unable* to raise Provisions for their Support, by their own Labour: That the said Inhabitants were called together by the said *Boltzius* to *sign their Petition,* dated *March* 13, 1739, and that they, or many of them, *would not* have signed it, had they not been *compelled* to do it by the said *Boltzius,* as they after told this Deponent, and, *repenting* their signing it, did several of them *leave* the Colony, as this Deponent believes the rest would do, were they able; for they are very uneasy under the *arbitrary Government of the said* Boltzius, who *judges* in all Causes, *gives to,* and *takes from,* whom *he pleases,* the said Inhabitants being deprived the Benefits of any Courts of *Judicature,* or *Magistrates,* having no such among them, except the said *Boltzius,* who takes upon him to *act* as *King, Priest* and *Prophet*; and who took this Deponent's Plantation Tools from him, on his coming away, *without Judge or Jury,* tho' he was nothing indebted to the said *Boltzius.* And farther this Deponent saith not.

South Carolina, ff.

Personally appeared the Deponent, *John Speilbeigler,* who on Oath declared, That the Contents foregoing are true.

Sworn this 16th Day of *Dec.*

1741, before me.

OTHNIEL BEALE.

I do hereby further certify, that I have employed the said *John Speilbeigler* at his Trade, being a Brick-layer, and that he performed to my Satisfaction, being (as far as I could discover) sober, diligent and faithful. Witness my Hand the Day above-mentioned.

OTHNIEL BEALE.

Number IX.

From Ebenezer.

Whereas the Inhabitants of *Ebenezer* in *Georgia*, have signed a Petition, setting forth their Dislike to Negroes, signifying that the Produce of their Lands answers the Labour bestowed on them, and that they are well pleased with their Condition; These are to certify, to all whom it may concern, that the Subscribers hereof, who are of the *oldest Settlers* in the said *Ebenezer*, have never yet been able to support themselves and Families by Cultivation; nor do they know an Instance of it, among all the said Inhabitants: And farther, that the Inhabitants in general think it hard, *that they have not free Titles to their Lands, nor a scrap of Writing,* shewing any Title at all to their Lands, which have cost them much Labour to improve: And further, that the Inhabitants in general of the said *Ebenezer, are* desirous of Negroes: That *they were called together* to sign their said Petition; and many of them have been heard by us to say, that they would not have done it, but that *our Minister would have been Angry* with them, if they had refused to do so: That they would yet sign a Petition for Negroes, were it not that Mr. *Boltzius,* our Minister, who *exercises an arbitrary Power* over us, *might make them very uneasie.*

> Christopher Ortman.
> John Michael Riser.
> Thomas Bicher.

Ebenezer, 20th
  Oct. 1741.

Number X.

From Augusta.

A List *of such Traders, Men, and Horses, as come from other Parts,
and only pass through or by* Augusta *in their Way
to the* Creek *Nation.*

	Men	Hor.
Mess. *Wood* and *Brown*, from *S. Carolina*	8	60
Daniel Clark, from Ditto	4	20
Archibald M'Gilvray, from Ditto	3	18
George Cossons, from Ditto	4	30
Jeremiah Knott, from Ditto	4	30
Messrs. { *Spencer*, from *Mount-pleasant*	3	16
{ *Gilmore*, from Ditto	4	20
Messrs. { *Barnett*, from Ditto	3	20
{ *Ladson*, from Ditto	3	20
James Cossons, from *South-Carolina*	5	30
George Golphin, from Ditto	4	25
William Sluthers, from Ditto	4	25
	49	314

A List *of the whole Inhabitants of the Township of*
Augusta *in* Georgia.

	Men	Wo.	Ch.
Mr. *Kennedy O Brien*	5	3	0
Thomas Smith	1	1	0
Messrs. *Mackenzie* and *Frazer*	5	1	0
John Miller	2	1	1
Thomas Goodale	2	1	2
Samuel Brown	2	1	1
Sanders Ross	2	0	0
A Sadler	1	1	1
A Taylor	1	1	0
William Clark	1	1	0
Henry Overstreet	1	1	4
Locklan M'Bean	2	2	1
William Gray	4	0	0
William Calahern	0	2	2
	29	16	12

A List *of* Traders, *Men,* and *Horses, employed from* Augusta *in the* Chickasaw *and* Creek *Trade.*

	Men	Hor.
George Mackay	4	20
Henry Elsey	3	20
Messrs. *Facey* and *Macqueen*	6	40
John Wright	4	20
John Gardner	3	20
William Calahern	3	15
Tho. Andrews in *Creek* and *Chickasaw* Nations	8	70
Thomas Daval	3	20
John Cammell	3	20
Paul Rundall	3	20
Nicholas Chinery	3	20
William Newberry	3	20
	46	305

Savannah, July,   JOHN GARDNER.
    14, 1741.

The Day above-written, *John Gardner,* of *Augusta, Indian* Trader, personally came and appeared before me *John Fallowfield,* one of the Bailiffs of the Town of *Savannah,* and made Oath, that the said several Accounts of Traders, Horses, and Men, employed in the *Creek* and *Chickasaw* Nations; And also the List of the white Persons, Men, Women and Children now living in the Township of *Augusta,* are, to the best of the said Deponent's Knowledge, *just and true*; and that the Persons residing in, and belonging to the *Fort* of *Augusta,* are not contained in the said Lists above, and on the other Side of this Paper Written.

JOHN GARDNER.

Sworn the Day and Year
    above-written at *Sa-*
    vannah aforesaid.
    JOHN FALLOWFIELD.

NUMBER XI.

From AUGUSTA.

THE Deposition of *Kennedy O Brien,* of *Augusta,* in the Colony of *Georgia,* Merchant, one of the first Inhabitants of the said Township, and a constant Resident therein, ever since the first Settlement thereof, who being duly sworn on the Holy Evangelists of Almighty God, saith, That whereas he hath been informed, that a *Representation* hath lately been made and transmitted to the Honourable the Trustees for establishing the said Colony of *Georgia*, setting forth the flourishing State and Condition of the said Colony in general, and of the said Township of *Augusta* in particular; and the said Deponent, being willing to undeceive any, or all, who may be thereby induced to give Credit to the said *Representation*, doth voluntarily, and of his own accord, declare and maintain the following Truths to be strictly just.

1. That there are not more than *forty white Men*, Inhabitants and Residents of the said Township of *Augusta*, save only the Soldiers in Garrison there, which are about fifteen or twenty more.

2. That *all*, or most of the *Corn* that hath been *made* and *raised* there, hath been wrought and *manufactured* by *Negroes*, belonging to the said Inhabitants, and those opposite to them on the North-Side of the River in *South-Carolina*.

3. That, at least, *one third Part of the Corn* reported to be raised in *Augusta* is raised in *South-Carolina* hard by the said Township.

4. That there are not more than *five hundred Horses* employed in the *Indian* Trade, that resort to *Augusta*, altho' it is esteemed the *Key* to the *Creek*, the *Chickasaw*, and the *Cherokee* Nations; and that the most of those Horses and Persons employed about them, and interested and concerned in them, do as often go to *New Windsor* in *South-Carolina* to *trade*, as to *Augusta*.

5. That there are now in *Augusta* but *three trading Houses*, and those in a State of *Decay* and languishing Condition; and that through the *ill Regulation* of the *Indian Trade*.

And this Deponent further saith, that no *Oyl*, *Wine*, nor *Olives*, hath ever been produced at *Augusta*, or hath ever been attempted to be raised or cultivated there, to the best of this Deponent's Knowledge. And further this Deponent saith not.

Kennedy O'Brien.

Subscribed and Sworn to be-
fore me this 9th Day of
July, 1741.
JOHN PYE, *Recorder.*

Number XII.

THE Deposition of Sir *Richard Everard*, Bart. who, being duly sworn, saith, That some time about the Evening of (to the best of this Deponent's Memory) the tenth of this present Month of *July*, he this Deponent had some Discourse with Mr. *Samuel Mercer* of the Town of *Savannah*, in the said Province of *Georgia*, in the Square of the said Town; amongst other Discourse this Deponent asked the said *Samuel Mercer*, how he could joyn in swearing to, and signing a *Representation* of the State of the Colony, when the said Representation contained many Things, of the Truth of which he could be no ways certain; and other Things which were in themselves absolutely (as this Deponent had been informed) false. The said *Mercer* said, that the Number of Men and Horses at *Augusta* were easily to be accounted for, that I counted only the *exact Number* of Men and Horses said to be there, which would not amount to near the Numbers mentioned in the Representation, but that he apprehended, that they had been counted every Man and Horse, as *often* as ever they *went* from, or *came* to *Augusta*, which would (he said) amount to the Numbers mentioned to be in the Representation. I told him, that they might have taken a shorter Method of counting, and not wait the Trouble of the Traders coming down from the Nation; that they had nothing more to do, but to make Capt. *Kent*, *Commander* of the Fort of *Augusta*, to march his Men in and out, as often as they pleased to count them, and they might make what Numbers they thought necessary for the Service of their Cause at any Time, or to that Effect. And this Deponent saith, that to the best of his Memory, this is the Substance of the Conversation he had at that time with the said *Samuel Mercer*. And he, this Deponent, further saith, that on *Monday* the 13th of this Instant, being in Company with several Gentlemen at the House of *Peter Morrell* in the Town of *Savannah* in *Georgia*, *John Ray* (who this Deponent was informed was) a Subscriber and Swearer to the above-mentioned *Representation*, being then there, he was asked how he came to swear to and subscribe the said *Representation*; after many weak and frivolous Excuses and Justifications, finding himself unable to defend the said Action, he said, and swore by God, that the *Honourable the Trustees owed him one hundred Pounds Sterling*, and that *he swore* to, and signed that *Representation*, in Hopes to get his Money from them, otherwise he never would have sworn to or sign'd the same; adding, that he hoped to have his *hundred Pounds* out of the *ten thousand* Pounds said to be voted by the Parliament for the Support of *Georgia*.

R. Everard.

Sworn before me this 14th
  Day of *July*, 1741.
    JOHN FALLOWFIELD.

NUMBER XIII.

Savannah, }
in *Georgia.* }   *From* SAVANNAH.

ANDREW NEILSON, Chief Mate, and *Thomas Conn*, one of the Mariners, of the Sloop *Oglethorpe*, belonging to St. *Christophers*, being duly sworn, on the Holy Evangelist of Almighty God, jointly and severally make Oath and say, That on or about the fourth Day of *May*, One thousand seven hundred and thirty-nine, these Deponents were *taken up* by a Warrant; and by Virtue thereof, brought before and examin'd by *Henry Parker* and *Robert Gilbert*, two of the Bailiffs of *Savannah* aforesaid, touching a Report that had been spread in the Camp of St. *Simons* in this Province. *To witt*, That General *Oglethorpe*, was under Confinement in *Charles Town*, which the Soldiers were glad of; and that the Soldiers should say, that if he should return to St. *Simons* he would be shot; and that if one would not shoot him, another would; and that when they had done it, they would fly to St. *Augustine*; all which Words and Report the said *Henry Parker* and *Robert Gilbert* charg'd these Deponents with, as the Authors; which Charge these Deponents utterly denied, and petition'd the said Bailiffs, that they might have Liberty to go to the Camp at St. *Simons* aforesaid, to answer to the said Charge before General *Oglethorpe*, which was accordingly granted; and these Deponents were next Day sent thither, under the Care of Lieutenant *William Horton*: And these Deponents further say, that some few Days after, they were brought before and examin'd by the said General *Oglethorpe*, at *Frederica*, on the said Island of St. *Simons*, concerning the said Report; the first part of which, *To witt*, That General *Oglethorpe* was under Confinement in *Charles-Town*: These Deponents acknowledg'd themselves to have uttered, and said in Vindication thereof, that so much of the said Report as last mention'd, was current in the Camp, and that these Deponents first heard it there; and as to the other Part of the said Report, these Deponents utterly denied to have ever so much as heard of the same, till they were charg'd therewith; whereupon the said *General Oglethorpe* examin'd these Deponents separately: And this Deponent *Andrew Neilson* for himself saith, that the said General *Oglethorpe* ask'd this Deponent, *if he never heard* his Owner, Mr. *Robert Williams*, spread the said Report, which this Deponent denying, the said General *Oglethorpe then insisted* that the said *Robert Williams*, *must have persuaded* this Deponent to have spread the said Report; which this Deponent again utterly denied, and said *it was hard to accuse an innocent Man:* And this Deponent *Andrew Neilson*, for himself further saith, that the said General *Oglethorpe*, after *having endeavoured to induce* this Deponent *to accuse the said* Robert Williams, as the *Author* of the said *Report*, by several *Cross Questions*; he then told this Deponent, that he the said General *Oglethorpe*, had been endeavouring to plead for him this Deponent, and would *put Words into his Mouth* if he had a Mind to save himself: But this Deponent still denying to accuse the said *Robert Williams*, the said General *Oglethorpe* then *endeavoured* to *intimidate* this Deponent, by *several Threats*; and among others, told this Deponent, that *unless he would say that the said* Robert Williams *had spoke or rais'd the aforesaid Report*, he *the said General* Oglethorpe, would *order* the Soldiers to be under Arms, and *would turn this Deponent loose among them*, and *leave him to their Mercy*. And this Deponent *Thomas Conn*, for himself saith, that the said General *Oglethorpe* asked this Deponent the *same Questions*, or to the *same Purpose;* and *endeavour'd to persuade* this Deponent to *accuse* the said *Robert Williams*, as the Author of the said Report, by *fair Words* and *Threats*, in the manner as the other Deponent *Andrew Neilson*, hath before deposed, or by Words to the very same effect, and meaning: And these Deponents both say, that after the said General *Oglethorpe* had examin'd them separately they were both brought before him together, and he then *again told* them, that *he would order* the Soldiers to be drawn out *under Arms*, and would *turn these Deponents loose among them*, and *leave them to their Mercy;* for there was not a Man among them but would dye for him. And lastly, these Deponents say, that the said General *Oglethorpe* cast several Reflections on the said *Robert Williams* about Cattle stealing; and a short time afterwards, Lieutenant *William Horton*, advised these Deponents to petition General *Oglethorpe* to be discharged, which they accordingly did; and soon after the said Lieutenant *William Horton* came and told them, that the said General *Oglethorpe ordered* that *they should make the best of their way for* Savannah; and that the said Lieutenant *William Horton* provided them a Passage in the Scout-Boat; and further these Deponents say not.

Andrew Neilson.
Thomas Conn.

Sworn this 20th Day
  of *May*, 1739, be-
  fore me,
  Tho. Christie, *Recorder.*

Number XIV.

From Savannah.

The Deposition of *John Pye*, of the Town of *Savannah*, who being duly sworn, on the Holy Evangelist of Almighty God, saith, that sometime in the Year 1739, the Honourable the Trustees for establishing the Colony of *Georgia*, sent over by Capt. *Thompson* into this Colony, twenty Casks of Copper Half-pence, Weight 230 lb each; in all about 400 *l.* Sterl. And this Deponent further saith, that he believes and is persuaded that the said Sum of 400 *l.* aforesaid was sent over into this Colony for *Change to the Inhabitants:* And this Deponent further saith, that sometime after *John Provoost*, came in to *Savannah* with a Cargoe of Provisions, which said Provisions, Mr. *Thomas Jones*, Store-keeper to the Honourable the Trustees, *purchas'd* and *paid down the Value in Copper;* and that the whole Quantity of Goods amounted to *fourteen or fifteen Casks of Copper, which* this Deponent *saw delivered* on board *Provoost's* Sloop, and further this Deponent saith not.

John Pye.

Sworn before me this
  24th Day of *July*,
  1741.
  John Fallowfield.

NUMBER XV.

From SAVANNAH.

JOHN SCOTT, late of *Savannah*, in the Province of *Georgia*, but now of *Charles-Town, South-Carolina;* maketh Oath and saith, That he went to work, and got up a House and Work-house, and was building a Forge; but *John West*, the then *Bailiff*, came to this Deponent, and *told him*, that *he should not build a Forge*, that *he would pull it down again*, for that *there should be no Forge* in Town *but his, he being by Trade a Blacksmith.*

John Scott.

Charles-Town, South-Carolina.
    Sworn before me this
    30th Day of *April*, 1740.
      THOMAS DALE.

NUMBER XVI.

From SAVANNAH.

James Oglethorpe, &c. to *John Lyndall.*

BY Virtue of Powers granted from his *Majesty*, George the Second, by the Grace of God, King of *Great-Britain, France* and *Ireland*, Defender of the Faith, *&c. I do appoint* you *John Lyndall*, to be *Tythingman* of the lower *New-Ward;* to train and exercise the Militia of the said Tythings, and to keep the Peace, and *obey* all such Orders as you shall receive from the Constable of the said *Wards*, or from *such* other *Person* or *Persons* as *I shall appoint* to *Command*, train and exercise the Militia: And *this shall continue* in *full Force*, until *I*, or such as shall succeed to my Commands, shall recall the same, and *then* it *shall cease* and *determine:* Given under my Hand and Seal at *Savannah*, in *Georgia*, the 19th Day of *October*, 1739.

James Oglethorpe.

This is a true Copy, examined the 26th of *October*, 1741, by us, Witness our Hands,

John Lyndall.
Thomas Ormston.

Number XVII.

ANDREW GRANT, late of the Province of *Georgia*, maketh Oath, that *he hath paid fourteen Shillings and three-pence per hundred* for Flour, which he bought out of the *Trustees Store-house* in *Savannah*, which Flour he believes cost the Trustees Storekeeper, *no more than ten Shilling per hundred*, that being the common Price in *Carolina* at that time: And further he saith, that he hath *paid eight-pence per Pound* for *New-York* or *Rhode-Island* Cheese, which he believes *cost but five-pence per Pound*, or *six-pence* at *the highest Rate;* and he hath likewise paid *four* Shillings per Gallon for *Madeira* and *Vidonia* Wines, which cost to the best of his Knowledge, not more than *three* Shilling per Gallon, that being the *highest* Rate given for such Wines in *Georgia* or *Carolina*, a great deal being bought *much cheaper:* And this Deponent saith further, that those extraordinary Prices *exacted* from the People for Provisions, and all other necessaries, occasioned (by the Trustees Storekeepers and their Agents) many and continual Complaints from the *whole* Inhabitants, *for the space of six Years and upwards;* that this Deponent lived in that Province: And this Deponent saith further, that to the best of his Knowledge, he *never* bought any Provisions from the Store aforesaid, but a considerable advance was made on the same, generally *not less* than *twenty-five per Cent.* neither doth he remember any other that ever did.

Andrew Grant.

Sworn at the Publick-
  Office, the 4th of
  January 1742. be-
  fore E. SAWYER.

Number XVIII.

From SAVANNAH.

JOSEPH SUMMERS, late of *Savannah* Town in the Province of *Georgia*, now of *Mount Pleasant* in *South Carolina*, Planter, maketh Oath, That in *March* 1734, he became a Freeholder in *Georgia* aforesaid, and continued there till *February* 1738, at which Time he came away, and left his Property there by reason of the very *unjust* and *bad Treatment* to the Generality of the Inhabitants and himself; That he was well acquainted with Capt. *Joseph Watson*, who he always thought to be a *sober, honest* Gentleman, and *no ways inclinable to Lunacy:* He this Deponent knew that the said *Watson* was settled, and kept a Store with *John Musgrove* at *Yamacraw Bluff*, whereon he had made great Improvements, and also that he was in Possession of Lands at *Grantham*, whereon he had built a good House and several Improvements.

This Deponent also was in Court in *November* 1734, when on the Trial of the said *Joseph Watson*, *Thomas Causton* (who acted as *Chief Judge*) came off the Bench, to become an Evidence against the said *Watson*, and treated him and the Jury with very indecent Language: And this Deponent well knows, and remembers, that the said *Joseph Watson* was kept in *Confinement under a strong Guard* for upwards of *two* Years, but the exact Time this Deponent cannot be certain to, not having kept any Minutes of the same.

This Deponent further saith, That he has heard Mr. *Thomas Causton*, when sitting on the Bench as *Judge*, declare, that he had no Business, *nor would be governed by the Laws of* England; but pulled out of his Pocket a Book, and said, "*Here are the Laws of* Georgia, *which I have from Mr.* Oglethorpe, *by which you are to be govern'd*," or Words to that Effect.

And this Deponent further saith, That he verily believes the said Captain *Joseph Watson* was a Well-wisher, and would have been of great Benefit to the *Georgia* Colony, and doth not think he ever had any evil Intention against it.

Joseph Summers.

Sworn at *Beaufort, Port Royal*,
   the First of *March* 1739,
  before me,
    THOMAS WIGG, J. Peace.

To the Bailiffs *and* Recorder *of the Town of* Savannah *in the Province of* Georgia *in* America.

THE Trustees very much approve of your Conduct in Mr. *Watson*'s last Affairs, and will always support those who act with Justice and Intrepidity, in putting the Laws in Execution, for the good of the Province, and Mr. *Causton* acted very judiciously in regarding the general Interest and

Safety, preferable to any private Consideration, in *justly* confining one Man rather than risquing the Safety of the Whole. Mr. *Watson*'s Behavior has been so Cruel, and has shewn so much premeditated Malice, that his destroying *Skee* with Rum, and the bragging of it, appears to the Trustees Murder; for killing a Man upon a Fore-thought, and with a malicious Design by means of any dangerous Liquor, is as much Murder, as killing him with any sort of Weapon: But *as the Jury have brought him in Lunatick*, and therefore incapable of making his Defence, The *Trustees direct* that *he shall be confined as a Lunatick*, and proper Care taken for his Recovery, until he shall be in a Condition to take his Trial; for which Trial, a Special Commission will be sent over; and *you at your Perils* must *take Care* that he shall be forth-coming, when such Commission shall arrive; and *no other* Proceeding *must* be had on his Affair until the arrival of the said Commission. The Trustees are apt to impute the Death of *Skee* (which has been a very great Detriment to the Province by the loss of so bold a Warrior, who both had been, and would have continued of the utmost Service, upon the *Spanish* Frontiers) to the Consequence of too great a Mildness, or rather Injustice, in letting Mr. *Watson* go off with so *slight* a Fine when he was first convicted for the Assault on *Esteeche*. You know, that *the Indians are very Nice in point of Honour*, and that they are not to be Insulted. — Had Mr. *Watson* at that time been *severely* fined, and bound to his good Behavior, it had very probably prevented him, from running into those Extravagancies, by which *he lost his Senses*, and from committing this Murder; and in the Consequence thereof, had prevented *Justus*, the Servant of Mr. *Musgrove*, from being killed. — *You see by this*, a foolish Tenderness is the greatest of Cruelties; it hath occasioned the Death of two Men, and if that kind of Spirit continue of not punishing the Guilty, you will destroy yourselves. — It is very surprizing to the Trustees, that any Magistrate could think of Bailing a Murderer, for Murder is not bailible, and *bailing of a Lunatick* is *an Act of Lunacy*; for his Distemper makes his Confinement necessary to Mankind: The new-started Opinion, that it is Cruel to imprison on account of an *Indian*, is itself very cruel and pernicious; for if Injustice is done to an *Indian*, the Person who does it should be more severely punished, for doing it to one who is helpless, from his Ignorance of our Language; and because it is a breach of Treaty, and an Act of Ingratitude to the first Possessors of the Land, who have always been exceeding friendly, and kind to the Colony in its first Weakness and Necessities. — And as for the Opinion that it is right, to let a guilty Man go out of the Province without Punishment, that is giving up at once those valuable Privileges of trying all Facts committed in it, and declaring yourselves incapable of supporting a Civil Government: If a Man is Guilty, you should punish him in the Province, according to his Deserts, and if he is not Guilty, you should acquit him: But you have no such thing as a Power of banishing a Man from the Colony, nor ought you to let a Criminal escape to another Colony in Safety. The Expences arising by Mr. *Watson*'s Confinement; and also for the taking Care of him and having a proper Keeper to watch him, will be defrayed by the Store-keeper at *Savannah*, *till such time as they can be defrayed out of his own Estate*, and he *being a Lunatick*, * it is impossible for him to carry on the *Indian* Trade, The Trustees hereby *recall his Licence*, and continue the Licence to Mr. and Mrs. *Musgrove*.

Signed by Order of the Common-Council of the Trustees the 17th of March, 1734–5.
BENJAMIN MARTYN, Secr.

Joseph Watson maketh Oath, that the above is a true Copy examined by himself with the Original Letter, which he, this Deponent, sent to *England* by the Rev. Mr. *John Wesley*.
JOSEPH WATSON.

Sworn, *April* 10, 1740,
  before me,
    THO. DALE.

From SAVANNAH.

Savannah, Oct. 20, 1737
WHEREAS on this Day a Court was holden at *Savannah* in the Province of *Georgia*, by Virtue of an Order from the Honourable the Trustees to pass Sentence on *Joseph Watson*, Gent. in Pursuance of a *Verdict* said to be given against him on *November* 20, 1734. And whereas the said *Joseph Watson had a Right* by the Laws of *England* to be heard as to what he

---

* There are no less than eight Affidavits from *Georgia*, besides Living Witnesses to prove, that he was *not* a Lunatick.

[320]

could offer, why Sentence should not be passed according to that Verdict: This is to certifie the *Honourable the Trustees*, that we, whose Names are underwritten, were then present in the said Court; and that the said *Joseph Watson* then offered to prove by Witnesses then in Court, who were of the said *Jury*, that the said *Verdict* had never been given, and that the *Verdict* delivered to the Court on *November* 20th aforesaid, was written in these and *no other* Words, "*Guilty of unguarded Expressions.*" And we do further certifie, that the said Court did absolutely refuse to permit those Witnesses to give their Evidence. Witness our Hands.

John Coates,	*Henry Garrat,*	his
Walter Fox,	*John Clark,*	*Hen. H Manly,*
John Lyndall,	*J. Fallowfield,*	mark
William Francis,	*Will. Aglionby,*	*Gilbert Becu,*
Henry Lloyd,	*Edward Bush,*	*John Kellay,*
John Burton,	*James Burnside,*	*Joseph Wardrop,*
Benj. Adams,	*Is. King Clark,*	*John Davis,*
John Wesley, Min-	*William Rigden,*	*W. Woodrose,*
ister of *Sa-*	*Richard Davis,*	*Will. Bradley,*
vannah,	*John Smith,*	*James Bland,*
George Row,	his	*Jacob Watts,*
Robert Potter,	*Ja. j. S. Smith,*	*David Snook,*
Robert Hows,	mark	*John Goldwire,*
Samuel Mercer,	*Ja. Cawpwell,*	*Hump. Bright,*
W. Brownjohn,	*George Buncle,*	*Thomas Salter*
Joseph Stanley,	*Thomas Neale,*	his
Richard Turner,	*William Elbert,*	*G. W Waterman.*
James Mears,	*James Carwele,*	mark

Georgia, Savannah, Sept. 12, 1737.

We whose Names are underwritten do assert, that being on the Petty Jury *Nov.* 20, 1734, in *Joseph Watson*'s Cause, we brought by our Foreman (*Elisha Dobree*) our written *Verdict*, "*Guilty of unguarded Expressions,*" what else was added was extorted by Menaces from *Thomas Causton*, Bailiff, and not assented to by us. Witness our Hands.

Jos. Stanley, John Clark.
Walter Fox, R. Lobb.

NUMBER XIX.

From SAVANNAH.

THOMAS NEALE, late of *Savannah* in *Georgia*, aged thirty-two Years and upwards, maketh Oath, and saith, that he lived in the Colony four Years and upwards, that holding a Lot in Right of *Katrine* his Wife, late Widow of *Paul Amatis*, who left a Son about sixteen Months old, who was Heir to the said Lot; this Deponent did on the Decease of the said Infant, apply to General *Oglethorpe* for a Right to the said Lot in his own Name, which the *said General* complying with, he ordered Mr. *John Fallowfield*, first Constable of *Savannah*, to give this Deponent Possession thereof; and the said *Fallowfield*, taking *Joseph Fitzwalter*, a Landholder of *Savannah*, for a Witness, did, in the Year One Thousand Seven Hundred and Thirty-Eight, give this Deponent Possession of the said Lot accordingly. That the said *General* did order *William Stephens*, Esq; Secretary for the *Trustees* Affairs in *Georgia*, to register it in this Deponent's Name. That being to clear the five Acre Lot belonging to the same within three Years thereafter, he agreed with a Person to do so, upon Consideration that this Deponent should pay him ten Pounds Sterling for his Labour, but not being able to get it done then, he did fully intend to clear it the next Spring, being One Thousand Seven Hundred and Thirty-Nine, *had he not been dispossessed thereof by Order of the said* General: That *he had fenced in the Town Lot, and built a good habitable Hut*, on the back of the same, and *made other Improvements*: That he *intended to build a large House* on the Front: That *he did both Watch and Ward, muster'd, and attended the Courts*: That *he paid Arrears for Guard Duty* for the said Lot before he came to it: That, when he was out of the Province, *Joseph Stanly undertook to do the said Duty*, for which this Deponent *paid the said* Stanly: That he never heard any Complaint made of Neglect, but has been well informed, that the said *Stanly* was punctual in so doing. That soon after he had Possession given him in his own Name, he put the Widow *Hughes* into the said Hut, which he had built. That the said Widow leaving the Colony, he did then leave Mr. *Martin* in it, who had cohabited with her in Possession thereof, and did agree with him that he might live in the said Hut, upon Condition, that he looked after it, and took Care of it in his Absence, and likewise did Guard Duty for the same. But that after some Months Absence, *having been sick in* Carolina, where *he went to buy Provisions for the Colony*; he did, on his Return to *Savannah*,

[322]

find the said *Martin* the Tenant turned out, and *Peter Jermain* in the Possession of the whole; and that the said *Jermain* had put in a Tenant of his own. That he was then informed by Mr. *Samuel Mercer*, Constable, and others of *Savannah*, that he, the said *Mercer, had given the said* Jermain *Possession of the said Lot*, in the manner that Possession had been given to this Deponent by Mr. *Fallowfield* aforesaid; and *that he did so by Order of the said* General. That he instantly applied to Mr. *Henry Parker*, and the other Magistrates, for Recovery of the said Lot; when they told him it was not in their Power to help him. That in *March* last *he made a Demand of the same* from the *said General, who only told him, that he ought to be there himself, when the said* Jermain *was put in Possession*. That he had *not* deserted the Colony, tho' he was *obliged* to go to *Carolina*, and trade betwixt the two Provinces, or do any thing for an honest Lively-hood, *not being able to support himself by Cultivation under the Restrictions in* Georgia, which have been *too severely felt by People in general*, as he can witness. And farther this Deponent saith not.

> Sworn to before *Thomas Wigg*, one of his Majesty's Justices as-
> signed to keep the Peace, in *Granville* County, *South Carolina*,
> this 26th Day of *January*, 1741–2.   Tho. Wigg.

No. 3. South.

SAMUEL DAVISON
J. O.

Mr. Bromfield to put Mr. *Amatis* into *Horne's* Lot, *which is forfeited*.
                                        J. Oglethorpe.

The Lot, late *William Hornes*, is now granted to *Paul Amatis*, by Order of *James Oglethorpe*, Esq;
The House Lot in *Jekyll* Tything, *Derby* Ward, No. 4.
The Garden lies South-East from the Town, No. 59.
The Farm is in the same Ward and Tything of Farmes, No. 5. Letter B.

> Witness *John Brownfield*, Register.

Savannah, June the 16th, 1736.

Number XX.

Joseph Watson, late of *Grantham*, Bailiff, in the Province of *Georgia*, aged forty Years and upwards, maketh Oath, and saith, that in the Year Seventeen Hundred Thirty-Four he bought some Cheese from the Store-house, commonly called the *Trustees Store*, in the Town of *Savannah*, in the said Province. That he was charged in his Account with the Trustees for establishing the said Colony, one Shilling Sterl. *per* Pound for the said Cheese. That he believes it was what in *London* is commonly called *Cheshire* Cheese. That the *Inhabitants in general* in the said Town and Neighbourhood thereof, *often* complained, that they paid the *same Price for the same Sort of Cheese*; and that the said Inhabitants did complain continually, That high Prices were advanced on all Sorts of Provisions, and other Necessaries, sold at the said Store. And farther this Deponent does not say.

Joseph Watson.

Sworn at the Publick
   Office 31st *December*, 1742, before
    R. Edward.

Number XXI.

Sarah Turner, late of the Colony of *Georgia*, maketh Oath and saith, That she arrived at *Savannah*, in the said Province, in *December* 1733, with her Husband *Richard Turner*; where she resided till *March*, 1739–40.

That from the Time of her Arrival, to *June* 1738, Mr. *Thomas Causton*, late *Magistrate*, *Store-keeper* and *Cashier* to the *Trustees* for *Georgia*, had the *sole* disposal of the Shop, commonly call'd the *Trustees Store*; where was always kept a large supply of all Provisions, Cloathing, Working Tools, and other Necessaries. That she has heard and doubts not, but that Cheese has been sold from the said Store, for One Shilling by the Pound; that she has herself bought Cheshire-Cheese (as she thinks it) of the said *Causton*'s Wife, (who kept a Chandler's Shop, which was generally thought, and she has great Reason to believe, was supply'd with Goods out of the said Store) for which she paid at the same time, in

Paper-Money of *South-Carolina*, after the Rate of Eight-pence Sterl. per Pound: That neither her Husband (as she knows of) nor herself, did ever receive any Part or Share of the Presents of Cattle, Provisions, &c. made to the first Settlers of *Georgia*, by the Provinces of *South-Carolina*, *Pensilvania*, &c. That neither she or her Husband (as she ever knew of) did ever receive a Cow or Sow, as promis'd to the said Setlers by the Trustees: That she has heard frequent Complaints among the first Settlers (to whom such Presents were said to be made) that they were made to pay for the same, as well as all other Sorts of Provisions and Necessaries, received at the Hands, or by the Order of the said *Causton*; and that they paid most extravagant Prices for the same.

That on the Removal of the said *Causton*, Mr. *Thomas Jones* was first made Store-keeper, and then Magistrate; which gave him an Opportunity of *exercising Cruelties* on the People, as *Causton* had done; and which were complain'd of by the People: That she has heard that the said *Jones* would allow one *Parker*, and other poor People, made Magistrates by the Trustees, no Provisions, when ever they differ'd in Opinion with him, *in a Case of Justice*; and he also sold all Sorts of Provisions from the said Store, at extravagant Prices; that he would not pay Labourers, and others employed in the publick Service in Money, but in Provisions at a dear Rate. That *John Graham* having sawed some Boards, the said *Jones* would pay him in Provisions only, which were not only dear, but *unwholesome*; and that she saw stinking Flour which was damaged, being black and full of Grubs, that had been deliver'd to others, for which they paid ten Shillings *per* hundred Pound; the Price of the best Flour being commonly about ten Shillings in the *Merchant*'s Warehouses.

That on her leaving the Province in *March* 1739, the People in general were complaining as much of the cruel Usage of the said *Jones*, as before they had been of the said *Causton*'s; and further this Deponent saith not.

Sworn the 6th Day of   *Sarah Turner*.
   January 1742, in
   Lincolns-Inn, before
     E. SAWYER.

Number XXII.

Extract of a Letter from Mr. Lobb.

SIR, *Chelmsford, Dec.* 1, 1742.

I send you a List of some Goods, with the Prices we were charged, at the Trustees Store-house in *Savannah.*

Coarse blue Duffles, at 4*s. per* Yard.
Cheese, 8*d. per* Pound.
Molasses, 2*s. per* Gallon.
Beef, at 2*d. per* Pound.
Bisket, at 2*d. per* Pound.
Ozenbrigs, at 10*d. per* Yard.
Rice, 3*l.* * Currency *per Cent.*

These Prices are what I can prove by their Bills. *Beef* about that time, *viz.* 1736, I bought in *Charles-Town,* the very best the Market afforded, at 9 *d.* † their Currency *per* Pound; *Biscuit* much about the same Difference; and *Ozenbrigs* at the meanest Retailers in *Charles-Town,* might be bought at 8 *d.* or under; the blue Duffles, I am inform'd, I might have for almost *half Price* in *Charles-Town.*   I am,
SIR,
Your humble Servant,
R. LOBB.

Number XXIII.

Extract of a Representation of the Grand Jury of SAVANNAH, *to the Honourable the Trustees.*

THAT the said *Thomas Causton,* by his Office of Store-keeper, hath the dangerous Power in his Hands of alluring weak-minded People, to comply with unjust Measures; and also *over-awing* others, from making just Complaints and Representations to your Honours; and the *known Implacability* of the said *Causton,* and his frequent threatning of such People, is to many weak-minded, tho' well disposed Persons, a strong Bul-

---

* Seven Shillings and Six-pence Sterling; Prime Cost about five Shillings.
† One Penny and one Eighth Sterling.

wark against their seeking Redress, by making proper Complaints, and just Representations to you, their Benefactors, Patrons and Protectors.

That the said *Causton*, has made *great Advancements* on Provisions and Goods, sold out of the Trustees Store, to the Inhabitants, contrary to Mr. *Oglethorpe*'s Promise, when he first settled this Colony; and contrary, as we apprehend to your Honour's good Intentions, and greatly detrimental to the Prosperity of the Colony; and that *he hath refused to pay the Publick Debts, otherwise than in Provisions at those dear Rates;* and *sometimes bad and unwholsome,* out of the publick Store, whereby the Inhabitants were *greatly distressed,* and *some have been obliged to leave the Province.*

In Witness, &c. *This first Day of* September, 1737.

Signed by the whole Grand Jury *of* 44 *Persons*

Number XXIV.

A Representation from the Grand Jury *to the Court of* Savannah.

Savannah, May 20, 1742.

The *Grand Jury* impannelled the 18th of this Instant *May,* for the Town and County of *Savannah,* humbly beg Leave to offer the following Reasons to this Court, why they think themselves obliged to present Mr. *Thomas Jones,* the *Second Bailiff* of this Town and County, and to examine Witnesses duly sworn thereon.

Imprimis. That in pursuance of the Oath, which they, as *Grand Jurors,* have solemnly taken, they are *obliged to present all such Matters and Things as shall come before them,* and that they *shall* leave *no one* Person *unpresented,* through *Fear, Favour* or *Affection.*

2*dly.* That the Matter of Complaint, against the said Mr. *Thomas Jones,* now before them, is (as they humbly conceive) a *Crime* of a *very heinous Nature,* and (if not duly enquired into by them) may be attended with very bad Consequence, highly detrimental to the *Liberties* and *Properties* of his Majesty's Liege People, inhabiting this Colony.

3*dly.* We humbly are of Opinion, that the *President* and *Assistants* taking Cognizance of any Crime or Misdemeanour, and representing the same to the Honourable the Trustees, *cannot discharge* the *Grand Jury,* from making due Enquiry into such Matters and Things as shall come before them, notwithstanding the said President and Assistants have Cognizance thereof; for if such Things should be once allowed, we humbly are of Opinion the Course of Justice would be diverted from its usual Channel, and thereby render *Grand* and *Petty Juries* entirely useless, contrary, as we humbly conceive, to the Rights and Privileges of our Mother Country.

4thly. We humbly are of Opinion, that the Court refusing to swear such Evidence, as the *Grand Jury* shall offer, in order to their further Enquiry into such Matters and Things, as are lying before them, will *prevent* them discharging that Duty incumbent on them by their *Oath;* whereby the greater Offenders may escape the Punishment due to their Offences.

5thly. We humbly are of Opinion that, if the Matter now before us relating to Mr. *Thomas Jones* be put off till the next Court, no Witnesses being examined upon Oath thereon, some unforeseen Accident (as the Death or Absence of one, perhaps the chief Evidence) may happen, whereby a *thorough Enquiry* into that Matter by the next Grand Jury *may be rendered ineffectual.*

Lastly, We humbly beg leave of this Court (if the aforesaid Reasons shall not be allowed sufficient) that it may be recorded, and laid before the Honourable the Trustees.

Samuel Mercer, Foreman.	*James Dormer,*
Thomas Salter,	*John Brownfield,*
John Wright,	*James Burnsides,*
John Sellie,	*Peter Morell,*
Thomas Bailie,	*Edward Bush,*
James Billou,	*William Woodrooffe,*
William Mears,	*James Carweles,*
John Lyndale,	*James Papott.*
John Penrose,	

Number XXV.

Extract of a Letter from Mr. William Ewen *to Mr.* Thomas Stephens.

Savannah, May 23, 1742.

MR. THOMAS JONES was at the Southward, when he was *indicted* by the Grand Jury, and on the 3d of this Instant there was a Court to be holden at *Savannah*, and Mr. *Jones* came, in order *to have taken his Place on the Bench;* which thing would have been objected against by all the People in the Town; neither would any * Man serve as Grand or Petty Jurors, while Mr. *Jones* sate on the Bench, till he had first taken his Trial, and cleared himself of the Charge laid against him. Mr. *Jones* told the *General* that there were *Spanish* Emissaries at *Savannah*, and that he went in Danger of his Life: This was done under a false Colour, *in order to introduce Soldiers into the Town and enslave the People.* General *Oglethorpe, in order to protect the Civil Power,* (tho' the Magistrates and other Officers here, knew nothing of the Matter, nor that there was any such Occasion) sent Lieutenant *Hugh M'Kay, Anthony Willy,* and *William Finley* with Mr. *Jones.* Lieutenant *Hugh M'Kay* had Orders in writing, signed by the *General,* for *to protect the Civil Power;* and, for his Assistants he was to take all the Forces that were at Fort *Argyle,* Captain *Matthews,* and what Men he had with him at *Savannah;* Captain *Wiggan* at *Paleachowlas* and his Men, and if these were not sufficient, for to send to Fort *Frederick* at *Beaufort,* to fetch Lieutenant *Sterling* and all the Men under his Command. I need not mention to you what *Concern* the Inhabitants were under, to find their Liberties so closely attacked; it was reported that these Forces were to assist Mr. *Jones* for to sit on the Bench; but Mr. *Parker,* and Mr. *Fallowfield,* in order to prevent any Noise or Disturbance, adjourned the Court to the 17th following. Mr. *Jones* then went back to *Frederica,* and told Colonel *Stephens* that the *General* and *himself* would be at *Savannah before the Court Sate again.*

* *Note,* Three Persons were sent to Gaol for refusing to act on the *Grand Jury* while *Jones* sat on the Bench without taking his Trial, and were fined 13*s.* 4*d.* each.

Number XXVI.

From Savannah.

THE Deposition of *John Pye, Recorder* of the Town of *Savannah* in *Georgia*, who being duly sworn, saith, That on *Thursday* the Tenth Day of *July* 1741, he, this Deponent, was at the House of Colonel *Stephens*, Secretary to the Honourable the Trustees for the Establishment of this Colony, Mr. *Henry Parker, first Bailiff* of the said Town, being then present, the said *Parker* did say to Mr. *Thomas Jones*, another of the *Bailiffs*, then also in Company, that he (the said *Henry Parker*) understood that the Grand Jury (who were then sitting) were about to *present the Representation of the State of this Colony, sent home to the Trustees by them*, some time in the Month of *December* last: And this Deponent further saith, that Mr. *Thomas Jones* said to *Henry Parker*, that *the said Grand Jury ought by all means to be discharged*; and the said *Henry Parker* replied to the said *Jones*, that the said Grand Jury had already concerned themselves in things they had nothing to do with, or Words to that Effect; and thereupon the said *Henry Parker consented to discharge the said Grand Jury:* And this Deponent further saith, that the Members of the said Grand Jury, were Men of the best Circumstances, Characters, and Fortune, that could be found within this County of *Savannah*, and summoned by virtue of a Warrant for that Purpose, issued by the said *Henry Parker*, and Mr. *John Fallowfield* two of the Bailiffs, in which said Warrant the Names of the said Grand Jury-men were expressly mentioned, and further this Deponent saith not.

John Pye.

Sworn before me this
  24th Day of *July*,
  1741.
    John Fallowfield.

Number XXVII.

Extract of a Letter from Mr. Patrick M'Kay, *to* Mr. Thomas Stephens, December 1741.

SIR,

Of the State of *Ebenezer*, its my Opinion, *they scarcely raise Provisions to supply their own Necessities*, and *Wants*, were they not *supported* by the

Charities of the *Pious in Europe:* It confirms me much in this Opinion, that Mr. *Boltzius,* even in *May* last, asked to *buy* Corn and Rice of me; which, as I had not to spare, he *Commissioned* me to *buy for him* at *Charles-Town,* for the supply of *Ebenezer;* tho' General *Oglethorpe* told me in *February* preceding, that Mr. *Boltzius* had sent him fine *Indian* Corn-flour, and told his *Excellency* that *he* would *supply his Regiment,* with what Quantities he pleased; and withal, that *he* thanked God he could now subsist *five Hundred* more of his Brethren, if they should be imported into *Georgia.* I mentioned this to Mr. *Boltzius,* when he *wanted* to *buy* Corn and Rice of me, but he *absolutely denyed,* that he had *ever said* or *wrote* so to the *General:* Whether the *General* or the *Parson* is to be *believed,* I leave it with you to determine.

You have yourself seen most of the Settlements in *Georgia* this Year, and what great Matters are done there; in a Word, laying aside *Augusta,* where *Planting is carried on by Negroes,* I dare affirm, I have raised *more* Provisions on my Plantation, in the Township of *Purrysburgh,* with *Twenty Slaves only,* than *All* the Colony of *Georgia* has done; including *Ebenezer* and *the General's own* Farm, which, after an Expence (as I am told) of *Sixty* or *Seventy* Pounds Sterling, returned him *ten* or *fifteen* Bushels of Corn, no Pease or Potatoes.

I am, SIR,
Your very humble Servant,
P A T R I C K   M A C K A Y.

N U M B E R   XXVIII.

Charles-Town, South Carolina, Oct. 12. 1741.

Dear Brother,

I take This Opportunity of acquainting you, that I have left *Georgia* and come to *Charles-Town, South Carolina,* where I am settled in my own Business. I have been here about 4 Months, and (I thank God) am got into very good Trade.

Georgia is very much deviated from what it was, when I first went there, especially in the *Government* of Affairs. I have told you, that at my first Arrival, I was appointed a *Magistrate,* in which Office, I continued till it was *a Crime to do Justice;* upon which, I begged leave of our *General,* to be excused, for that I would act no more, since to act according to my *Oath* and *Conscience* was *displeasing* to him; upon which he made one of his *waiting* Boys a *Magistrate* in my stead, a *Boy* that was *not Nineteen* Years of Age: after which, the *General* turn'd my utter *Enemy*, hindering me, in every Shape, of getting my *Livelihood*, which he has not only done by me, but by *all* those, who *will not consent to wash their Hands in such Water as he thinks proper*. I left but *two* People behind me, that were of my Disposition, and they are both coming away, and then, at *Frederica*, they'll be *like my Lord Thomound's Cocks*. In short, *his Magistrates durst not decide a Cause* without first going to *him* to ask *which* Party is to *suffer*; and, those that happen to be most in his Favour at that time, are sure to get the better on't, *right* or *wrong*. There is also *a Set* of People now left, that, if any Paper is drawn up, and contains the greatest of *Falsities* (in order *to keep still in Darkness the Parliament, the Trustees, and the People of England*) are all ready to *sign*, nay even to make *Oath*, to the Truth of it; and those that *cannot digest those hard Pills, must not stay there*.

I have also an Account of *One hundred Thirty-nine* Pounds Sterling which, when settled, there will be due to me between *Ninety* and *One hundred* Pounds. "*He* swore the Account should not be settled, neither would he ever pay me a Farthing:" But I intend to send my Case home, by a Gentleman who is now gathering up the *true* State of *Georgia* (*much against his Excellency's Inclinations*) in order to lay it before this next Sitting of the *Parliament*, who, the whole *Colony* expects, will relieve them from *Tyranny* and *Oppression*, and *arbitrary Government*, which is too much practised there, and consequently very disagreeable to so young a Settlement. However strange these Things may appear to you *People of England*, I do assure you they are *nothing but Truth*. Nay a whole Volume might be filled with *worse Relations* of that Place, than I have mentioned; which made me think sometimes, we had *lost our Way*, and come to the *wrong Georgia*, and had not got to that *fine Place*, so much talk'd of in *England* some Years ago. Neither *Law* nor *Gospel* find any Encouragement there; our *Minister* (who is a very *worthy Gentleman*) was obliged (*thro' ill Treatment from the General*) to leave the Place, and return Home. You may perhaps wonder why I did not give you so just an Account of these Proceedings before; the Answer to which is, that it is too common a Practice to *open all Letters*, that are sent from thence; and such as speak well of the Place, may perhaps get a Passage according to their Superscriptions, and those that speak ill of the Place, are committed to the Mercy of the Flames. What emboldens me now to *speak the Truth* is, my being arrived in a *Land* of *Liberty; but there (if it please God to keep me in my right Senses)* they never shall get me again, unless there is an Alteration in the Government, not even to view my Estate, which is now lett for 15 *l.* a Year Sterling. When I left *England,* I intended (if pleased God) to have returned in *Ten* Years, but making my first Voyage to the *mistaken Georgia,* where I lost a good part of the Time, I believe I must intrude upon your Patience two or three Years longer, in order to retrieve the lost Time before-mentioned.

Your ever loving Brother,
SAMUEL PERKINS.

NUMBER XXIX.

Extract of a Letter from General Oglethorpe's *Secretary.*

Dear SAM.   *Frederica, Sept.* 13, 1741.

I Would have wrote to you by *Lullams,* had I not at that time, been very busy in writing Letters for the *General,* which I am determined never to do again, unless he will pay me a pretty Sum of Money, which, last Night I wrote to him for; and to which, I have not yet received any Answer. I am tired of this *Way of living;* and am only employed, when his other *Secretaries* * are ill, which often happens after their *frequent* Debauches.

I am *weary* of this *cursed Place,* and will endeavour to get out of it as soon as I can, for it looks as though I was marked out for a *Sacrifice,* in not being able to receive a farthing of my Salary, when there is so much due to me.

Every thing here goes on *as usual,* that is to say, with the *utmost Confusion.* The other Day, whilst the *General* was gone on a Cruize, I happened to hear one of our *worthy* Justices † *cursing* and *swearing,* "that the *General* had used him ill, and that unless he would recall some Words, which he had publickly spoken, he never more would be a *Tool to him* as he had been, in *receiving Instructions privately,* how to behave with Regard to the *unhappy* Mrs. *Norbury* in particular, and then publickly denying that the *General* knew any thing of their Proceedings, but that

* *Marriott,* whom the *General* lately made Magistrate.
† Dr. *Hawkins.*

[333]

they went according to *Law* and their *own* Reason." He also came over to a great many People, who were with *Davidson* in his *Bed Stable*, * and seeing the *Constable* there, he ordered him to bring no more Affairs before him as a *Justice*, for that he would act no more; and accordingly the *Constable* gave him no more trouble, but carried all Affairs before Mr. *Marriott.* When the *General* return'd to *Frederica*, the *Justice returned to his Duty;* in which *he* and his *Wife* have been very assiduous, insomuch that they caused a *Negroe* on board Mrs. *Wood*'s Schooner, to be seiz'd, which was accordingly done: That occasioned two of Mr. *Jeny*'s also to be seiz'd, as would a Girl also of Mrs. *Lyford*'s, who was too cunning for them, and had sent it away. However a petty (*pretty*) *Sessions* was held, when the Masters of *Jeny*'s and Mrs. *Wood*'s Boats having sworn, that they would not have brought any *Negroe*, could they have got white Men to hire; and also, that they would not have been in this Province at the time the *Negroes* were seized, had it not been for a violent Storm, or Hurricane, that we have lately had; and producing their Clearances, *Jeny*'s signed by *Patterson*, and Mrs. *Wood*'s by his *Excellency*, they thereupon *in form*, clear'd the *Negroes* under their Hand-Writing. However, it was reported, that the Slave on board Mrs. *Wood*, was not Colonel *Flowers*'s, as had been sworn to, but belonged to Mrs. *Wood*, and by her hired for the Service of the Schooner; upon which, another Warrant was issued by the *Triumvirate*, † (after a *long Advice given by the Dictator*) to take up the *Negroe* on board Mrs. *Wood*, under a Pretence, that he was cleared by a wrong Name: He is now in *our Guard-House*, ‡ and next Week, I believe will be sold at *Vendue*; notwithstanding Captain *Lyford*, and some other Persons, will swear that the said *Negroe* was employed not long since, (for some Months on board the same Boat, and by the said Name that he always went) in going up and down the River for Oyster-shells, for Tappy-work.

Thus stands the Case with Mrs. *Wood* and our *Civil Power*, whose Character is already known *so well* abroad, that every one almost is *afraid* to come near us; and we, who are on the Spot, want to be out of the *reach* of it. Last time Mrs. *Wood* was here, she had a Servant (*Willy Cormach*) taken from her in a *more unjust* manner (if possible) than her *Negroe* was this Voyage. I hope *this*, and *several other Instances*, of the

* See Number 4.
† The three Magistrates.
‡ The Soldiers Guard.

Usage of Georgia, will not escape *young Stephens;* who, if he has Authority, will I dare say, *not want Matter of Fact* to be laid before him. You, to be sure will quietly sit down, and not speak a Word against *this Place! How ungrateful must you be, if you are not sensible of the good Usage you receiv'd here?* Mr. *Davidson* is now sending his Family to *Port Royal*, along with Mrs. *Wood:* As he designs soon to follow, I will not trouble you with an imperfect Account of the Cause of his so sudden Departure, when you will soon have the Satisfaction, of hearing it from his own Mouth; I will only say, that *"his Case is a perfect Georgian";* and will, I hope, come under the Cognizance of Mr. *Stephens*, to whom I cannot give my Reasons for leaving the Colony; but should be very glad to acquaint him with the Reasons, of my Design to get out of this *destructive Place*, as soon as I can. It is currently reported here (and *I know part of it to be true*) that one or two Children have *died* here, for want of Medicines, which were refused them; and Mrs. *Hawkins* order'd her Husband's Mates, at *their Peril*, not to deliver a bit out of the Chest. If that W - - - n is to be *punished* in this World, *for her Wickedness, how dreadfull will the Example be?* I grow sick with the Thoughts of her, and must therefore conclude, desiring your frequent Correspondence, than which nothing can be more agreeable to,

Dear SAM,
*Thy trusty Friend, well Wisher,
and faithful humble Servant,*
F. MOORE.

To Mr. *Samuel
Perkins.*

NUMBER XXX.

A Letter from the Magistrates of Frederica, *to the commanding Officer at the Camp, on St.* Simons.

SIR,   *Frederica, May, 5* 1740.
The Reason of our troubling you is this. *Jonathan Edge*, having been this Day convicted of breaking the *King*'s *Stores*, breaking open a Lock of a Trunk, and stealing 17 *l.* in Money; and having receiv'd Sentence of Death for the same; and we having no Place proper for the Confinement of a Person in his Condition, beg leave to desire your help, in ordering him

to be taken due care of, (so as he might not escape) until such time as *the General is pleased to order him to be executed.*

We are, SIR,
Your obedient humble Servants,
Samuel Perkins.
Francis Moore.

To the Officer, commanding
General *Oglethorpe*'s Regiment, at St. *Simons.*

NUMBER XXXI.

SIR,
Jonathan Edge was lately *executed* here, for breaking open and robbing of *John Dick*'s House. He confess'd the Fact, and was very sorry that he should come to so an unhappy an end. I am sorry to tell you, that he declared at the same time, that "*if the* General *had paid him what he owed him, he should have had no Occasion for to have done it.*" Whether this is true or not, that the *General* owed him the Money, I can say, that I heard the rest of those that were employed with him at the same time, complain of their not being paid; from your assured Friend,

Joseph Cannon.

Frederica, September,
the 8th, 1740.
To Mr. *Henry Buckley*, in *Carolina.*

NUMBER XXXII.

Extract of a Letter from Mr. * William Ewen,
to Mr. Thomas Stephens.

SIR, *Grange, Aug.* 21, 1742.
I shall give you an Account of the present *deplorable State* of *Savannah;* every one was in the utmost Confusion, for to carry his Wife, Family and Goods out of the Town; some to *Ebenezer,* some to *Abercorn,* some to

* One of the Correspondents appointed by the People.

Purrisburgh, and some to Captain *Mackay's* Plantation: *Our Council did not talk of fighting, neither did they take one Step for the Defence of the Place;* but on the contrary, had concluded, when they heard the *Spaniards* were coming, for *to have tumbled the great Guns into the River, and then to have gone away on Horseback: They kept their Horses ready bridled and saddled all the time.* Mr. *Boltzius* offered his People to come down, which if they had, and joined the *English* and *Dutch* that were in *Savannah*, they would have made about two hundred Men; who, under the Conduct of a good Commander, might have repuls'd six or seven hundred of the *Enemy*, if any had come. *They were so far from defending the Town, that, in the midst of the Alarm, there was no Guard kept for two Nights.* What little Substance the People had, is now *exhausted;* nor is there any Business going on, either publick or private; so that the People are now in a very low State; many of them are dead, and more I am apt to think will dye, for several People are now dangerously ill. Mr. *Fallowfield*, Mr. *Ormston*, Mr. *Penrose*, Mr. *Townsend*, Mr. *Elbert*, and *several others*, including Men, Women and Children, to the Number of thirty-five Persons, have already left the Colony, besides several of the *Dutch;* many others are also intending to go very soon.

SIR,
Your most humble Servant,
William Ewen.

Number XXXIII.

SIR,
We should be wanting in Point of Gratitude, did we not, in behalf of those We * *represent*, as well as of ourselves, thankfully acknowledge your unwearied Endeavours for the *Publick Welfare* of those, who can no other Way repay you, than by putting up their Prayers to the *Almighty*, to reward and bless you in all your generous Undertakings in their Behalf; and tho' our *Circumstances* are *such*, as give us little Hopes of staying here to see the Accomplishment of your Negotiations; yet it is our *earnest Request*, that you will still continue to sollicit our Affairs in such a Man-

---

* These Gentlemen are three of the Correspondents appointed by the People.

ner, as (*with the Blessing of the Almighty*) may be the Means of *settling* this *unhappy* Colony, upon a firm and lasting Basis, which will transmit your Name to Posterity, as the *Restorer* of *Civil Rights* and *Priviledges*, and thereby render your Name ever dear.

Whatever you may think necessary to be done in our Behalf, we must leave to your Discretion, hoping you will do nothing therein, but what is consistent with your Character, as our Agent.

We are, SIR,
Your most humble Servants,

Savannah, 21st
   August, 1742.
To Mr. *Thomas Stephens.*

William Woodrooffe.
William Ewen.
John Lyndall.

NUMBER XXXIV.

Appointment for an Agent on Behalf of the People of *Georgia.*

Georgia,
   At a Meeting of Landholders, Settlers and Inhabitants at Savannah, *the Seventh Day of* October *in the Fifteenth Year of the Reign of our Sovereign Lord* GEORGE *the Second, by the Grace of God of* Great-Britain, France *and* Ireland, *King, Defender of the Faith,* &c. Annoque Domini, *One Thousand Seven Hundred and Forty One.*

Whereas many of his Majesty's Subjects, who are settled in, and are belonging to the Province of *Georgia,* have, as well singly, as in joint Numbers, from time to time presented to the Trustees for establishing the Colony of *Georgia,* divers *Remonstrances, Representations* and *Petitions,* with *repeated* Complaints of Grievances, which have never been effectually redress'd. And whereas, for Want of timely Remedies to the Evils set forth in the said *Representations, &c.* being apply'd, the said Province is greatly deserted by many of her Inhabitants, by Reason of the *Restrictions that render them wholly incapable of raising Provisions for their Support;* and whereby those, who still remain in the said Province, are unable to subsist themselves and Families by *Cultivation,* as are some of them barely in *any Shape.* We, whose Names are hereunto subscribed, being Settlers and Inhabitants of the said Province, are unanimously of Opinion, that, in order to the effectually settling and establishing the said Province, and to remove all those Grievances and Hardships we now labour under, *It is expedient for Us to appoint an Agent* for representing, transacting and soliciting in *Great-Britain* those Affairs of so great Importance. Wherefore, Mr. *Thomas Stephens* being thought by us to be a Person fitly qualified for the said Purpose, in Behalf of ourselves, and many others of his Majesty's poor distressed Subjects, now residing in, and belonging to the said Province, We do hereby constitute and appoint the said *Thomas Stephens*. And he is hereby nominated and declared *Agent,* to represent and transact the Affairs aforesaid. And further, it being necessary, that We the said Inhabitants, or some of us do correspond with the said *Thomas Stephens*. We do in Behalf of Ourselves and others aforesaid, hereby nominate and appoint *William Woodrooffe, Thomas Ormston, Peter Morell, John Lyndal,* and *William Ewen,* or any three of them to correspond with the said *Agent;* and he is hereby impowered and authorized to pursue such Instructions, as he shall from time to time receive from the said Persons, hereby appointed to correspond with him in Relation to the Complaints of Grievances of the People in the aforesaid Colony of *Georgia;* and this *Appointment* to remain in full Force and Vertue, during the Pleasure of the said Inhabitants. GIVEN under our Hands at *Savannah* the Day and Year above-written.

Signed by Landholders	123
Letters from those absent at the time	18
	141

Instructions *to Mr.* Thomas Stephens, *Agent for the People of* Georgia *in* America.

We do in Behalf of ourselves, and the rest of his Majesty's Subjects, who have settled in this Province, request and desire, that you Mr. *Thomas Stephens* will, on your Arrival in *England, apply, petition, and solicit for Redress of Grievances,* in such manner as you shall think most advisable, (*Application to the Trustees only excepted*) and in particular for obtaining the following Articles, which We apprehend to be necessary in order for the more effectually establishing this Province; and which the *Charter* granted by his Majesty to the *Trustees impowers them* to give us, *viz.*

That a *regular Government* be established in *Georgia*, as in others of his Majesty's Provinces in *America*.

That upon Consideration, that *Georgia* is intended as a Barrier to *South-Carolina*, all *Grants of Lands* be at *least* as extensive, and not inferior in any Respect to those of that Province.

That the *Quit Rents* in *Georgia* be not greater than in others of his Majesty's Provinces, the *Land being in no kind better* than in *South-Carolina*.

That the *Use of Negroes*, under such Restrictions as shall be thought proper, be allowed for cultivating our Lands.

That Incouragement be given for the making *Pot-ash, Silk, Wine, Oil, Indigo, Hemp, Flax*, or other Commodities that might be raised in *Georgia* in *America*, and greatly *increase* the *Trade* and *Navigation* of *Great-Britain*.

That, if you should not obtain such an *Alteration in the Constitution*, as shall enable the Inhabitants to support themselves by *Cultivation*, to pray, "*that the* Money, *which may hereafter be granted for the Use of the Colony, may be applied for removing them to some other Part of his Majesty's Dominions, where they may be able to support themselves and Families, and be of Use to the Publick, instead of a Burthen to it, as they are now.*"

William Woodrooffe.
Thomas Ormston.
Peter Morel.
William Ewen.
John Lyndall.

Savannah, 27th
Oct. 1741.

Number XXXV.

A List *of* Complainants, *who are stiled a few* Clamorous Malecontents.

A.	B.
John Amory	John Brownfield
Benjamin Adams	John Burton
Thomas Andrews	Charles Britain
Thomas Atwell	James Burnside
Thomas Antrobus	Francis Brooks
James Anderson	Matthew Bright
Gasper Aughester	Robert Bradley
Hugh Anderson.	William Bradley

Mich. Burghalter, *sen.*
James Bland
William Barbo
Peter Baillou
Edward Bush
Giles Becu
James Baillou
George Buncle
Peter Beller
Michael Burghalter
Thomas Bailey
Andrew Bell
Thomas Baillie
Harry Buckley
John Brown
William Blechman
Ambrose Barr
Thomas Bicher.

C.

William Calvert
William Carter
James Carwels
Thomas Cross
William Colthred
John Clarke, *sen.*
Philip Courtney
John Cundale
William Cooksey
Isaac-King Clark
James-Collyer Collins
James Campell
Jacob Curl
Anthony Camuse
Thomas Clyatt
Joseph Cannon
James Cotneck
John Cuthbert
Isaac Coln

Tho. Christie, *Recorder*
John Clark.

D.

James Dormer
John Desborough
Richard Davis
John Desborough, *jun.*
Francis Dalgrass
Edward Desborough
Andrew Duché
Thomas Dawson
James Dodds
John Dudding
David Douglas
Samuel Davison
William Davy
James Dean
Ph. Delegal, *jun.*
Edward Davison
James Dodds
Christian Dasher.

E.

William Elbert
Thomas Eggerton
John Evans
William Ewen
Thomas Ellis
Peter Emery
William Evans.

F.

Hugh Frazer
Joseph Fitzwalter
Henry Fletcher
William Francis
John Fallowfield, *Magistrate.*
Walter Fox

Elisha Foster
Thomas Fraser
John Foulds.

G.

Robert Gilbert, *Magistrate*.
Peter Gordon, *Magistr*.
Patrick Grhame
John Grhame
David Guinder
William Greenfield
Christopher Greenfield
James Gallway
Archibald Glen
Michael Germain
James Gould
John Grinter
George Gorsand
Thomas Gantlett
Samuel Goff
William Grickson
Henry Green
Charles Grimaldi
Andrew Grant
John Goldwire.

H.

Robert Howes
Samuel Holmes
James Haslefoot
Theoph. Hetherington
Robert Hainkes
John Heirinmam
James Houston
Gasper Herbough
Jacob Herbough.

J.

James Jeansack

Peter Joubert
Edward Jenkins
Edward Jenkins, *jun*.

K.

John Kelly
William Kennedy.

L.

Samuel Lacey
Richard Lobb
Richard Lawley
Henry Lloyd
John Lyndall
James Landree
Samuel Lyon
John Landry
Thomas Lee
Adrian Loyer
Adrian Loyer, *jun*.

M.

Samuel Mercer
Stephen Marrauld
Henry Manley
Stephen Mountford
Thomas Mellichamp
John M'Donald
Peter M'Kay
Benjamin M'Intosh
John M'Intosh
Daniel M'Kay
James Mure
John Miller
Anthony M'Brid
Jacob Matthews
Henry Moulton
Peter Maillier
William Meers

Farguhar M'Guilvery
Peter Morell
Richard Mellichamp
Thomas Morris
Daniel M'Donald
John M'Leod, *Minister of* Darien.
Alexander Monro
James Miller
James Marsh
John M'Intire
Owen M'Leod
Matthew Mauve
Peter Miller.

N.

Thomas Neale.

O.

Thomas Ormston
Christother Ortman
Kenedy O Brien.

P.

Henry Parker, *Magistrate.*
William Parker
Samuel Parker
John Priestwood
John Pye, *Recorder*
Robert Parker
John Penrose
William Pendricks
James Papot
Jean Pirebreton
Samuel Perkins
George Philip.

R.

Simon Rieuwere
Richard Rogers

John Robe
George Rush
John Rae
Alexander Rose
John Roberson
Alexander Rantowle
William Rigden
Hugh Ross
Alexander Reynolds
John Michael Riser.

S.

Lewis Stamon
William Starflichet
Joseph Stanley
Donald Stewart
James Smith
Alexander Simes
Joseph Summers
John Smith
John Sellie
Thomas Salter
James Scott
John Smalley
Thomas Sparnell
David Snook
George Stevens
Joseph Stringer
John Scott
William Stirling
John Speilbeigler
Joseph Smithers
William Stenhouse.

T.

Peter Tector
Edward Townsend
George Tyrrel
Stephen Tarrian

John Teasdale
Jacob Truan
Thomas Tripp
Thomas Tebbut
Patrick Tailfer
Alexander Taylor
Samuel Teasdale.

U.

Thomas Upton
Oliver Upsall.

W.

James Williams
Jacob Watts
Samuel Ward
George Waterman
James Willson
William Williamson

William Wood
James White
Thomas Wattle
Andrew Walker
William Woodrooffe
Thomas Webb
Joseph Wardrope
John Warwick
Joseph Watson
John Wackfeld
Robert Williams.

Y.

Isaac Young, *Sen.*
Isaac Young, *Jun.*
John Young
Thomas Young, *Sen.*
Thomas Young, *Jun.*

If it be asked, why all these did not sign the Appointment for an Agent? the Answer is, a few of them are dead, and many deserted.

A List *of those who are deemed the Body of the People, and who were either bribed or compelled to sign Petitions in Opposition to those stiled* Malecontents.

From EBENEZER.

John Martin Boltzius
Israel Christian Gronau
Gabriel Maurer
John Maurer
George Kogler
Paulus Zittrauer
Peter Renter
Stephen Rottenberger
Ambrosii Zubli
John Jacob Zubli
§ Christopher Ortmann
Ruprecht Kalcher
Leonard Rauner
Christian Riedelsperger
Fridrick Willhelm Moller
Martin Hortzug
Christian Hessler
John Pletter
Frank Sigismund
John Hernberger
George Bruckner
Carl. Sigismund Ott
Matthias Zettler
Ruprecht Eischberger
John Peter Arnsdorff

Bartholomeus Rieser
Bartholomeus Zant
Thomas Gsohwandel
Simon Reiter
Matthias Brandner
Christian Leimberger
Martin Lackner
Luprecht Steiner
Veit Lemmenhoffer
John & Car. Floerel
Ruprecht Zimmerman
Simon Steiner
George Schwaiger
John Schmidt
Leonard Crause
Peter Gruber
Jacob Schartner
Joseph Leitner
John Cornberger
Andreas Grimmiger
Matthias Burgsteiner
Veit Landselder
Joseph Ernst
§ John Michel Rieser
§ Thomas Pichler
§ John Spielbiegler.

From DARIEN.

John Mackintosh Moore
John Mackintosh Lynvilge
Ranald M'Donald
Hugh Morrison
John M'Donald
John Maclean
John Mackintosh *Son to L.*
John Mackintosh Bain

James M'Kay
Daniel Clark, *first*
Alexander Clarke
Donald Clark, *third*
Joseph Burges
Donald Clark, *second*
Archibald M'Bain
§ Alexander Munro
William Munro
John Cuthbert.

A List *of those who signed a State of the Province of* Georgia, *attested upon Oath.*

✳ Patrick Graham, *Apothecary to the Trustees.*
✳ Joseph Fitzwalter, *Gardner to them.*
✳ James Carwells, *Gaoler.*
§ Thomas Upton, *Commands a Garrison of 5 Men.*
§ Giles Becu, *Baker to the Trustees Store-keeper.*
§ Thomas Egerton, *Grandson of the Trustees Wheelwright.*
Thomas Cundell, *a Boy under Age.*
§ Anthony Camuse, *Silkman.*
✳ John Burton, *a Town Officer in the Pay of the Trustees.*
Joseph Pavey, *in Pay at Fort* Augusta.
§ Robert Hainks, *a Town Officer.*
John Millidge, *one of the General's Servants.*
§ Thomas Bayley, *Smith to the Trustees.*
George Johnson, *Sawyer to the Trustees.*
✳ Samuel Parker, *Son-in-Law to* Samuel Mercer.
Thomas Palmer, *Sawyer to the Trustees.*
William Stephens, *the Trustees President and Secretary.*
✳ Henry Parker, *a Magistrate and Assistant to the President.*
Thomas Jones (✳) *Magistrate, Assistant, Accomptant, Overseer. Store-keeper and Cashier to the Trustees.*
Samuel Mercer (†), *Constable and Assistant.*

✳ App. No. XXIV, XXV, XXVI, *&c.*
† App. No. XII.

§ James Campbel, *late Gaoler*.
John Rae (*), *Scout Boat-man*.
Noble Jones, *Commands a Garrison near Captain* Upton.
§ Thomas Young, *Wheelwright to the Trustees*.
§ Thomas Ellis, *Surveyor*.

Those marked ✻ signed the Representation of 117 in 1738.

Those marked § have since repented and signed the *Agent*'s Appointment, and the rest have ever been dependant.

N. B. The State of the Colony attested by the above 25, only shews how far the People have gone towards improving the Colony, and what it may be made capable of; but does not shew the *present*, *real* and *true* State of it, since it has made no mention of its *ruinous* and *deserted* Plantations.

Number XXXVI.

SIR,   *Georgia-Office, Westminster*.
Your forgetting the Duty of a *Magistrate*, to preserve Peace, and Authority of Government, and heading a discontented Party to become *Petitioners* with yourself, *against the Trustees Conduct*, setting up yourselves as *Dictators*, and prescribing Rules to bring all Order into Confusion, is an *Offence of that Nature* to the *Trustees*, who appointed you a *Magistrate* for *other Purposes*, that they thought fit to *discharge* you from the Office of *Second Bailiff*, and one of the *Assistants* at *Savannah*, and have sent over their Constitution for another Person in your Room.

Persons not content with Government, are equally unable to *govern* themselves, as *choose* their own Governors; and the *Trustees* having no farther Service for you, who take upon you *thus to act*, directed my acquainting you therewith.

I am SIR,
Your most humble Servant,
Herman Verelst, *Accomptant*.
Feb. 16, 1741.

To Mr. John Fallowfield.

Finis.

* App. No. XII.

Select Bibliography

Aldridge, Alfred O., "George Whitefield's Georgia Controversies," *Journal of Southern History*, IX (Aug. 1943), 357–80.

Berriman, William, *Two Pamphlets on the Province of Georgia: A sermon preach'd before the Honorable Trustees for Establishing the Colony of Georgia, and the associates of ... Dr. Bray ... by W. Berriman* (1739) and *An enquiry into the state and utility of the Province of Gerogia* [sic] (1741), California State Library, Occasional Papers, Reprint Series, no. 13.

Church, Leslie F., *Oglethorpe: A Study of Philanthropy in England and Georgia* (London, 1932).

Coulter, E. Merton, ed., *The Journal of William Stephens 1741–1745* (2 vols., Athens, 1958–9).

Ettinger, Amos A., *James Edward Oglethorpe, Imperial Idealist* (Oxford, 1936).

Fant, H. B., "The Labor Policy of the Trustees," *Georgia Historical Quarterly*, XVI (March, 1932), 1–16.

Heath, Milton S., *The Role of the State in Economic Development in Georgia to 1860* (Cambridge, 1954).

Lonn, Ella, *The Colonial Agents of the Southern Colonies* (Chapel Hill, 1945).

McCain, James R., *Georgia as a Proprietary Province: The Execution of a Trust* (Boston, 1917).

Miller, Randall M., "The Failure of the Colony of Georgia under the Trustees," *Georgia Historical Quarterly*, LIII (March, 1969), 1–17.

Northen, William J., ed., *Men of Mark in Georgia* (3 vols., Atlanta, 1907–11).

Spiller, Robert E., *et al.*, eds., *Literary History of the United States* (revised edition in one volume, New York, 1953).

Stevens, William B., *A History of Georgia from its first discovery by Europeans to the adoption of the present constitution in 1798* (2 vols., New York and Philadelphia, 1847 and 1859).

Temple, Sarah B. Gober, and Kenneth Coleman, *Georgia Journeys: Being an Account of the Lives of Georgia's Original Settlers and Many Other Early Settlers from the Founding of the Colony in 1732 until the Institution of the Royal Government in 1754* (Athens, 1961).

Tyler, Moses Coit, *A History of American Literature 1607–1765* (New York, 1878; revised edition, Ithaca, 1949).

Ver Steeg, Clarence L., ed., *A True and Historical Narrative of the Colony of Georgia* (Wormsloe Foundation Publications no. 4; Athens, Ga., 1960).

White, George, *Historical Collections of Georgia* (3rd edn., New York, 1855).

Trevor R. Reese teaches at the University of London Institute of Commonwealth Studies. He is author of *Colonial Georgia: A Study in British Imperial Policy in the Eighteenth Century* (Athens, 1963). All of the original documents for this new edition of the Malcontents controversy have come from the collection of the University of Georgia Library Special Collections, at Athens. § This book was planned and edited at Savannah, Georgia, by The Beehive Press, which publishes sources and studies of Georgia history and literature. Its pressmark, which appears above and pictures bees busy at their hive, expresses the enthusiasm of this work; the source of the pressmark is one of the pamphlets printed in this present volume, *An Impartial Enquiry into the State and Utility of the Province of Georgia*. § This book was printed at Lunenburg, Vermont, by The Stinehour Press.

THE BEEHIVE PRESS
321 Barnard Street
Savannah, Georgia